Papillon

Miwa Ueda

Translated and adapted by Elina Ishikawa
Lettered by North Market Street Graphics

DEL
REY

Ballantine Books · New York

Papillon volume 3 is a work of fiction. Names, characters, places, and incidents are the products of the author's imagination or are used fictitiously. Any resemblance to actual events, locales, or persons, living or dead, is entirely coincidental.

A Del Rey Manga/Kodansha Trade Paperback Original

Published in the United States by Del Rey, an imprint of The Random House Publishing Group, a division of Random House, Inc., New York.

DEL REY is a registered trademark and the Del Rey colophon is a trademark of Random House, Inc.

Publication rights arranged through Kodansha Ltd.

First published in Japan in 2007 by Kodansha Ltd., Tokyo

ISBN 978-0-345-50807-2

Printed in the United States of America

www.delreymanga.com

4 6 8 9 7 5 3

Translator/Adapter: Elina Ishikawa
Lettering: North Market Street Graphics

CONTENTS

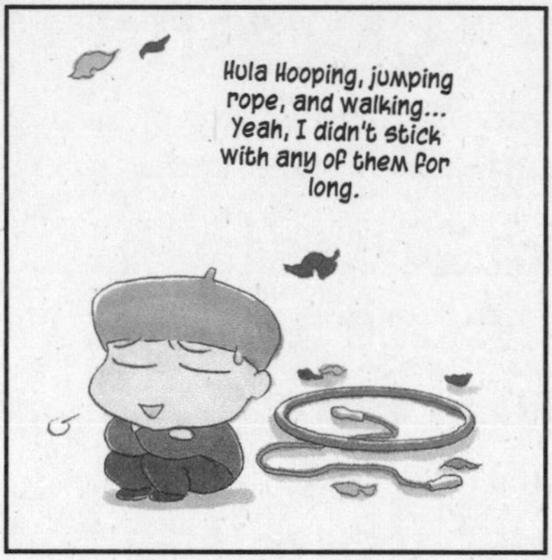
Hula Hooping, jumping rope, and walking... Yeah, I didn't stick with any of them for long.

When I go to psychology courses and seminars for work, I find myself feeling comforted, which helps me forget about upsetting incidents in the past. Then very pleasant and peaceful days go by, but there is one problem: It becomes harder to draw the emotionally difficult scenes in my manga. I can't help thinking there is no need to worry. Still I believe that these scenes are necessary in story development. So every day I go to my desk and try to remember what it was like to be a teenager.

—Miwa Ueda

Honorifics Explained

Throughout the Del Rey Manga books, you will find Japanese honorifics left intact in the translations. For those not familiar with how the Japanese use honorifics and, more important, how they differ from American honorifics, we present this brief overview.

Politeness has always been a critical facet of Japanese culture. Ever since the feudal era, when Japan was a highly stratified society, use of honorifics—which can be defined as polite speech that indicates relationship or status—has played an essential role in the Japanese language. When you address someone in Japanese, an honorific usually takes the form of a suffix attached to one's name (example: "Asuna-san"), is used as a title at the end of one's name, or appears in place of the name itself (example: "Negi-sensei," or simply "Sensei!").

Honorifics can be expressions of respect or endearment. In the context of manga and anime, honorifics give insight into the nature of the relationship between characters. Many English translations leave out these important honorifics and therefore distort the feel of the original Japanese. Because Japanese honorifics contain nuances that English honorifics lack, it is our policy at Del Rey not to translate them. Here, instead, is a guide to some of the honorifics you may encounter in Del Rey Manga.

-san: This is the most common honorific and is equivalent to Mr., Miss, Ms., or Mrs. It is the all-purpose honorific and can be used in any situation where politeness is required.

-sama: This is one level higher than "-san" and is used to confer great respect.

-dono: This comes from the word "tono," which means "lord." It is an even higher level than "-sama" and confers utmost respect.

-*kun:* This suffix is used at the end of boys' names to express familiarity or endearment. It is also sometimes used by men among friends, or when addressing someone younger or of a lower station.

-*chan:* This is used to express endearment, mostly toward girls. It is also used for little boys, pets, and even among lovers. It gives a sense of childish cuteness.

Bozu: This is an informal way to refer to a boy, similar to the English terms "kid" and "squirt."

Sempai/
Senpai: This title suggests that the addressee is one's senior in a group or organization. It is most often used in a school setting, where underclassmen refer to their upperclassmen as "sempai." It can also be used in the workplace, such as when a newer employee addresses an employee who has seniority in the company.

Kohai: This is the opposite of "sempai" and is used toward underclassmen in school or newcomers in the workplace. It connotes that the addressee is of a lower station.

Sensei: Literally meaning "one who has come before," this title is used for teachers, doctors, or masters of any profession or art.

-*[blank]:* This is usually forgotten in these lists, but it is perhaps the most significant difference between Japanese and English. The lack of honorific, known as *yobisute,* means that the speaker has permission to address the person in a very intimate way. Usually, only family, spouses, or very close friends have this kind of permission. It can be gratifying when someone who has earned the intimacy starts to call one by one's name without an honorific. But when that intimacy hasn't been earned, it can be very insulting.

Papillon

Miwa Ueda

CONTENTS

The Story So Far

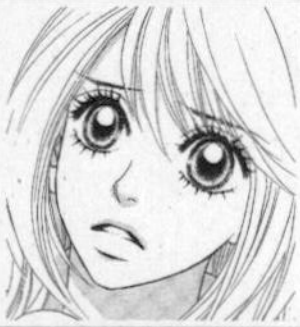

Ageha Mizuki
(a.k.a. Chrysalis)

Our heroine, one of the twins, kindhearted and honest.

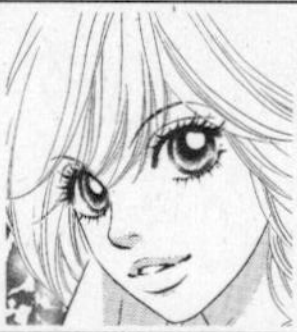

Hana Mizuki

Ageha's twin sister. She picks on Ageha.

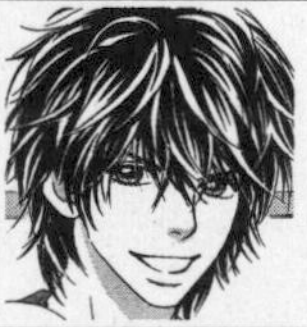

Hayato Ichijiku
(a.k.a. Kyû-chan)

A counselor-in-training and a graduate student.

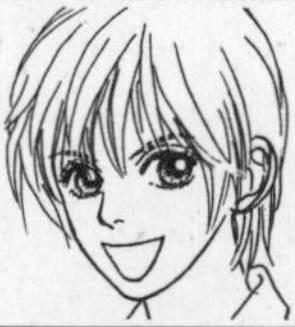

Ryûsei Koike

Ageha's childhood friend, goes out with Hana.

Summary: Ageha has always had a crush on Ryûsei, but she loses all hope after her sister, Hana, steals him away from her. But after meeting her school counselor, Kyû-chan, Ageha develops a positive attitude. Realizing her growing feelings for Kyû-chan, Ageha finds herself confessing to him at the end of a "practice" date at the amusement park. Will Kyû-chan respond to her declaration of love?

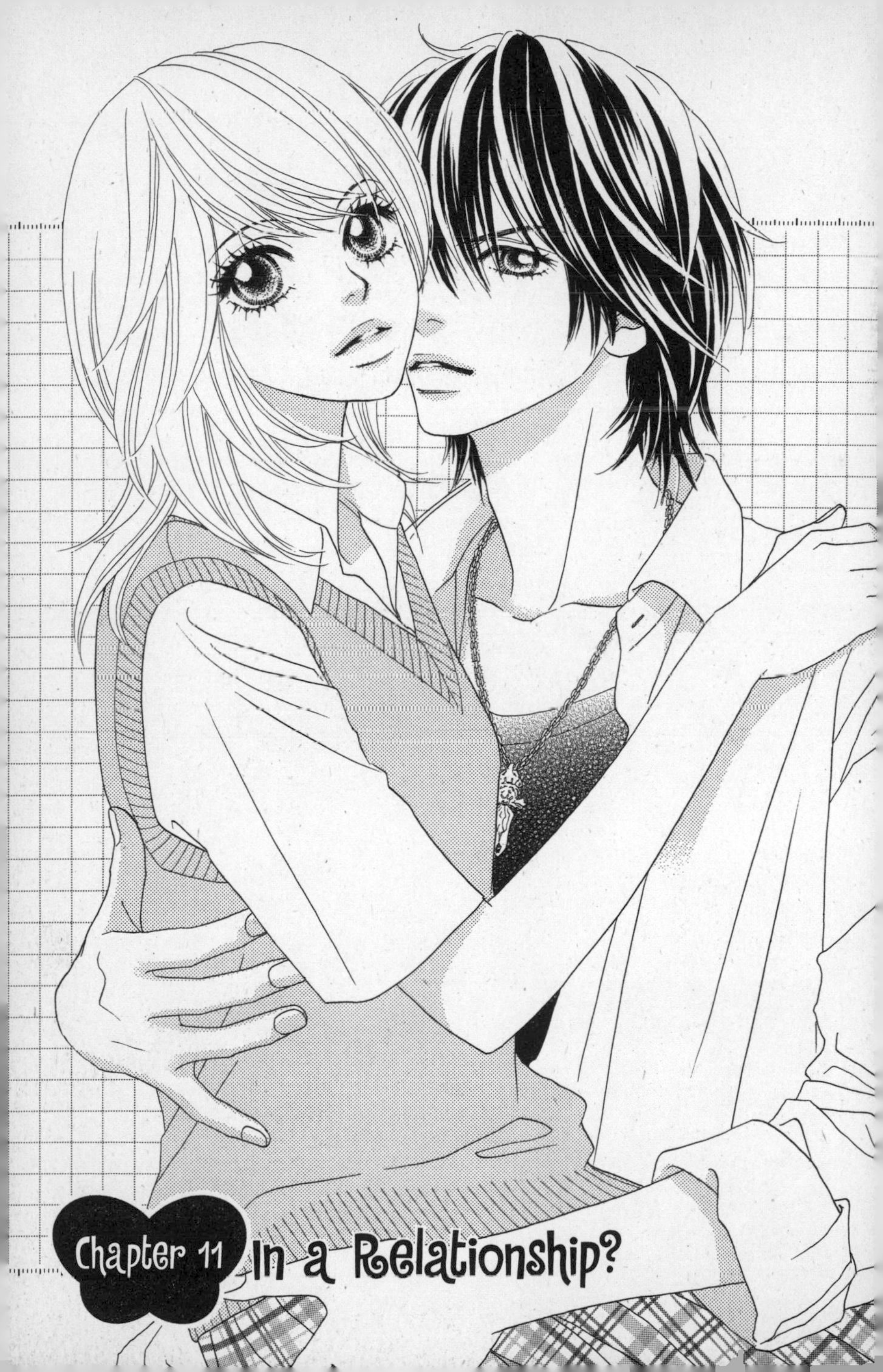
Chapter 11
In a Relationship?

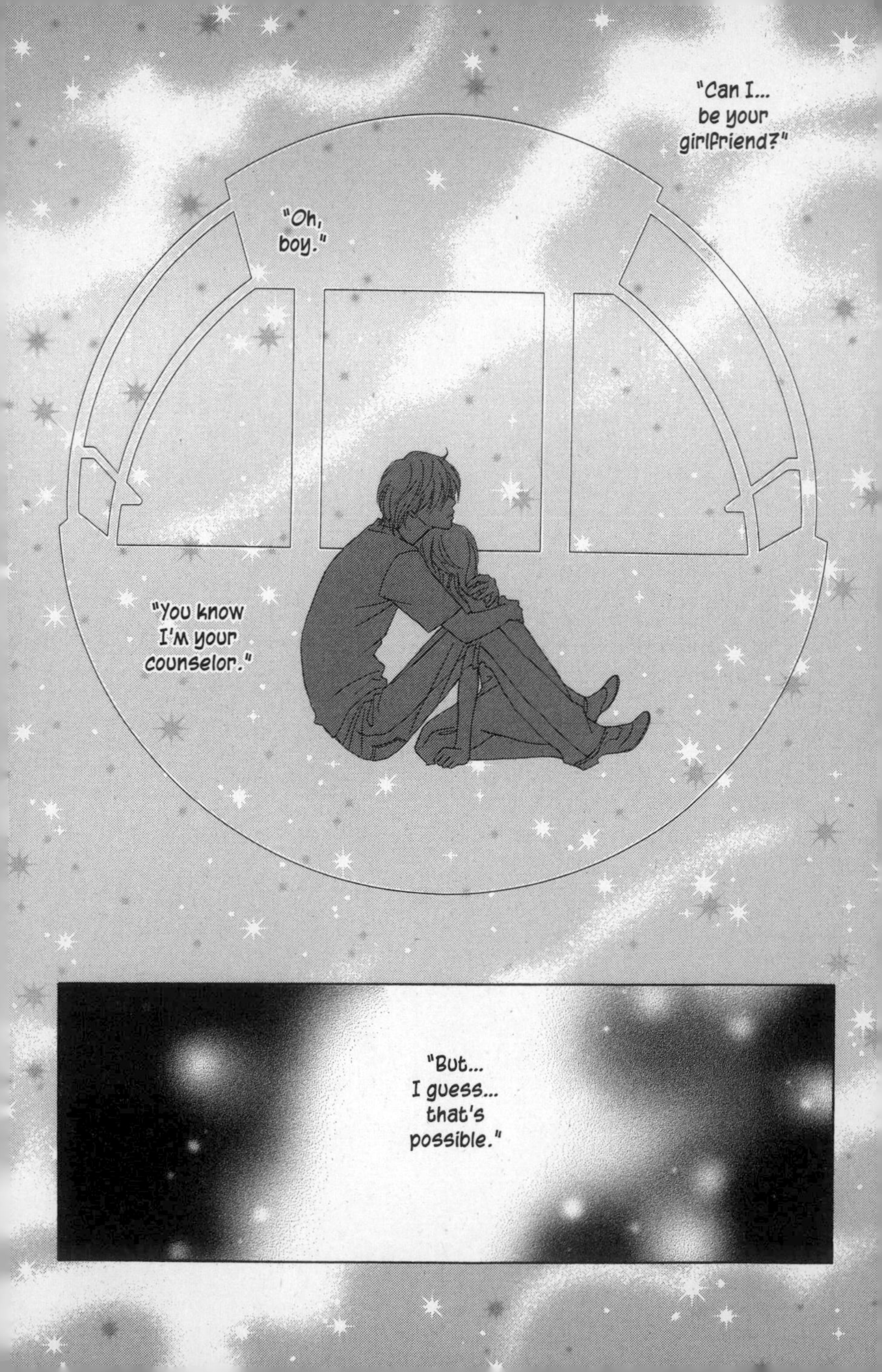
"Can I... be your girlfriend?"
"Oh, boy."
"You know I'm your counselor."
"But... I guess... that's possible."

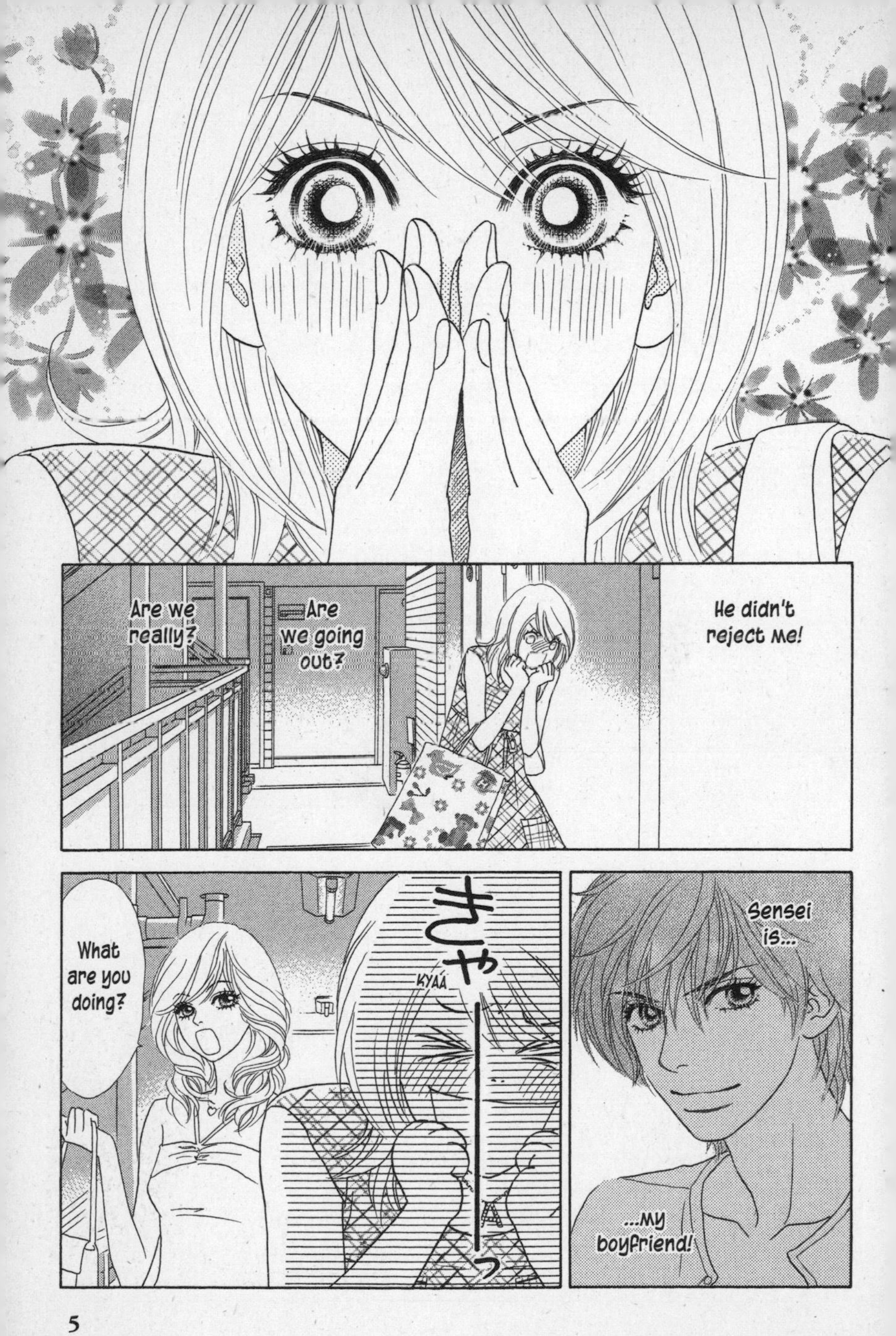
He didn't reject me!
Are we going out?
Are we really?
Sensei is...
...my boyfriend!
きゃーっ
KYAA
What are you doing?

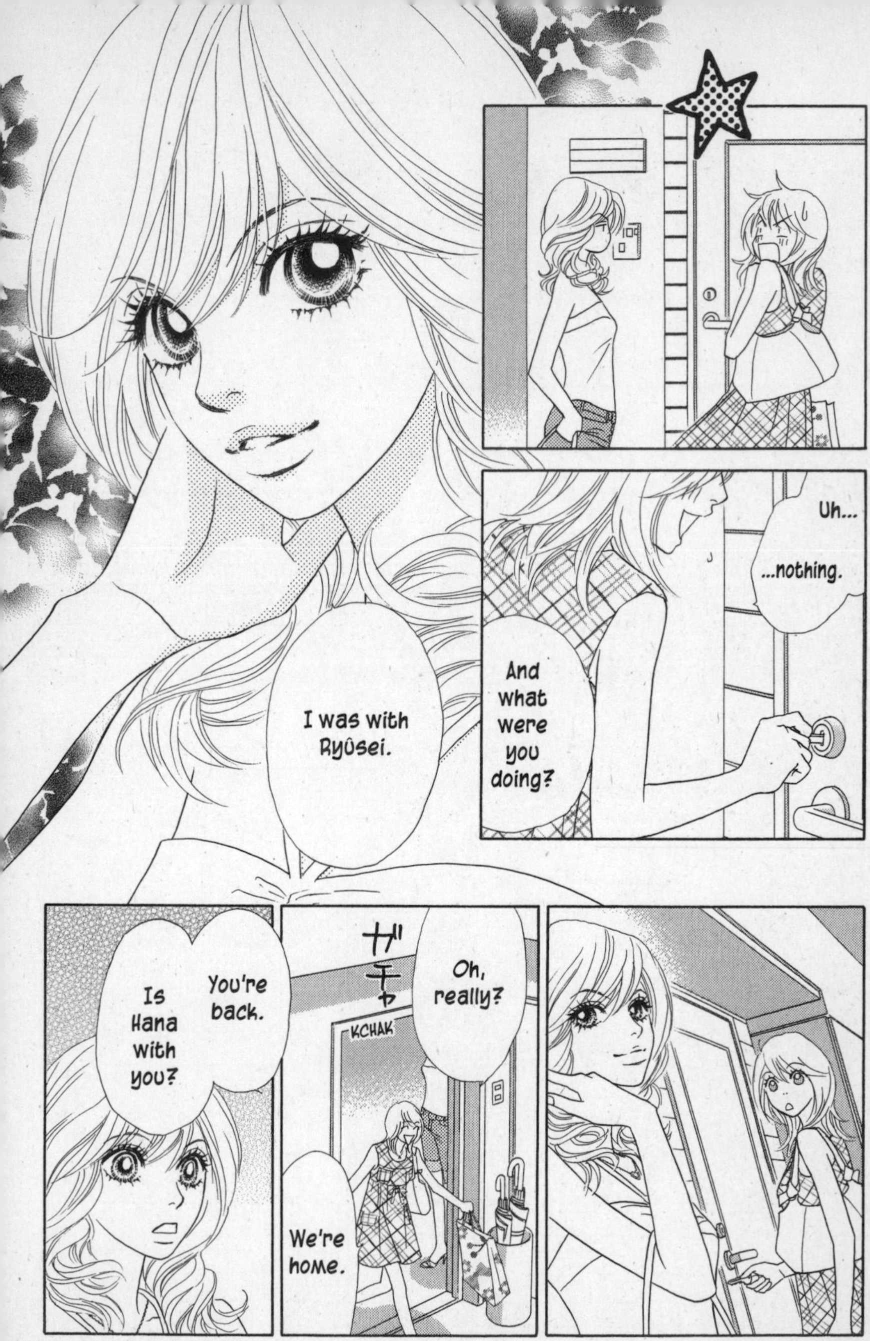

Uh...
...nothing.
And what were you doing?
I was with Ryûsei.
Oh, really?
ガチャ
KCHAK
We're home.
You're back.
Is Hana with you?

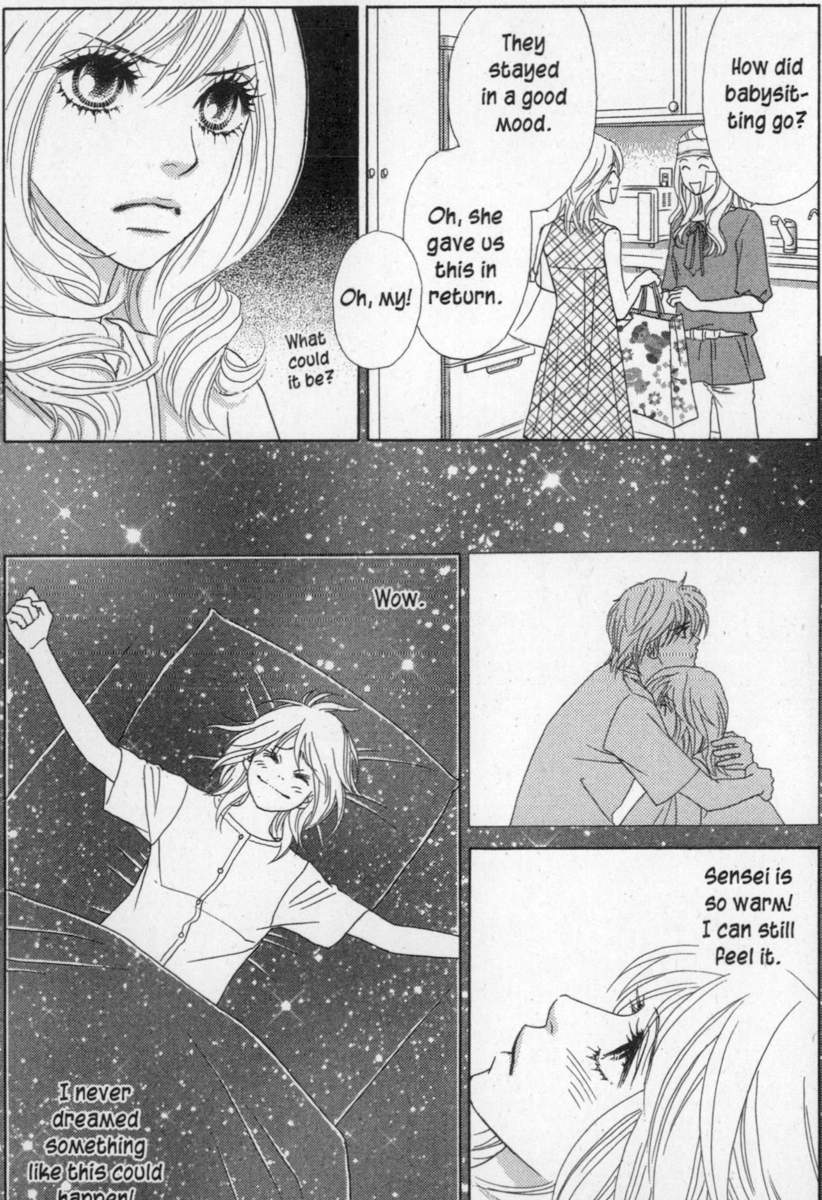
How did babysit-ting go?
They stayed in a good mood.
Oh, she gave us this in return.
Oh, my!
What could it be?
Sensei is so warm! I can still feel it.
Wow.
I never dreamed something like this could happen!

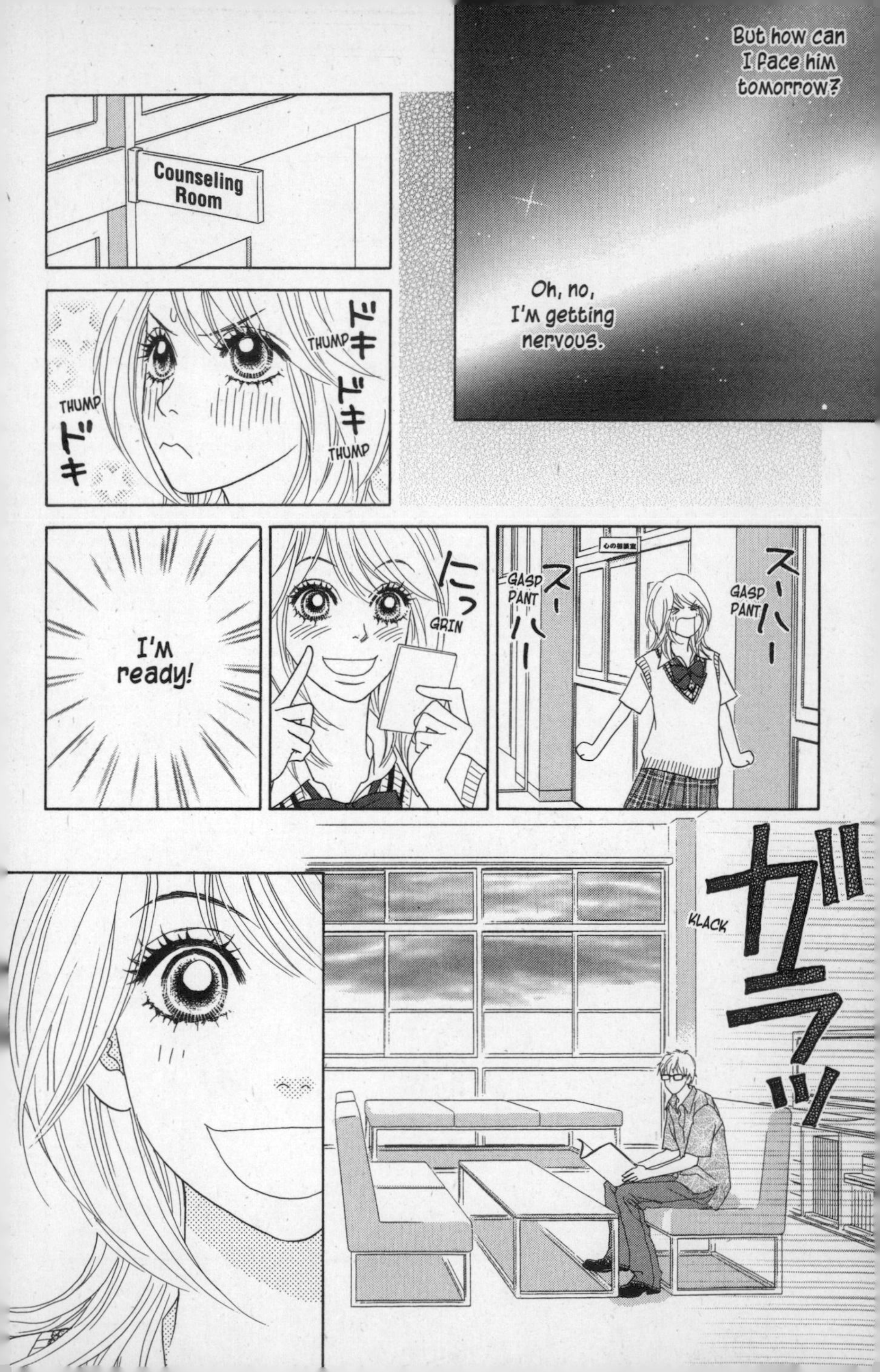
But how can I face him tomorrow?
Oh, no, I'm getting nervous.
Counseling Room
ドキ THUMP
ドキ THUMP
ドキ THUMP
GASP PANT スー ハー
GASP PANT スー ハー
にっ GRIN
I'M ready!
ガラッ KLACK

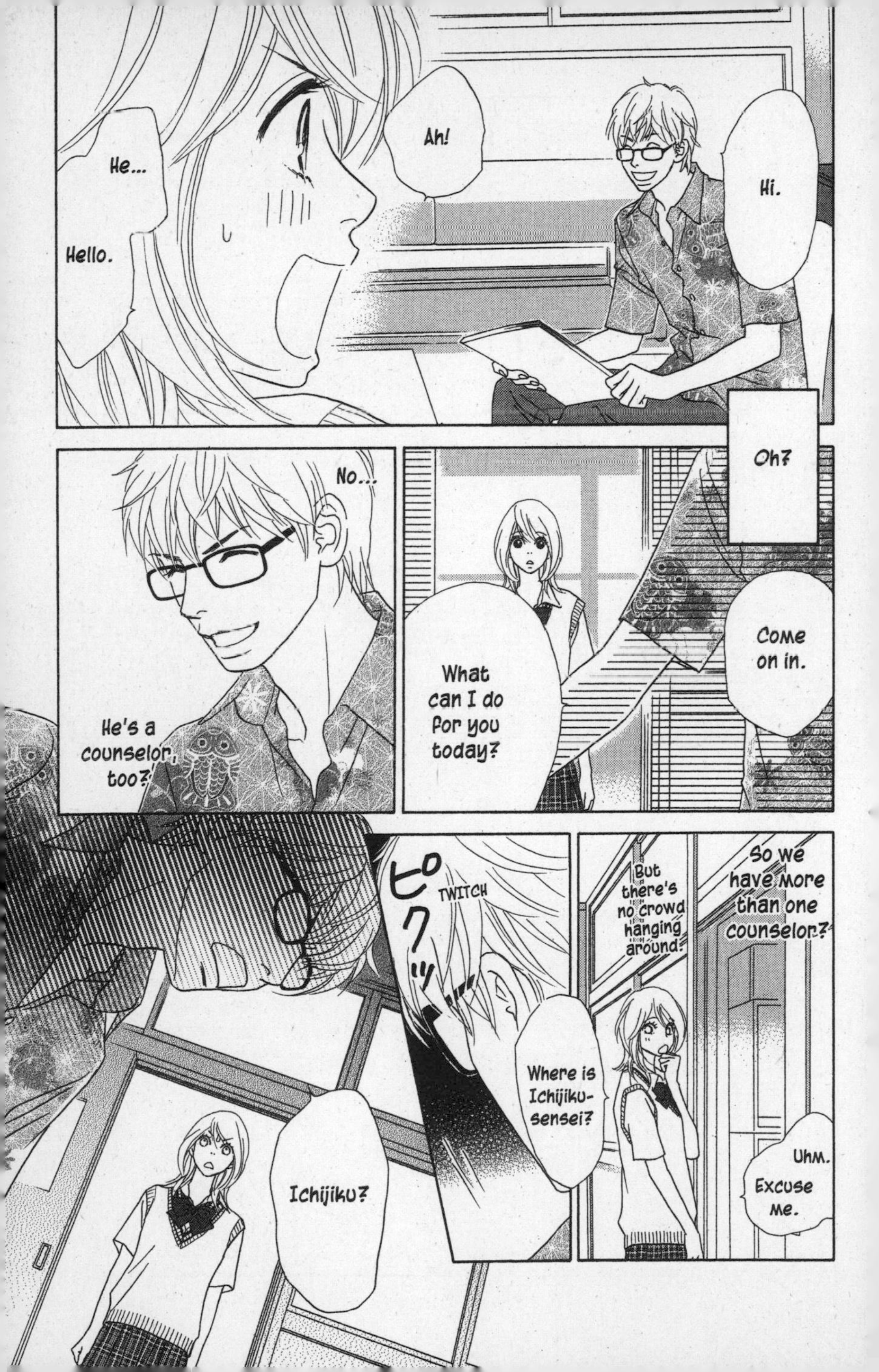
Hi.
Ah!
He...
Hello.
Oh?
Come on in.
What can I do for you today?
No...
He's a counselor, too?
Uhm. Excuse me.
So we have more than one counselor?
But there's no crowd hanging around.
Where is Ichijiku-sensei?
TWITCH
Ichijiku?

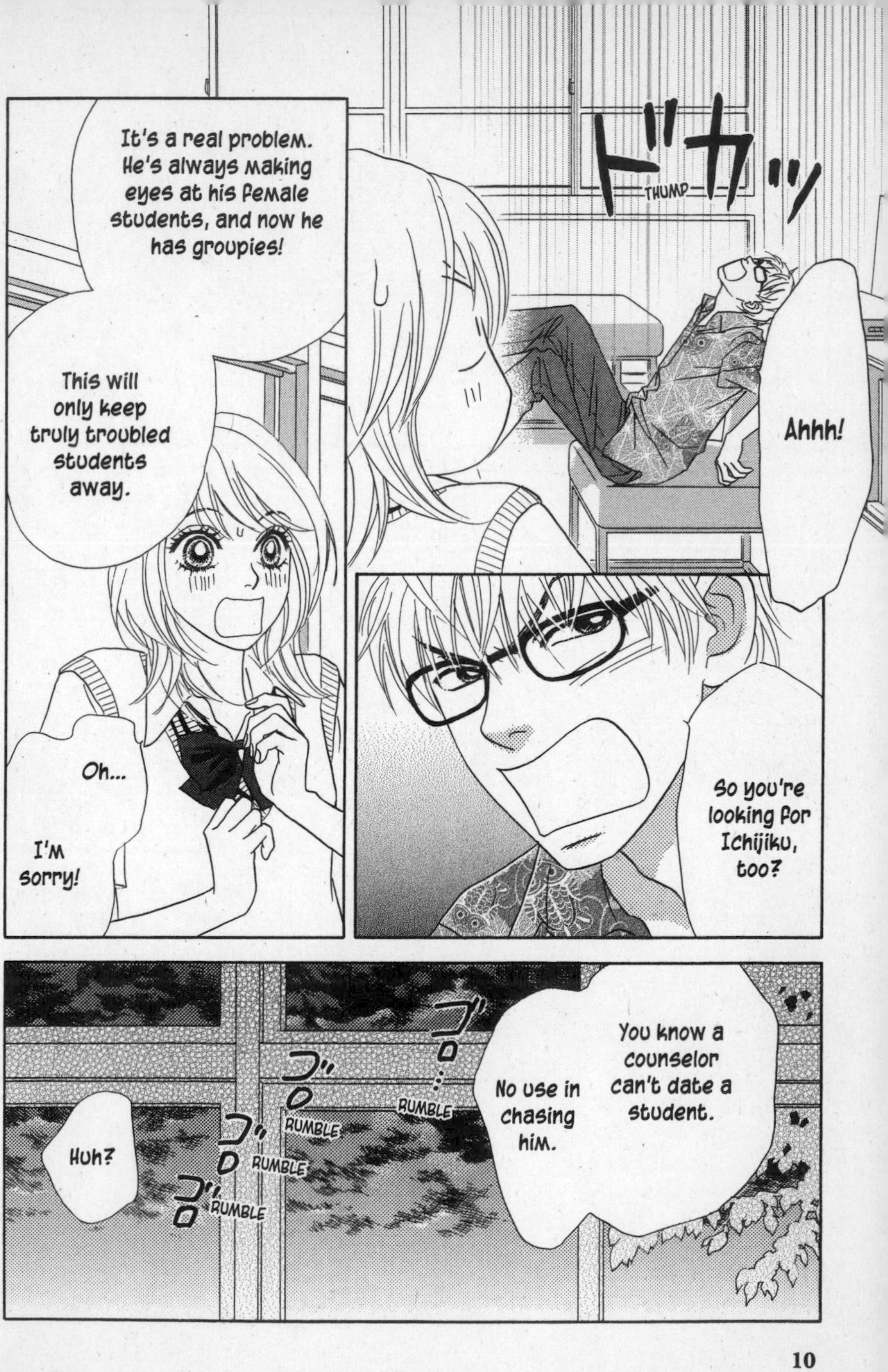
ドカッ
THUMP
Ahhh!
So you're looking for Ichijiku, too?
It's a real problem. He's always making eyes at his female students, and now he has groupies!
This will only keep truly troubled students away.
Oh...
I'm sorry!
You know a counselor can't date a student.
No use in chasing him.
ゴロ...
RUMBLE
ゴロ
RUMBLE
ゴロ
RUMBLE
ゴロ
RUMBLE
Huh?

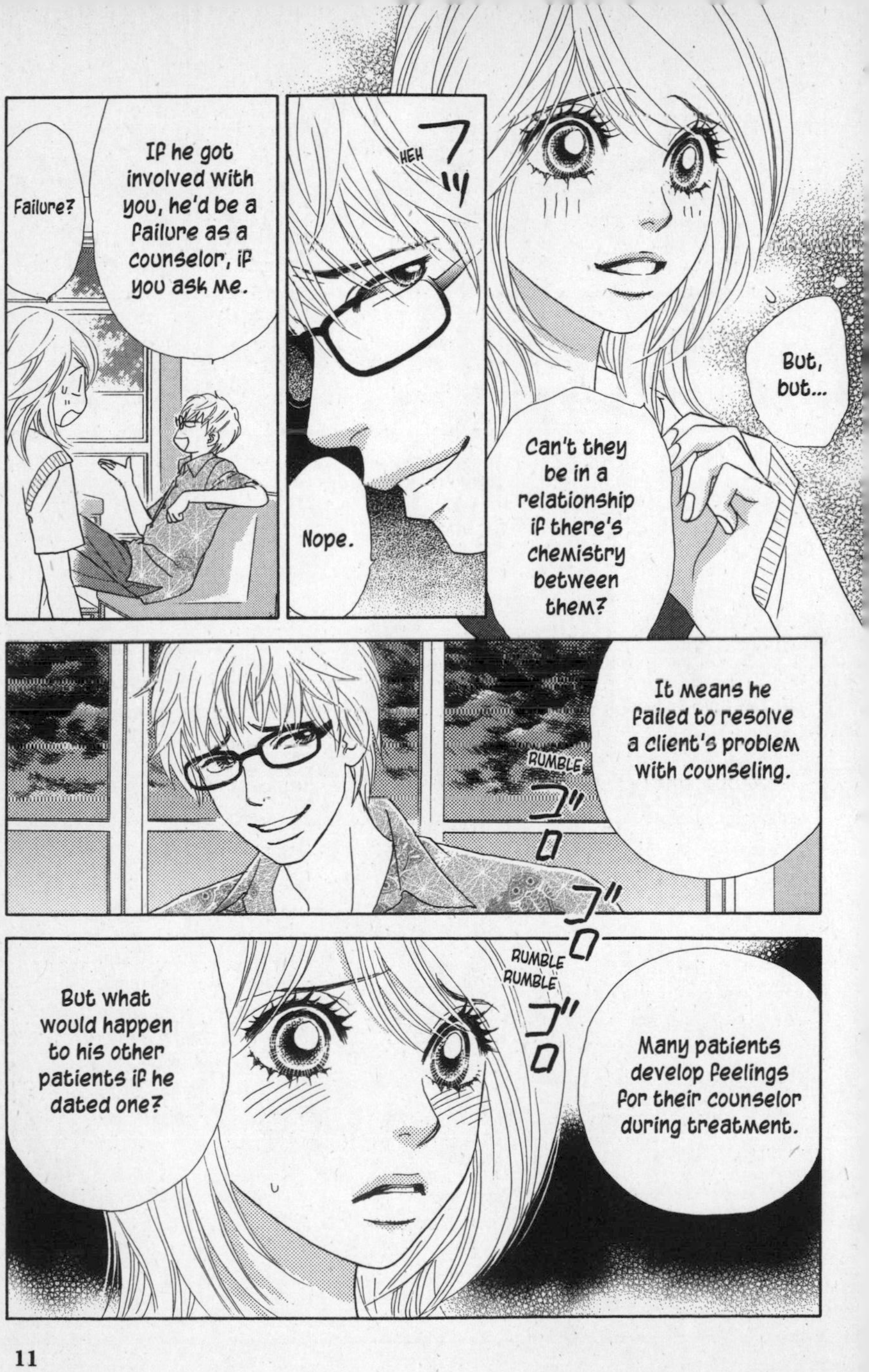
But, but...
Can't they be in a relationship if there's chemistry between them?
HEH
Nope.
If he got involved with you, he'd be a failure as a counselor, if you ask me.
Failure?
It means he failed to resolve a client's problem with counseling.
RUMBLE
Many patients develop feelings for their counselor during treatment.
RUMBLE RUMBLE
But what would happen to his other patients if he dated one?

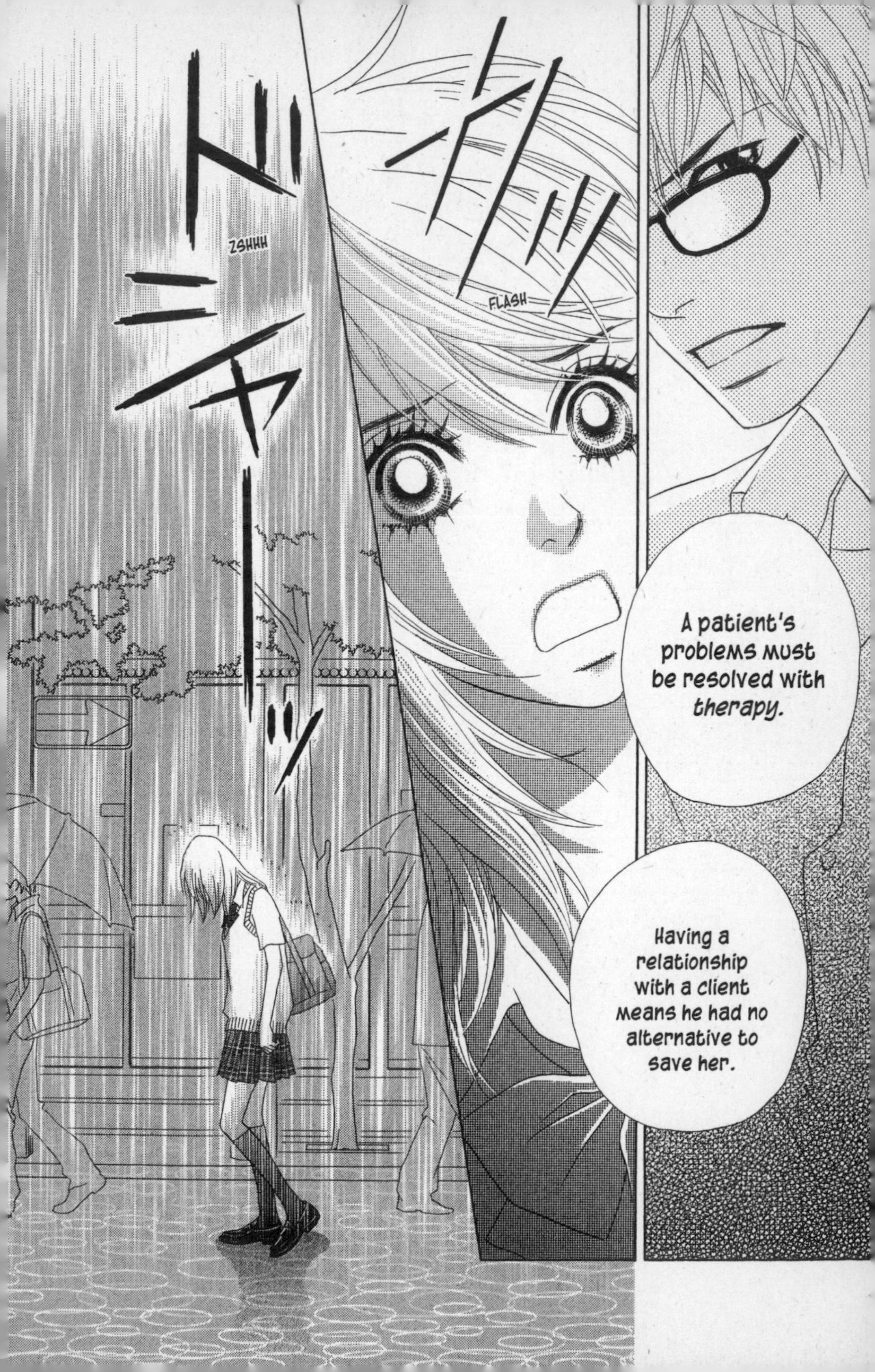
A patient's problems must be resolved with *therapy.*
Having a relationship with a client means he had no alternative to save her.
FLASH
ZSHHH

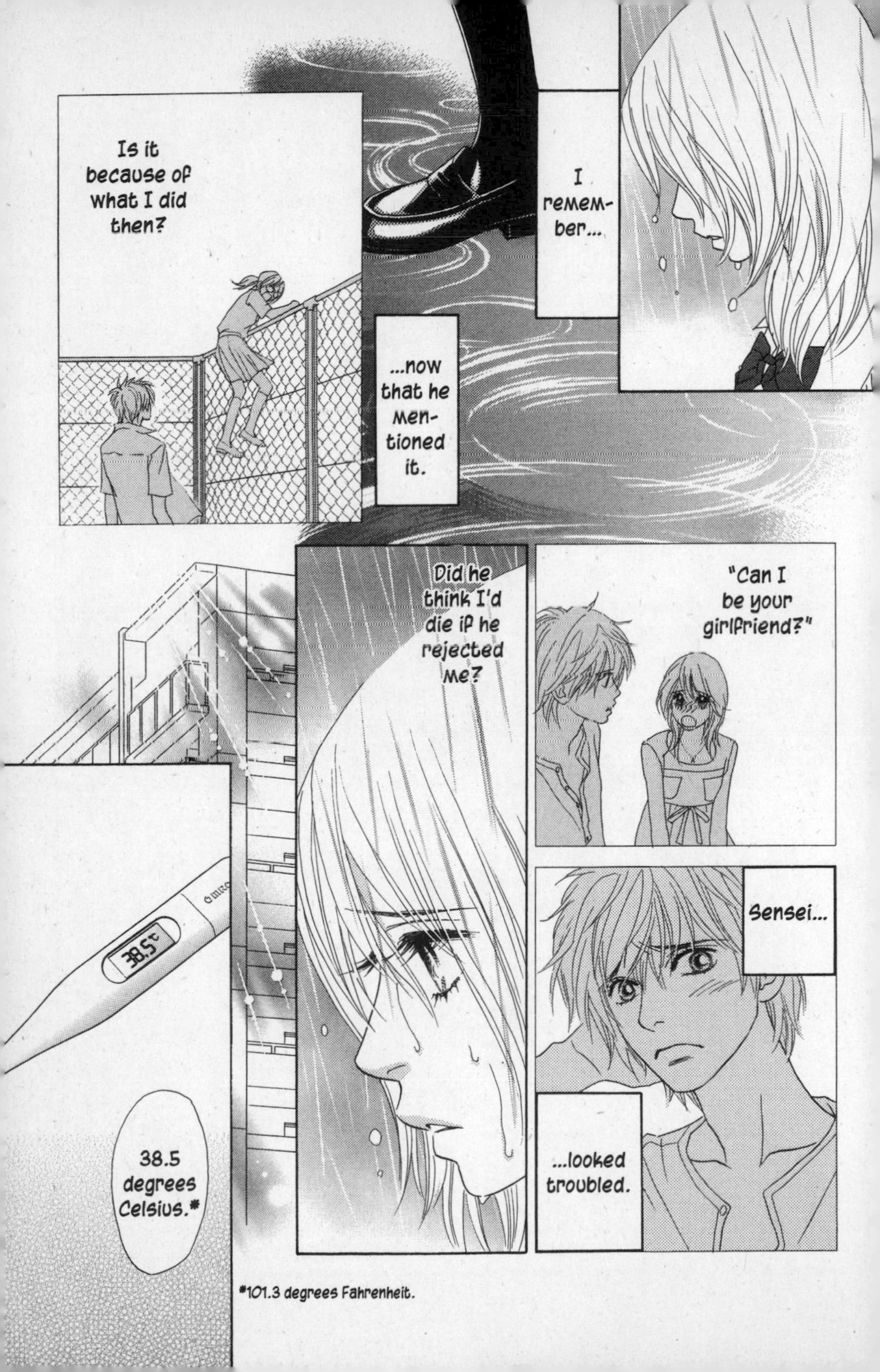
I remember...
...now that he mentioned it.
Is it because of what I did then?
"Can I be your girlfriend?"
Sensei...
...looked troubled.
Did he think I'd die if he rejected me?
38.5
38.5 degrees Celsius.*

*101.3 degrees Fahrenheit.

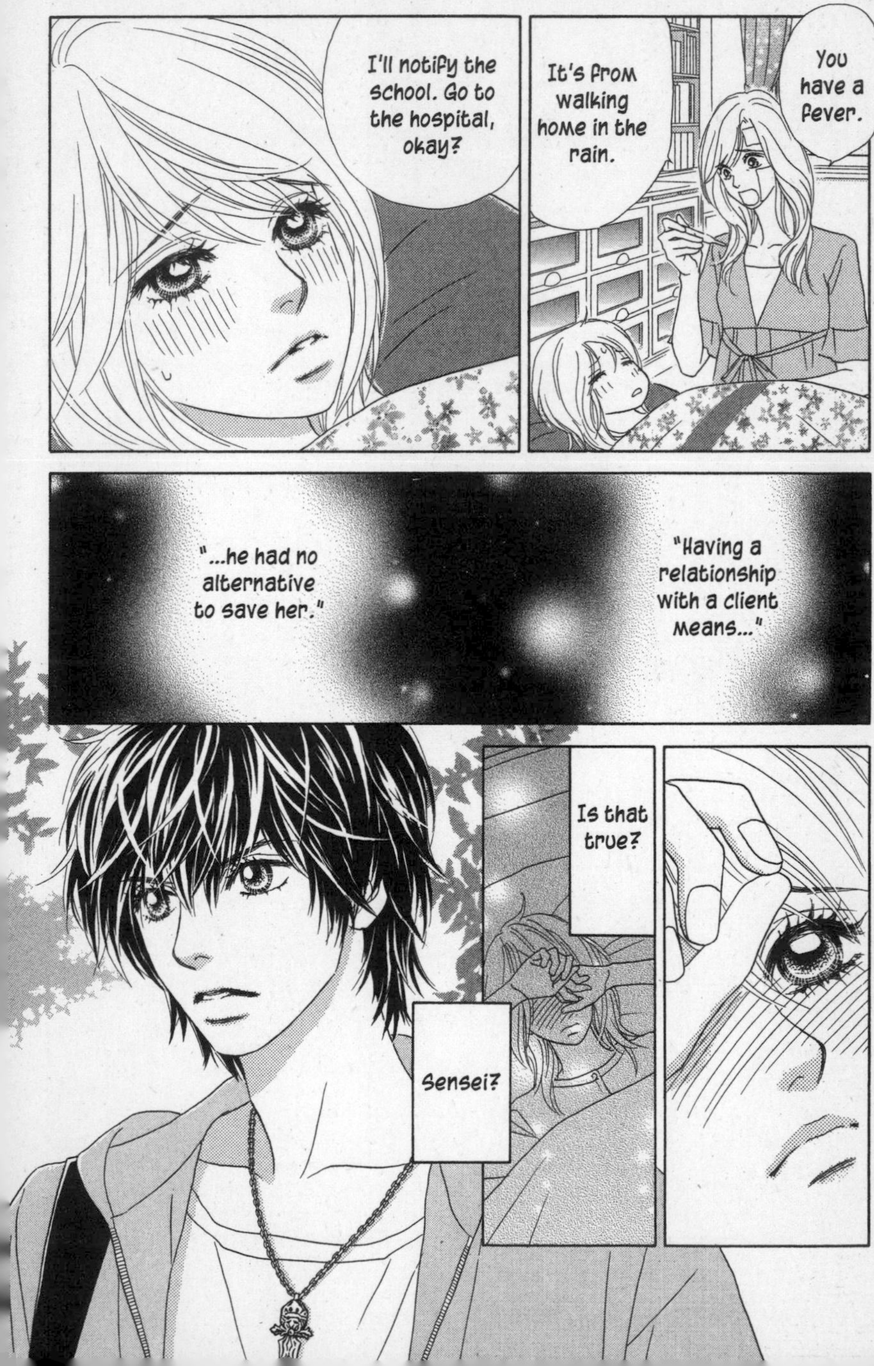
You have a fever.
It's from walking home in the rain.
I'll notify the school. Go to the hospital, okay?
"Having a relationship with a client means..."
"...he had no alternative to save her."
Is that true?
Sensei?

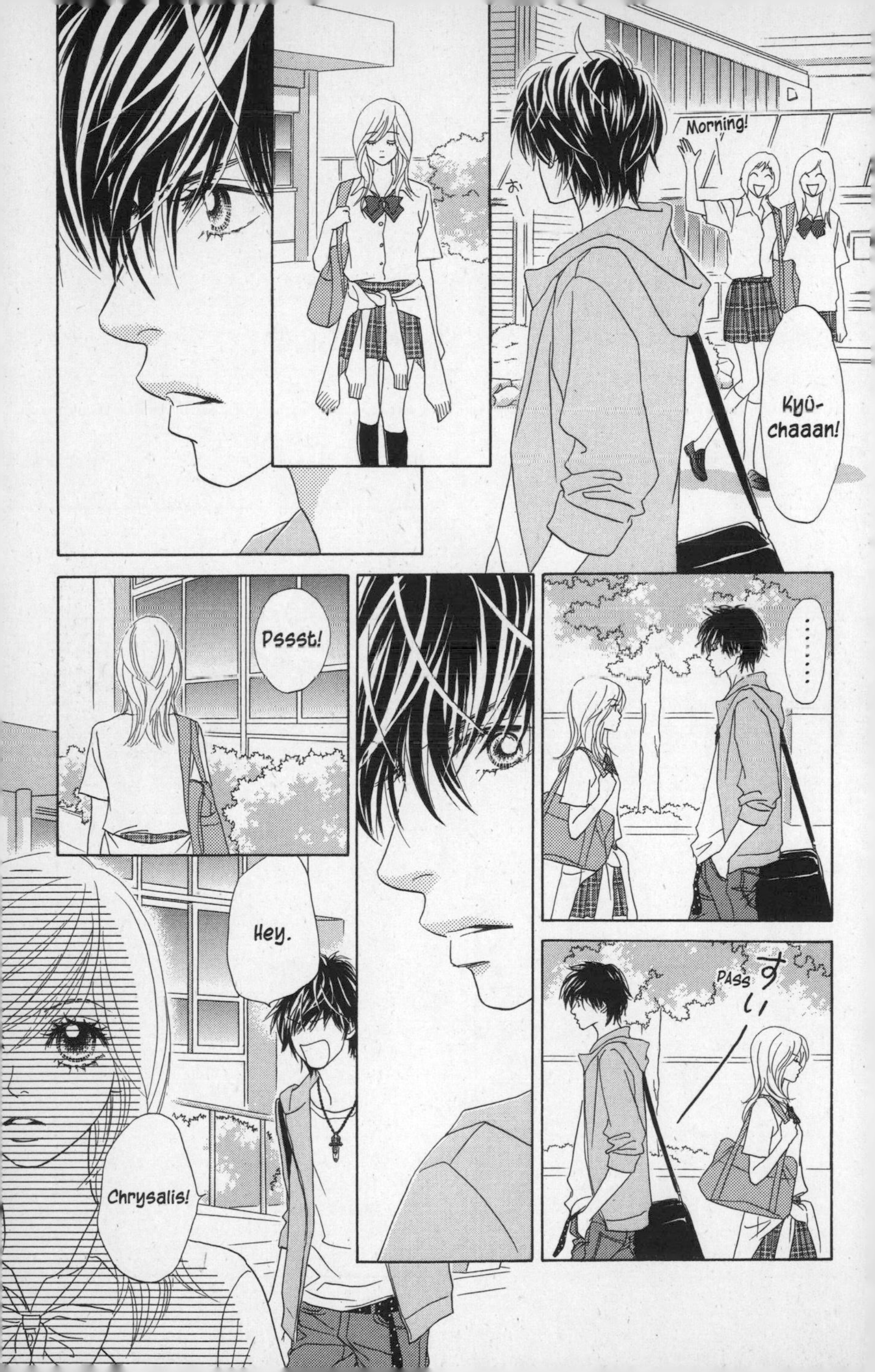

Morning!
お
Kyû-chaaan!
......
PASS
すい
Pssst!
Hey.
Chrysalis!

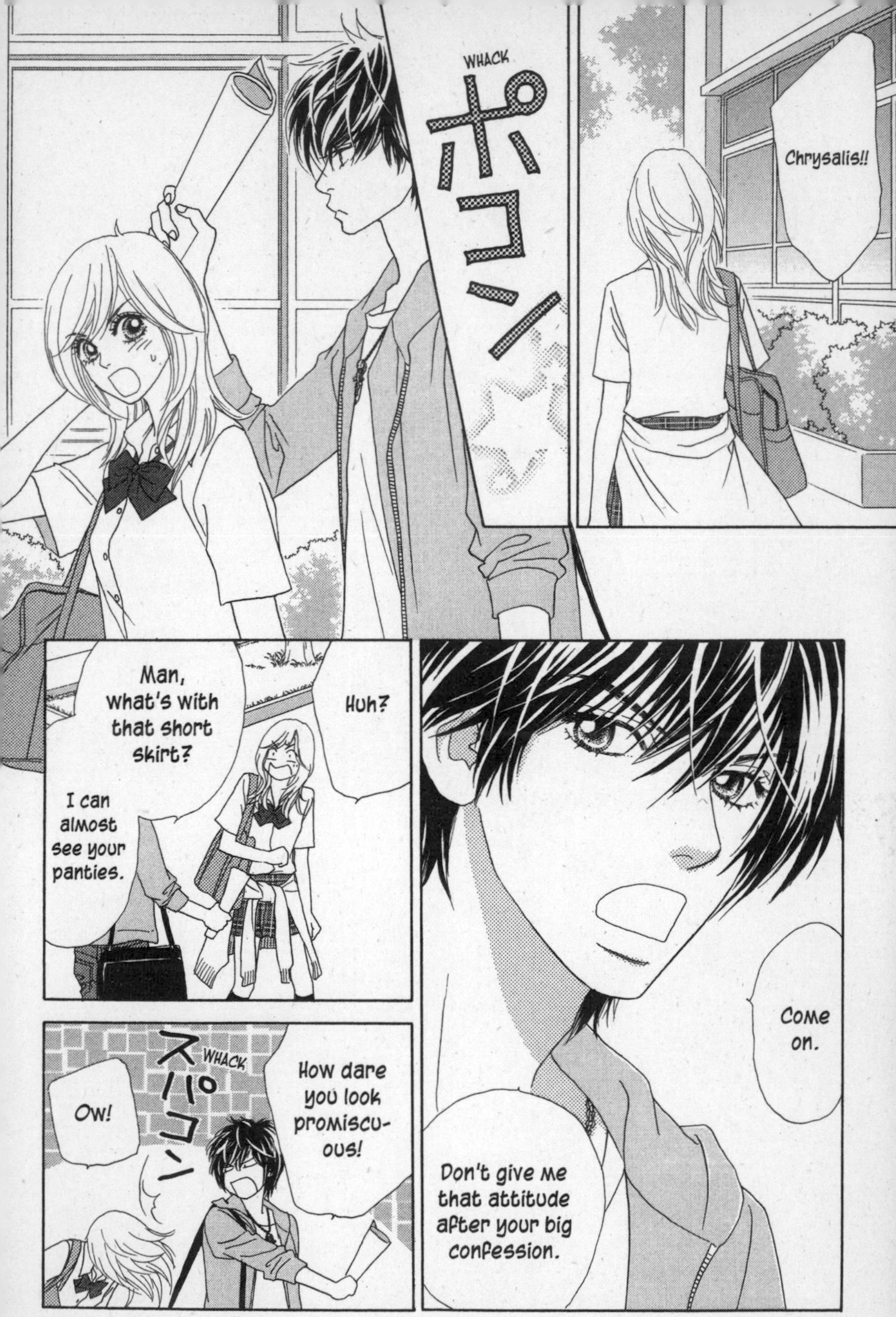
Chrysalis!!
WHACK
ポコン
Come on.
Don't give me that attitude after your big confession.
Man, what's with that short skirt?
I can almost see your panties.
Huh?
How dare you look promiscuous!
WHACK
スパコン
Ow!

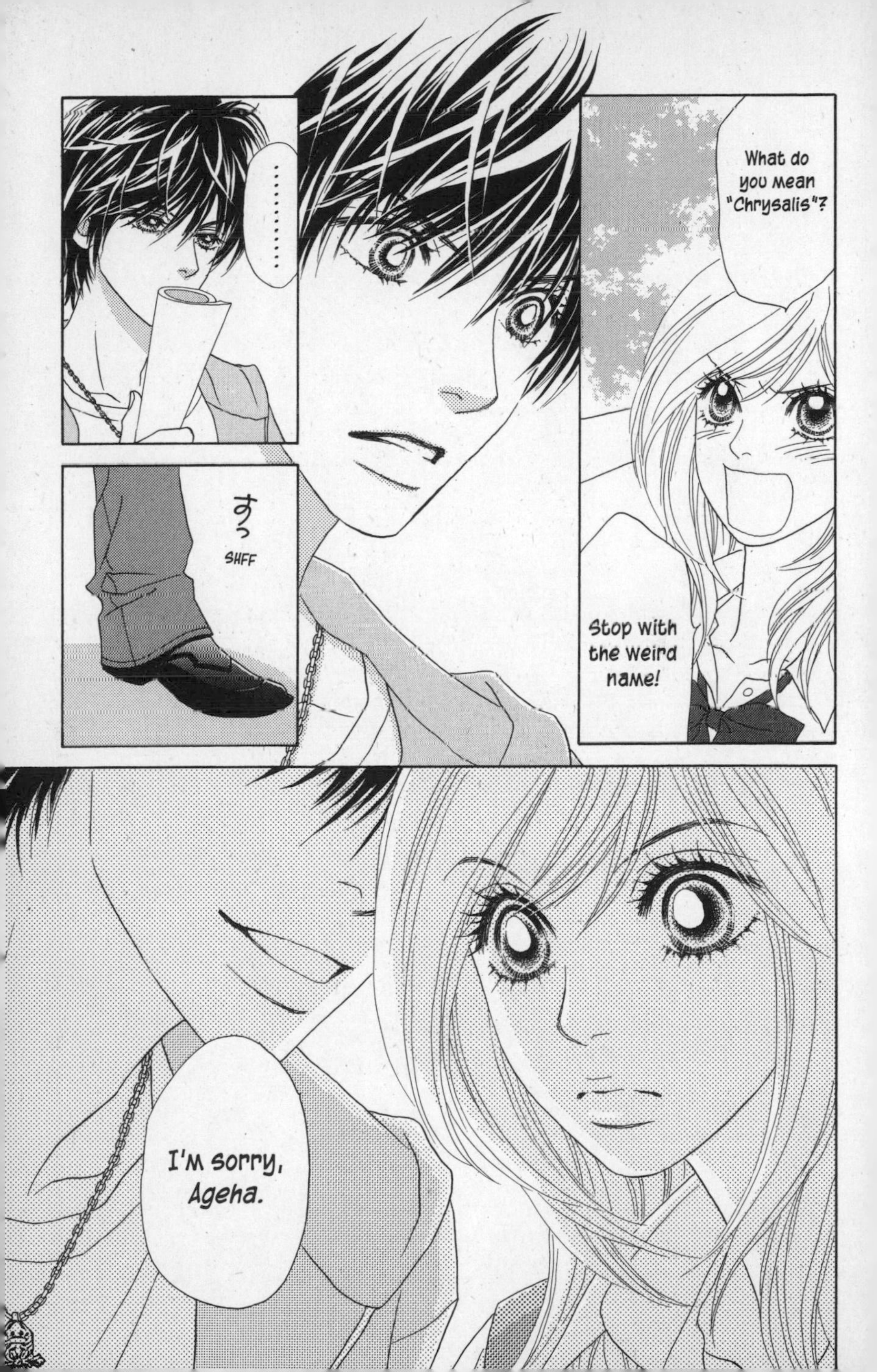
What do you mean "Chrysalis"?
Stop with the weird name!
......
すっ
SHFF
I'm sorry, Ageha.

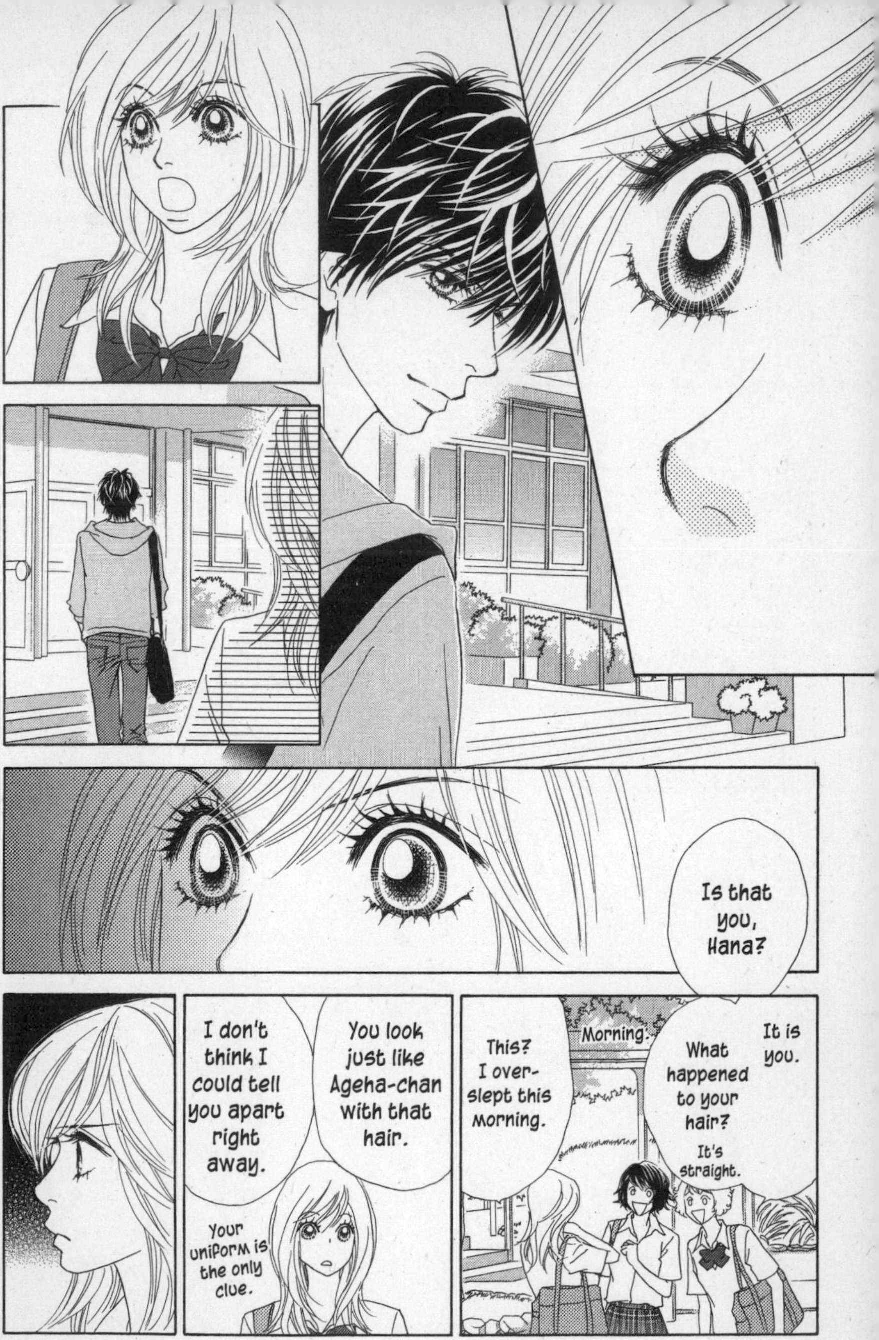
Is that you, Hana?
It is you.
What happened to your hair?
It's straight.
Morning.
This? I over-slept this morning.
You look just like Ageha-chan with that hair.
I don't think I could tell you apart right away.
Your uniform is the only clue.

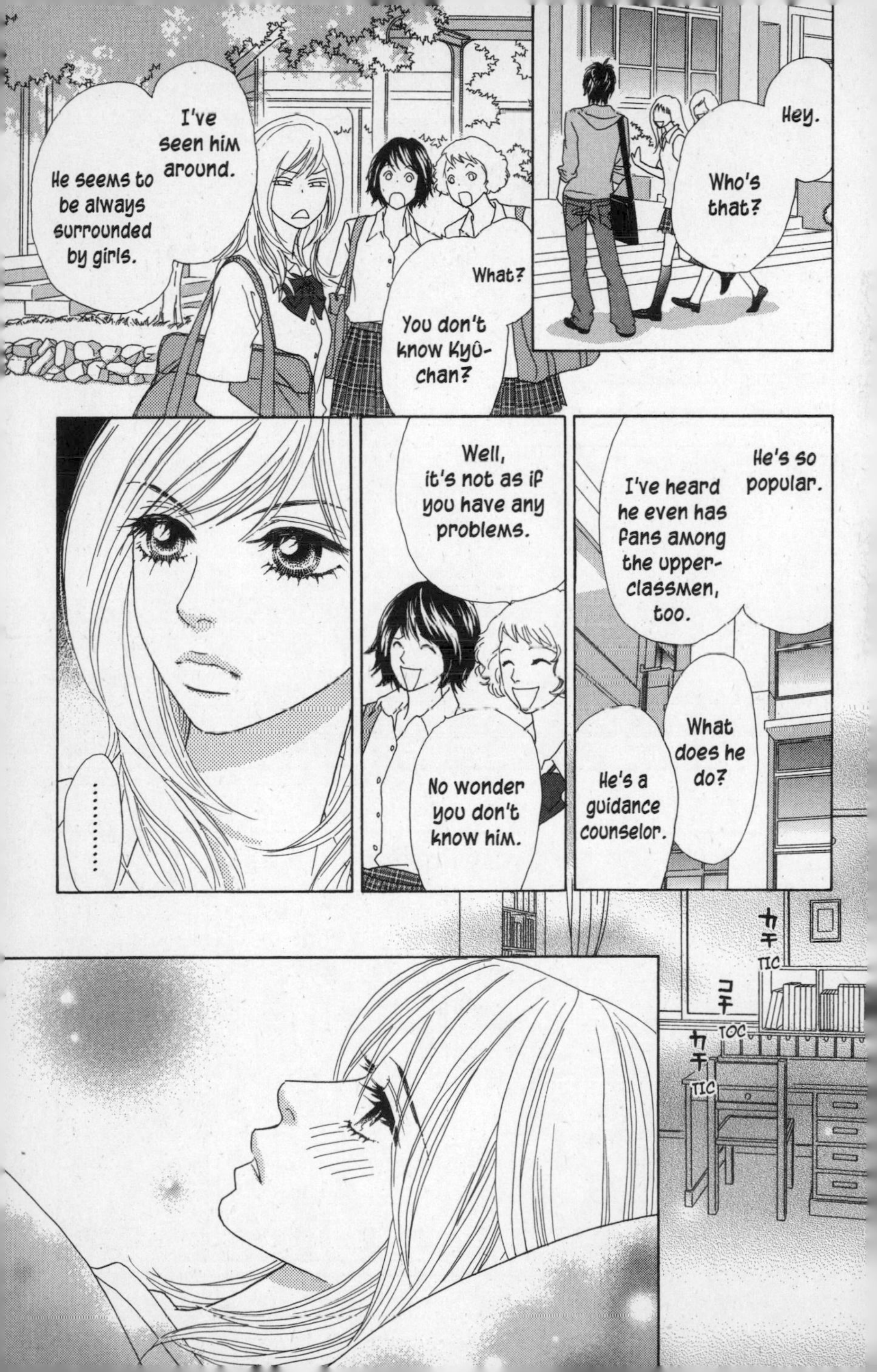
Hey.
Who's that?
What?
You don't know Kyû-chan?
I've seen him around.
He seems to be always surrounded by girls.
He's so popular.
I've heard he even has fans among the upperclassmen, too.
What does he do?
He's a guidance counselor.
Well, it's not as if you have any problems.
No wonder you don't know him.
......
カチ TIC
コチ TOC
カチ TIC

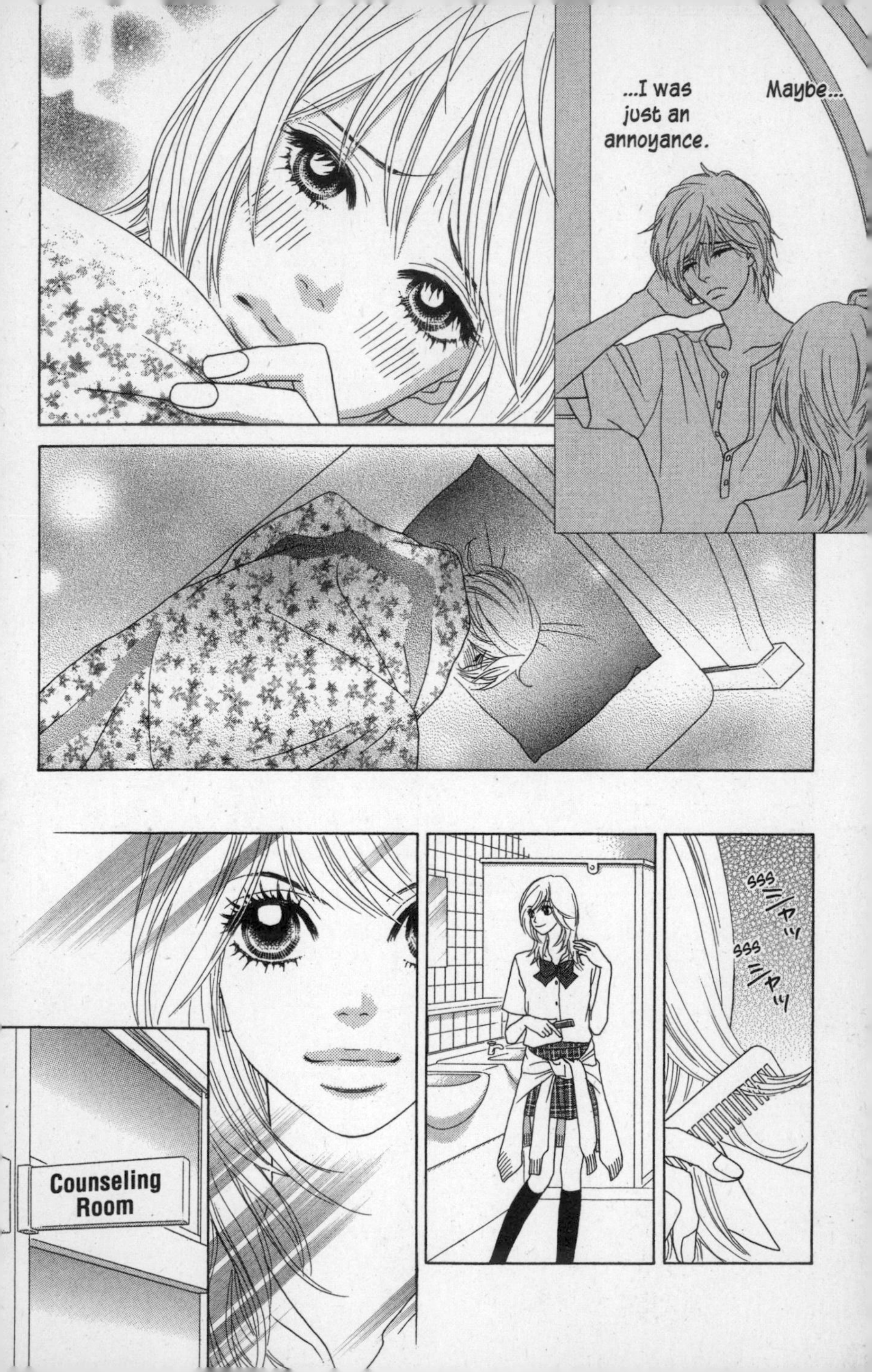
Maybe...
...I was just an annoyance.
sss
シャッ
sss
シャッ
Counseling Room

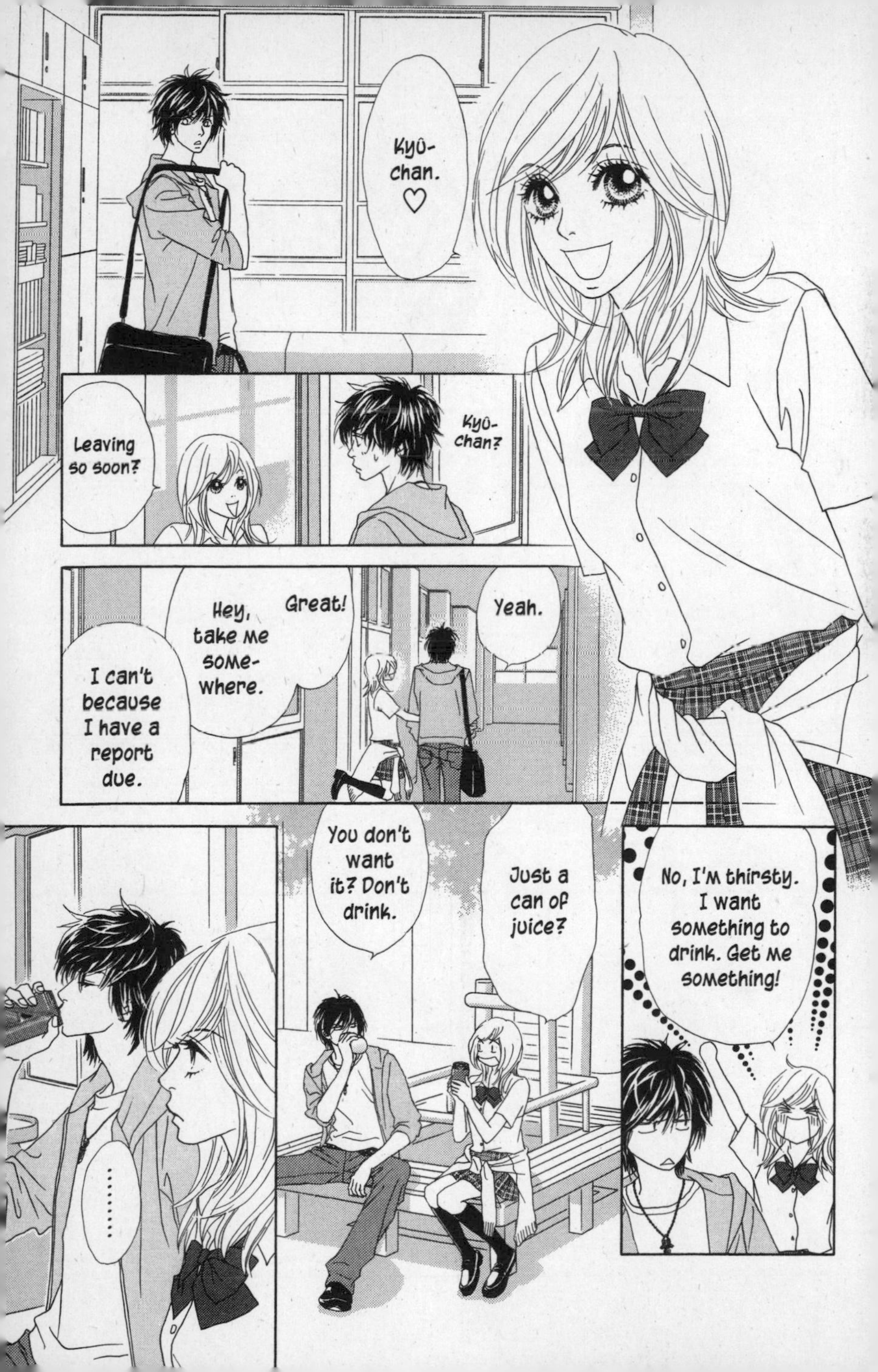
Kyû-chan. ♡
Kyû-chan?
Leaving so soon?
Yeah.
Great!
Hey, take me some-where.
I can't because I have a report due.
No, I'm thirsty. I want something to drink. Get me something!
Just a can of juice?
You don't want it? Don't drink.
......

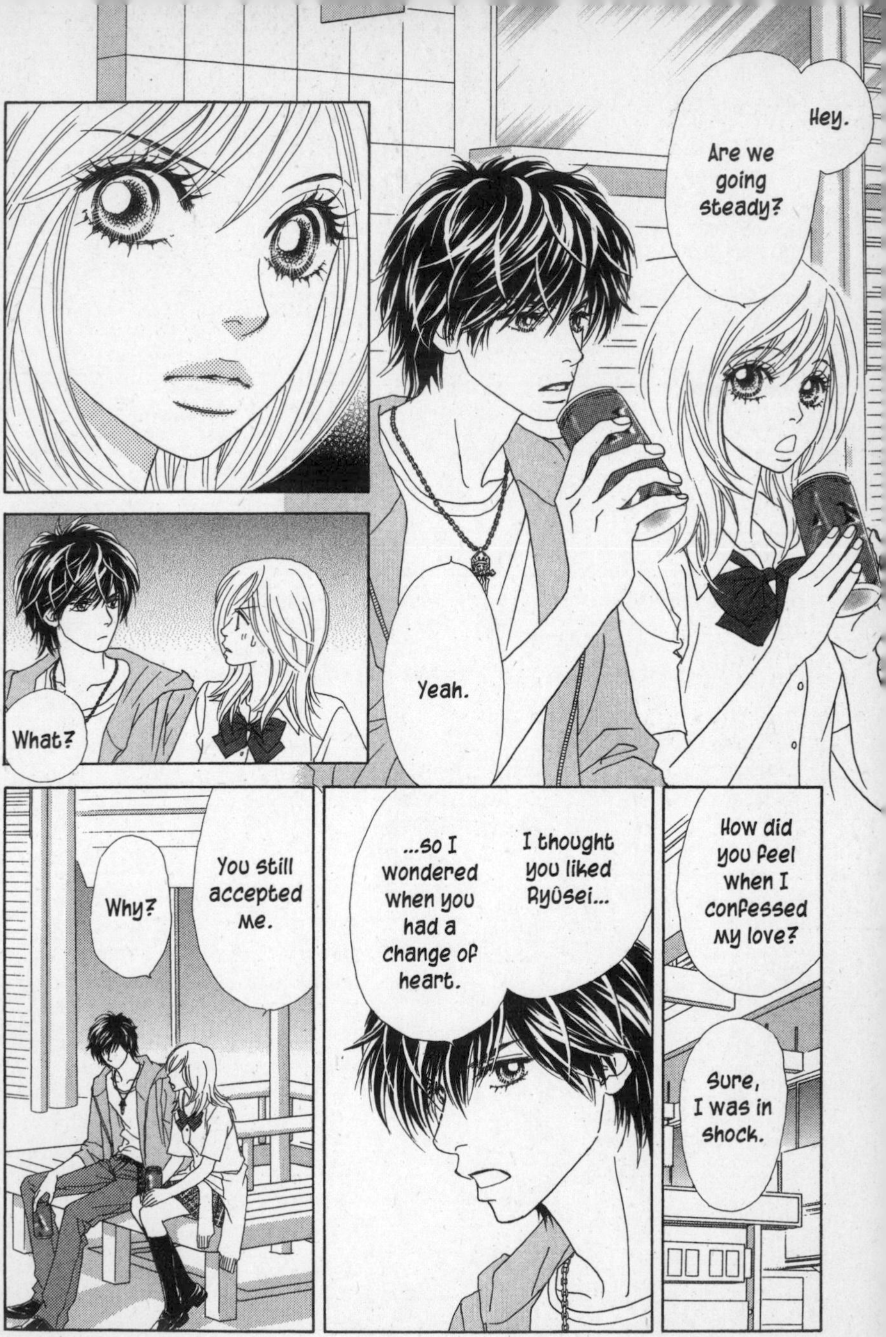
Hey.
Are we going steady?
Yeah.
What?
How did you feel when I confessed my love?
Sure, I was in shock.
I thought you liked Ryûsei...
...so I wondered when you had a change of heart.
You still accepted me.
Why?

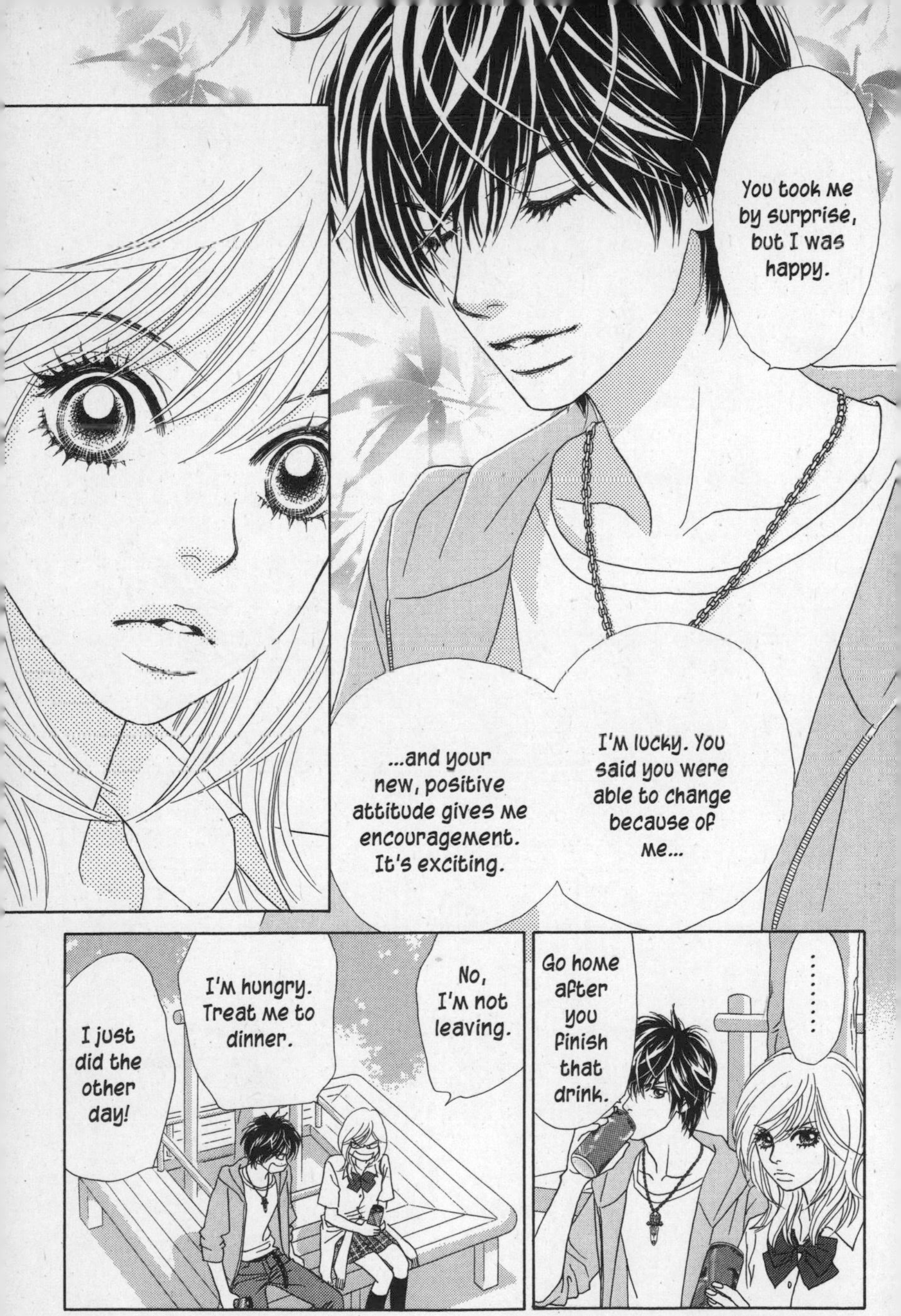
You took me by surprise, but I was happy.
I'm lucky. You said you were able to change because of me...
...and your new, positive attitude gives me encouragement. It's exciting.
....
Go home after you finish that drink.
No, I'm not leaving.
I'm hungry. Treat me to dinner.
I just did the other day!

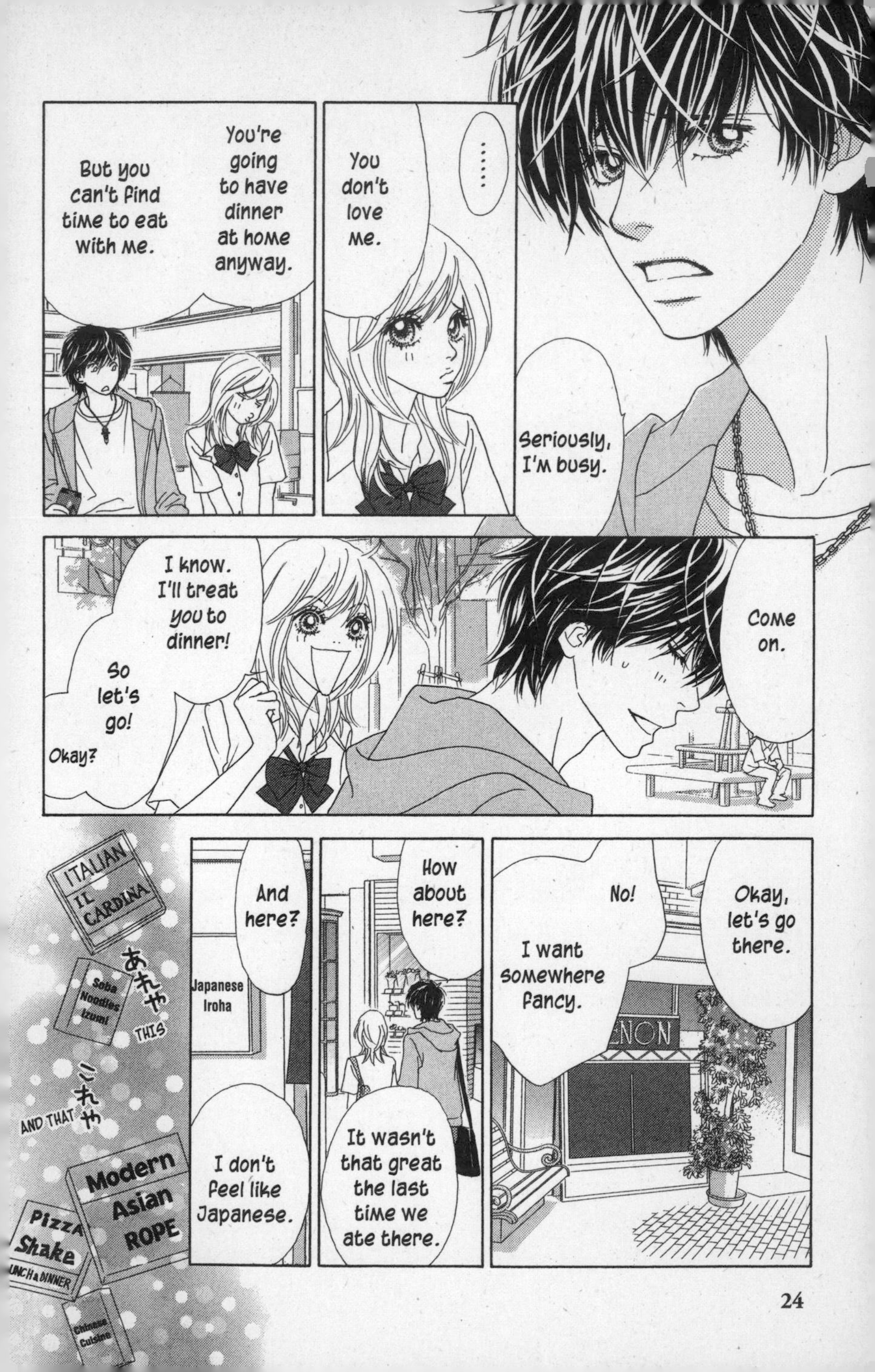
Seriously, I'm busy.
......
You don't love me.
You're going to have dinner at home anyway.
But you can't find time to eat with me.
Come on.
I know. I'll treat you to dinner!
So let's go!
Okay?
Okay, let's go there.
No!
I want somewhere fancy.
How about here?
It wasn't that great the last time we ate there.
And here?
Japanese Iroha
I don't feel like Japanese.
ITALIAN IL CARDINA
Soba Noodles Izumi
あれや
THIS
これや
AND THAT
Modern Asian ROPE
Pizza Shake
LUNCH & DINNER
Chinese Cuisine

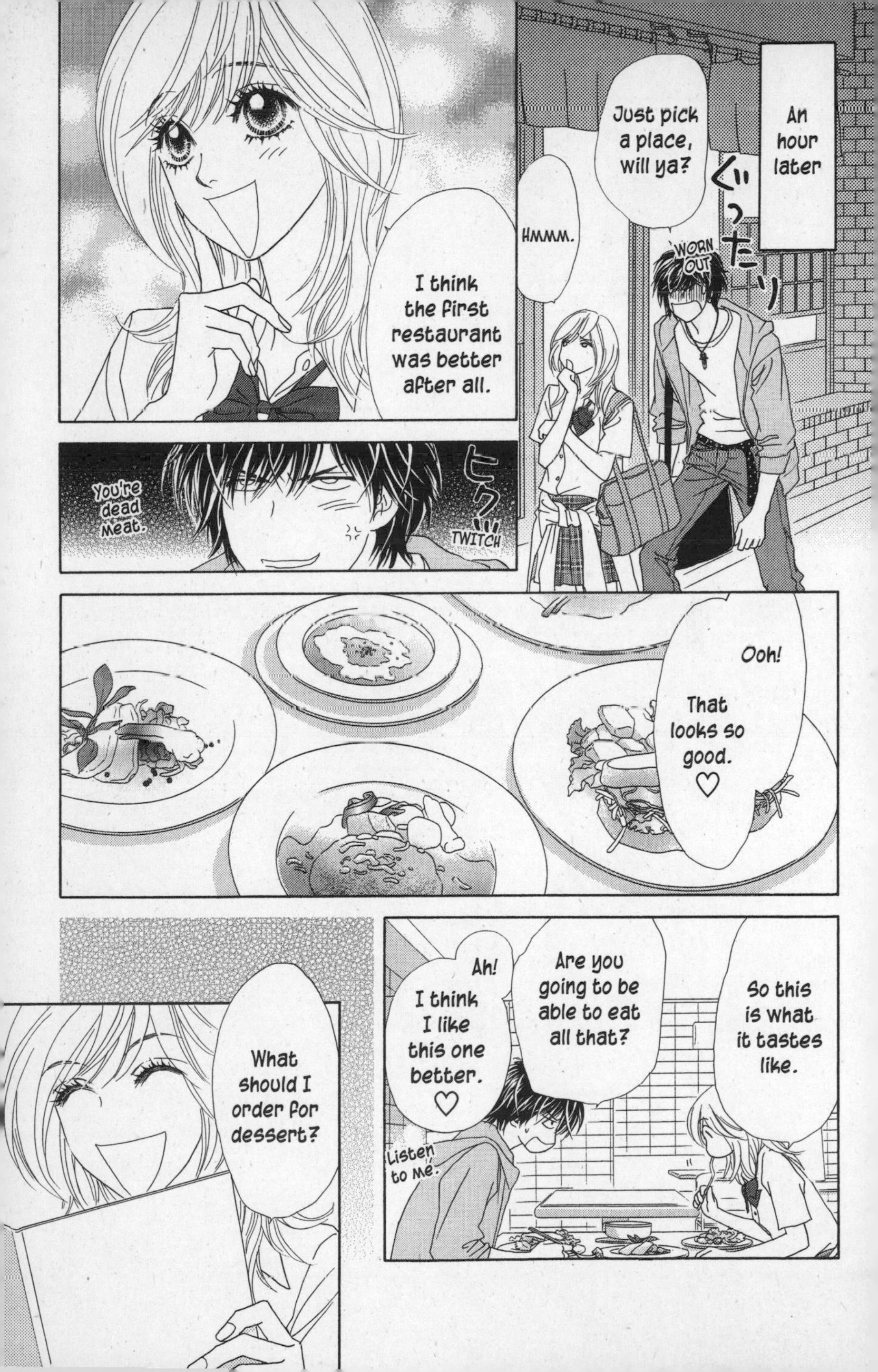
An hour later
ぐったり
Just pick a place, will ya?
HMMM.
WORN OUT
I think the first restaurant was better after all.
ヒク
TWITCH
You're dead meat.
Ooh!
That looks so good. ♡
So this is what it tastes like.
Are you going to be able to eat all that?
Ah! I think I like this one better. ♡
Listen to me.
What should I order for dessert?

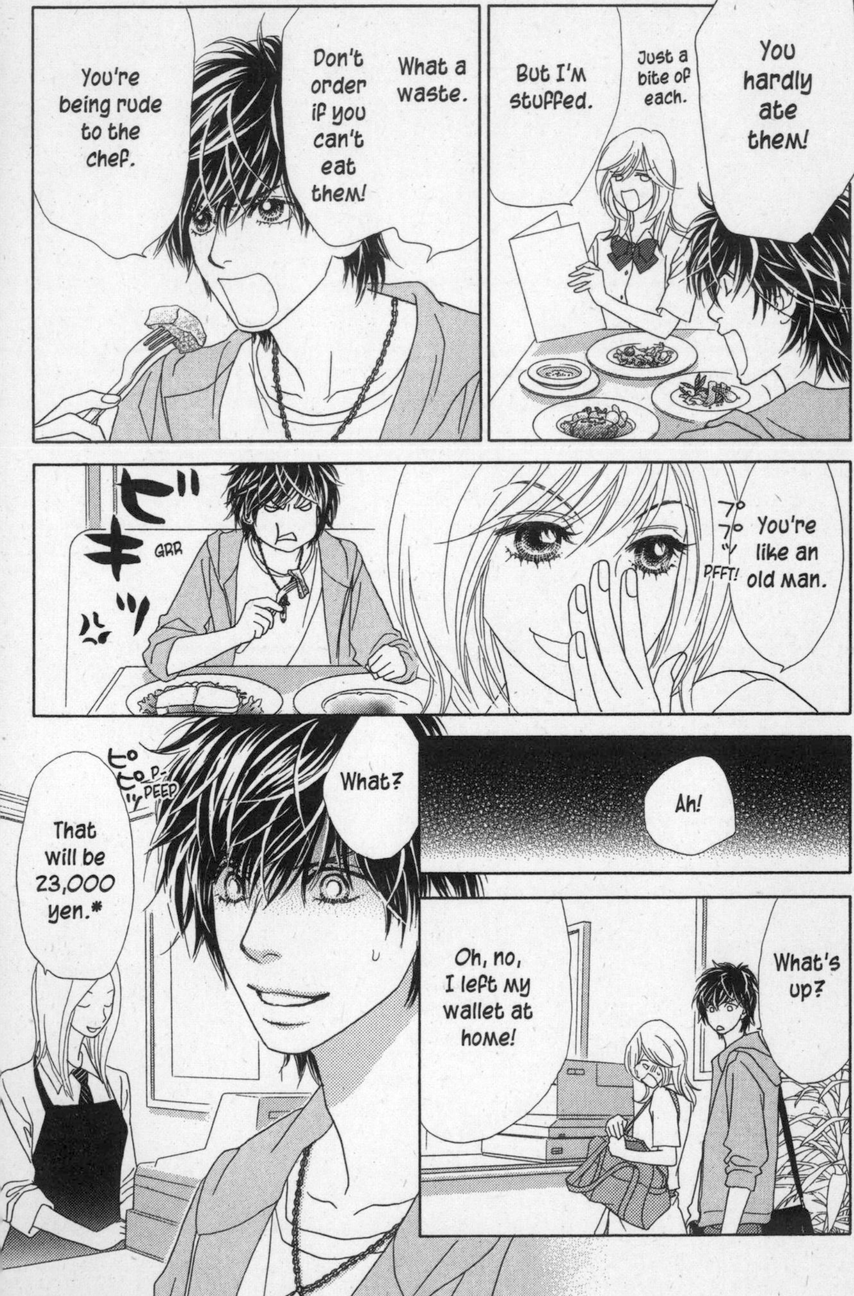
You hardly ate them!
Just a bite of each.
But I'm stuffed.
What a waste.
Don't order if you can't eat them!
You're being rude to the chef.
You're like an old man.
ププッ
PFFT!
ビキッ
GRR
Ah!
What's up?
Oh, no, I left my wallet at home!
What?
ピピッ
P-PEEP
That will be 23,000 yen.*

*Approximately $230.

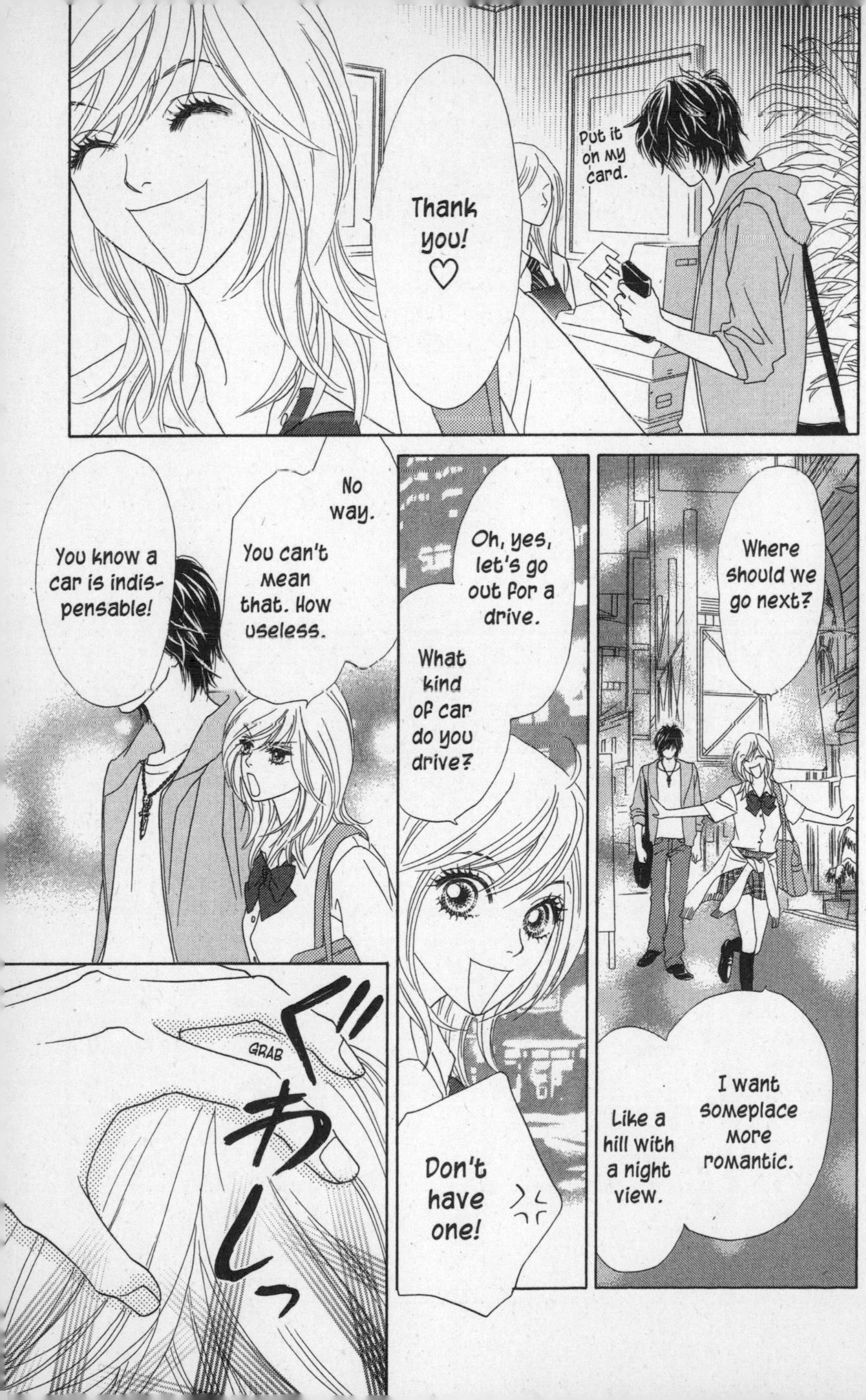

Put it on my card.
Thank you! ♡
Where should we go next?
I want someplace more romantic.
Like a hill with a night view.
Oh, yes, let's go out for a drive.
What kind of car do you drive?
Don't have one!
No way.
You can't mean that. How useless.
You know a car is indispensable!
ぐわしっ
GRAB

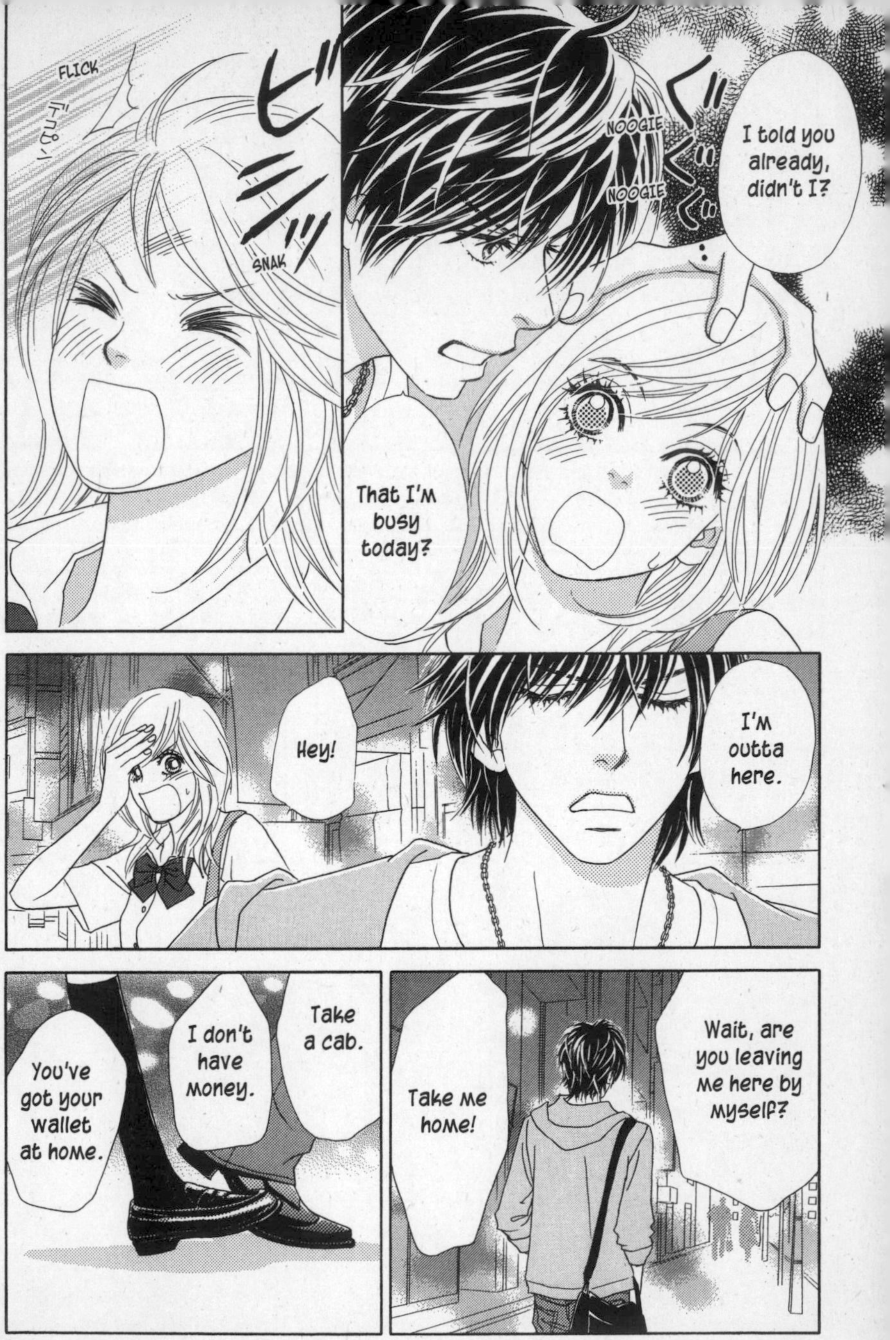
NOOGIE
NOOGIE
I told you already, didn't I?
That I'm busy today?
FLICK
SNAK
I'm outta here.
Hey!
Wait, are you leaving me here by myself?
Take me home!
Take a cab.
I don't have money.
You've got your wallet at home.

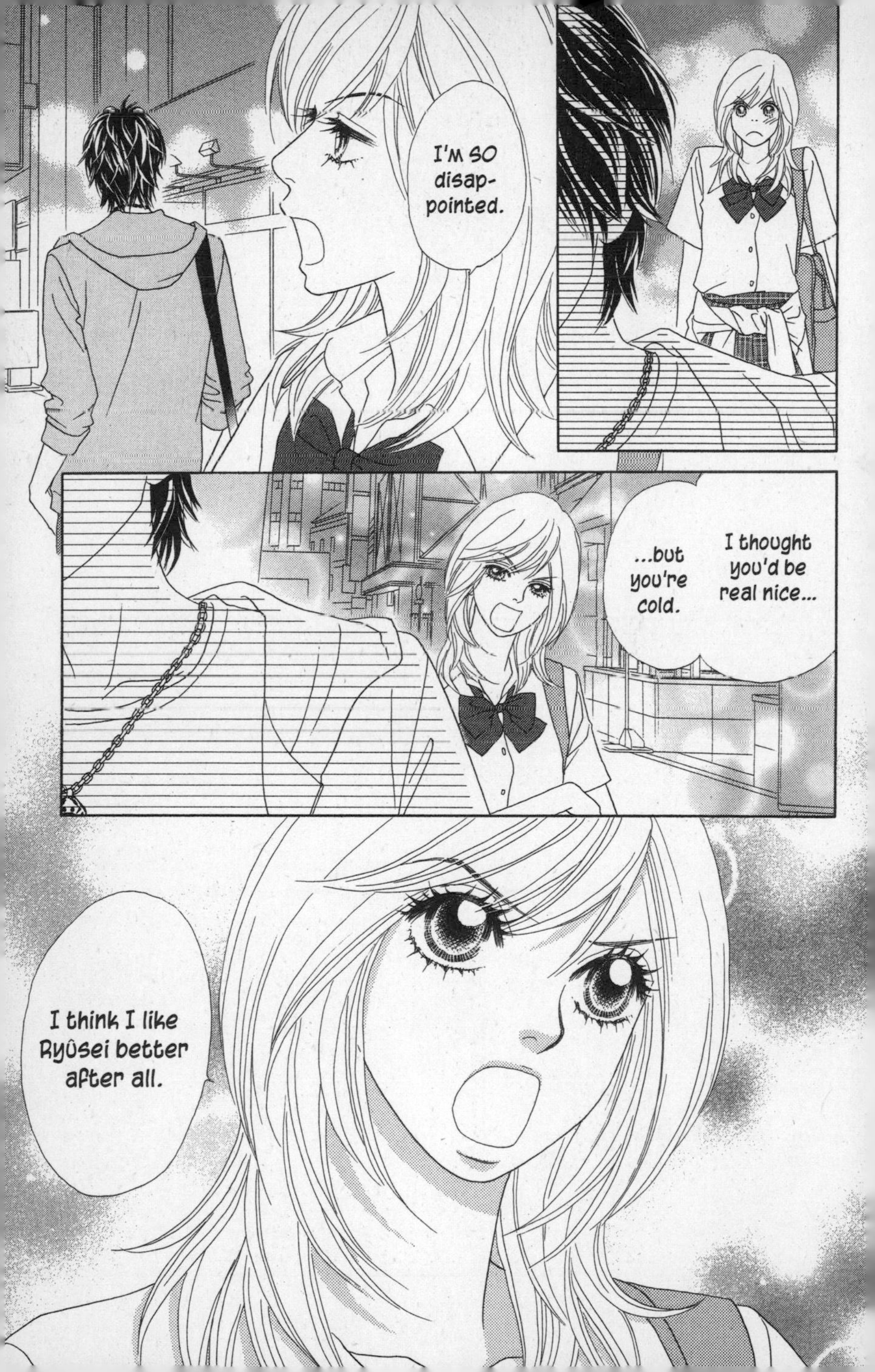
I'M SO disap-pointed.
I thought you'd be real nice...
...but you're cold.
I think I like Ryûsei better after all.

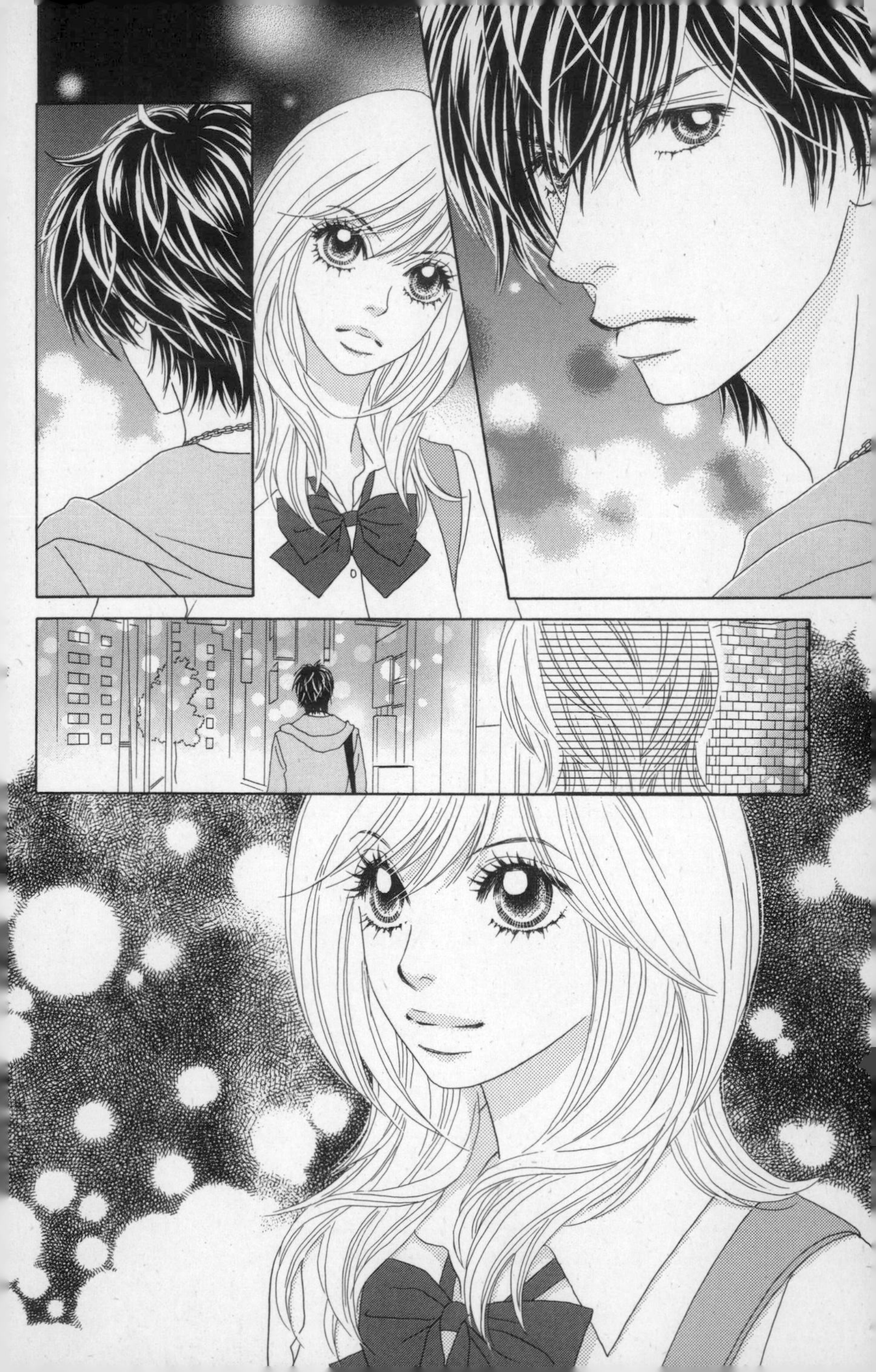

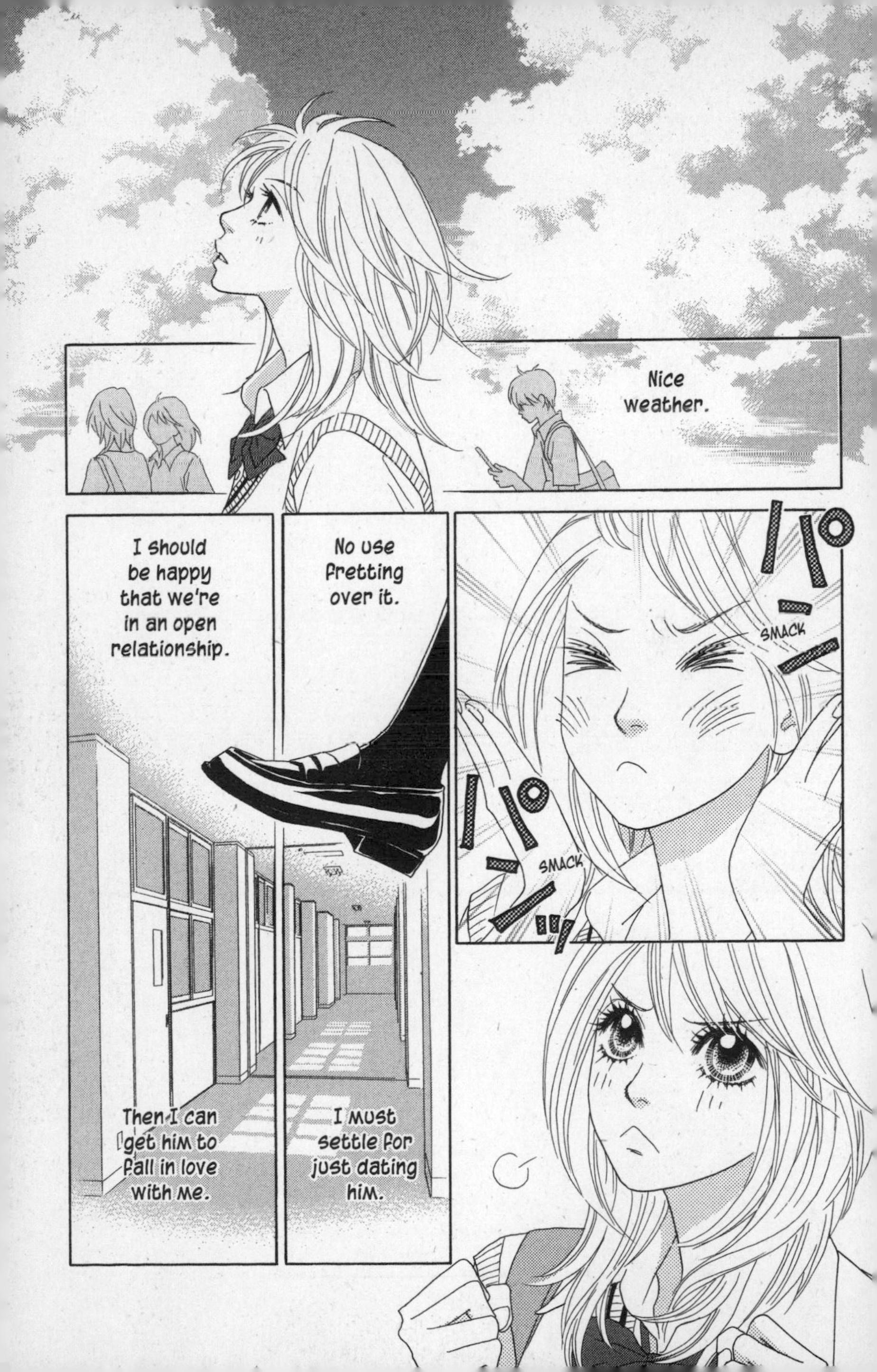
Nice weather.
SMACK
SMACK
No use fretting over it.
I must settle for just dating him.
I should be happy that we're in an open relationship.
Then I can get him to fall in love with me.

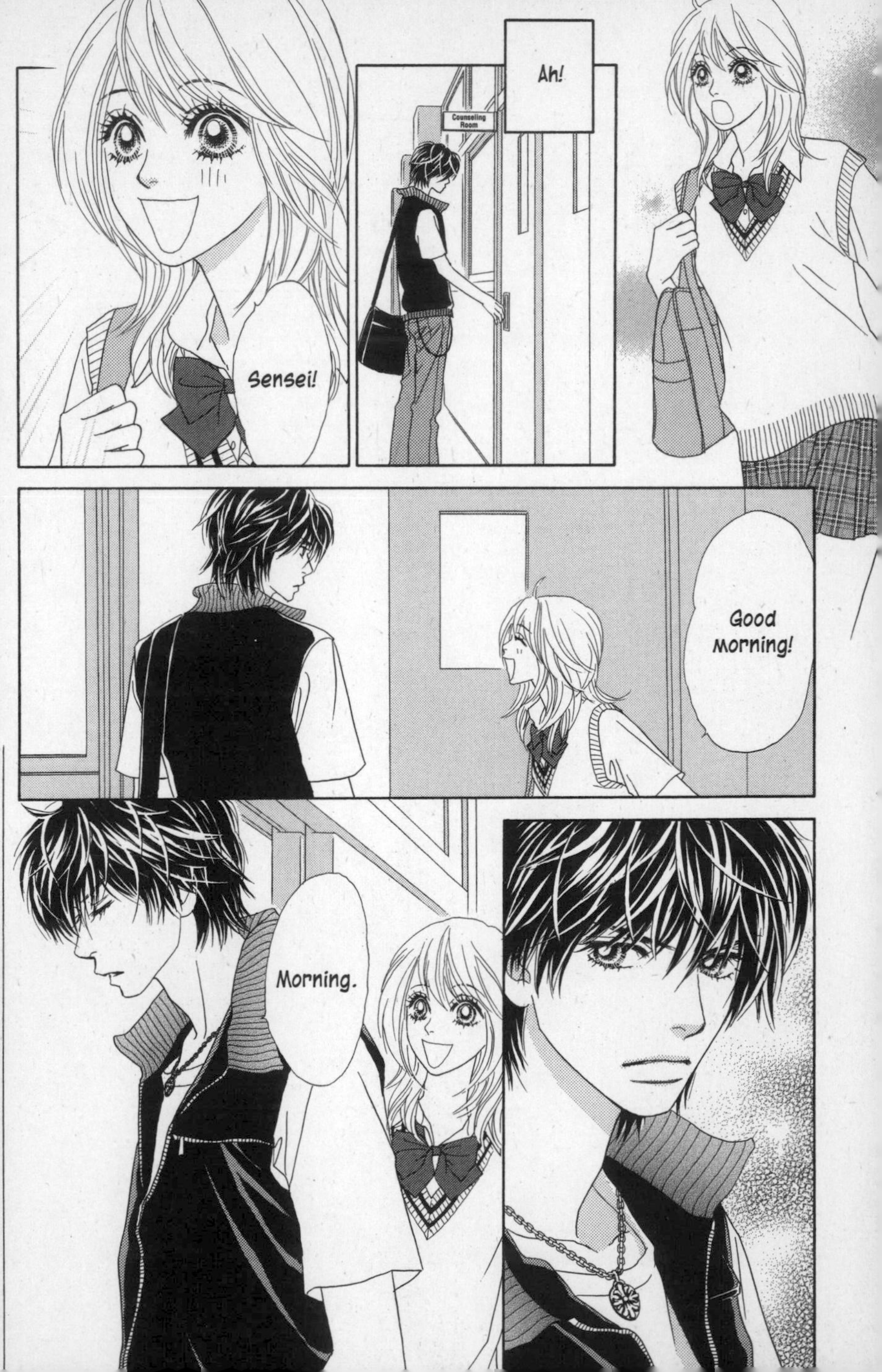
Ah!
Counseling Room
Sensei!
Good morning!
Morning.

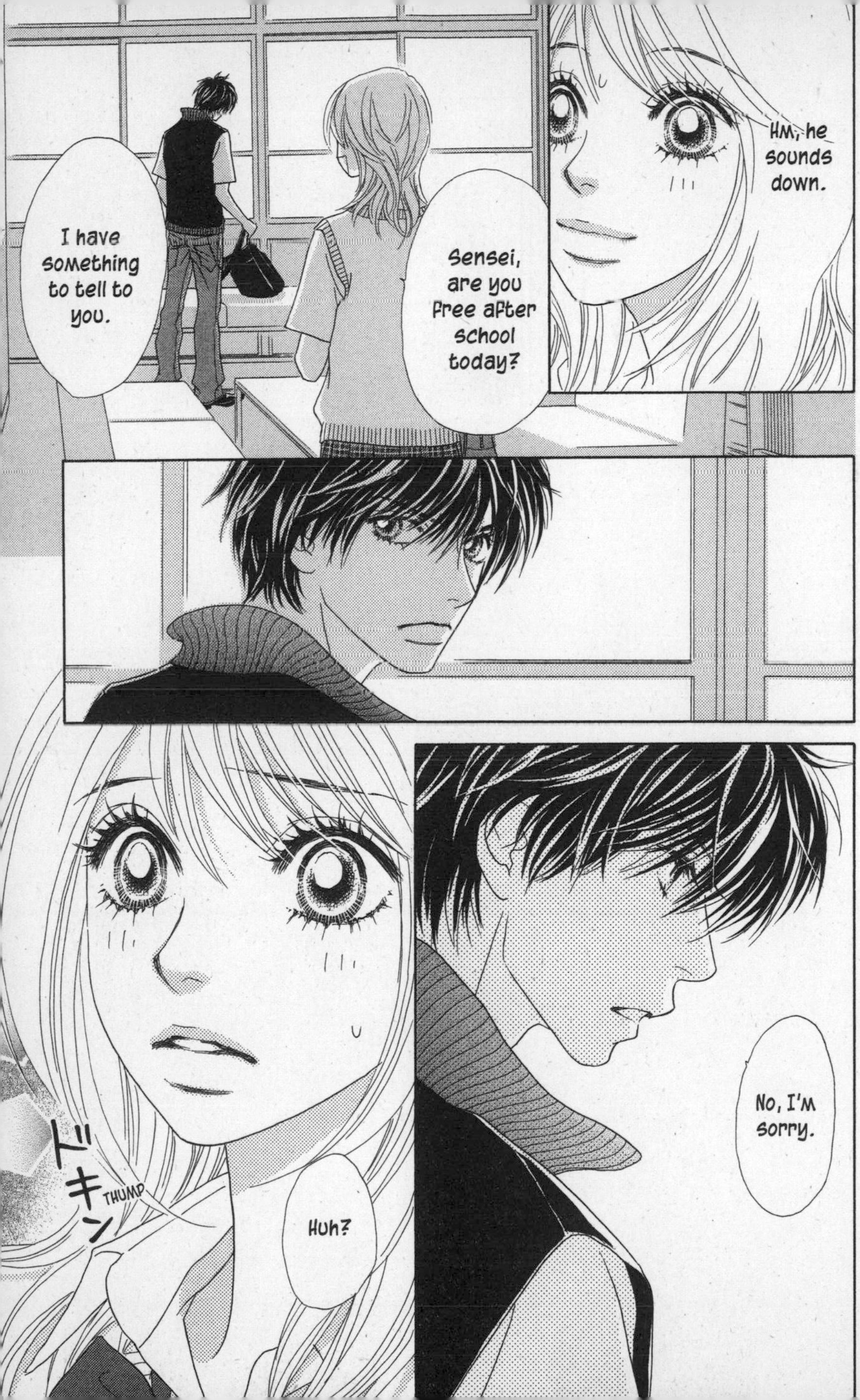
Hm, he sounds down.
Sensei, are you free after school today?
I have something to tell to you.
No, I'm sorry.
ドキン THUMP
Huh?

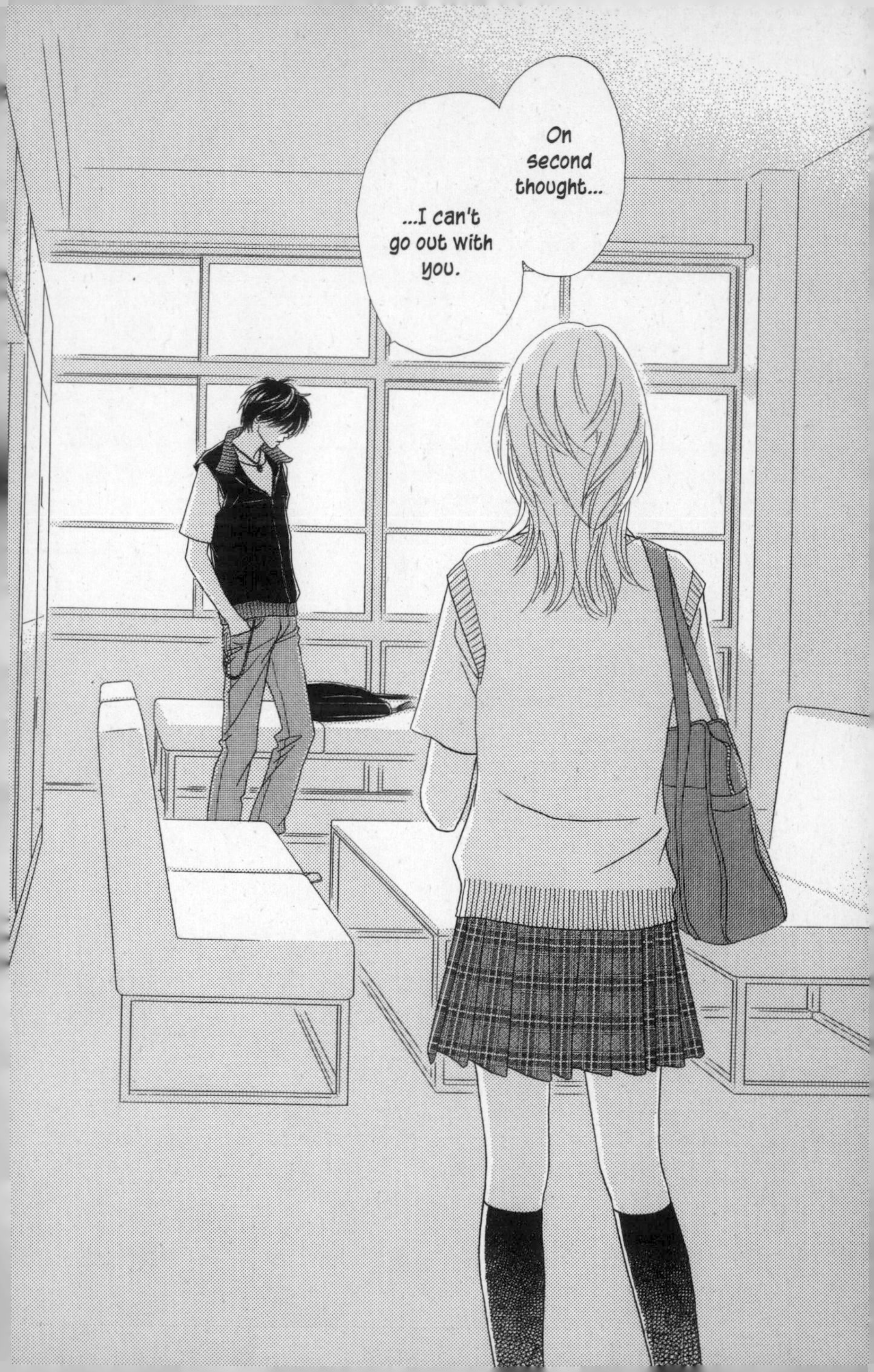
On second thought...
...I can't go out with you.

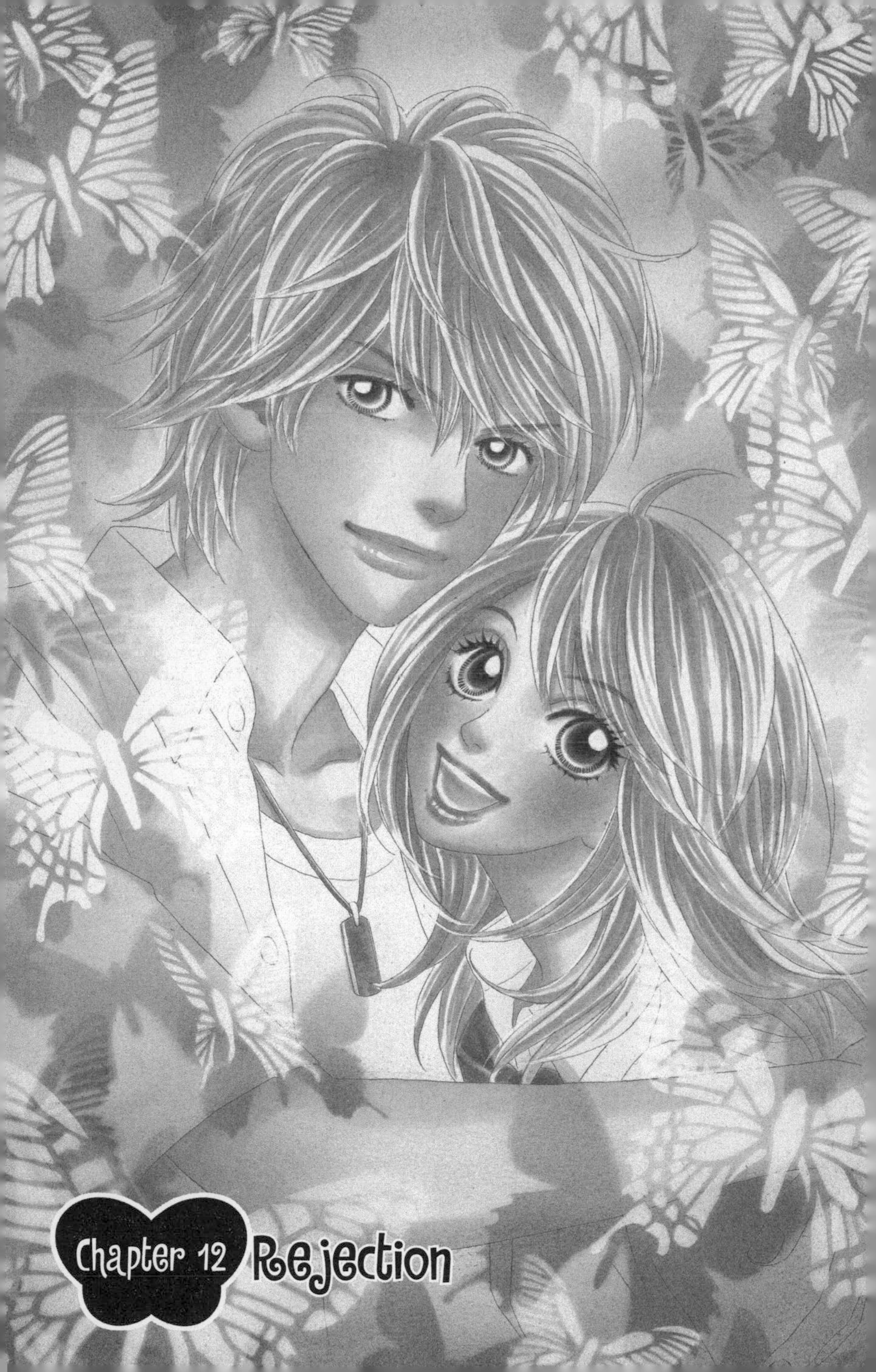
Chapter 12 Rejection

Papillon

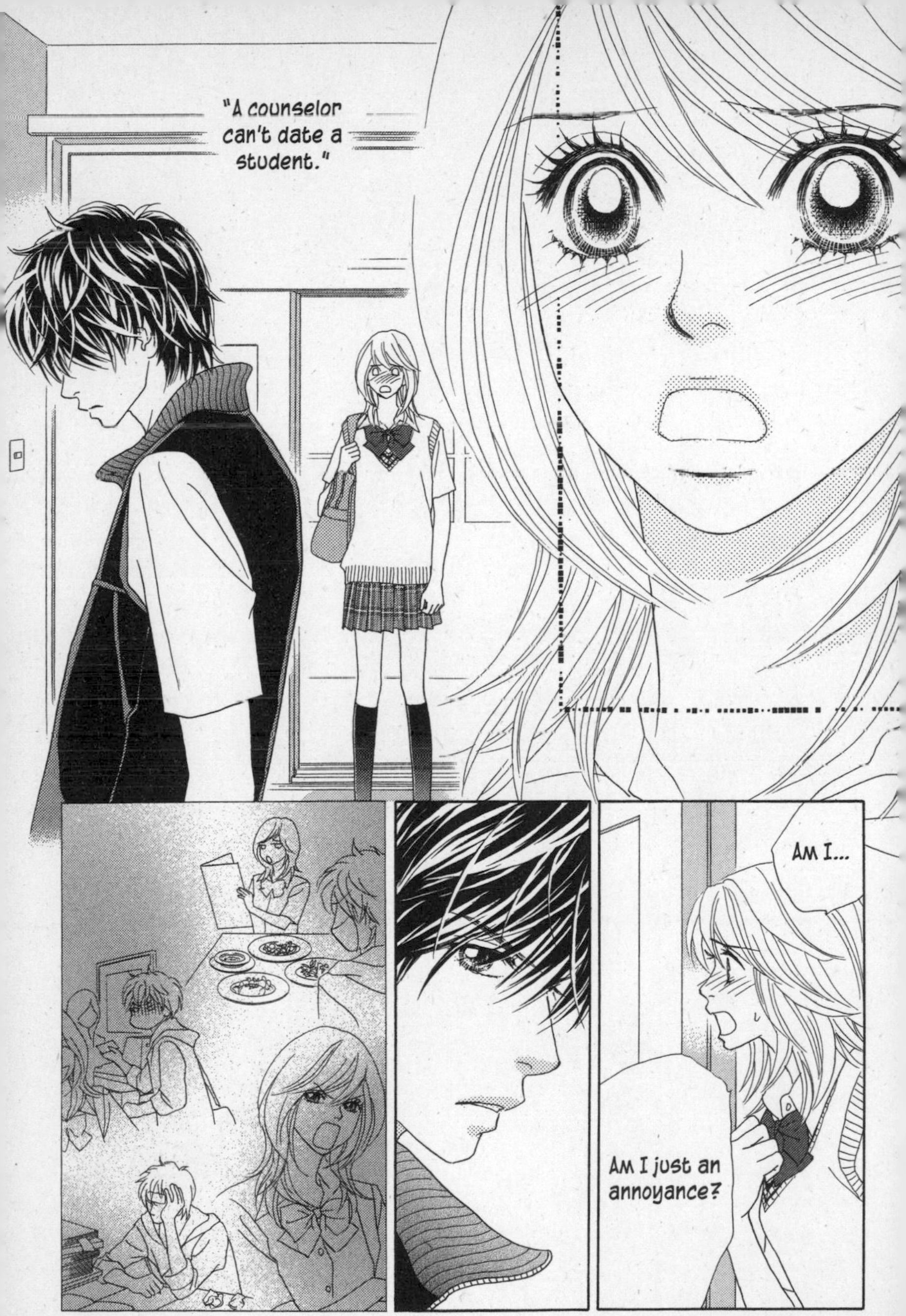
"A counselor can't date a student."
Am I...
Am I just an annoyance?

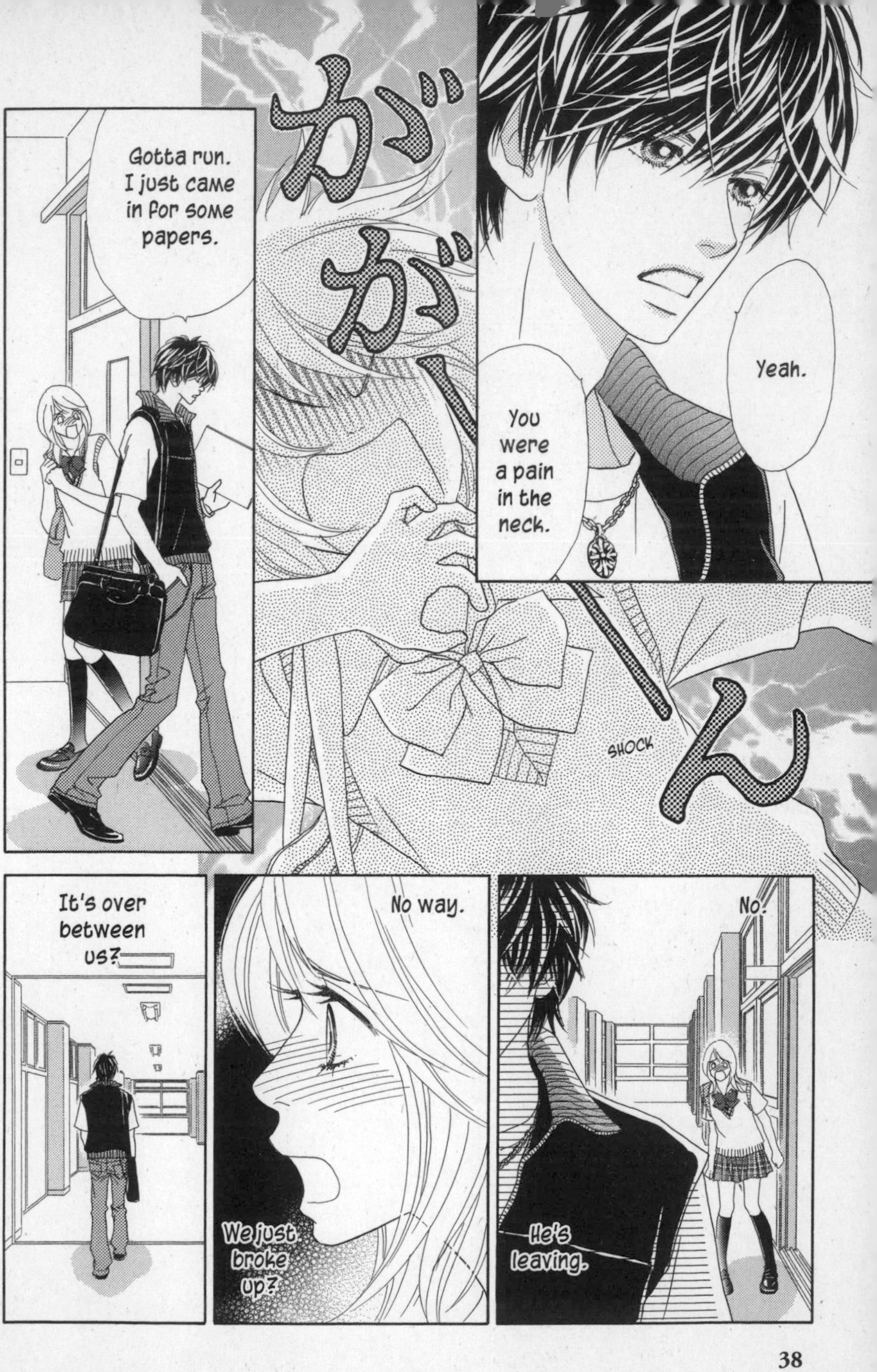
Yeah.
You were a pain in the neck.
ががーん
SHOCK
Gotta run. I just came in for some papers.
No.
He's leaving.
No way.
We just broke up?
It's over between us?

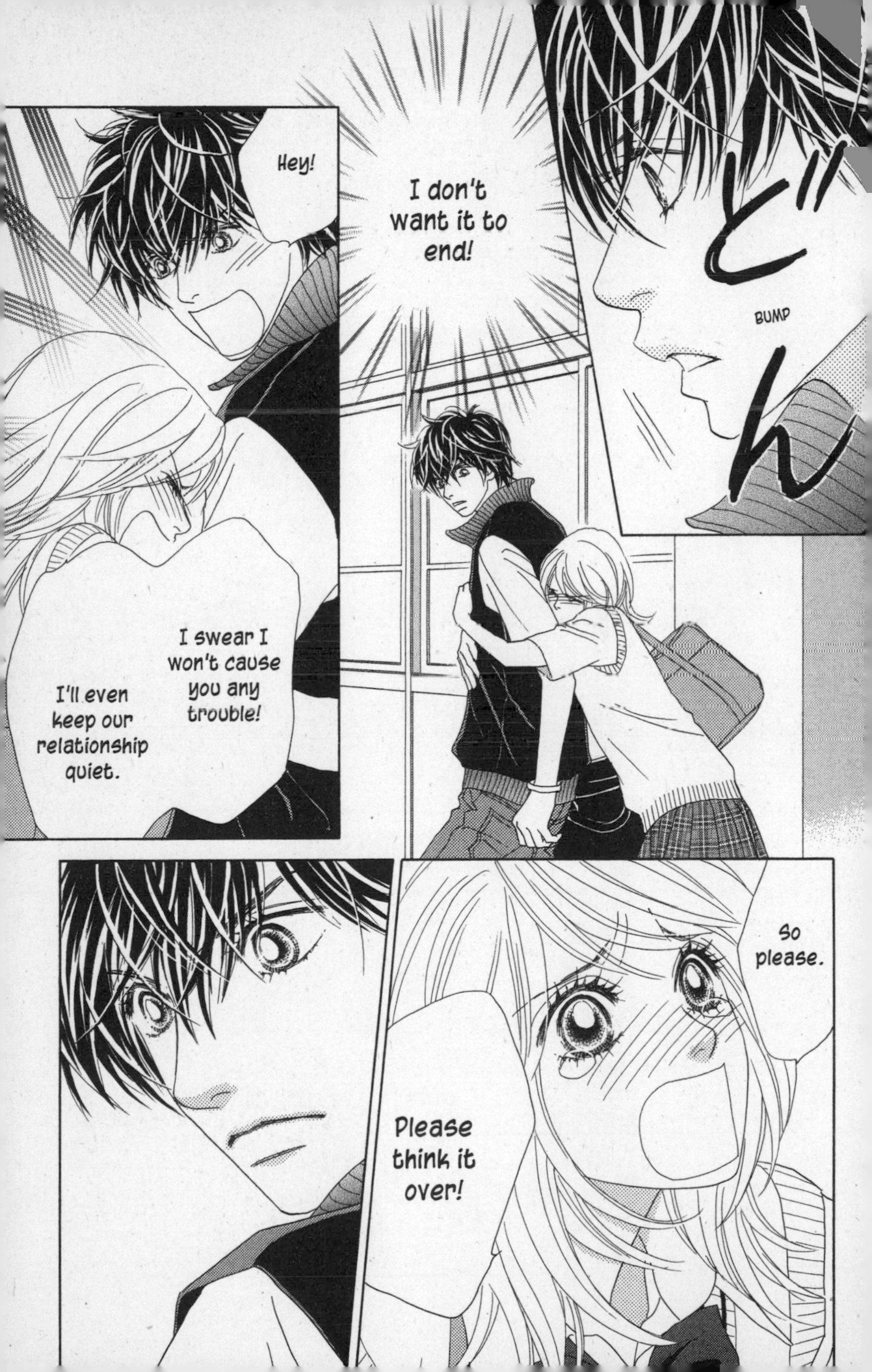
どん
BUMP
I don't want it to end!
Hey!
I swear I won't cause you any trouble!
I'll even keep our relationship quiet.
So please.
Please think it over!

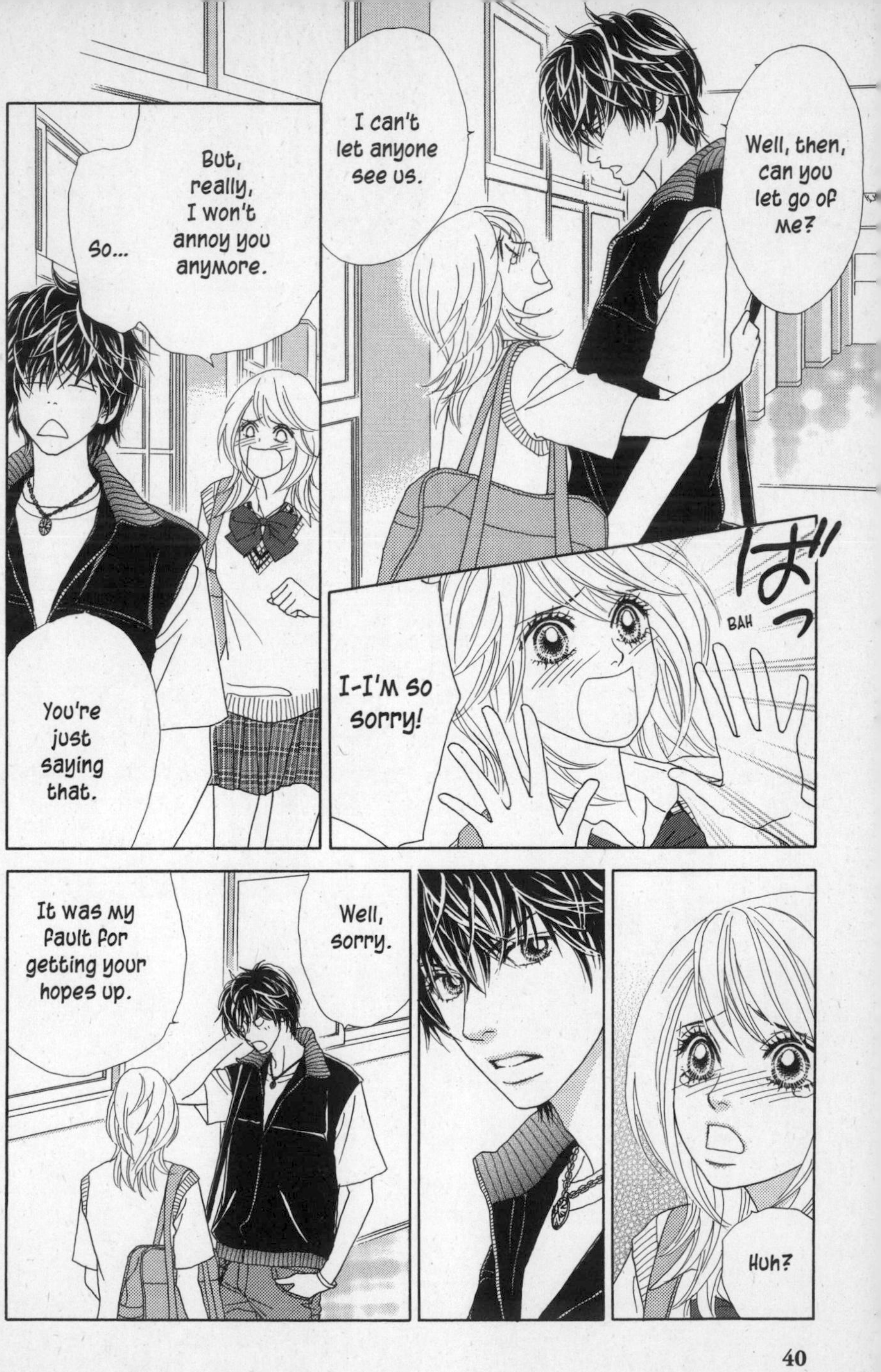
Well, then, can you let go of me?
I can't let anyone see us.
ばっ
BAH
I-I'm so sorry!
But, really, I won't annoy you anymore.
So...
You're just saying that.
Huh?
Well, sorry.
It was my fault for getting your hopes up.

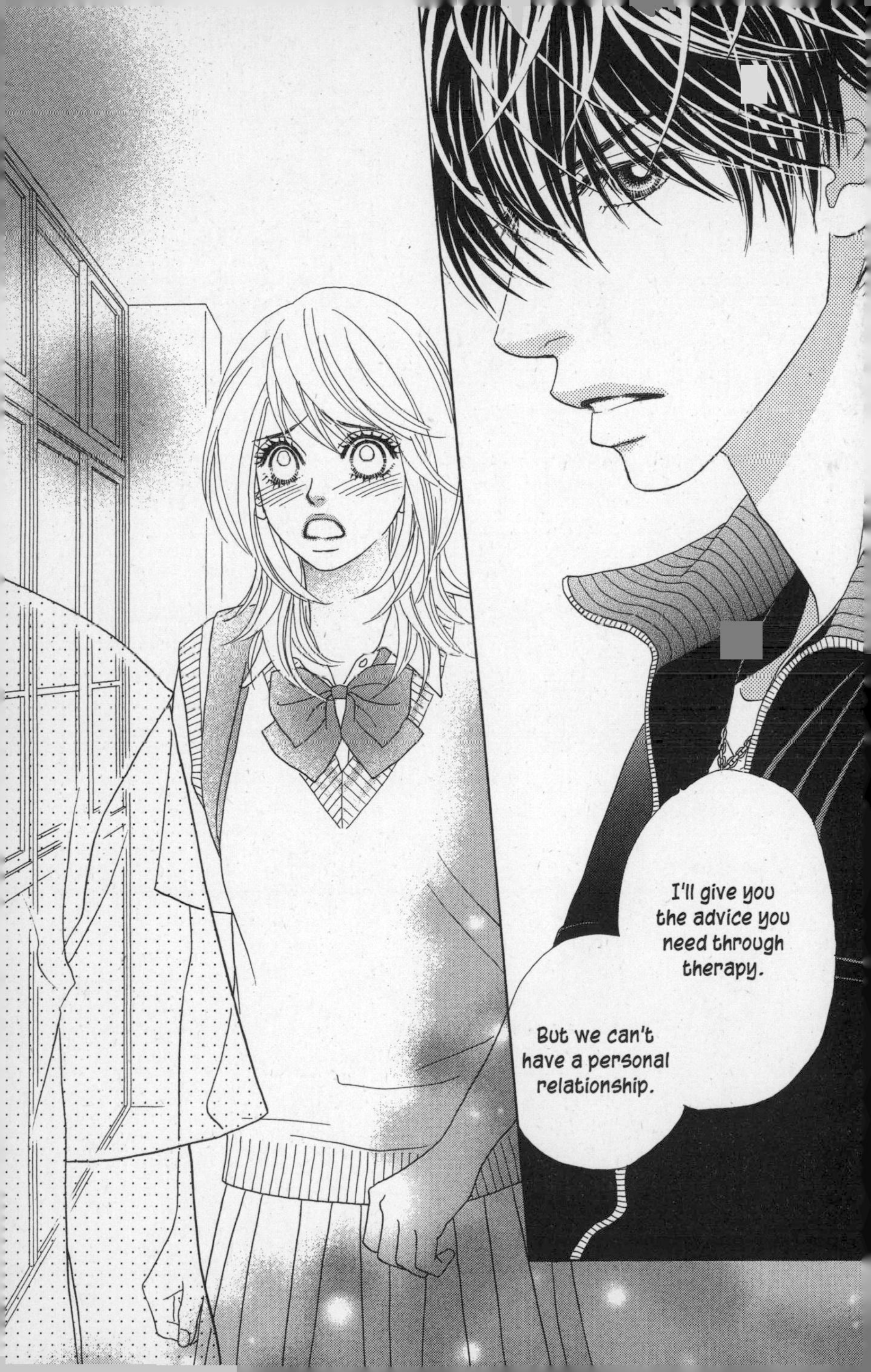
I'll give you the advice you need through therapy.
But we can't have a personal relationship.

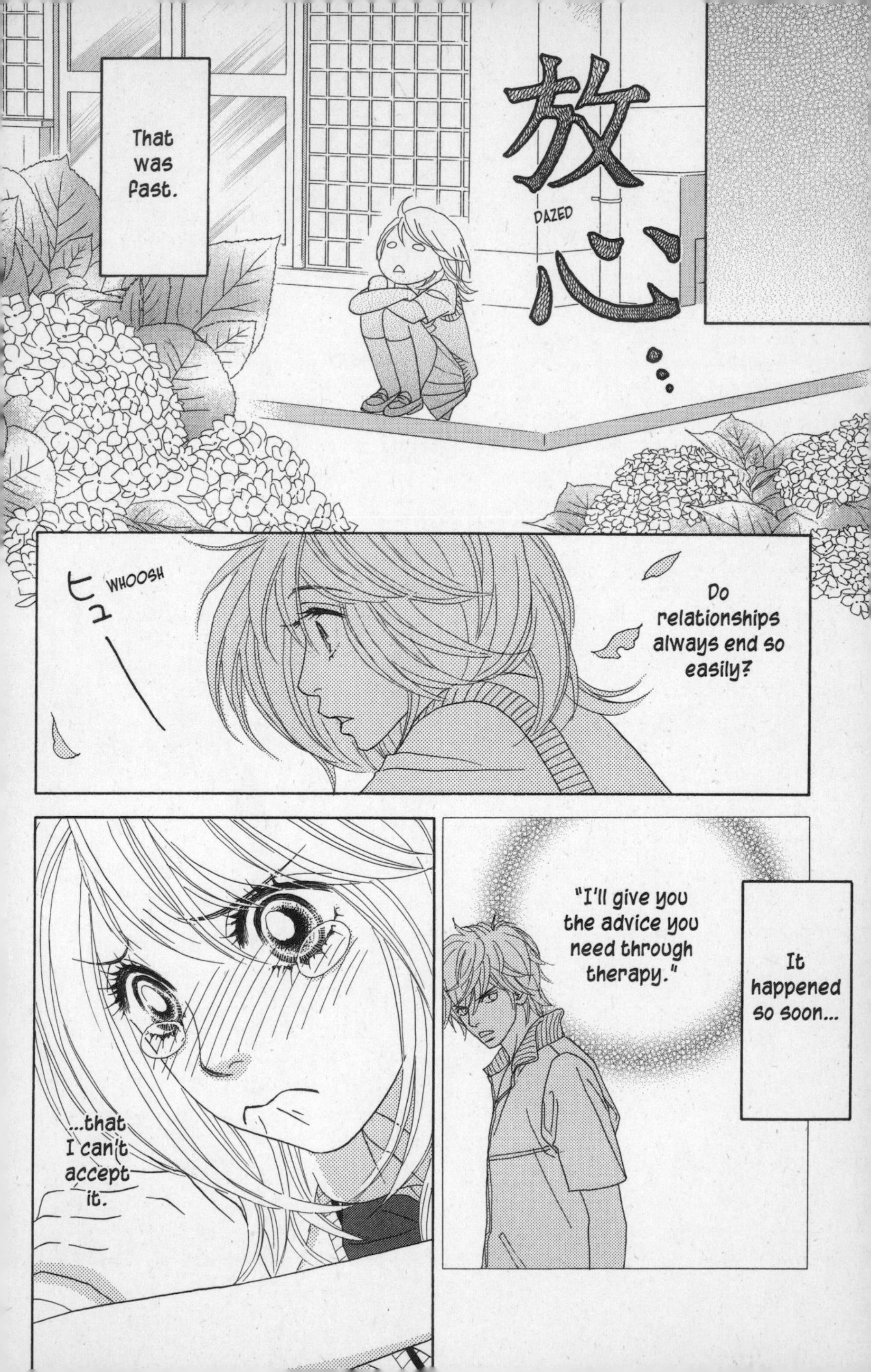
放心
DAZED
That was fast.
Do relationships always end so easily?
ヒュー
WHOOSH
It happened so soon...
"I'll give you the advice you need through therapy."
...that I can't accept it.

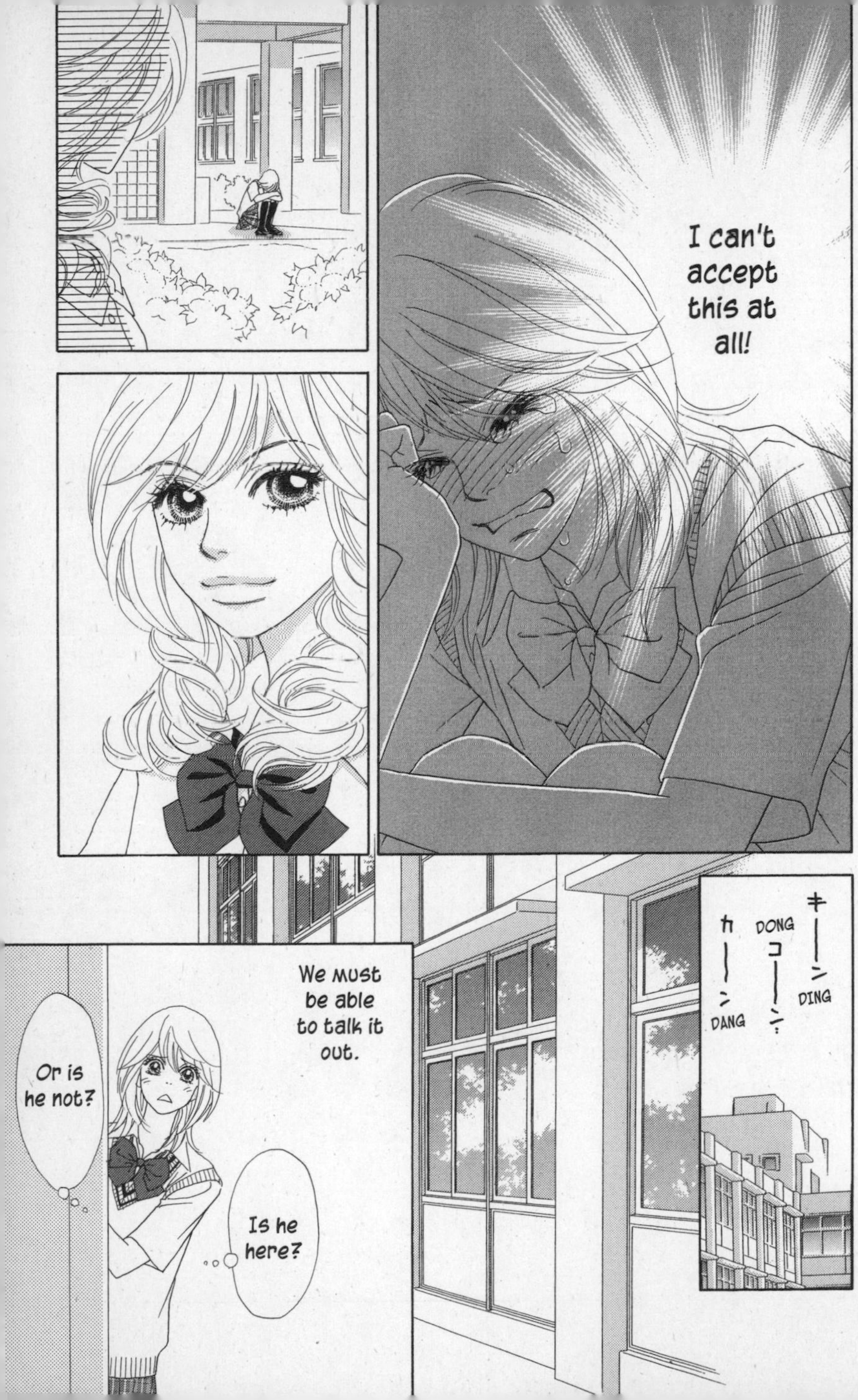
I can't accept this at all!
キーン
DING
コーン
DONG
カーン
DANG
We must be able to talk it out.
Is he here?
Or is he not?

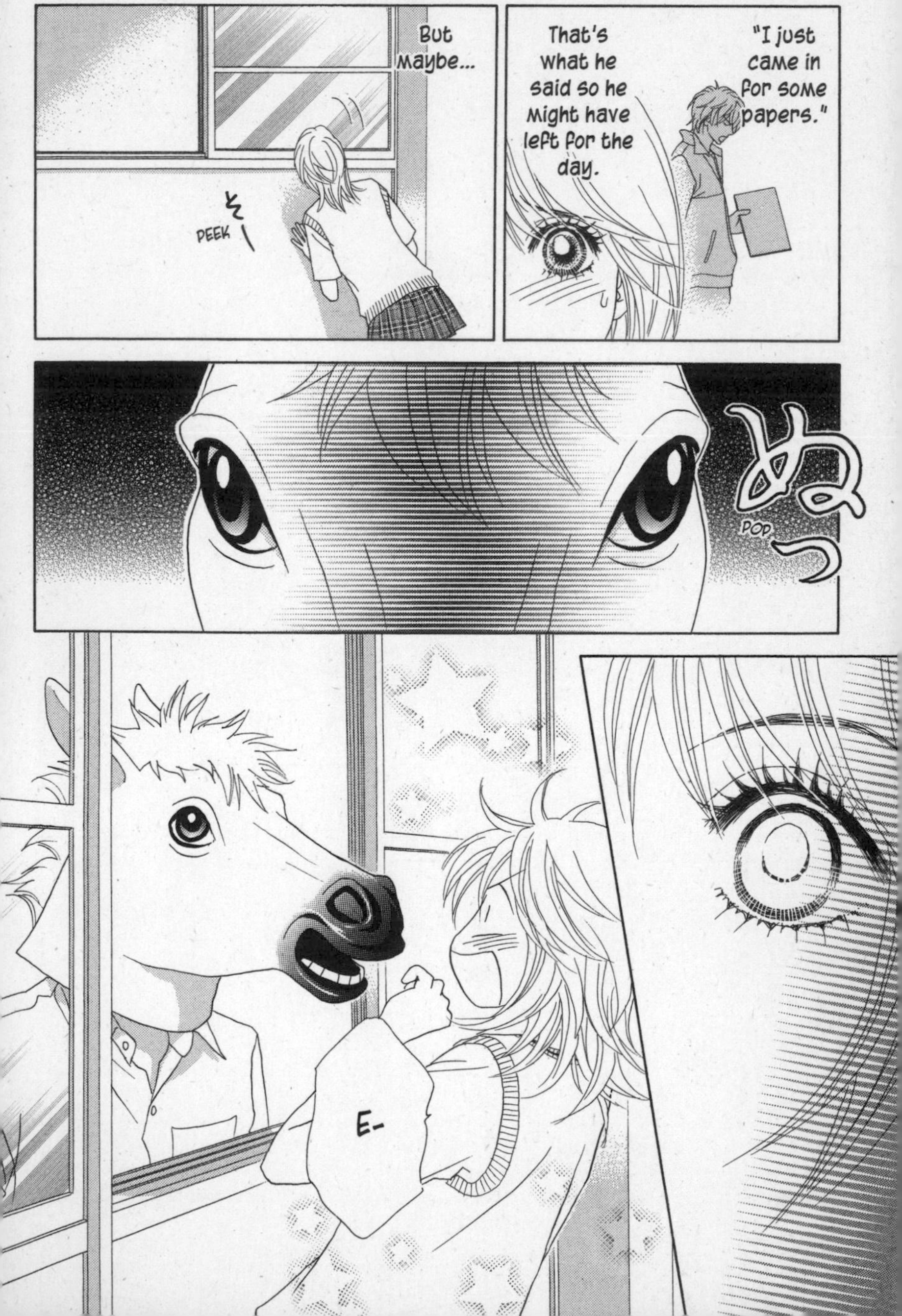
"I just came in for some papers."
That's what he said so he might have left for the day.
But maybe...
PEEK
ぬっ
POP
E-

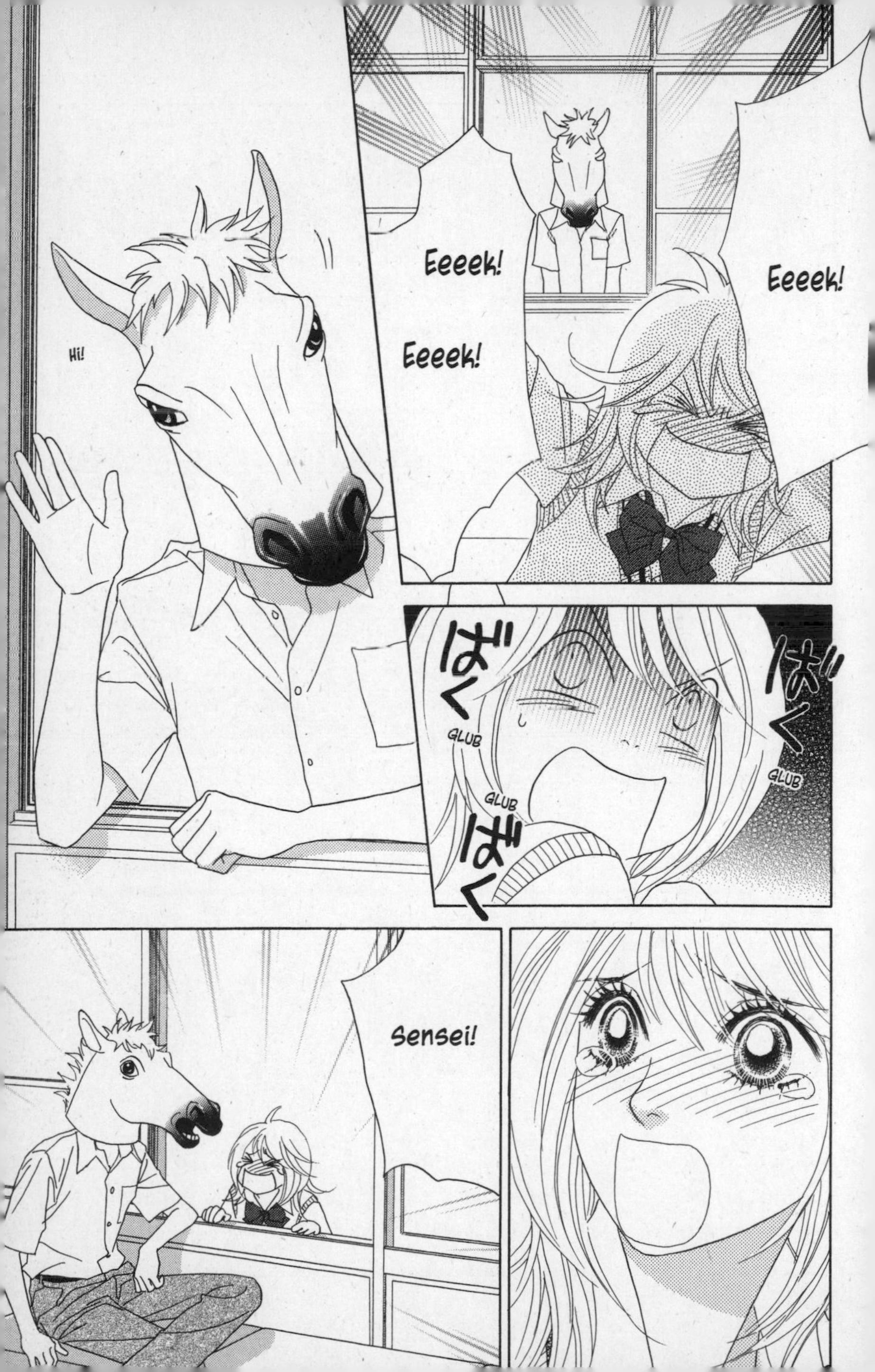
Eeeek!
Eeeek!
Eeeek!
ばく
GLUB
ばく
GLUB
ばく
GLUB
Hi!
Sensei!

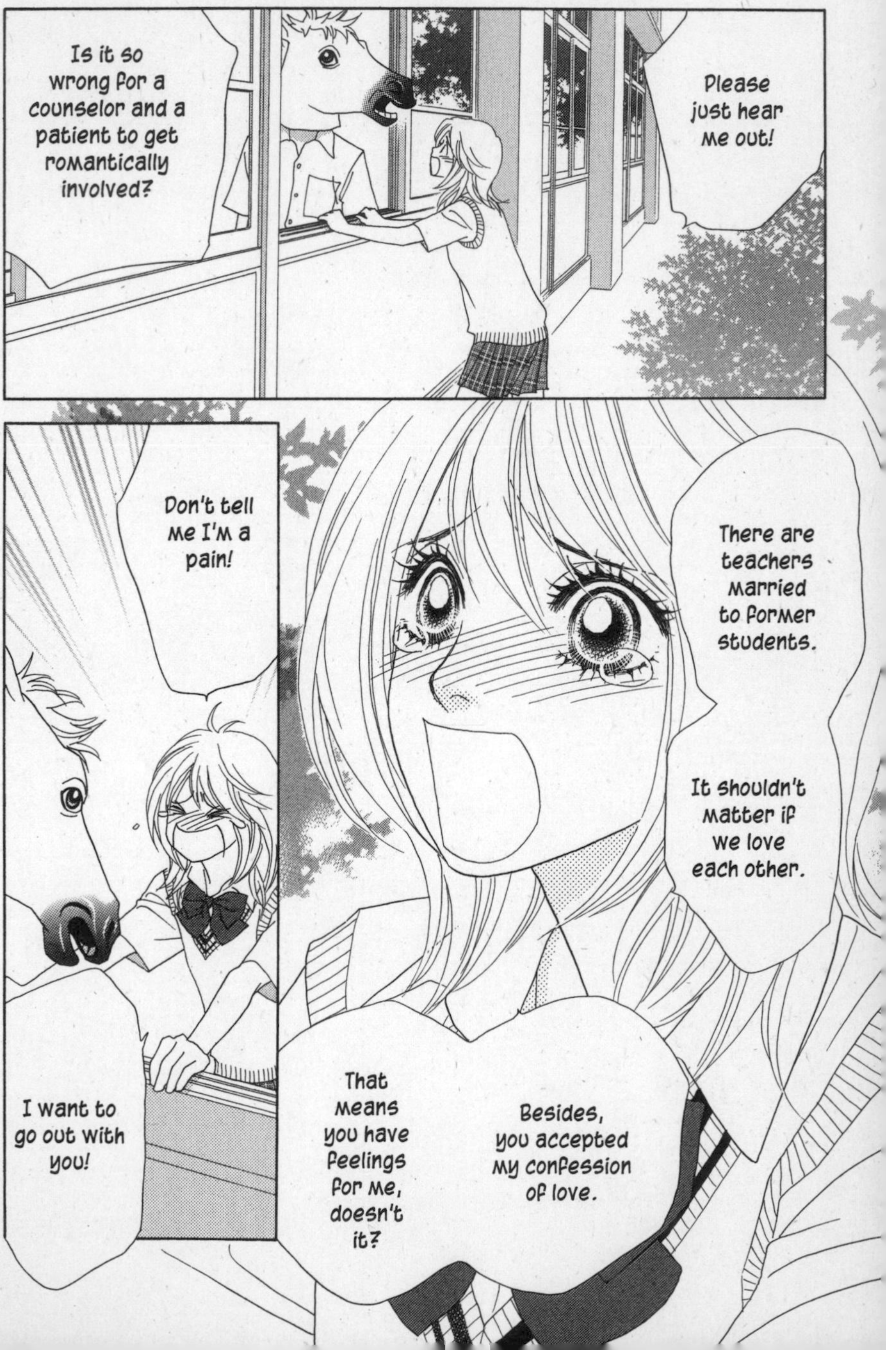
Please just hear me out!
Is it so wrong for a counselor and a patient to get romantically involved?
There are teachers married to former students.
It shouldn't matter if we love each other.
Besides, you accepted my confession of love.
That means you have feelings for me, doesn't it?
Don't tell me I'm a pain!
I want to go out with you!

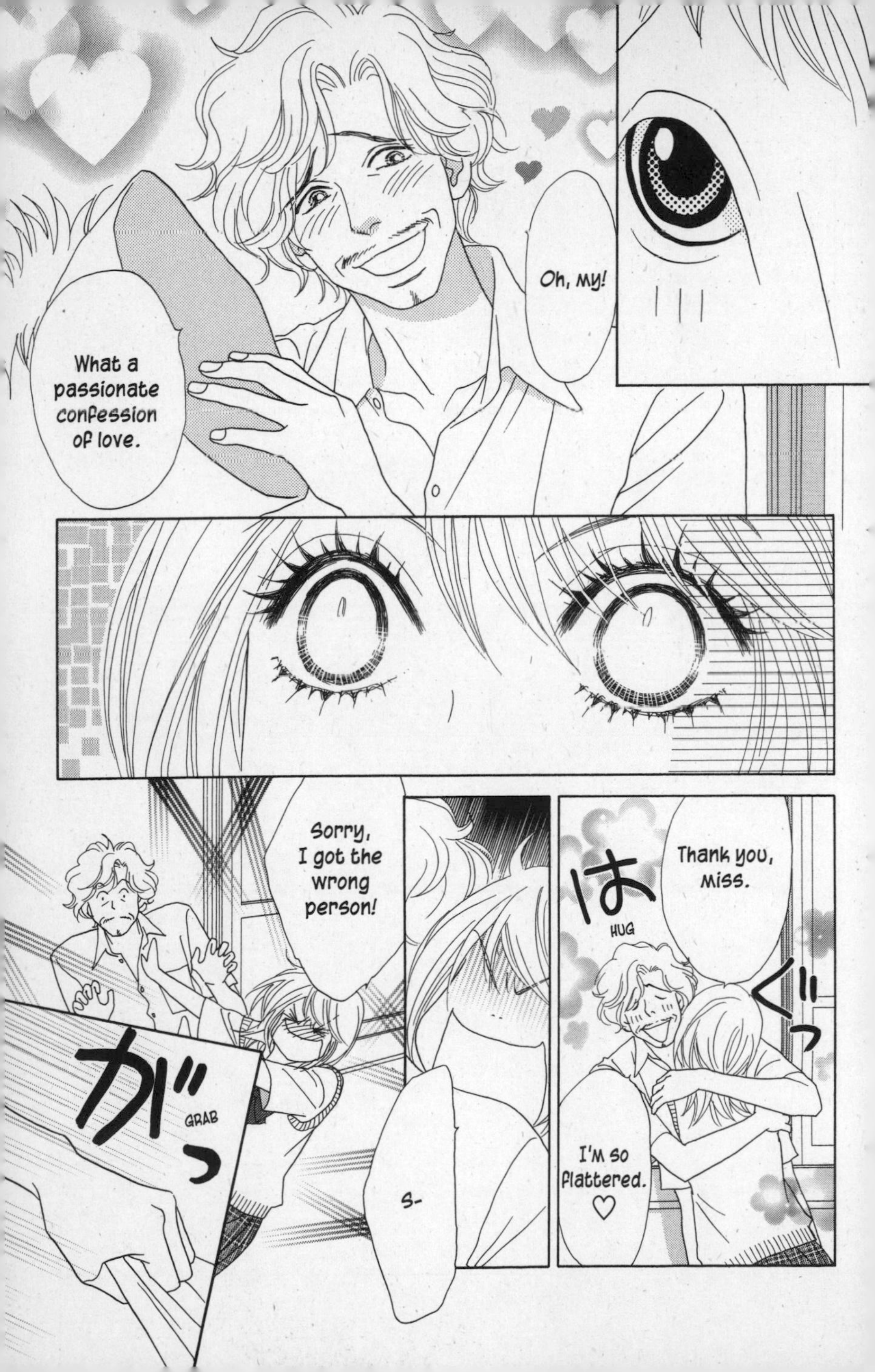
Oh, my!
What a passionate confession of love.
Thank you, miss.
は
HUG
ぐっ
I'm so flattered. ♡
S-
Sorry, I got the wrong person!
がっ
GRAB

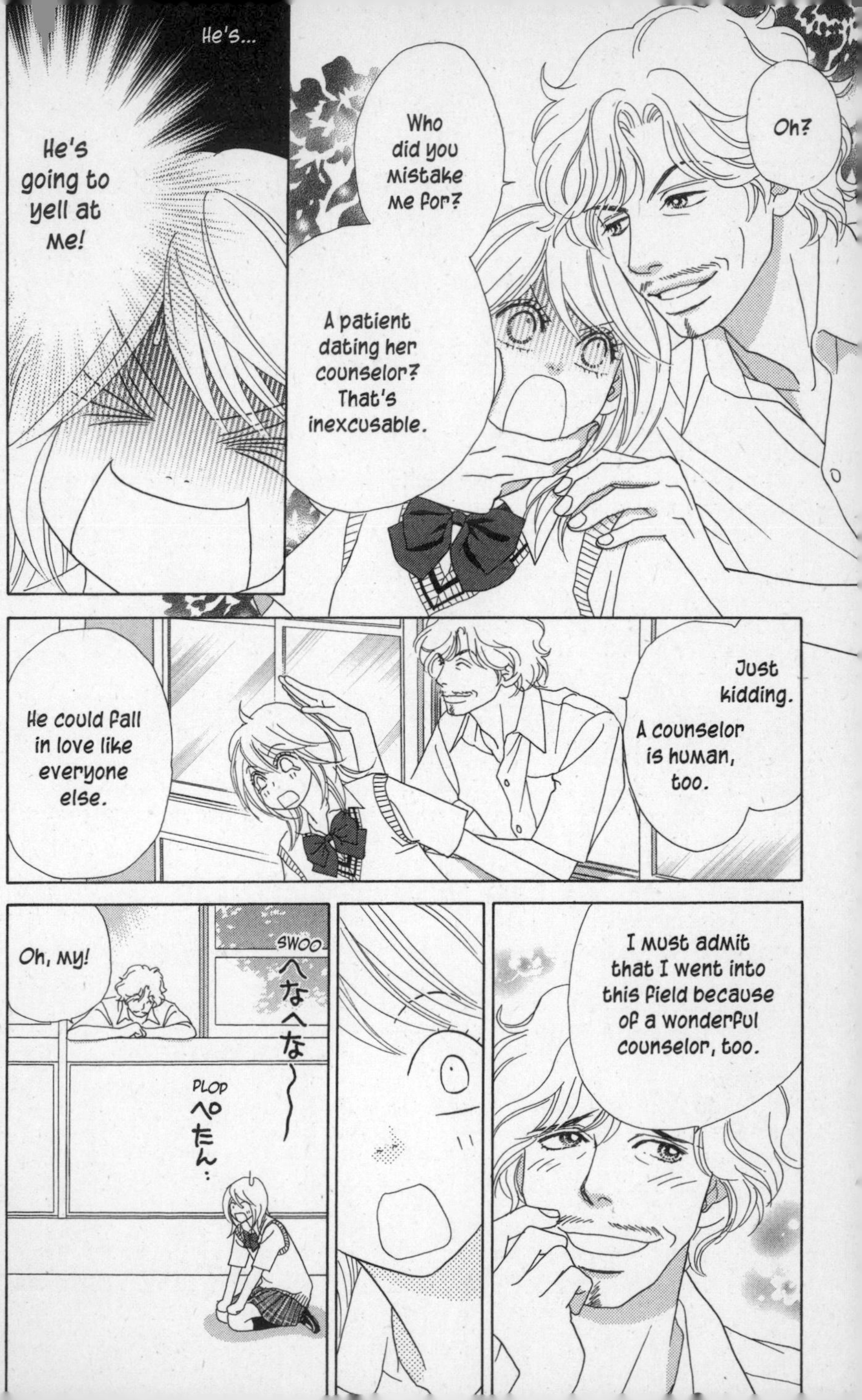
Oh?
Who did you mistake me for?
A patient dating her counselor? That's inexcusable.
He's...
He's going to yell at me!
Just kidding.
A counselor is human, too.
He could fall in love like everyone else.
I must admit that I went into this field because of a wonderful counselor, too.
SWOO
へなへな〜
Oh, my!
PLOP
ぺたん..

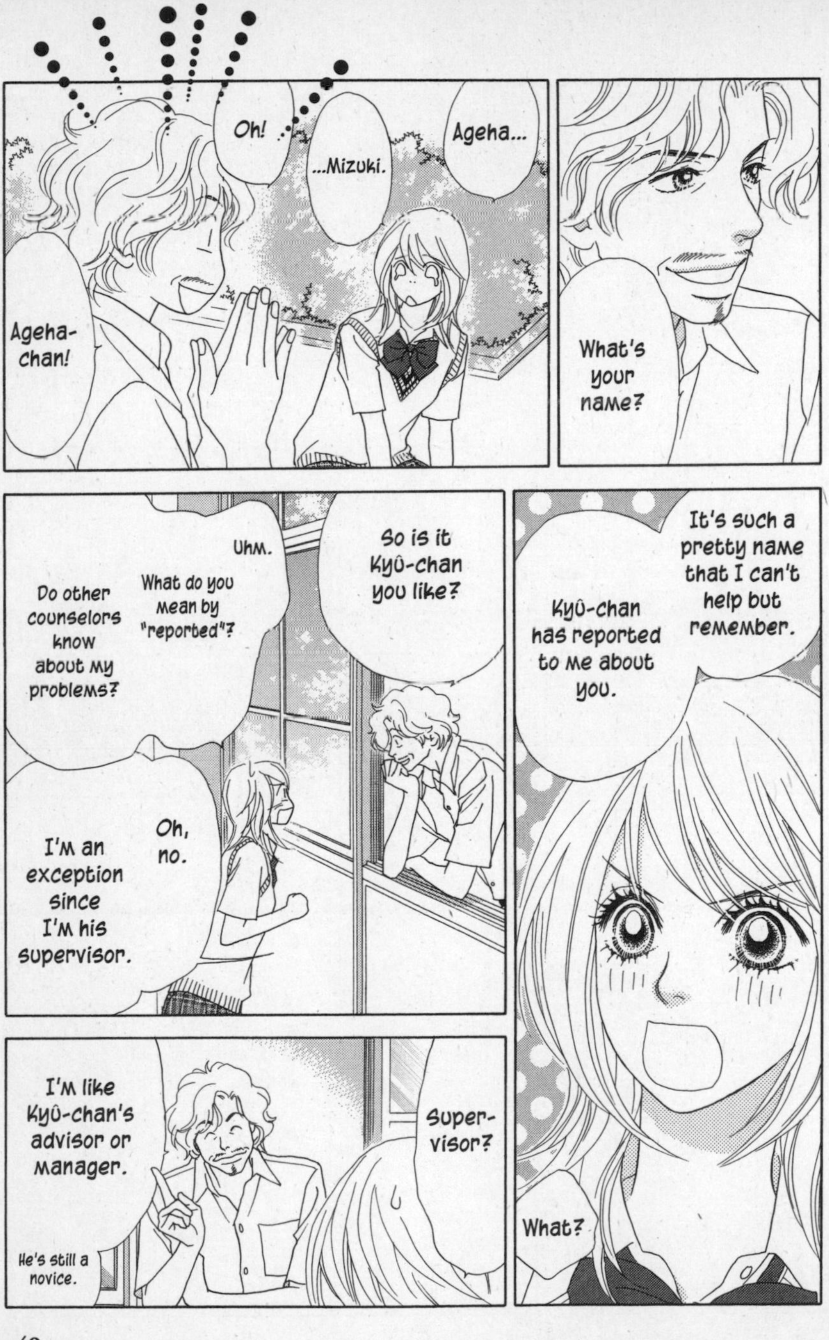
What's your name?
Ageha...
...Mizuki.
Oh!
Ageha-chan!
It's such a pretty name that I can't help but remember.
Kyû-chan has reported to me about you.
What?
So is it Kyû-chan you like?
Uhm.
What do you mean by "reported"?
Do other counselors know about my problems?
Oh, no.
I'm an exception since I'm his supervisor.
Super-visor?
I'm like Kyû-chan's advisor or manager.
He's still a novice.

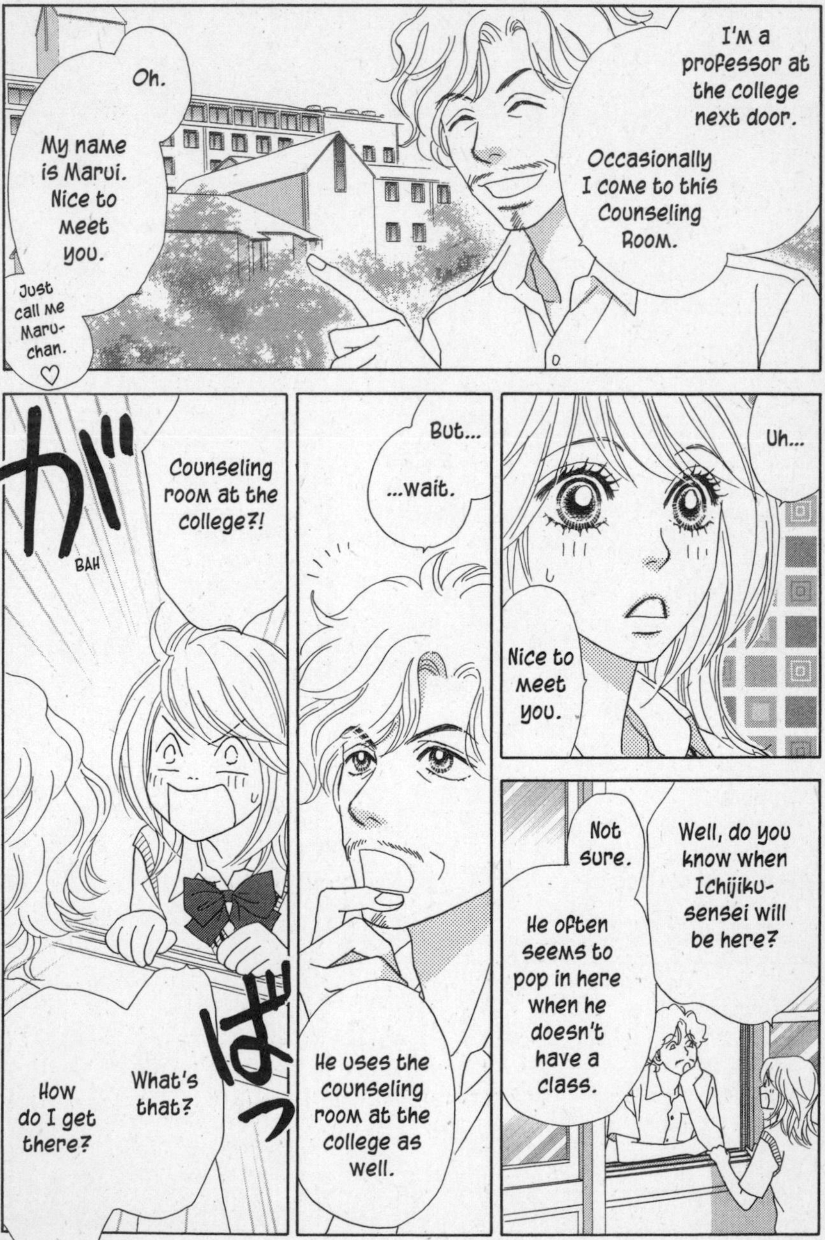
I'm a professor at the college next door.
Occasionally I come to this Counseling Room.
Oh.
My name is Marui. Nice to meet you.
Just call me Maru-chan. ♡
Uh...
Nice to meet you.
Well, do you know when Ichijiku-sensei will be here?
Not sure.
He often seems to pop in here when he doesn't have a class.
But...
...wait.
He uses the counseling room at the college as well.
ばっ
Counseling room at the college?!
が
BAH
What's that?
How do I get there?

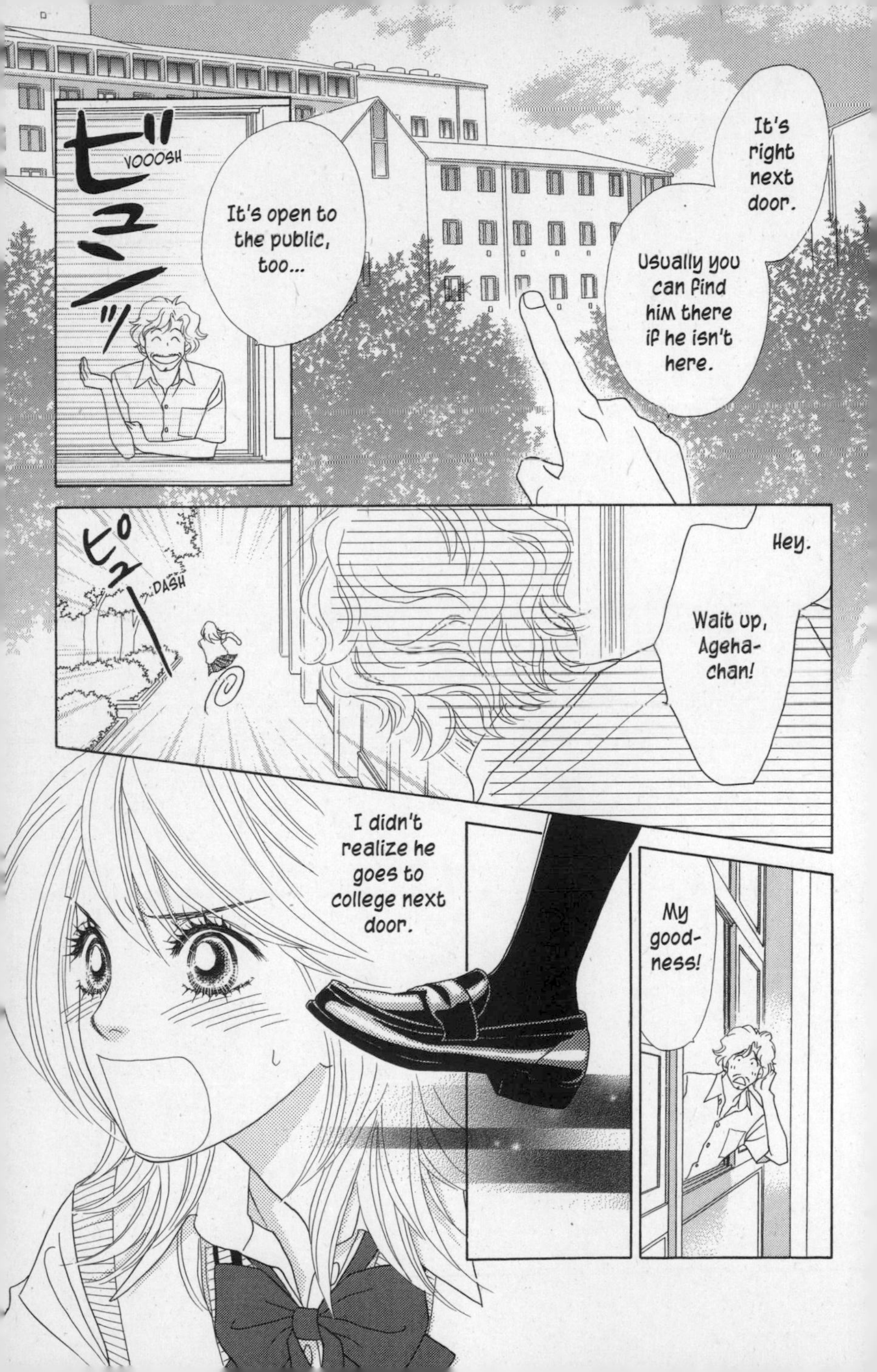
It's right next door.
Usually you can find him there if he isn't here.
It's open to the public, too...
VOOOSH
Hey.
Wait up, Ageha-chan!
DASH
My goodness!
I didn't realize he goes to college next door.

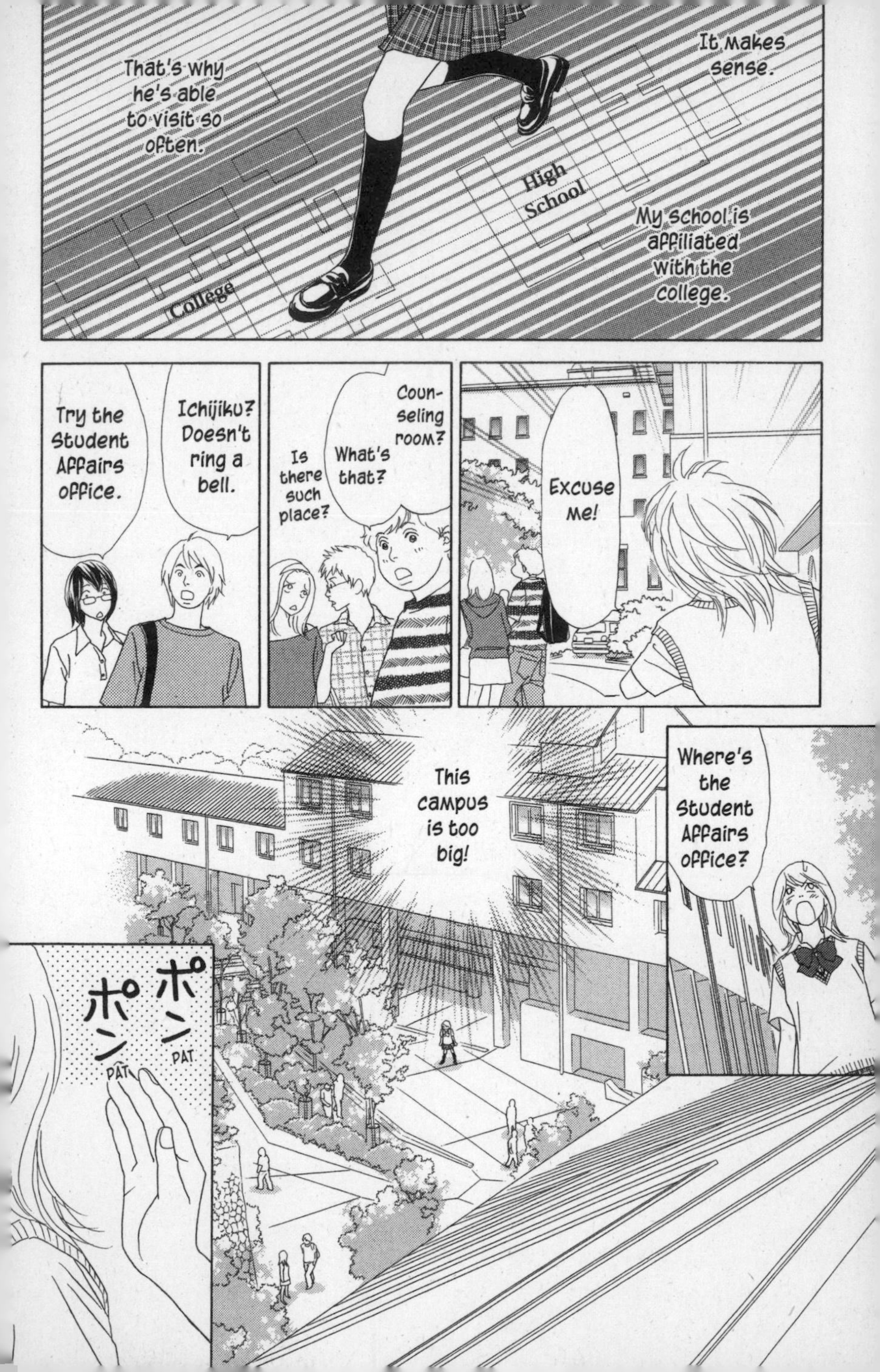
It makes sense.
High School
My school is affiliated with the college.
That's why he's able to visit so often.
College
Excuse me!
Coun-seling room?
What's that?
Is there such place?
Ichijiku? Doesn't ring a bell.
Try the Student Affairs office.
Where's the Student Affairs office?
This campus is too big!
ポン
ポン
PAT
PAT

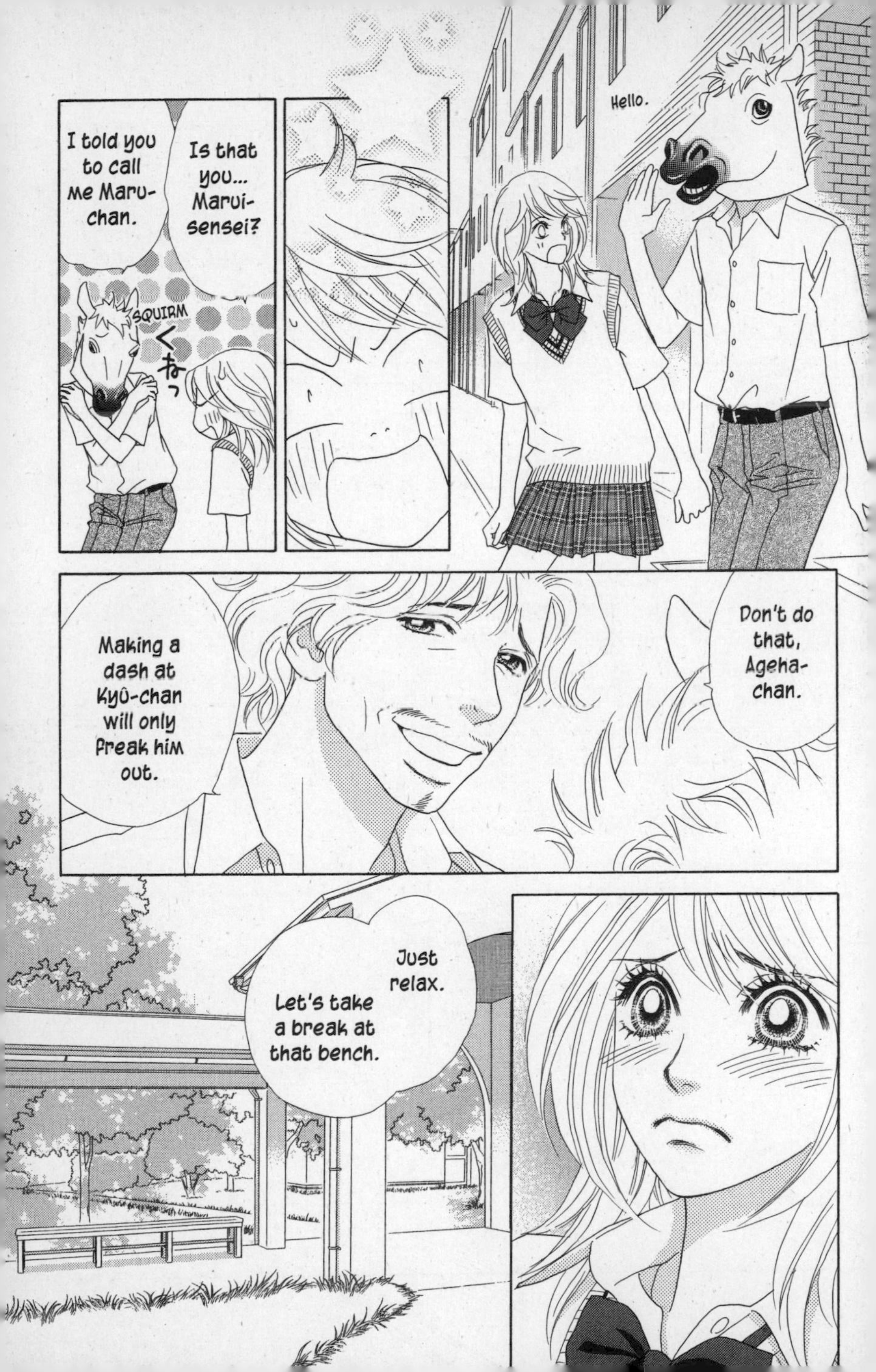
Hello.
Is that you... Marui-sensei?
I told you to call me Maru-chan.
SQUIRM くねっ
Don't do that, Ageha-chan.
Making a dash at Kyû-chan will only freak him out.
Just relax.
Let's take a break at that bench.

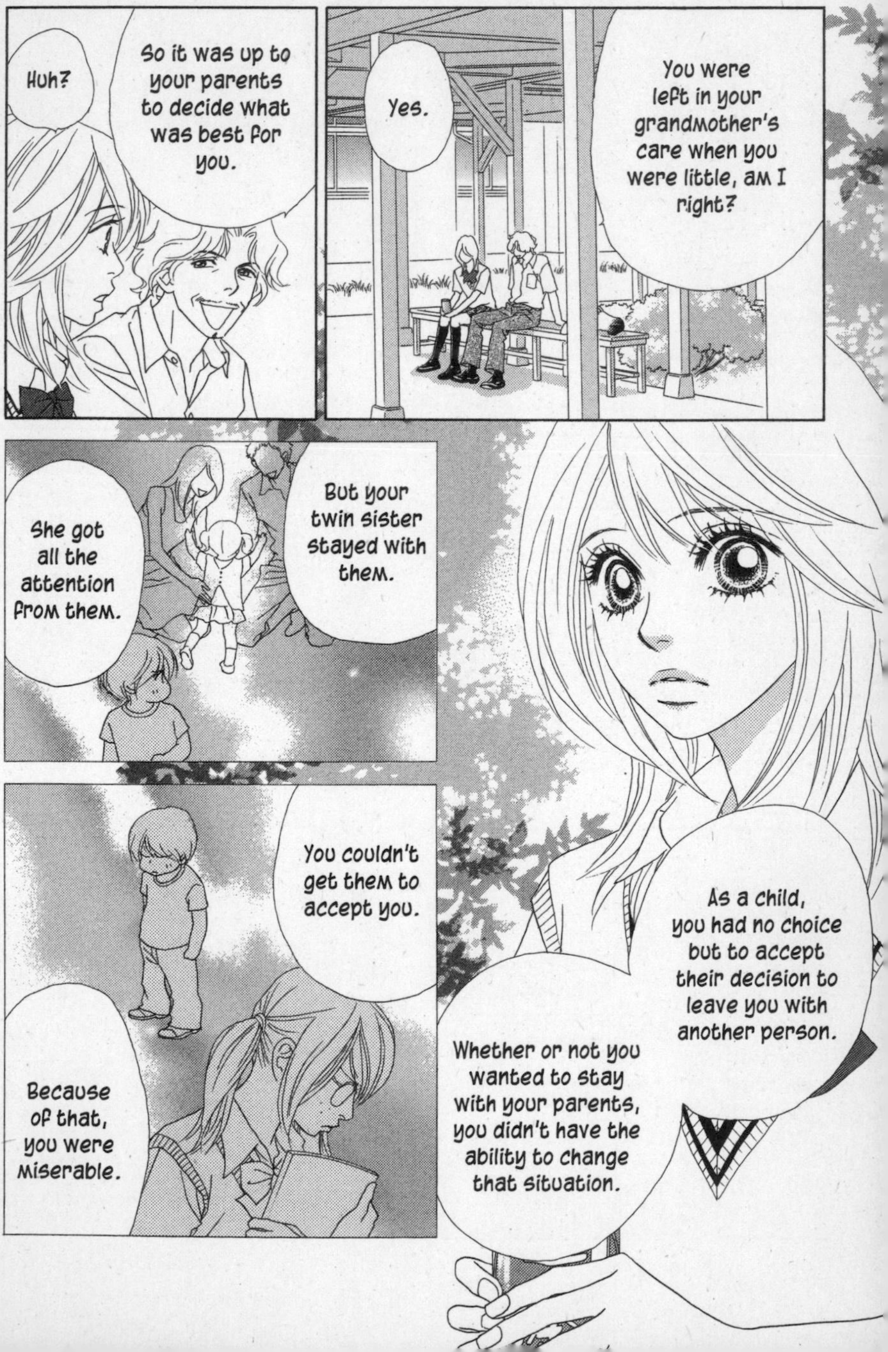
You were left in your grandmother's care when you were little, am I right?
Yes.
So it was up to your parents to decide what was best for you.
Huh?
As a child, you had no choice but to accept their decision to leave you with another person.
Whether or not you wanted to stay with your parents, you didn't have the ability to change that situation.
But your twin sister stayed with them.
She got all the attention from them.
You couldn't get them to accept you.
Because of that, you were miserable.

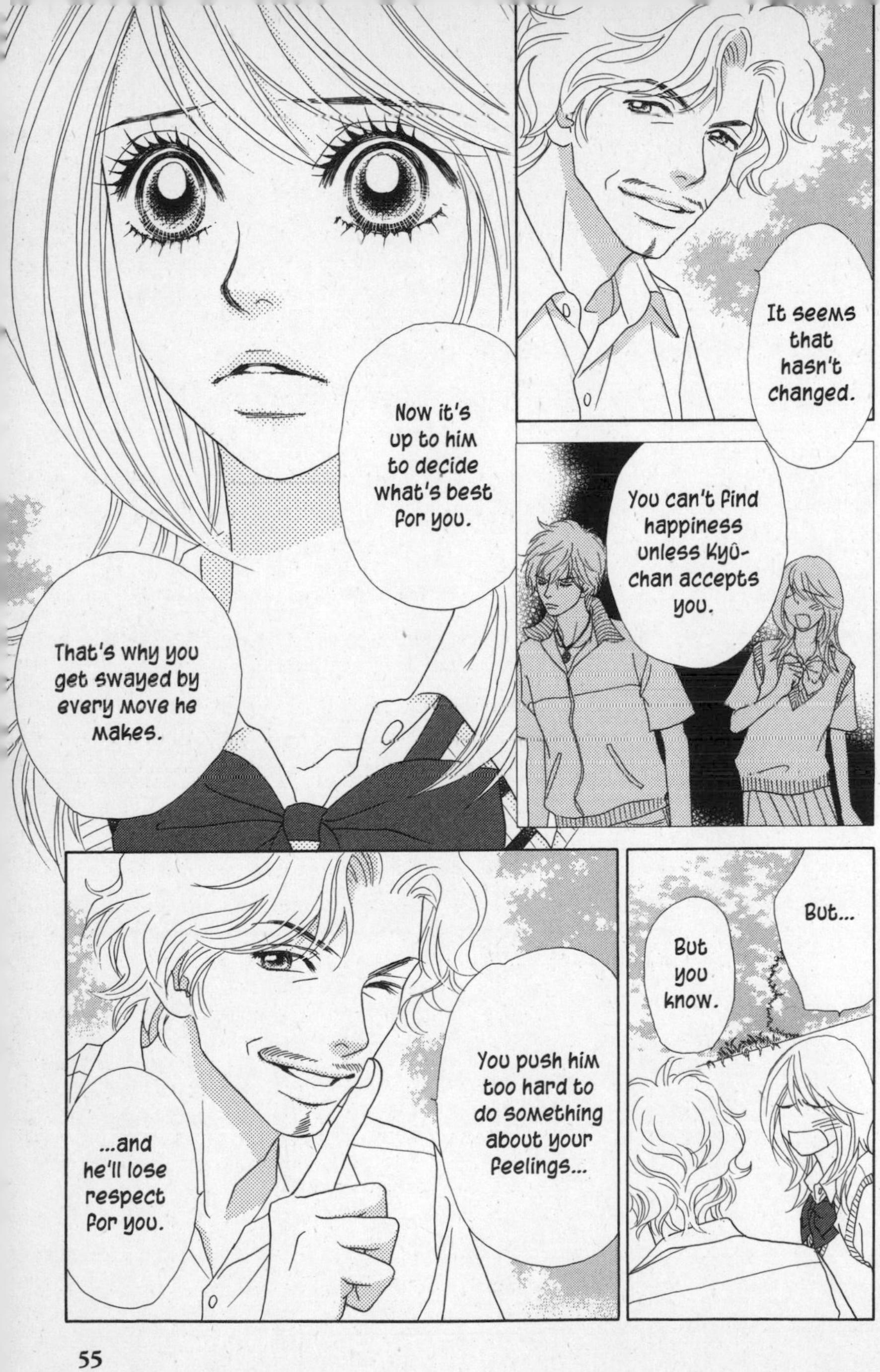
It seems that hasn't changed.
You can't find happiness unless Kyû-chan accepts you.
Now it's up to him to decide what's best for you.
That's why you get swayed by every move he makes.
But...
But you know.
You push him too hard to do something about your feelings...
...and he'll lose respect for you.

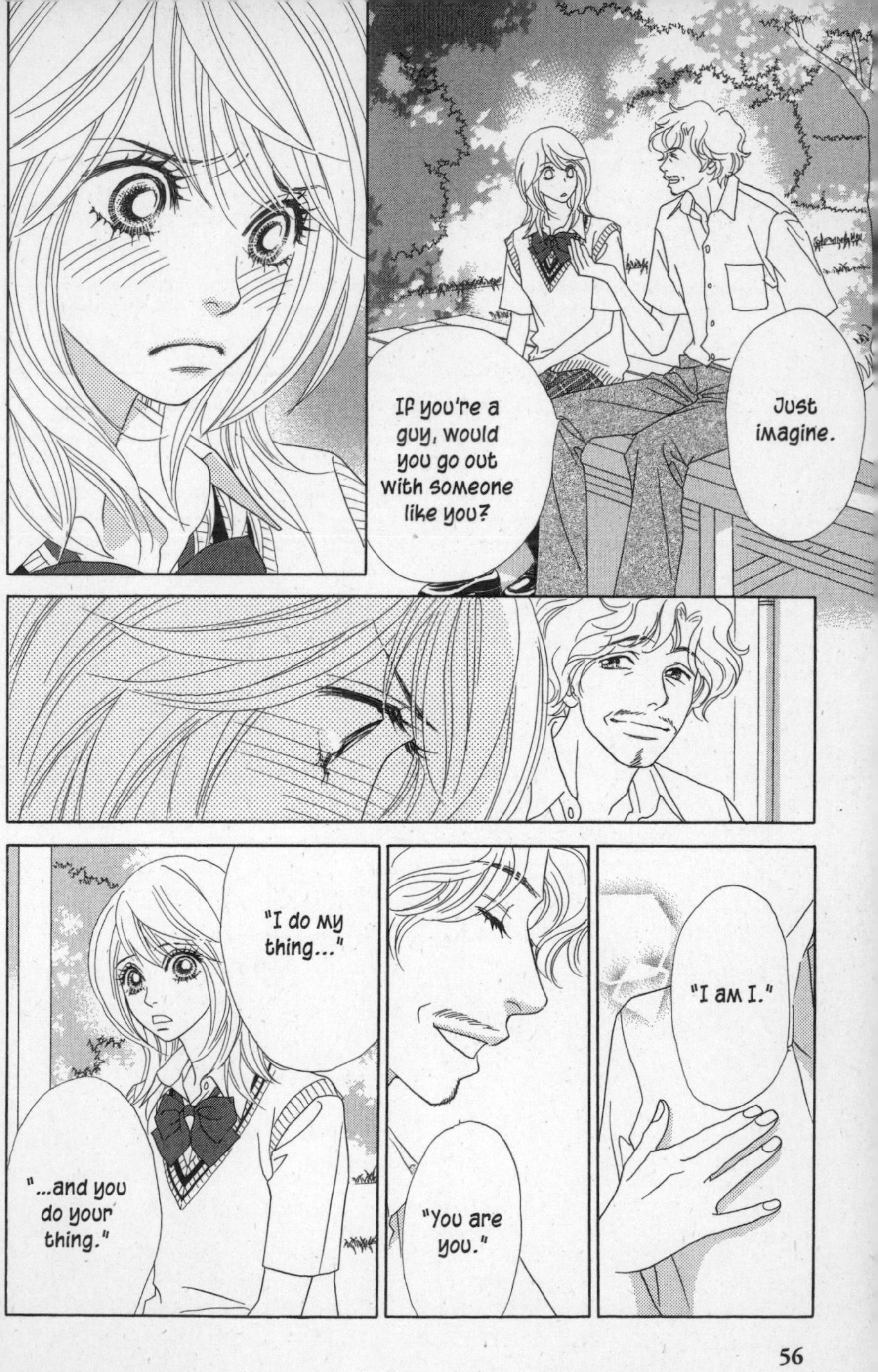
Just imagine.
If you're a guy, would you go out with someone like you?
"I am I."
"You are you."
"I do my thing..."
"...and you do your thing."

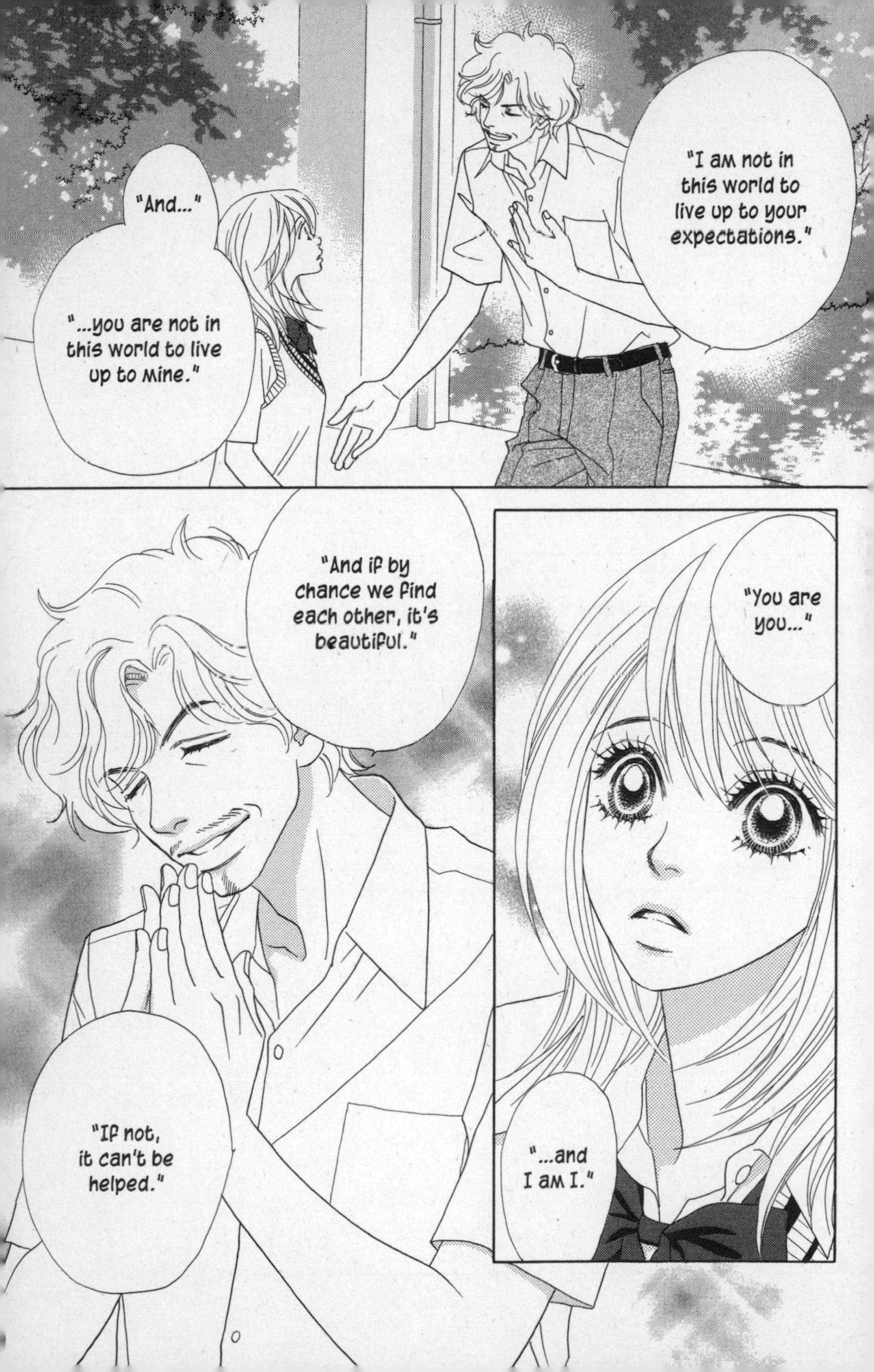
"I am not in this world to live up to your expectations."
"And..."
"...you are not in this world to live up to mine."
"You are you..."
"...and I am I."
"And if by chance we find each other, it's beautiful."
"If not, it can't be helped."

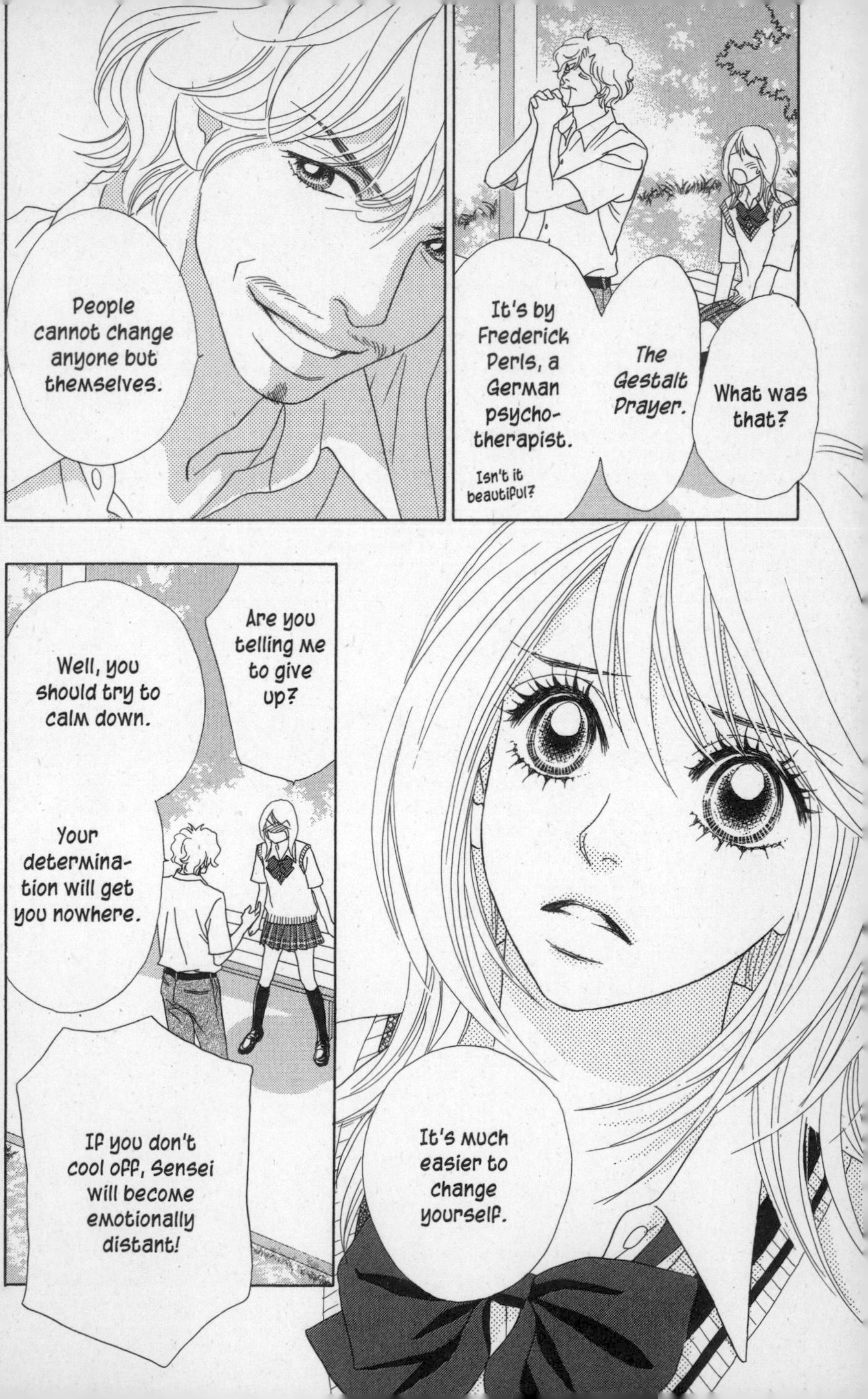
What was that?
The Gestalt Prayer.
It's by Frederick Perls, a German psycho-therapist.
Isn't it beautiful?
People cannot change anyone but themselves.
It's much easier to change yourself.
Are you telling me to give up?
Well, you should try to calm down.
Your determina-tion will get you nowhere.
If you don't cool off, Sensei will become emotionally distant!

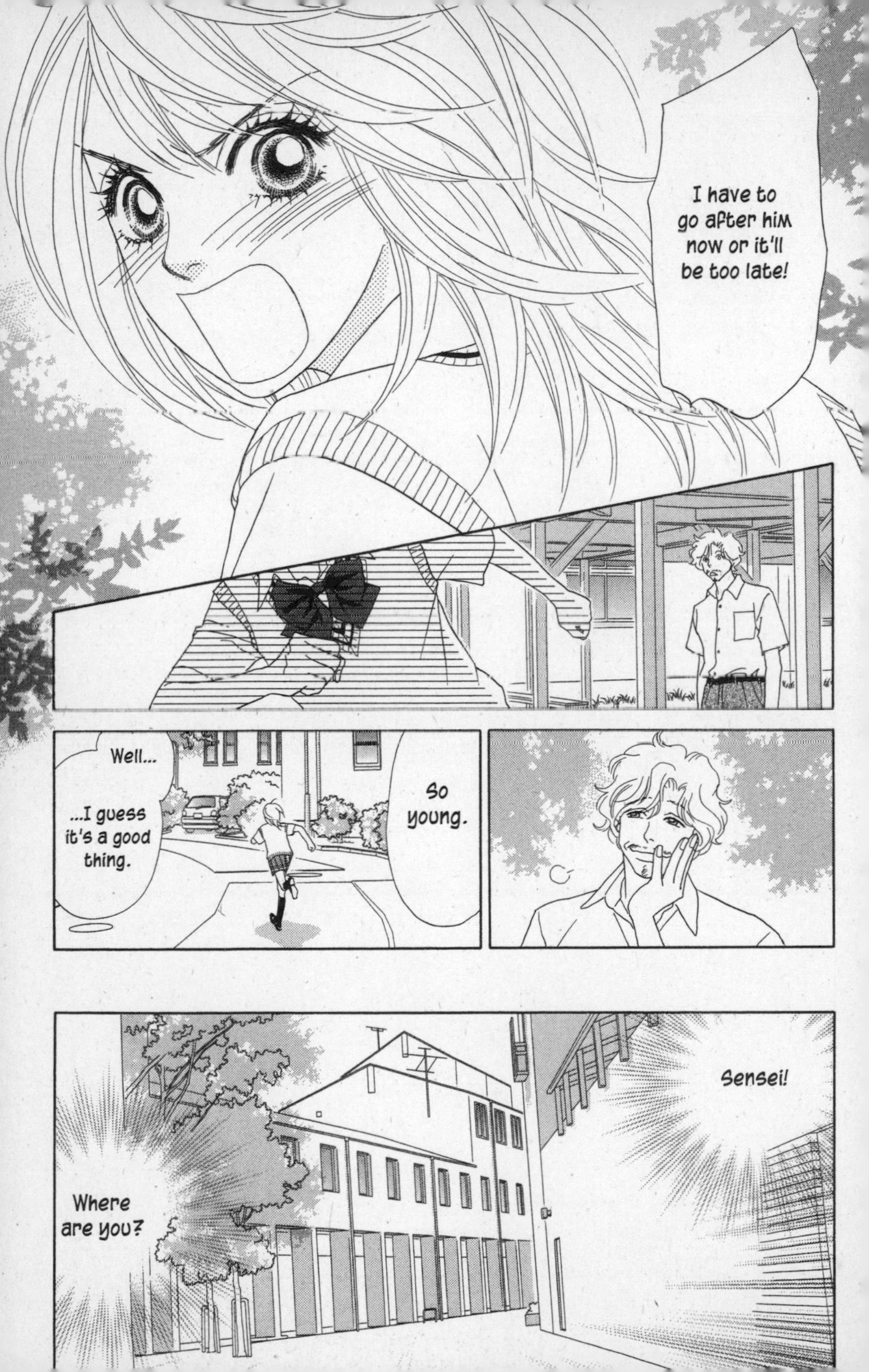
I have to go after him now or it'll be too late!
So young.
Well...
...I guess it's a good thing.
Sensei!
Where are you?

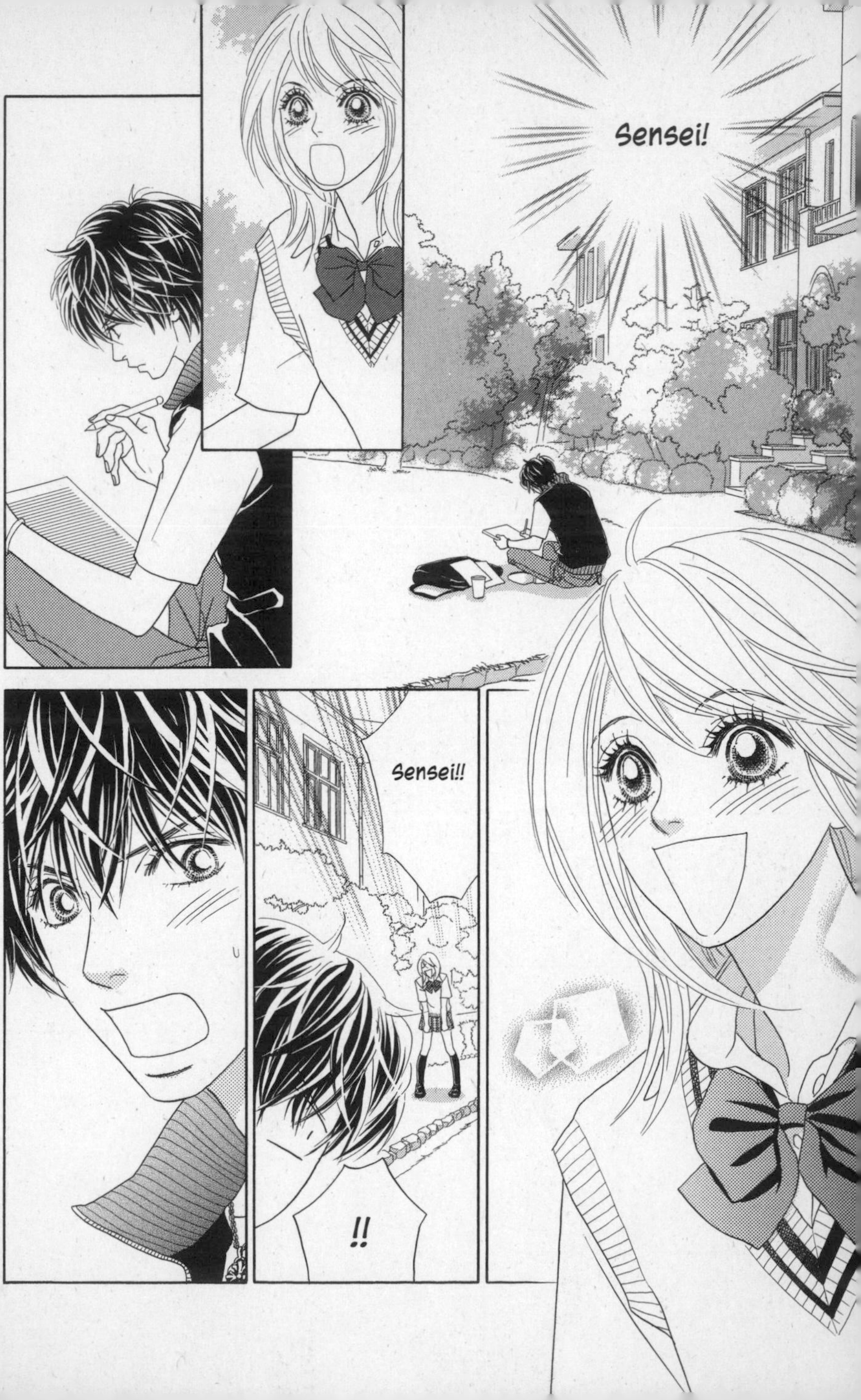
Sensei!
Sensei!!
!!

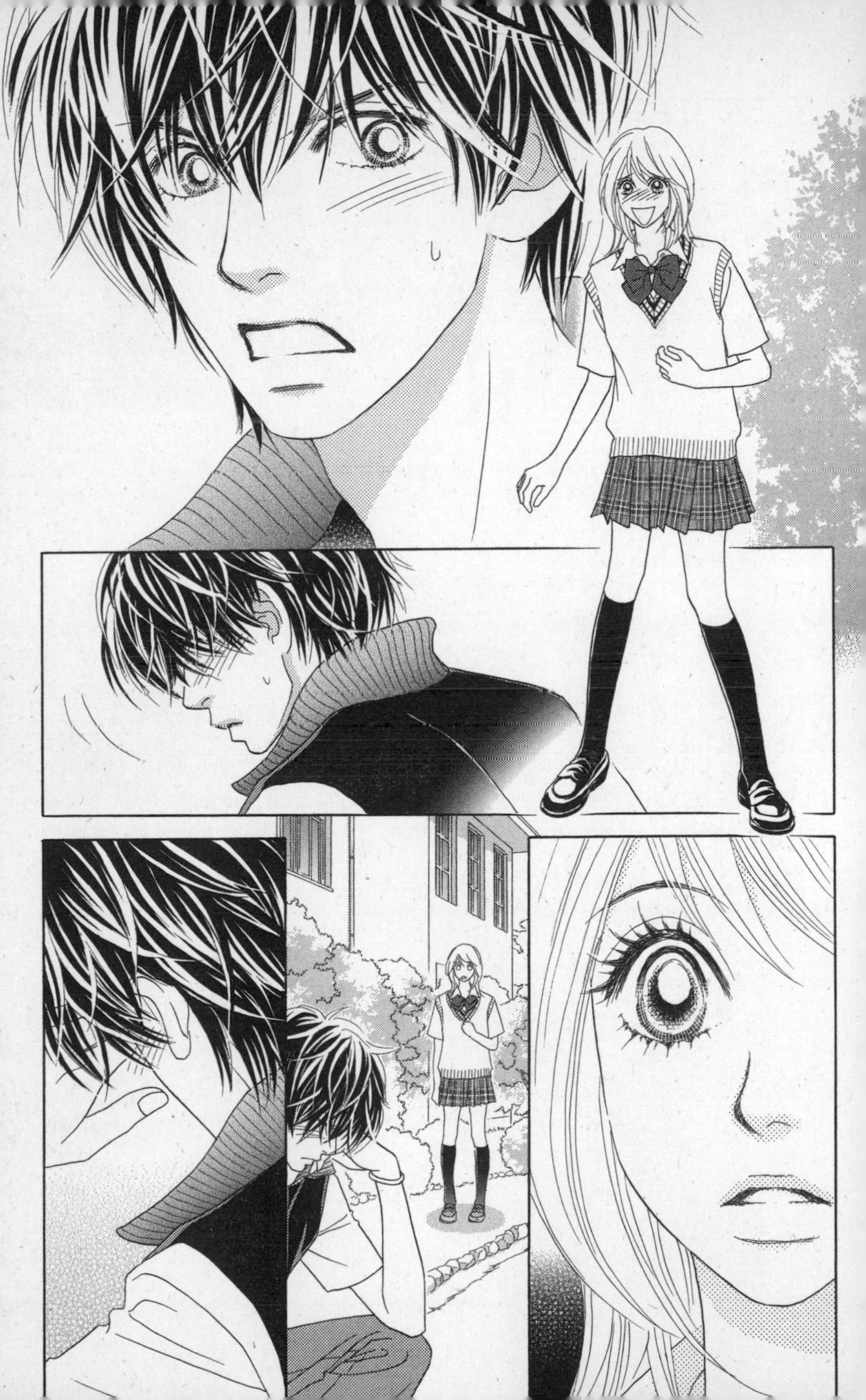

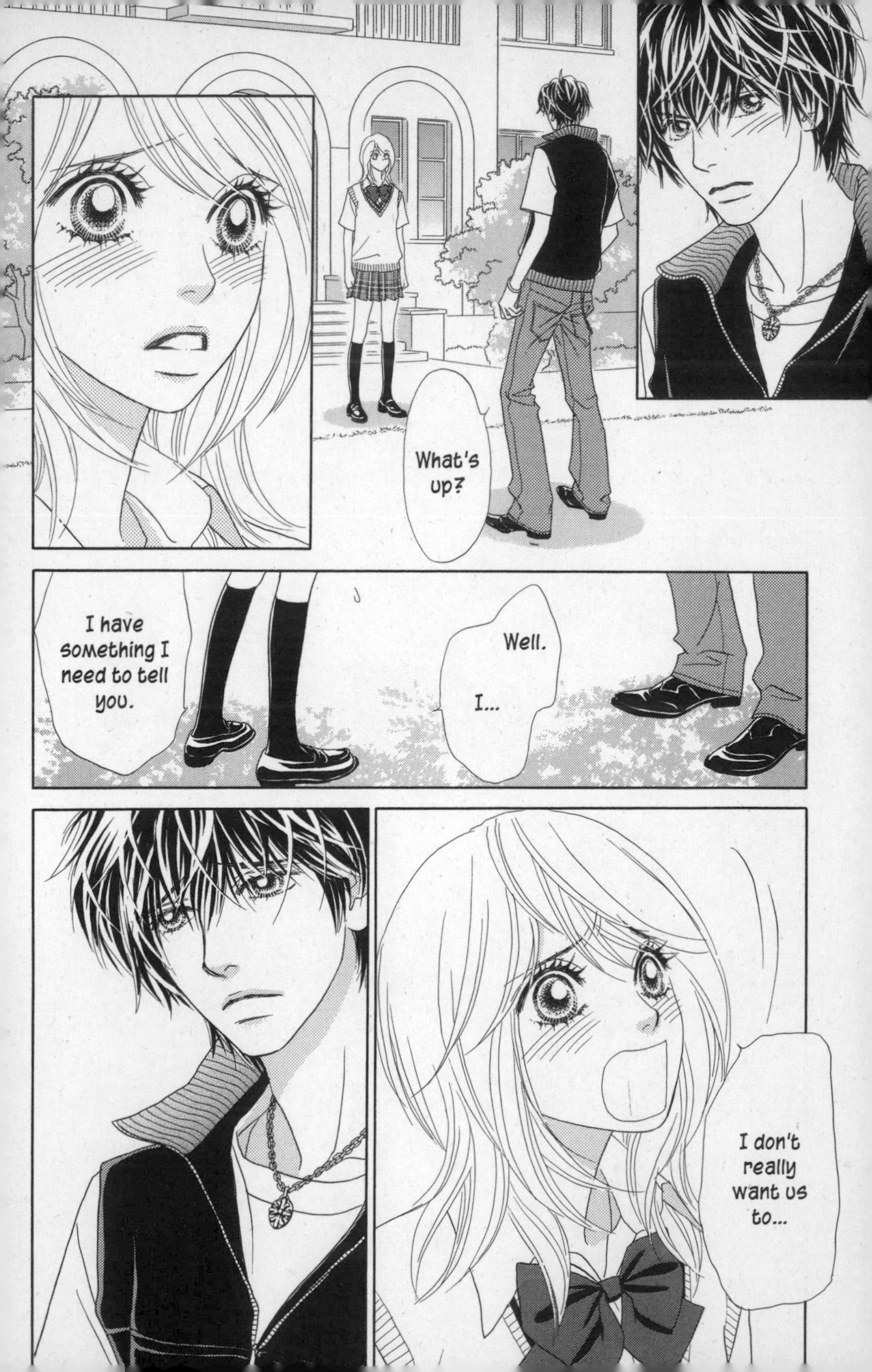
What's up?
Well. I...
I have something I need to tell you.
I don't really want us to...

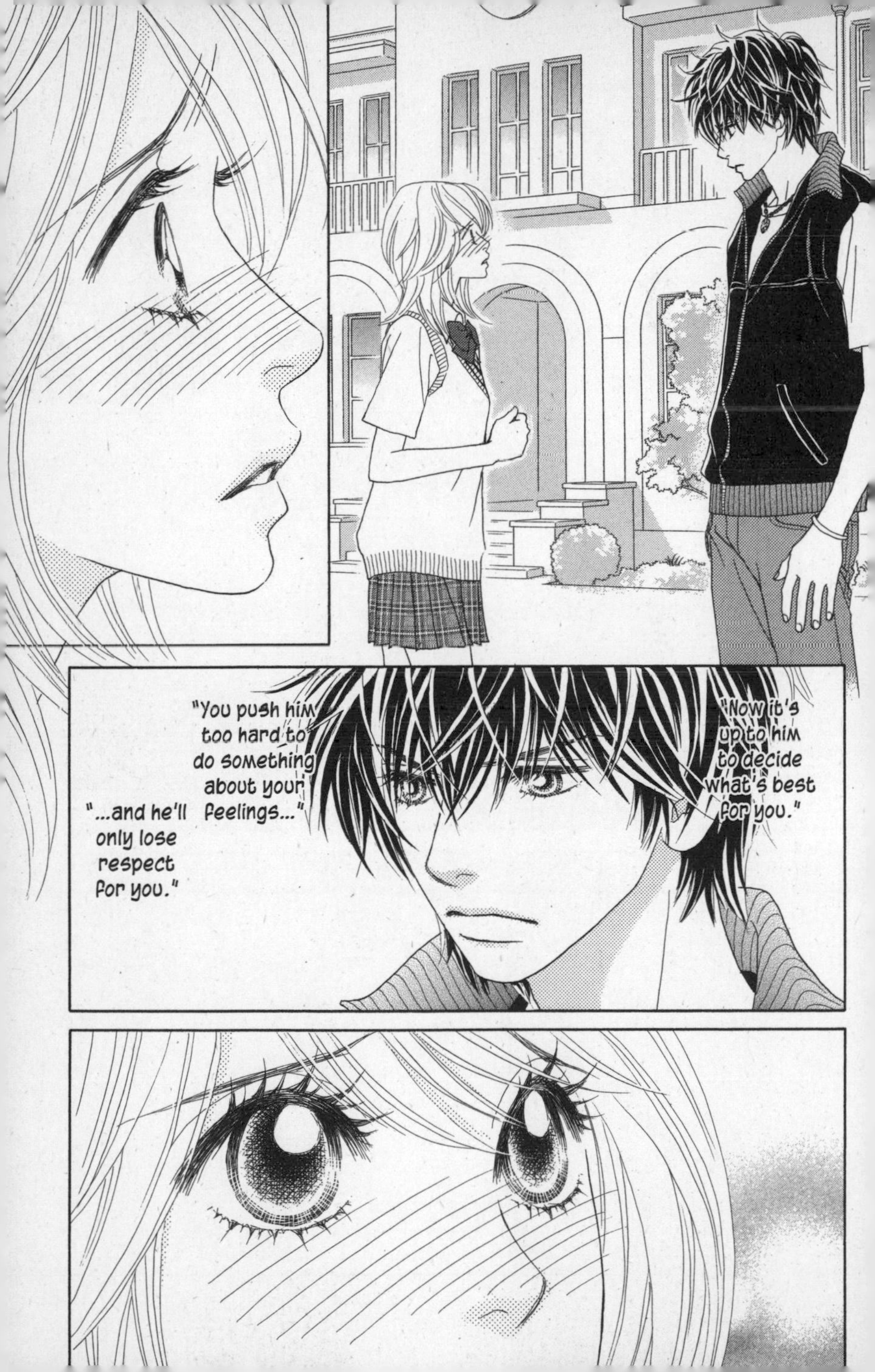
"Now it's up to him to decide what's best for you."
"You push him too hard to do something about your feelings..."
"...and he'll only lose respect for you."

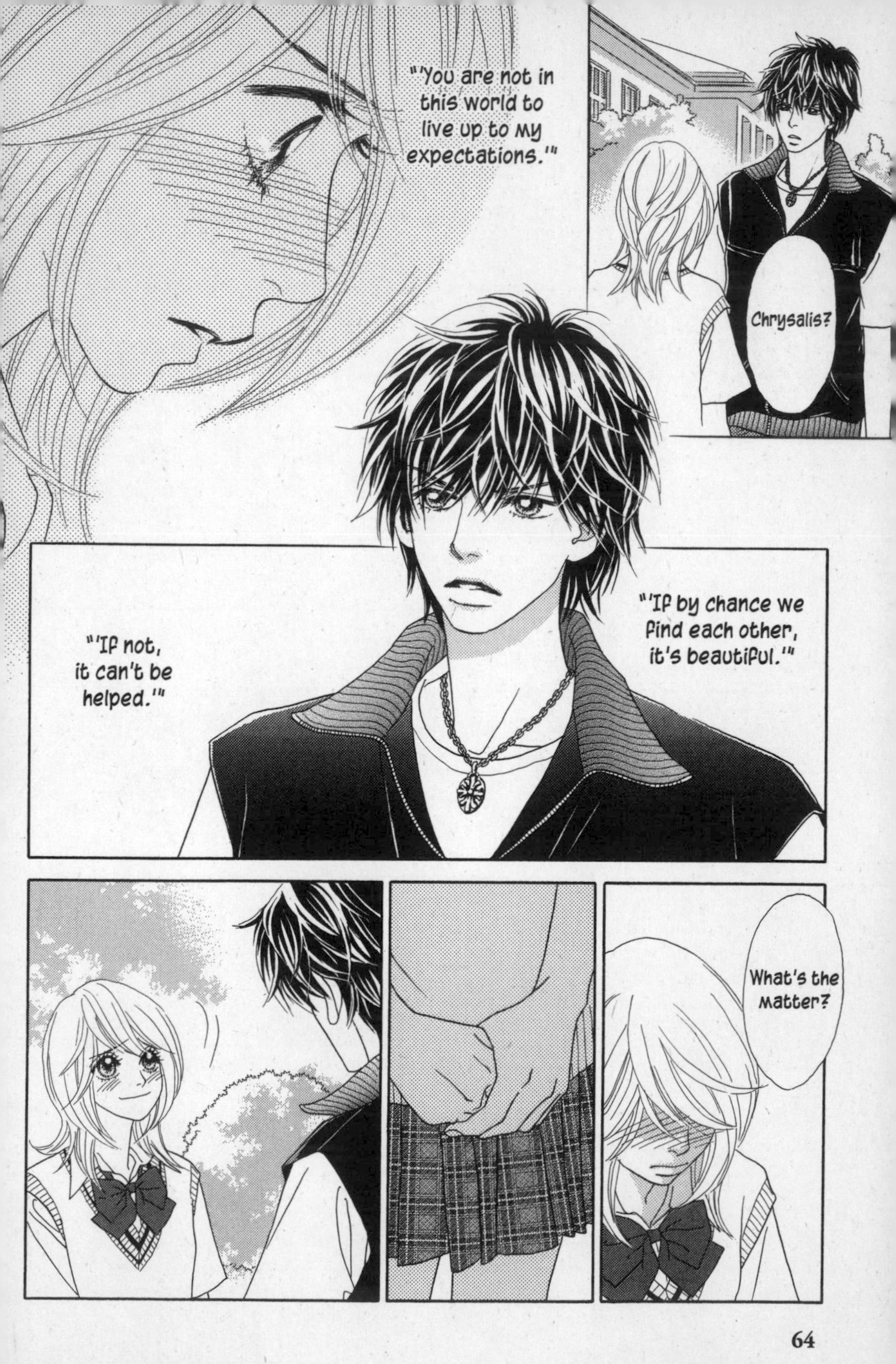
Chrysalis?
"'You are not in this world to live up to my expectations.'"
"'If by chance we find each other, it's beautiful.'"
"'If not, it can't be helped.'"
What's the matter?

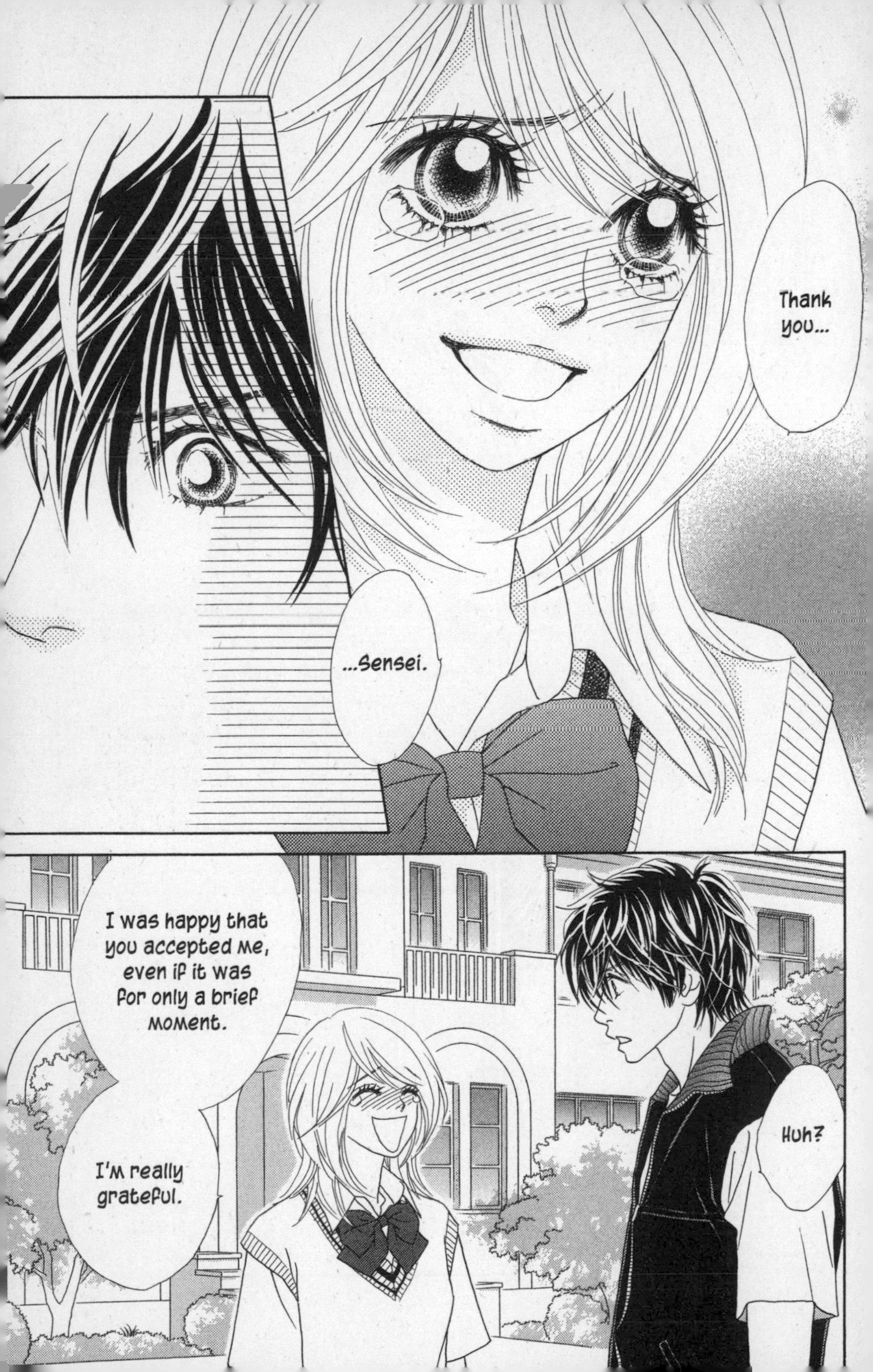
Thank you...
...Sensei.
I was happy that you accepted me, even if it was for only a brief moment.
I'm really grateful.
Huh?

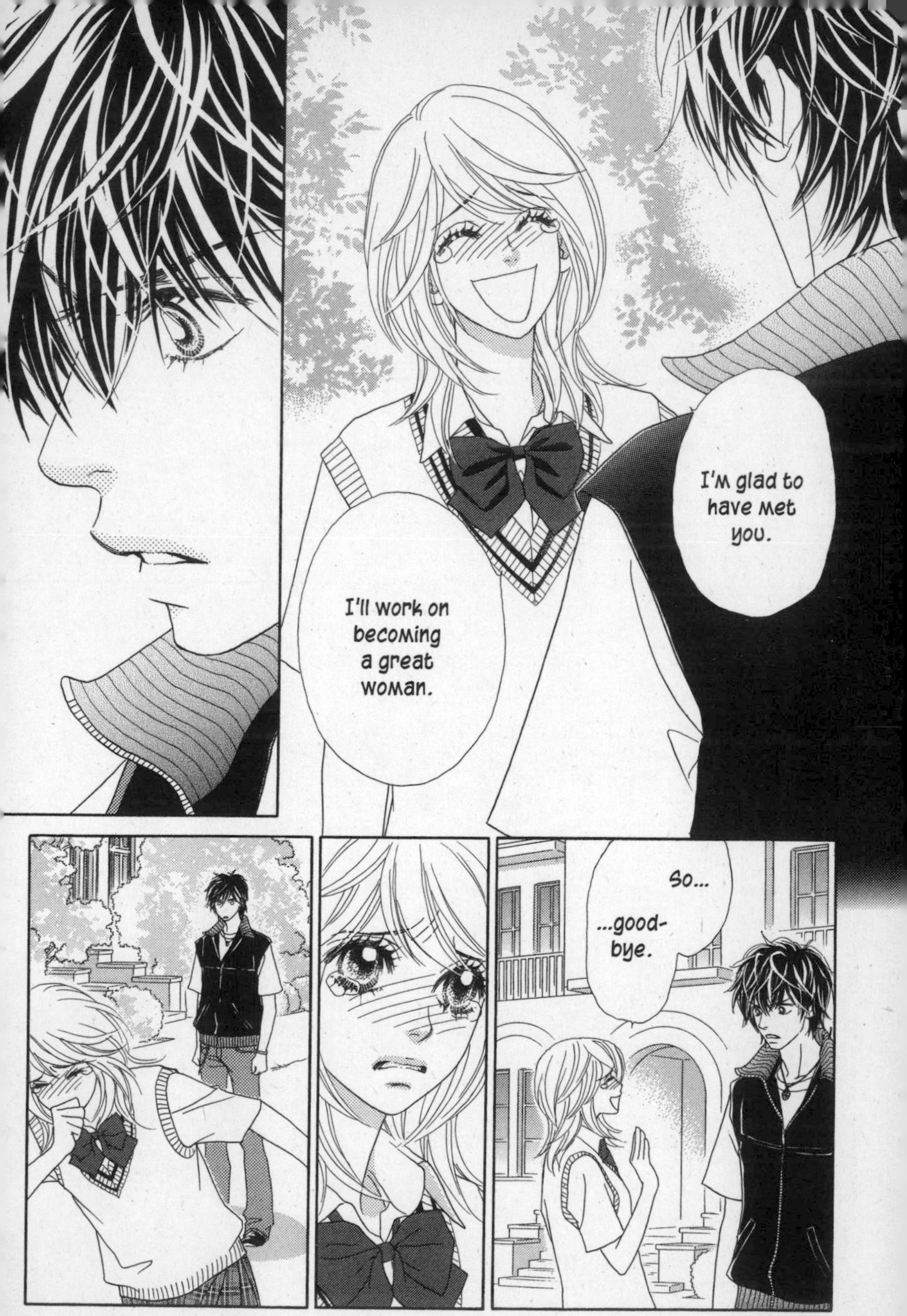
I'm glad to have met you.
I'll work on becoming a great woman.
So...
...good-bye.

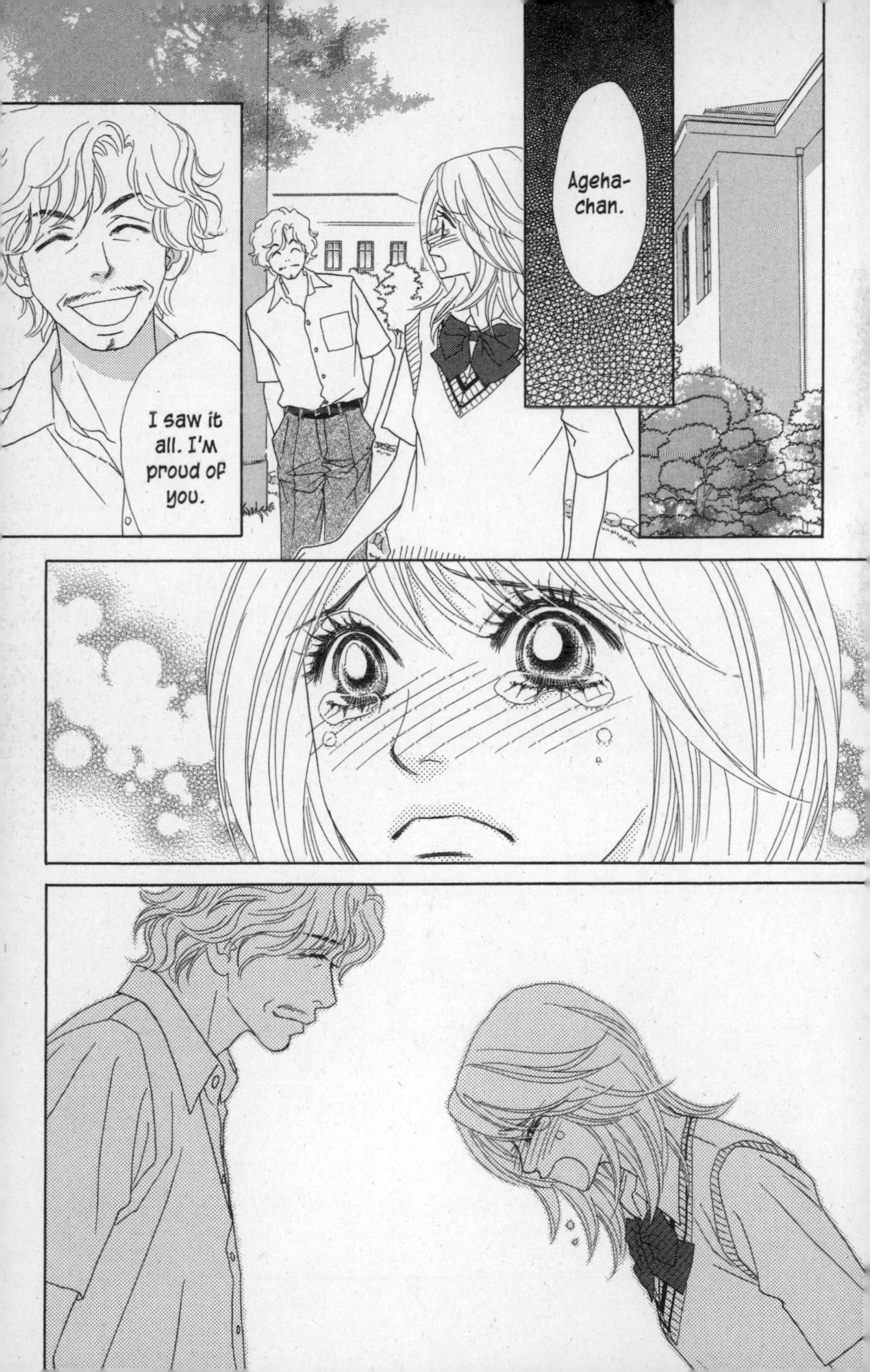
Ageha-chan.
I saw it all. I'm proud of you.

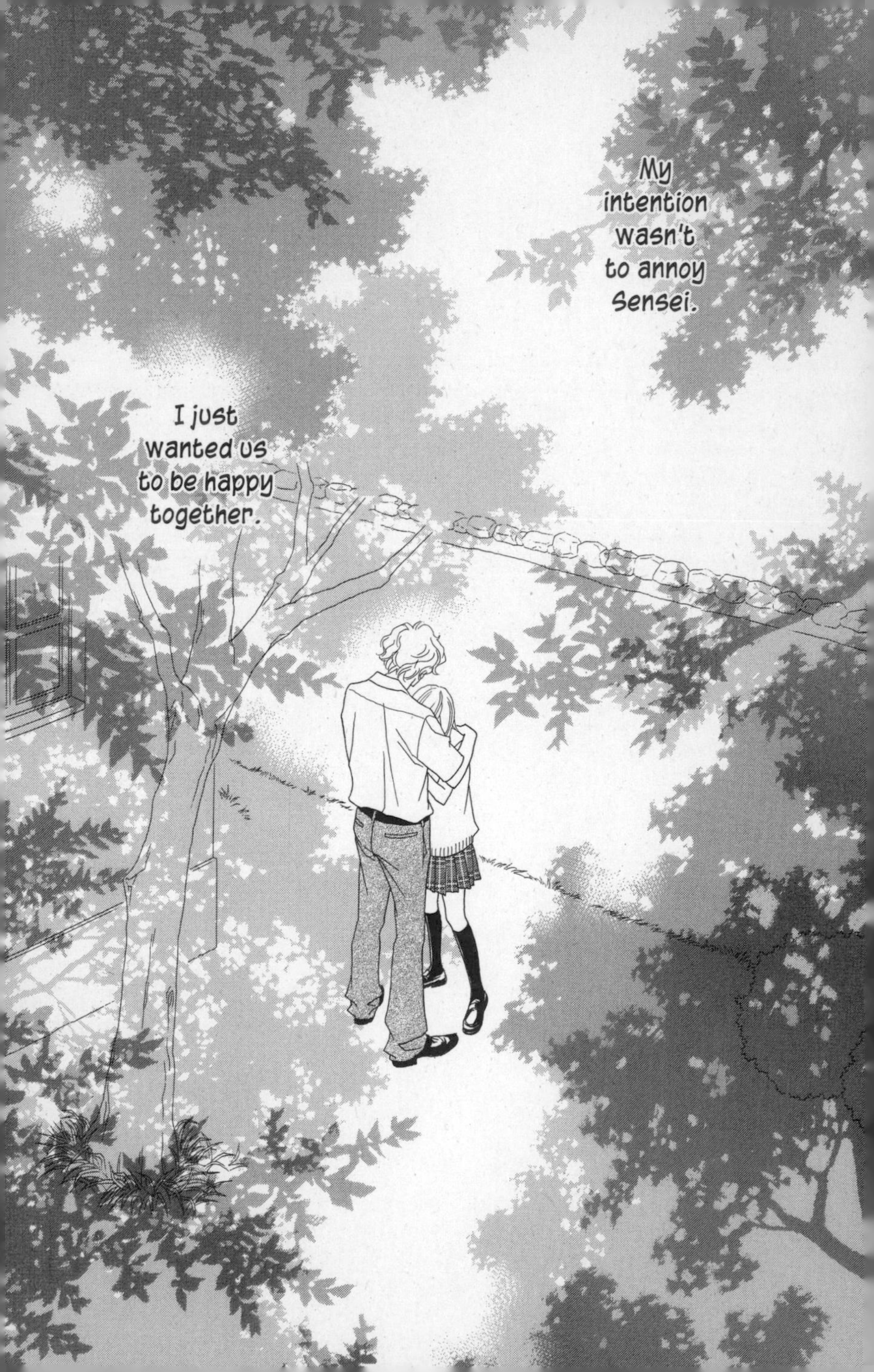
My intention wasn't to annoy Sensei.
I just wanted us to be happy together.

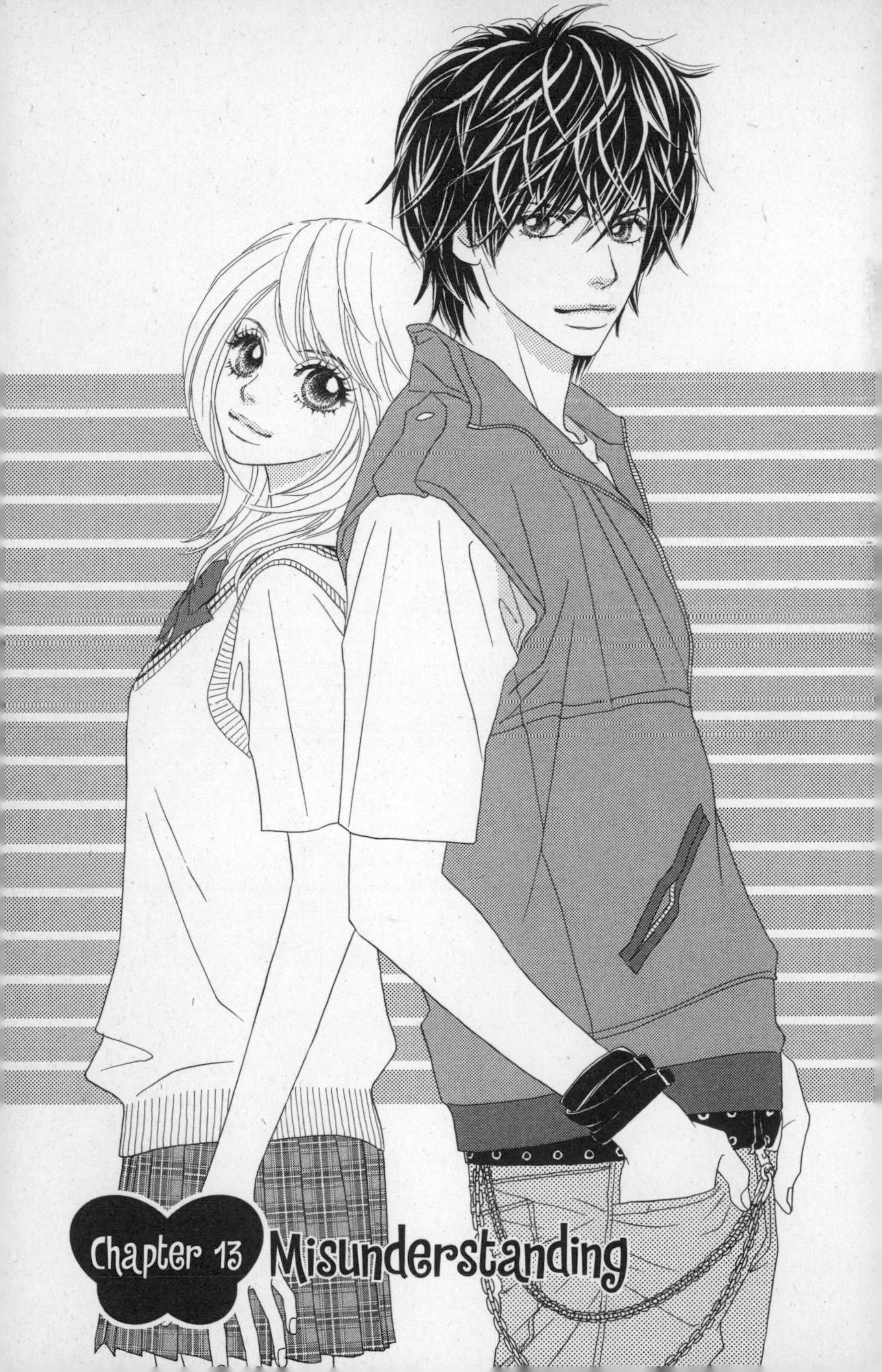
Chapter 13
Misunderstanding

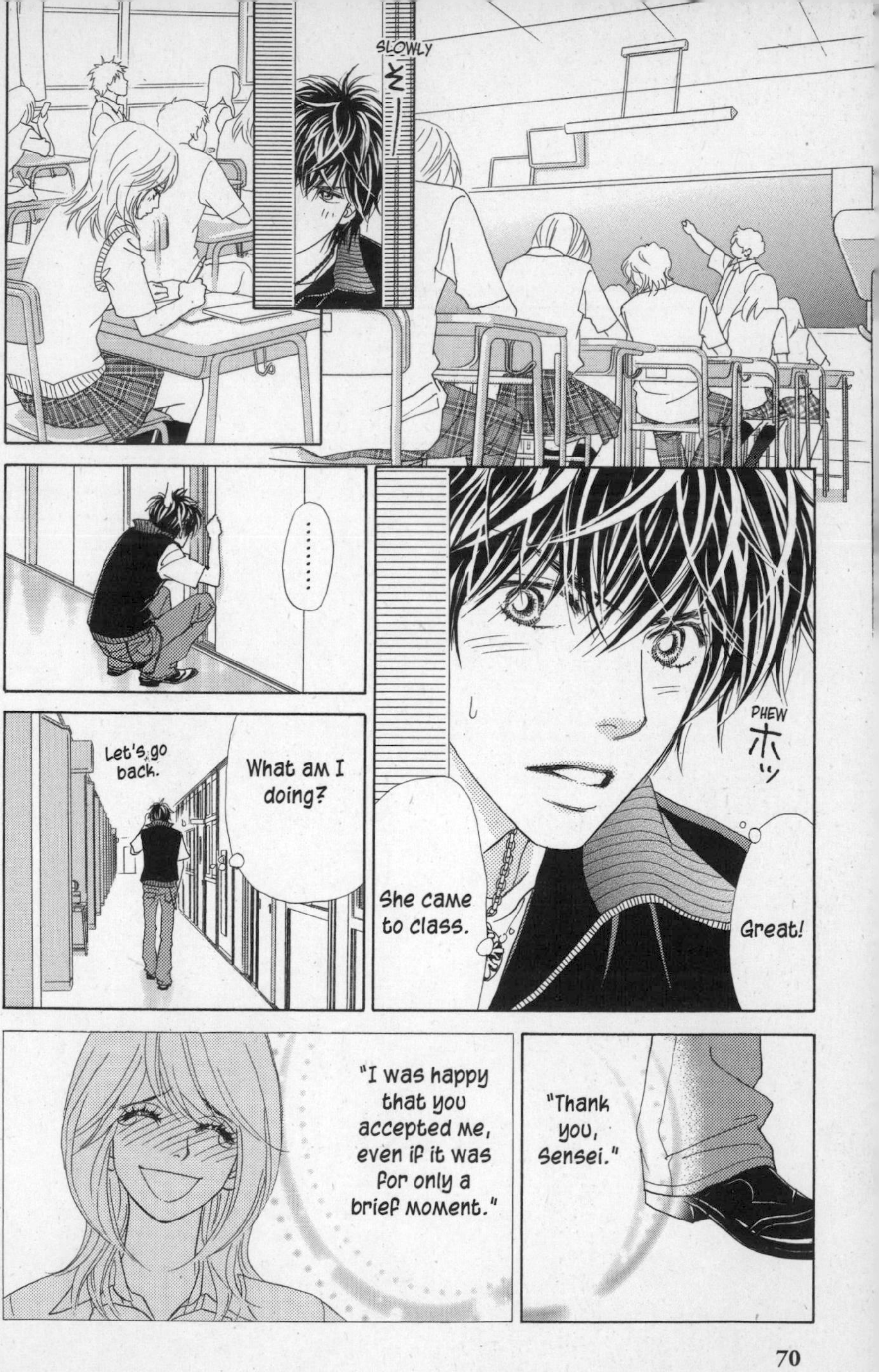
SLOWLY
PHEW
ホッ
Great!
She came to class.
……
What am I doing?
Let's go back.
"Thank you, Sensei."
"I was happy that you accepted me, even if it was for only a brief moment."

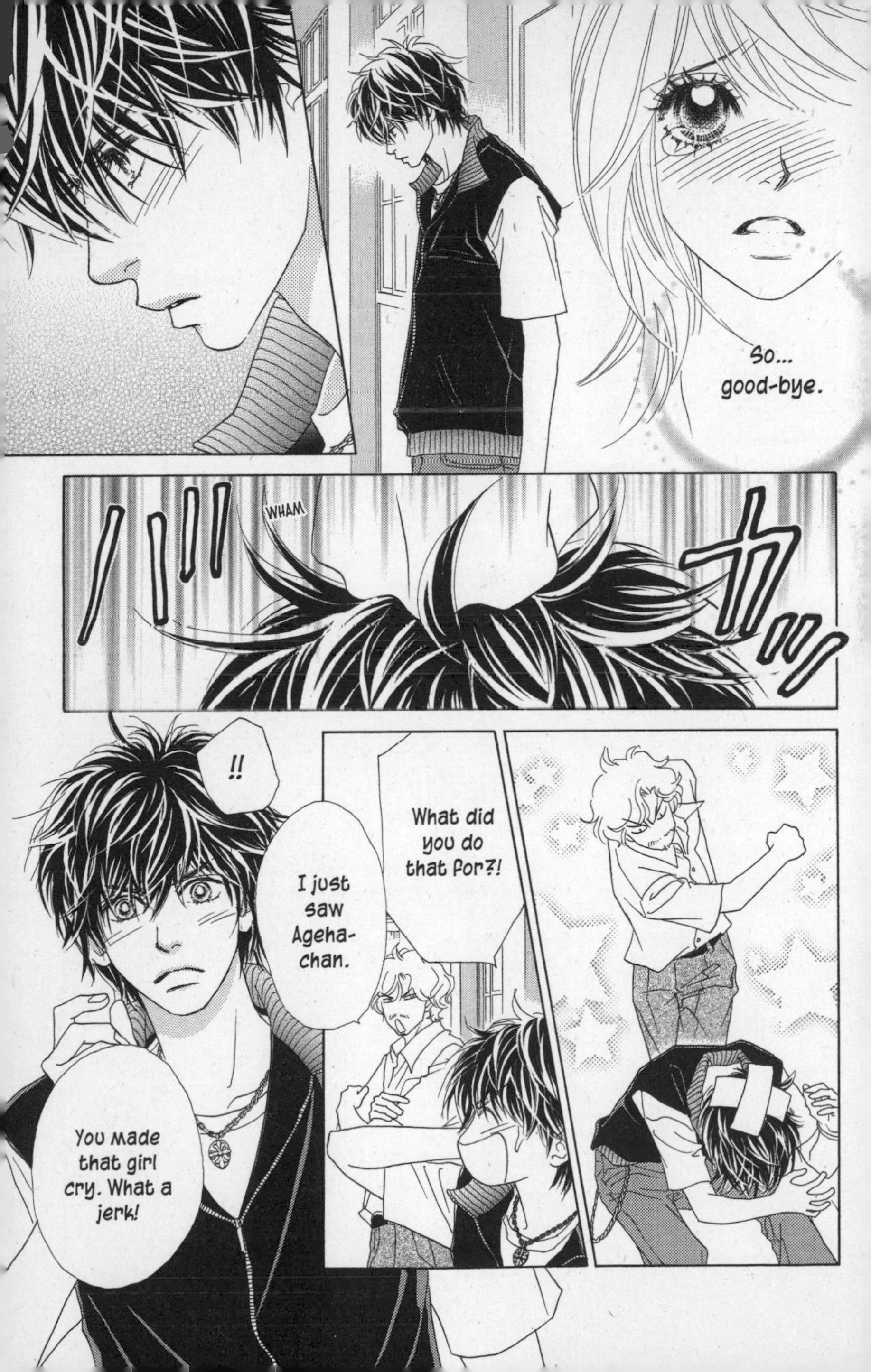
So... good-bye.
カッ
WHAM
What did you do that for?!
!!
I just saw Ageha-chan.
You made that girl cry. What a jerk!

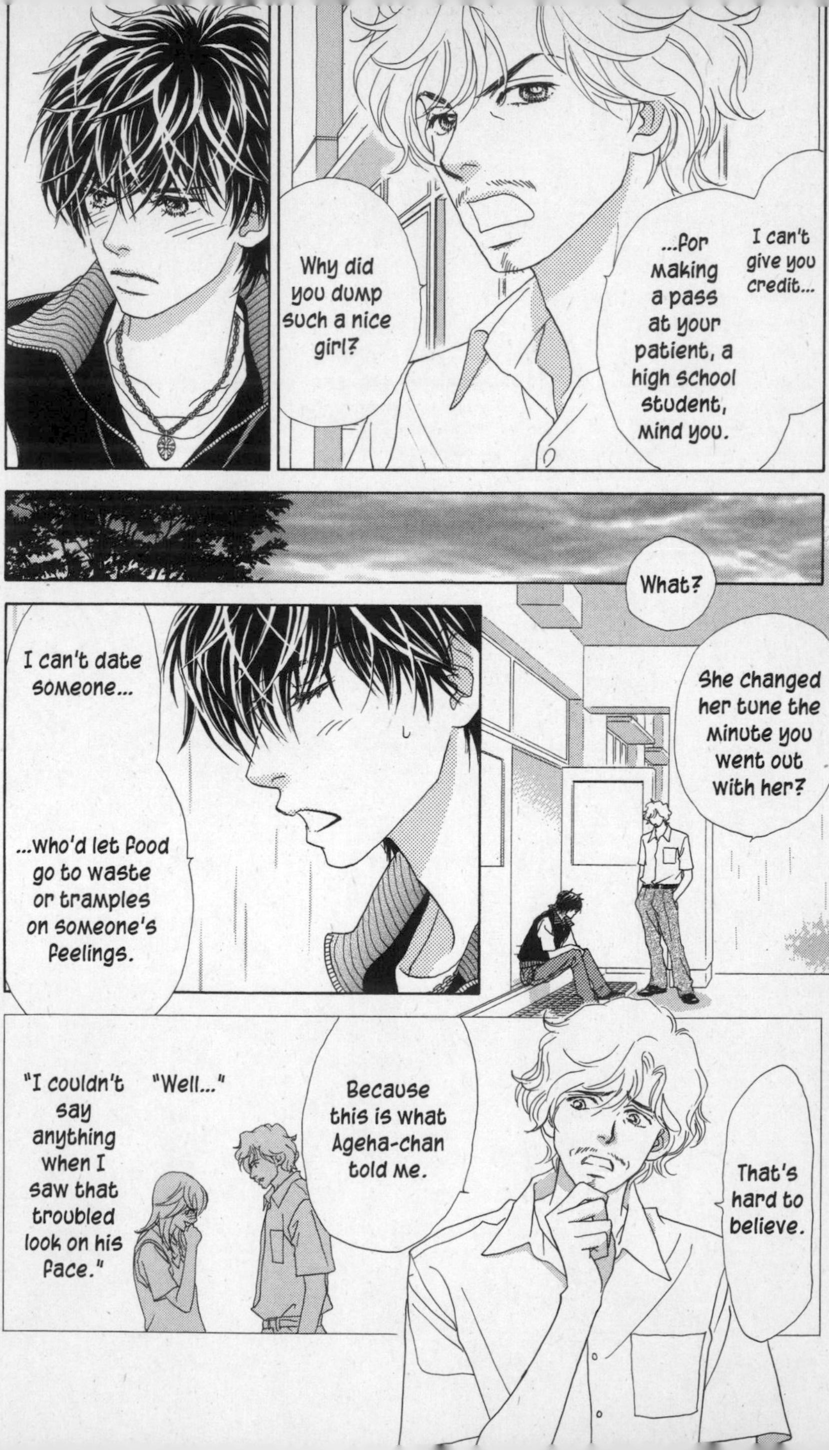
I can't give you credit...
...for making a pass at your patient, a high school student, mind you.
Why did you dump such a nice girl?
What?
She changed her tune the minute you went out with her?
I can't date someone...
...who'd let food go to waste or tramples on someone's feelings.
That's hard to believe.
Because this is what Ageha-chan told me.
"Well..."
"I couldn't say anything when I saw that troubled look on his face."

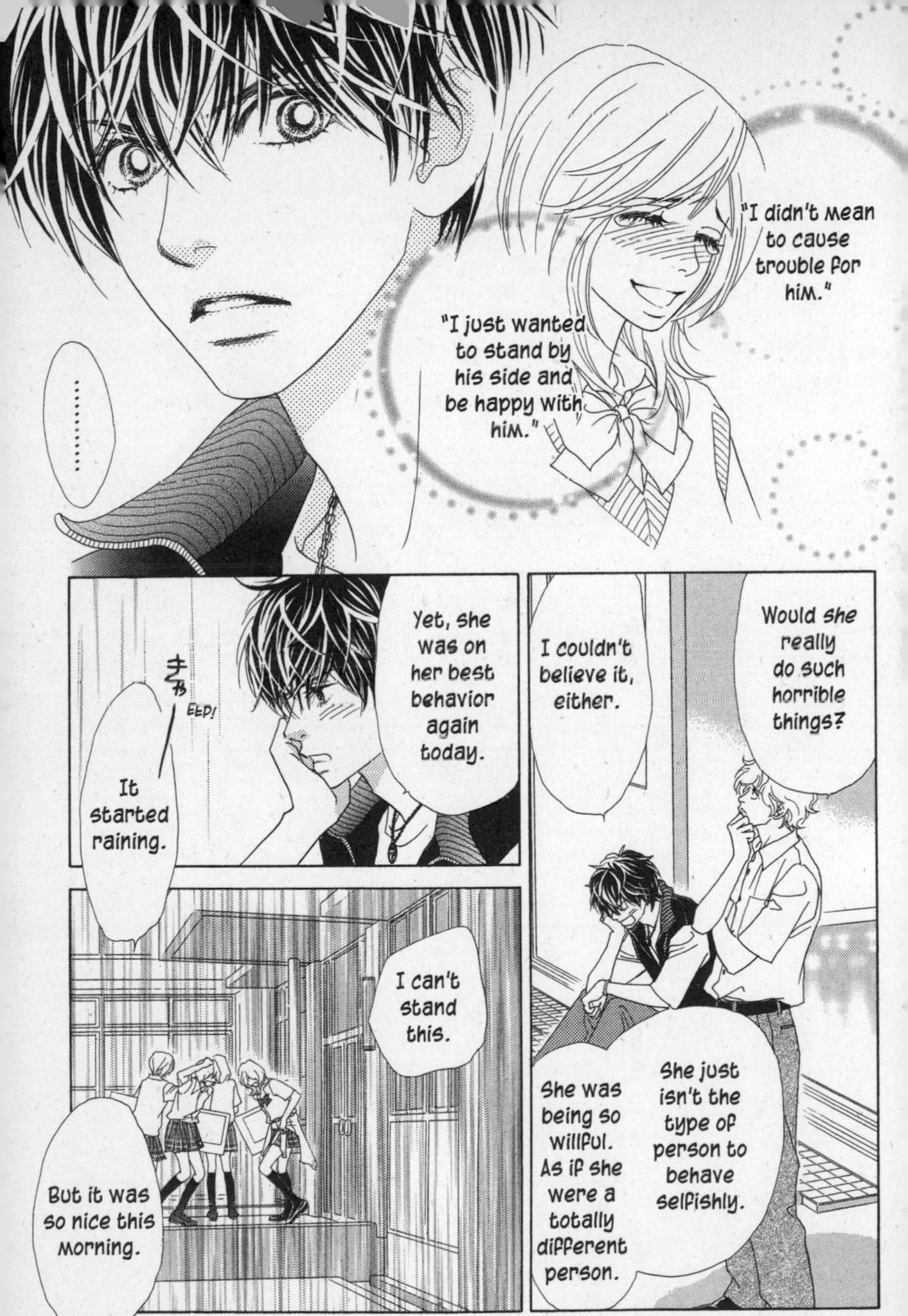
"I didn't mean to cause trouble for him."
"I just wanted to stand by his side and be happy with him."
......
Would she really do such horrible things?
I couldn't believe it, either.
She just isn't the type of person to behave selfishly.
She was being so willful. As if she were a totally different person.
Yet, she was on her best behavior again today.
EEP!
It started raining.
I can't stand this.
But it was so nice this morning.

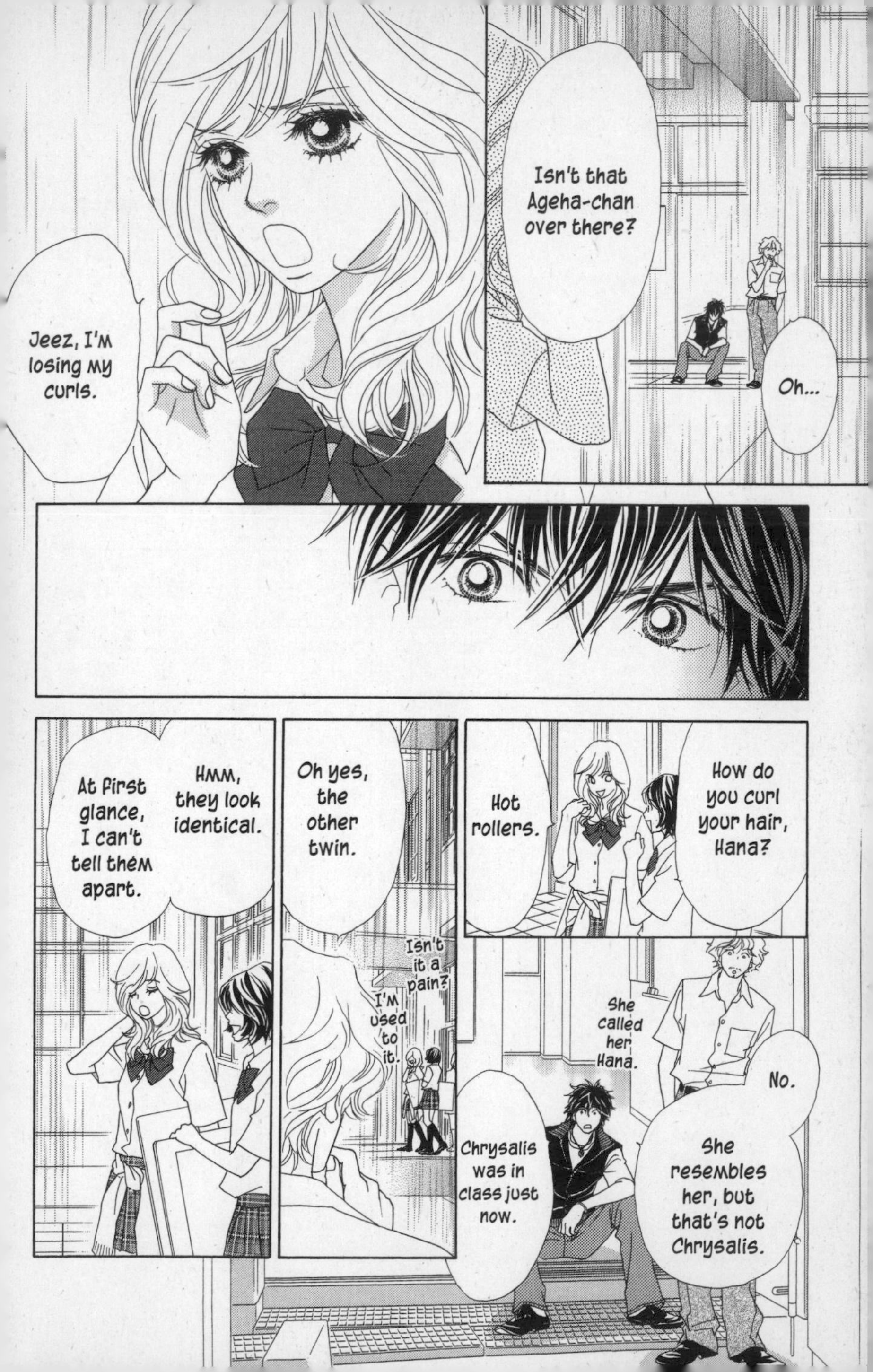
Isn't that Ageha-chan over there?
Oh...
Jeez, I'm losing my curls.
How do you curl your hair, Hana?
Hot rollers.
She called her Hana.
No.
She resembles her, but that's not Chrysalis.
Chrysalis was in class just now.
Oh yes, the other twin.
Isn't it a pain?
I'm used to it.
Hmm, they look identical.
At first glance, I can't tell them apart.

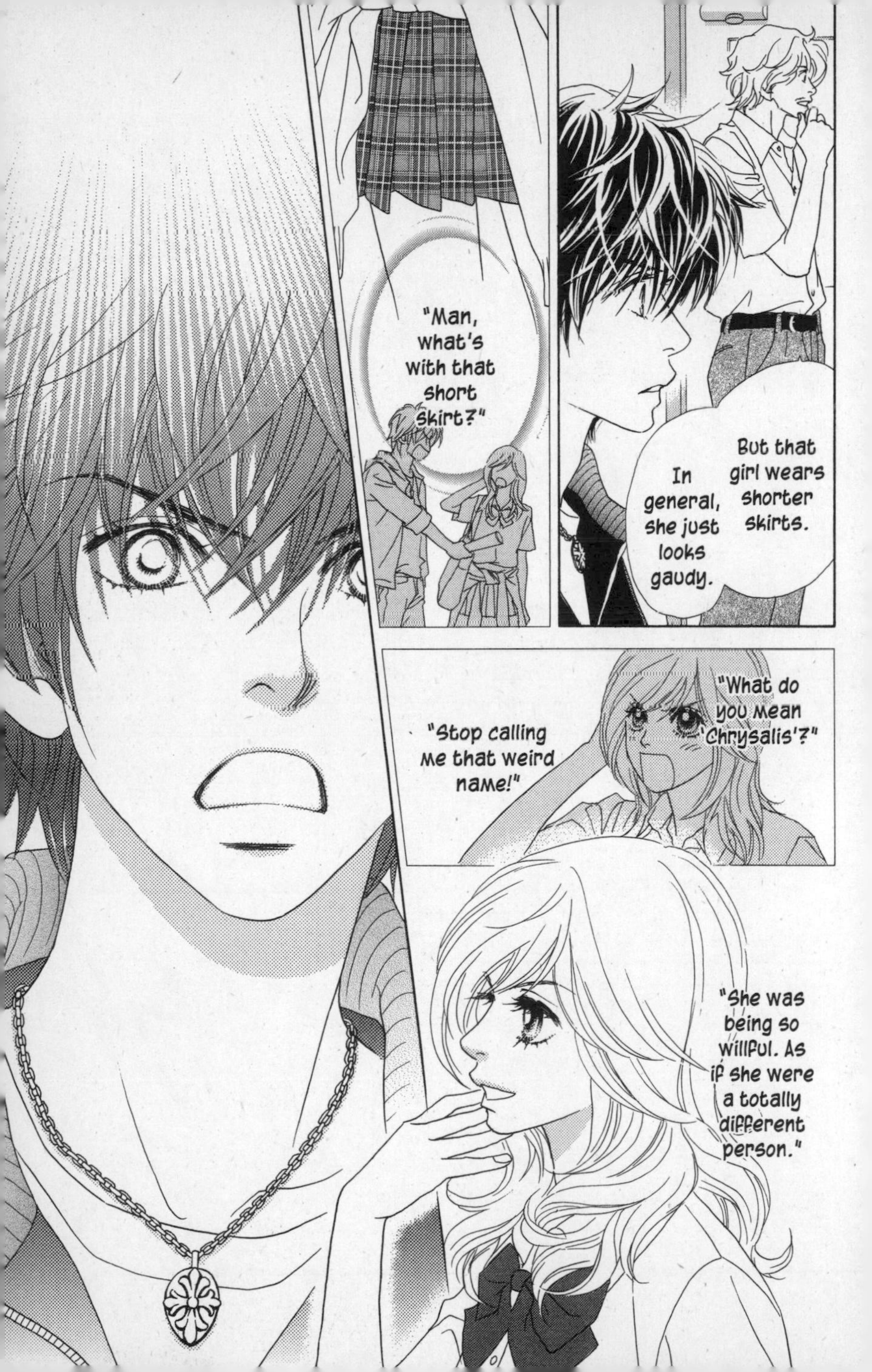
But that girl wears shorter skirts.
In general, she just looks gaudy.
"Man, what's with that short skirt?"
"What do you mean 'Chrysalis'?"
"Stop calling me that weird name!"
"She was being so willful. As if she were a totally different person."

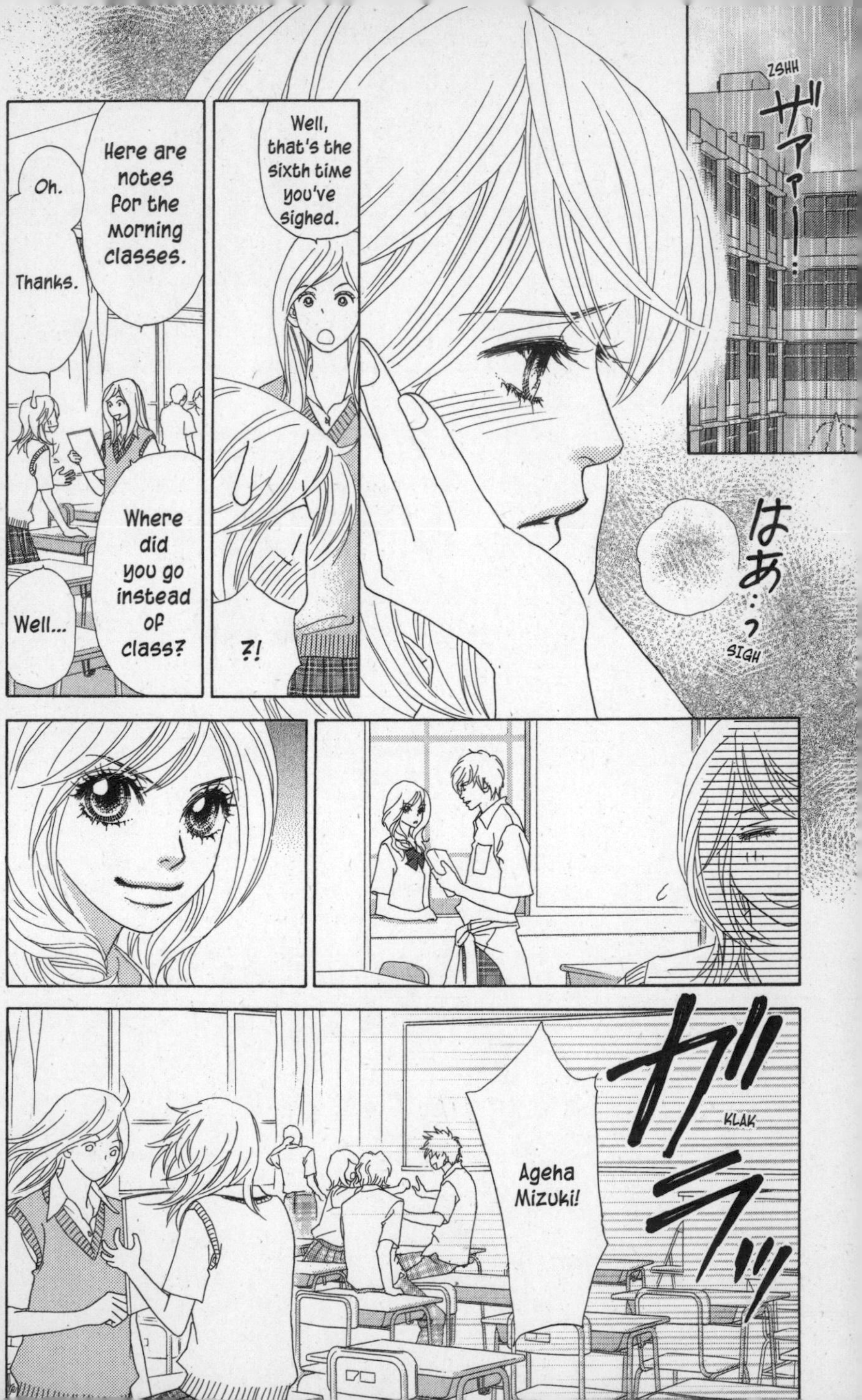
ZSHH
ザァァー…!
はあ…っ
SIGH
Well, that's the sixth time you've sighed.
?!
Here are notes for the morning classes.
Oh.
Thanks.
Where did you go instead of class?
Well...
ガラッ
KLAK
Ageha Mizuki!

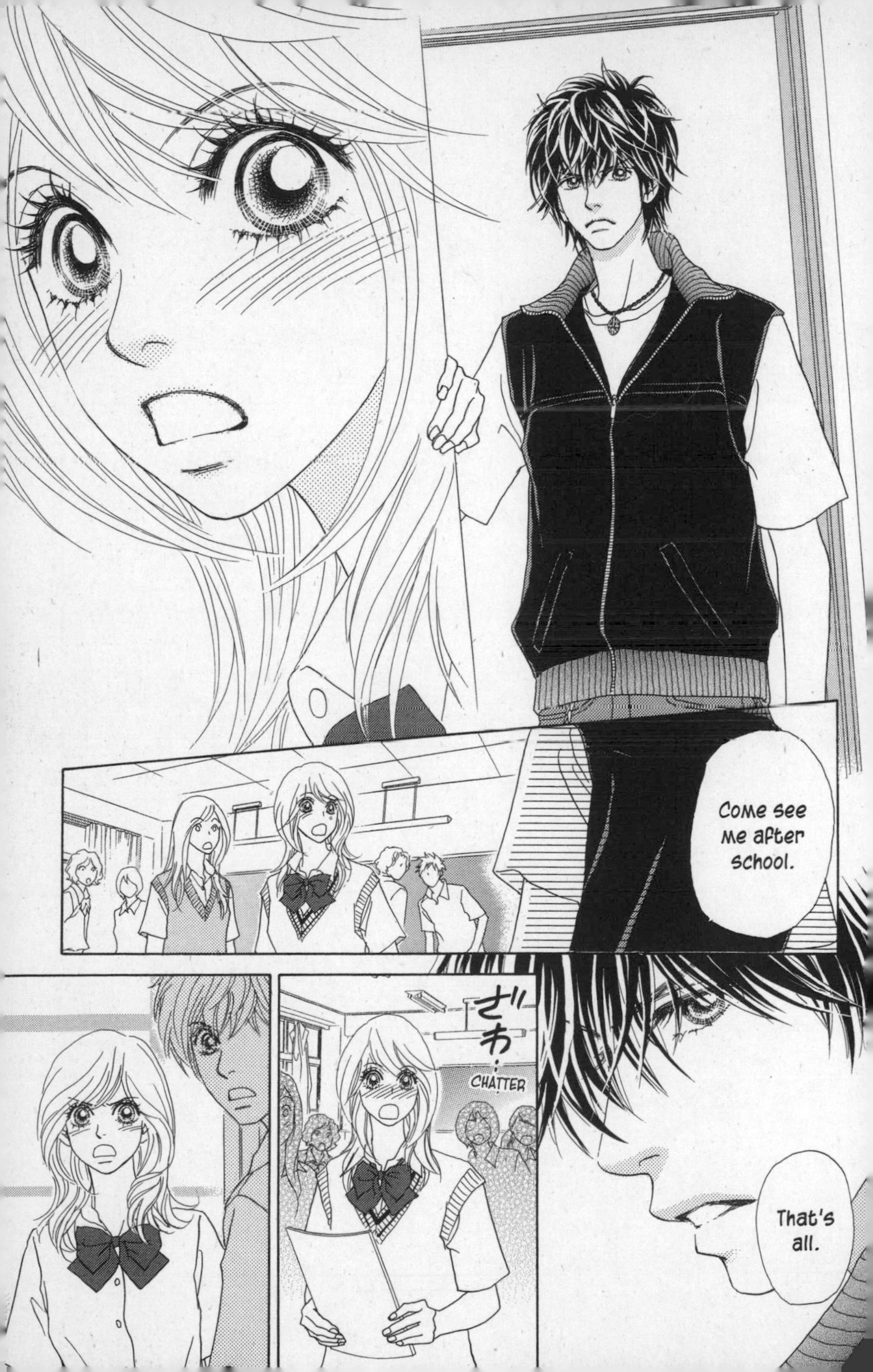
Come see me after school.
That's all.
ざわ
CHATTER

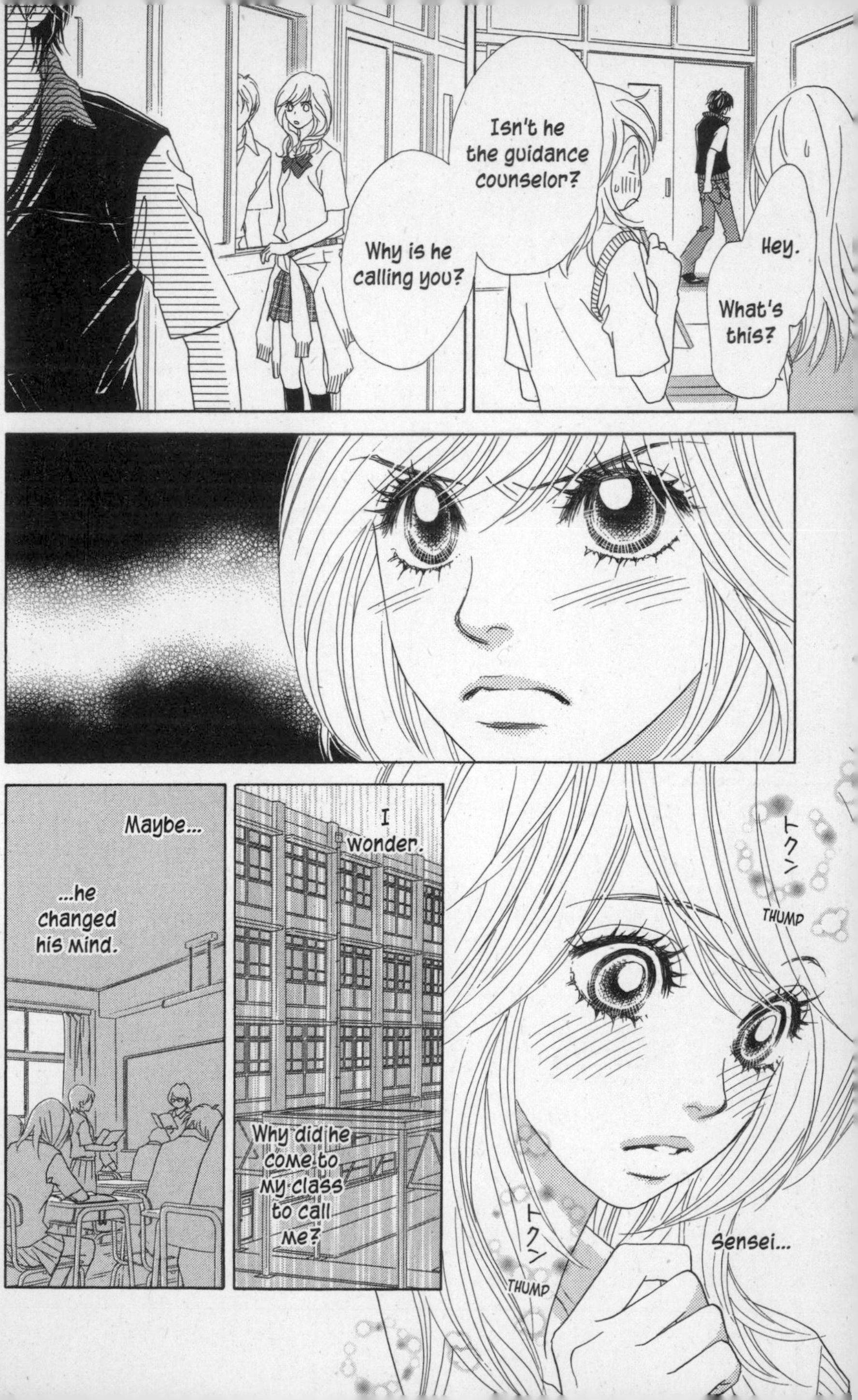
Hey.
What's this?
Isn't he the guidance counselor?
Why is he calling you?
トクン
THUMP
トクン
THUMP
Sensei...
I wonder.
Why did he come to my class to call me?
Maybe...
...he changed his mind.

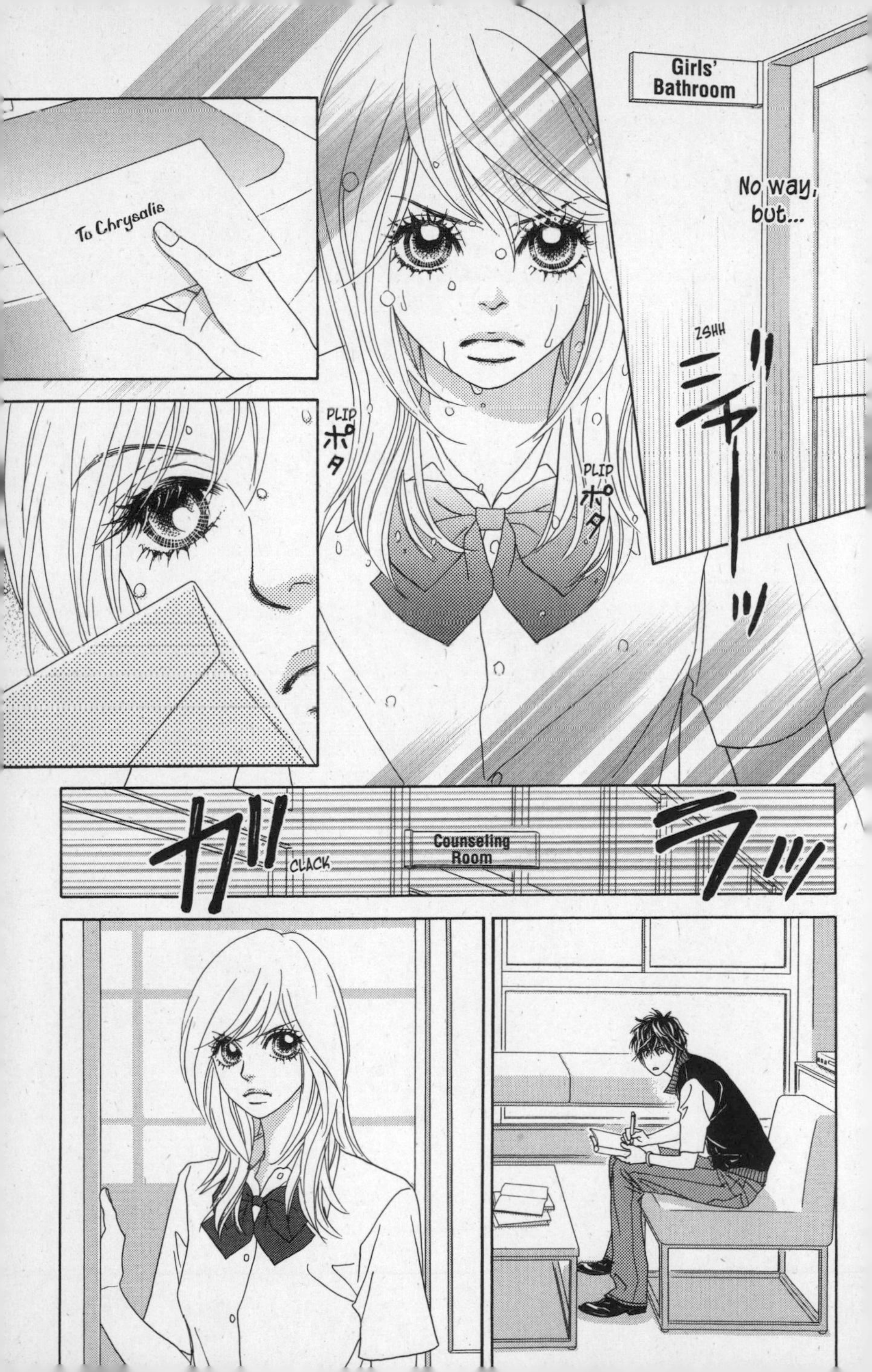
Girls' Bathroom
No way, but...
ZSHH
ジャーッ
PLIP
ポタ
PLIP
ポタ
To Chrysalis
CLACK
ガラッ
Counseling Room

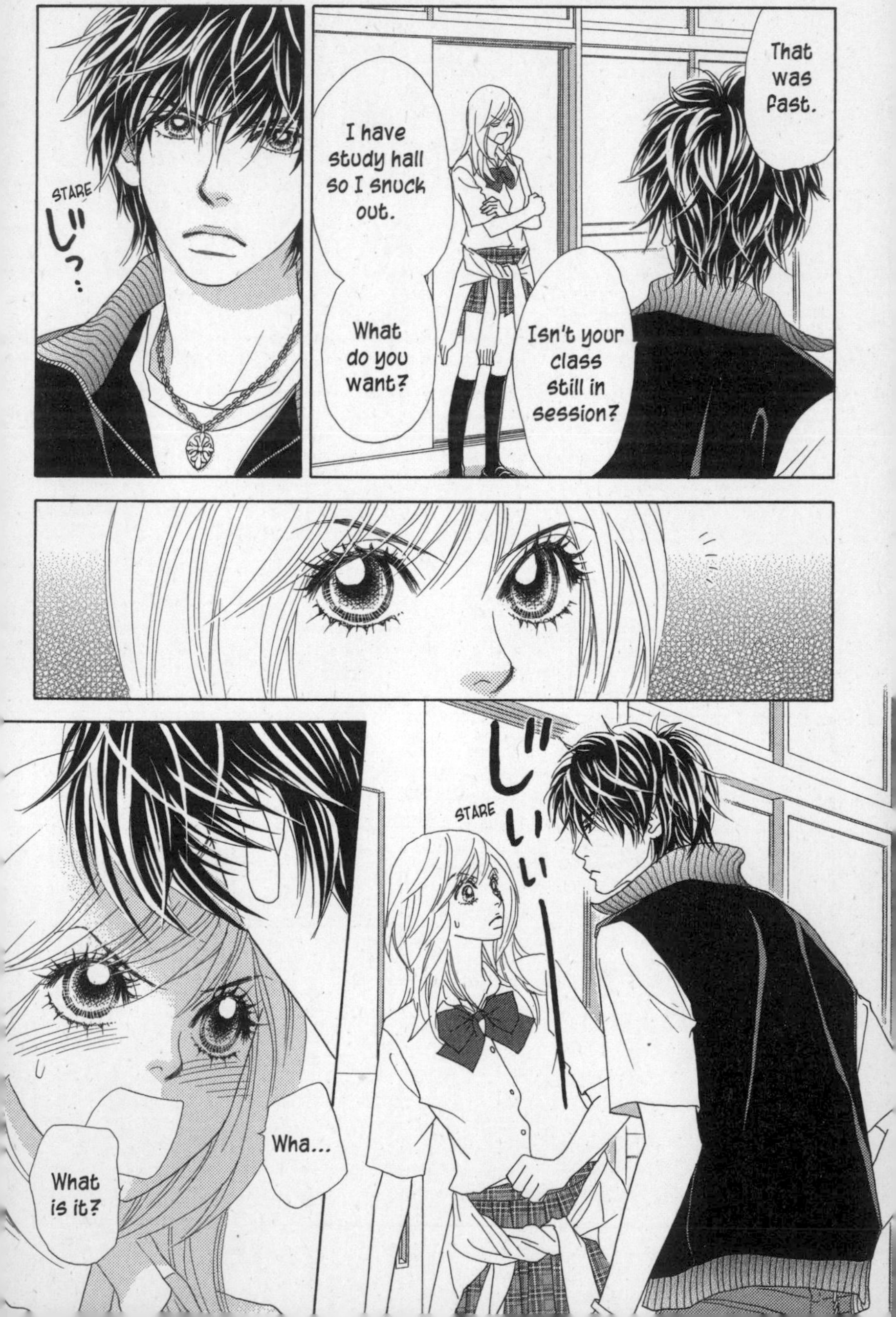
That was fast.
Isn't your class still in session?
I have study hall so I snuck out.
What do you want?
STARE
STARE
Wha...
What is it?

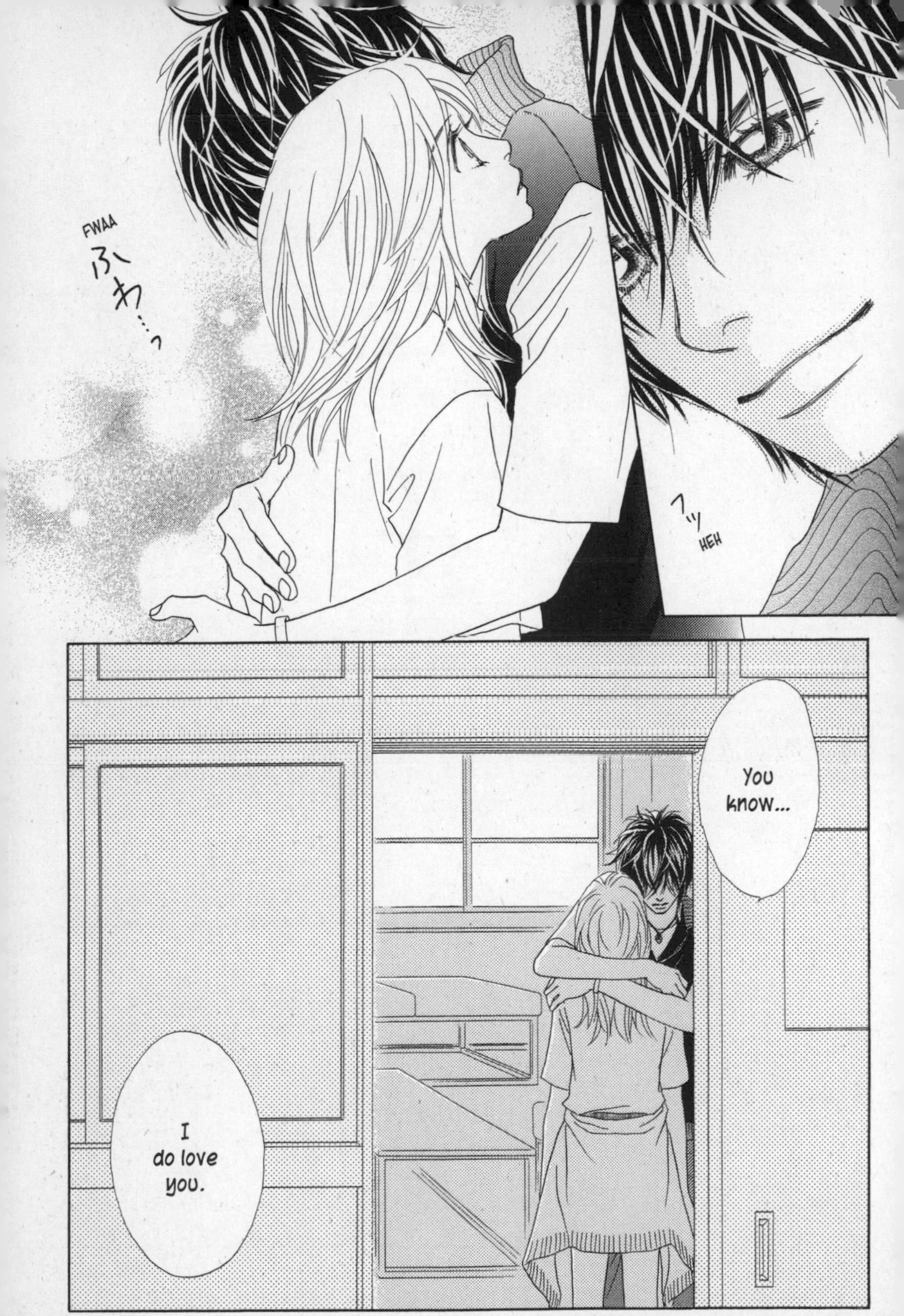
FWAA
ふわ…っ
フッ
HEH
You know...
I do love you.

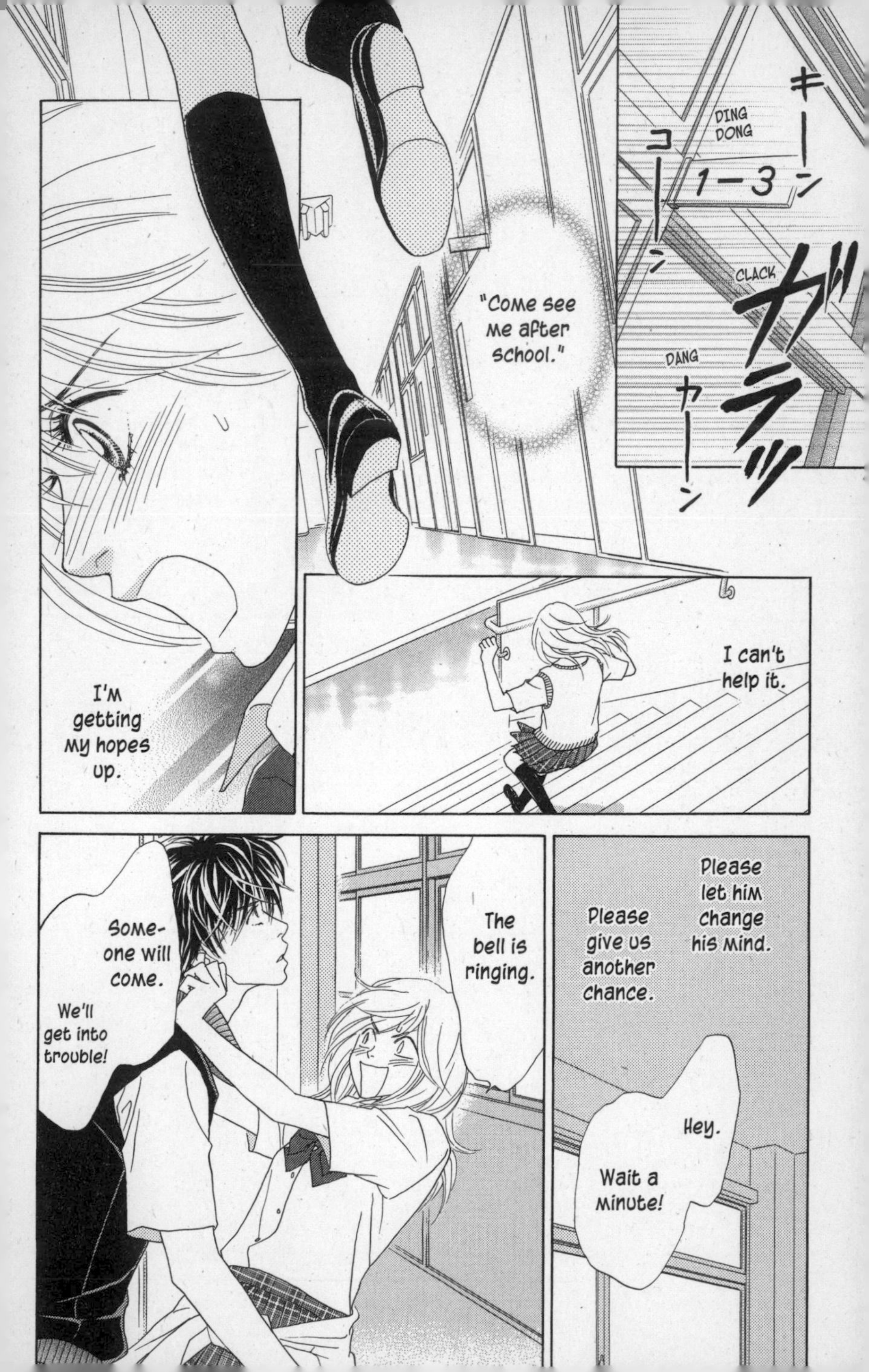
キーン
コーン
DING DONG
1-3
ガラッ
CLACK
ヤーン
DANG
"Come see me after school."
I can't help it.
I'm getting my hopes up.
Please let him change his mind.
Please give us another chance.
Hey.
Wait a minute!
The bell is ringing.
Some-one will come.
We'll get into trouble!

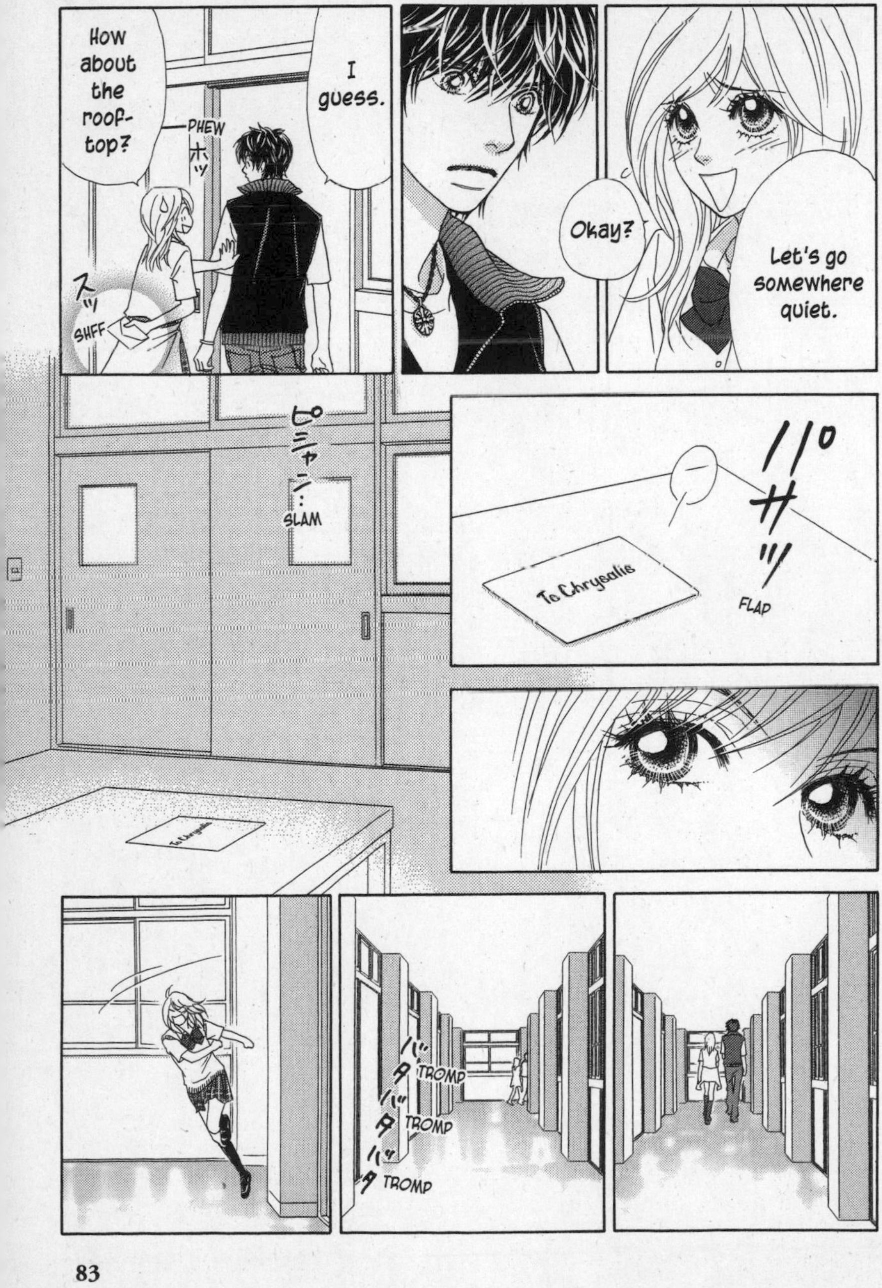
Let's go somewhere quiet.
Okay?
How about the roof-top?
I guess.
ホッ
PHEW
スッ
SHFF
パサッ
FLAP
To Chrysalis
ピシャン…
SLAM
To Chrysalis
バタ
TROMP
バタ
TROMP
バタ
TROMP

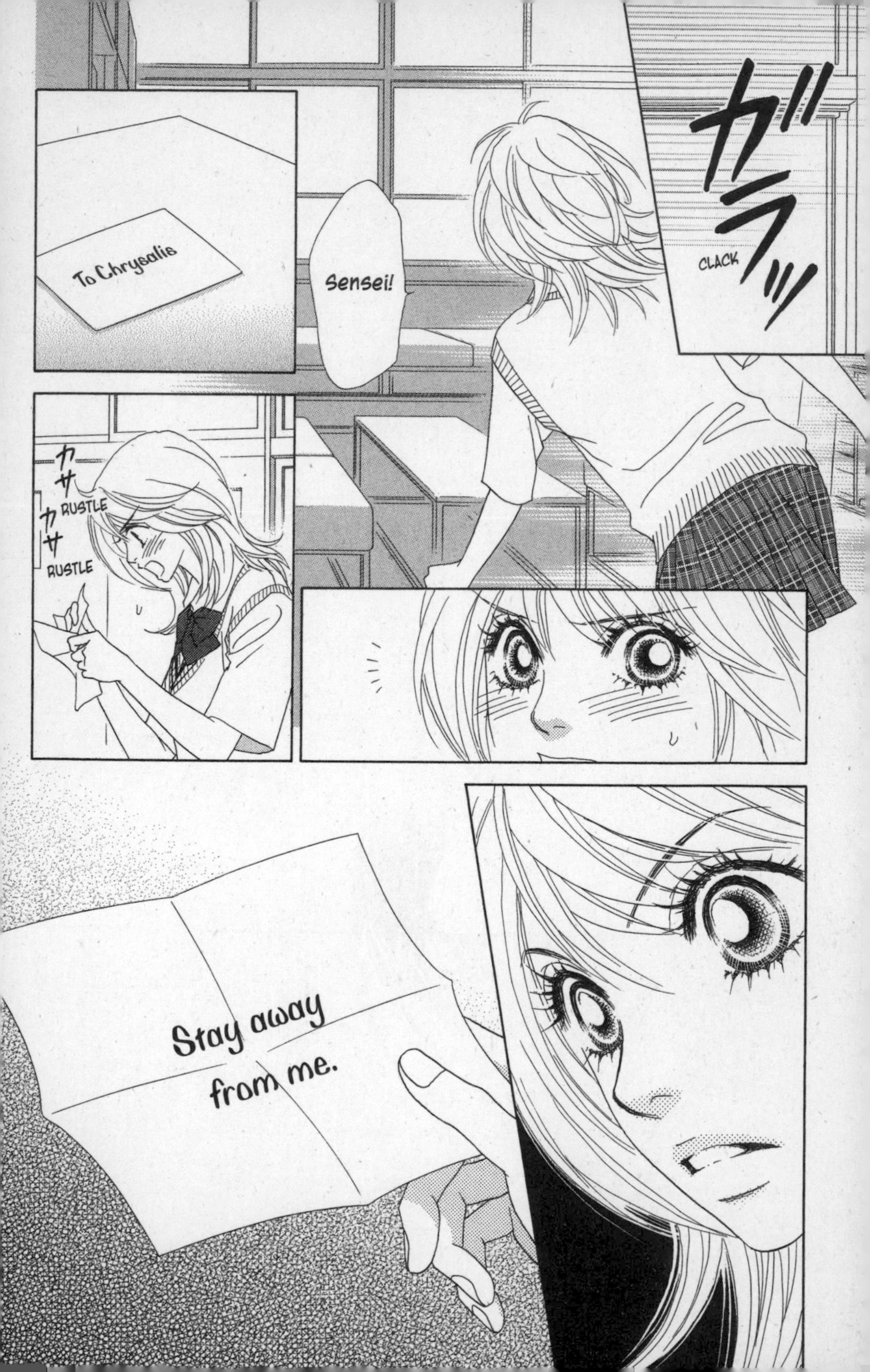
ガラッ
CLACK
Sensei!
To Chrysalis
カサ
RUSTLE
カサ
RUSTLE
Stay away from me.

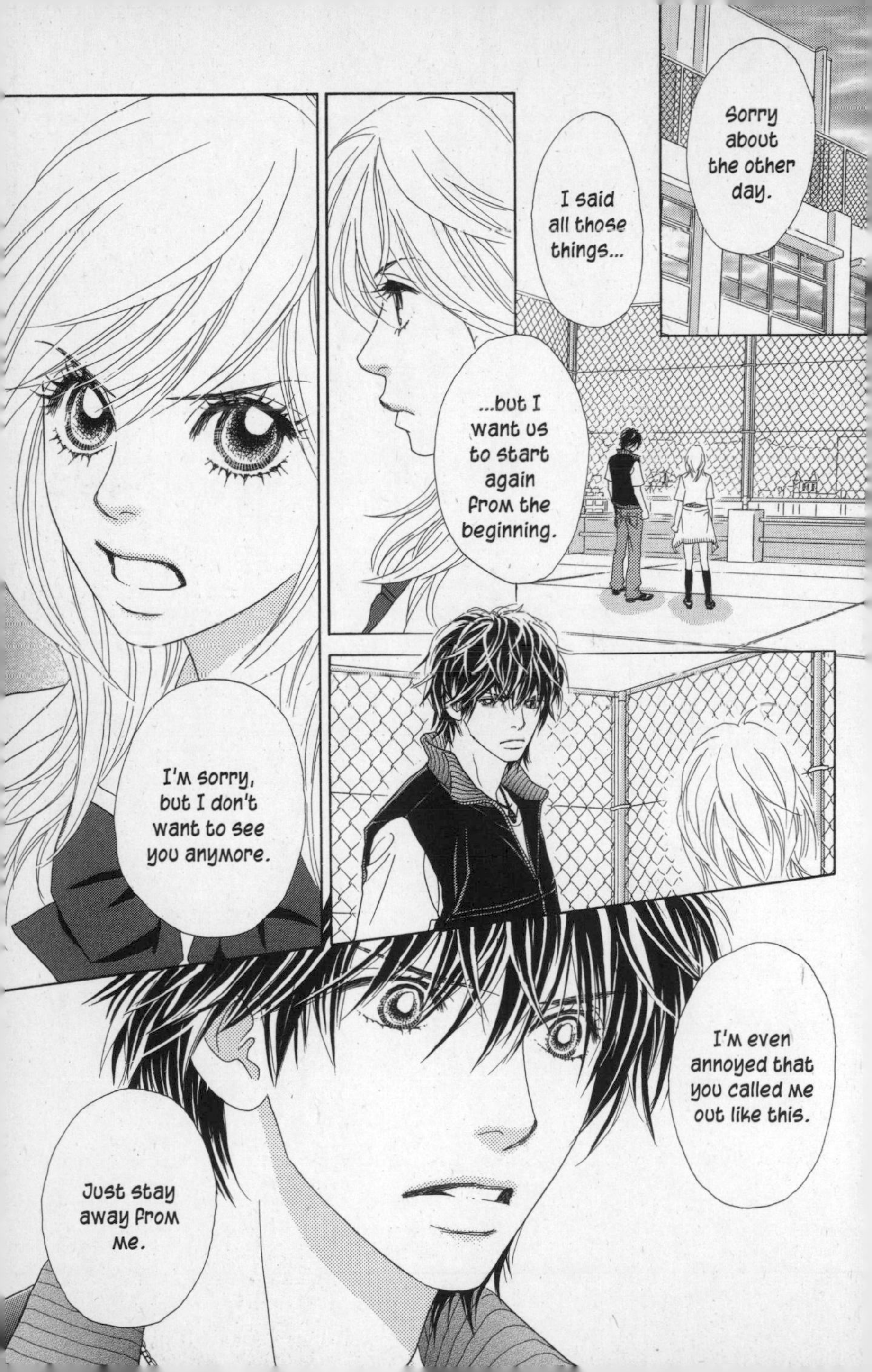
Sorry about the other day.
I said all those things...
...but I want us to start again from the beginning.
I'm sorry, but I don't want to see you anymore.
I'm even annoyed that you called me out like this.
Just stay away from me.

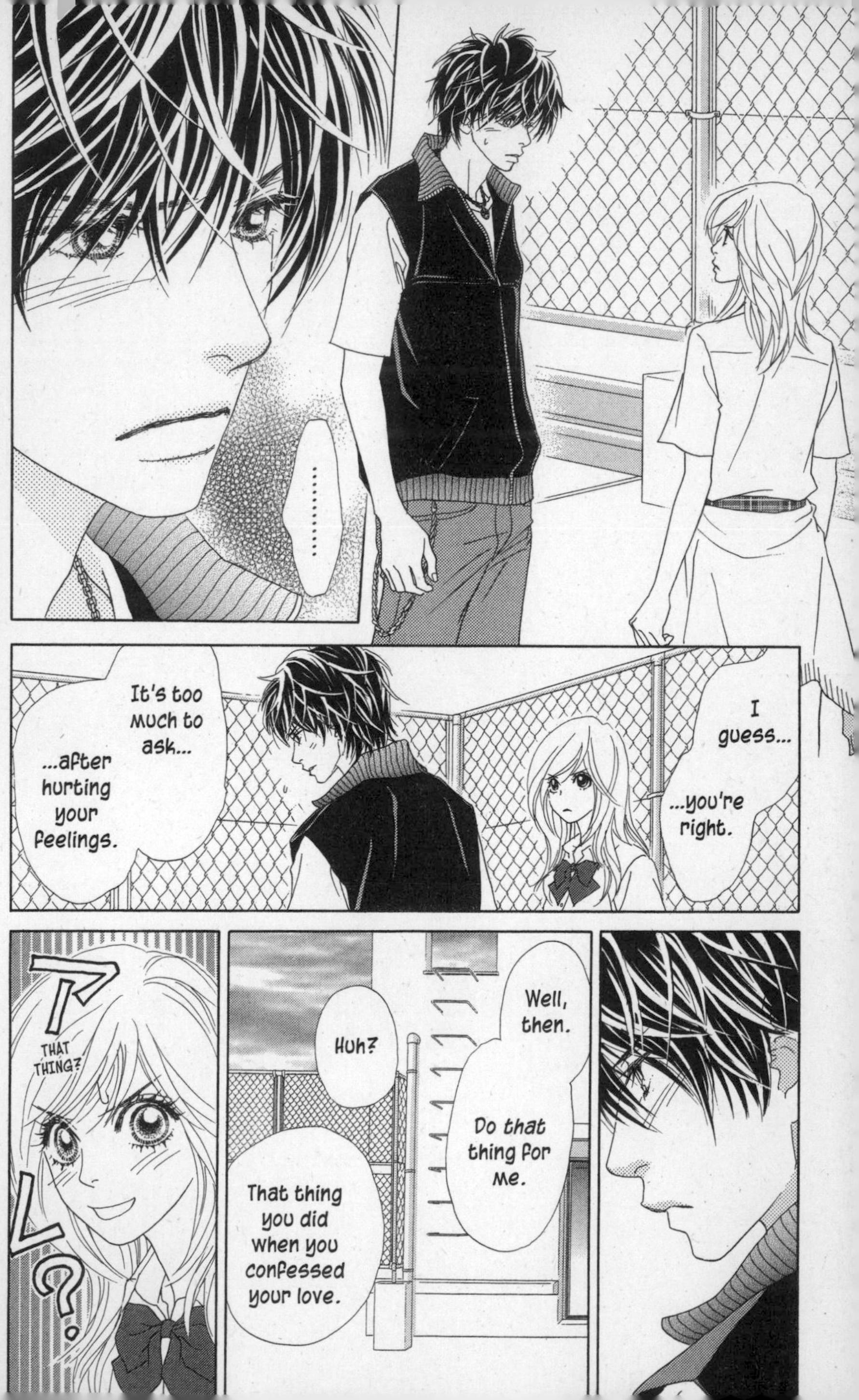
......
I guess...
...you're right.
It's too much to ask...
...after hurting your feelings.
Well, then.
Do that thing for me.
Huh?
That thing you did when you confessed your love.
アレ?
THAT THING?

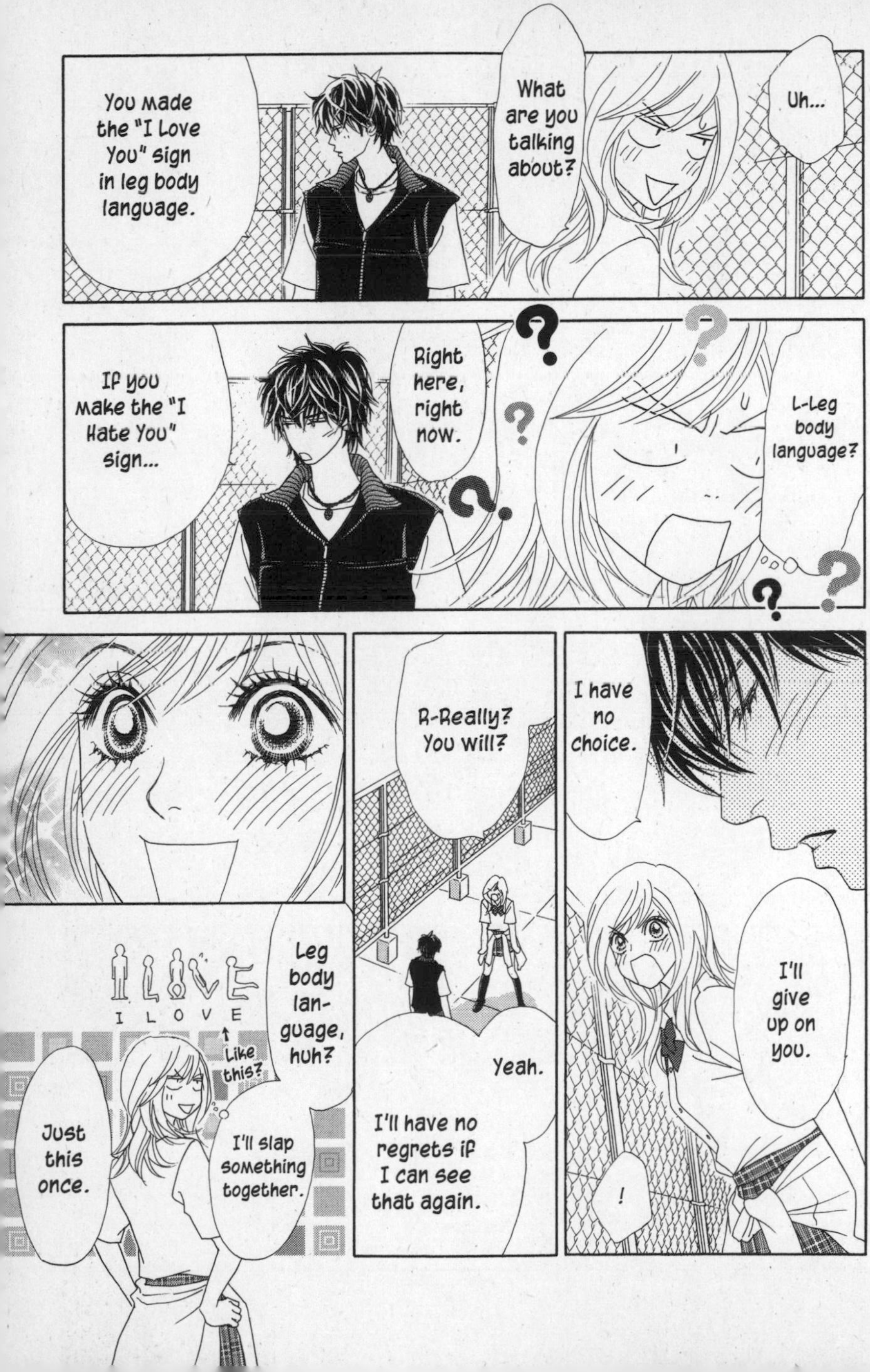
Uh...
What are you talking about?
You made the "I Love You" sign in leg body language.
L-Leg body language?
Right here, right now.
If you make the "I Hate You" sign...
I have no choice.
I'll give up on you.
!
R-Really? You will?
Yeah.
I'll have no regrets if I can see that again.
Leg body lan-guage, huh?
I L O V E
Like this?
I'll slap something together.
Just this once.

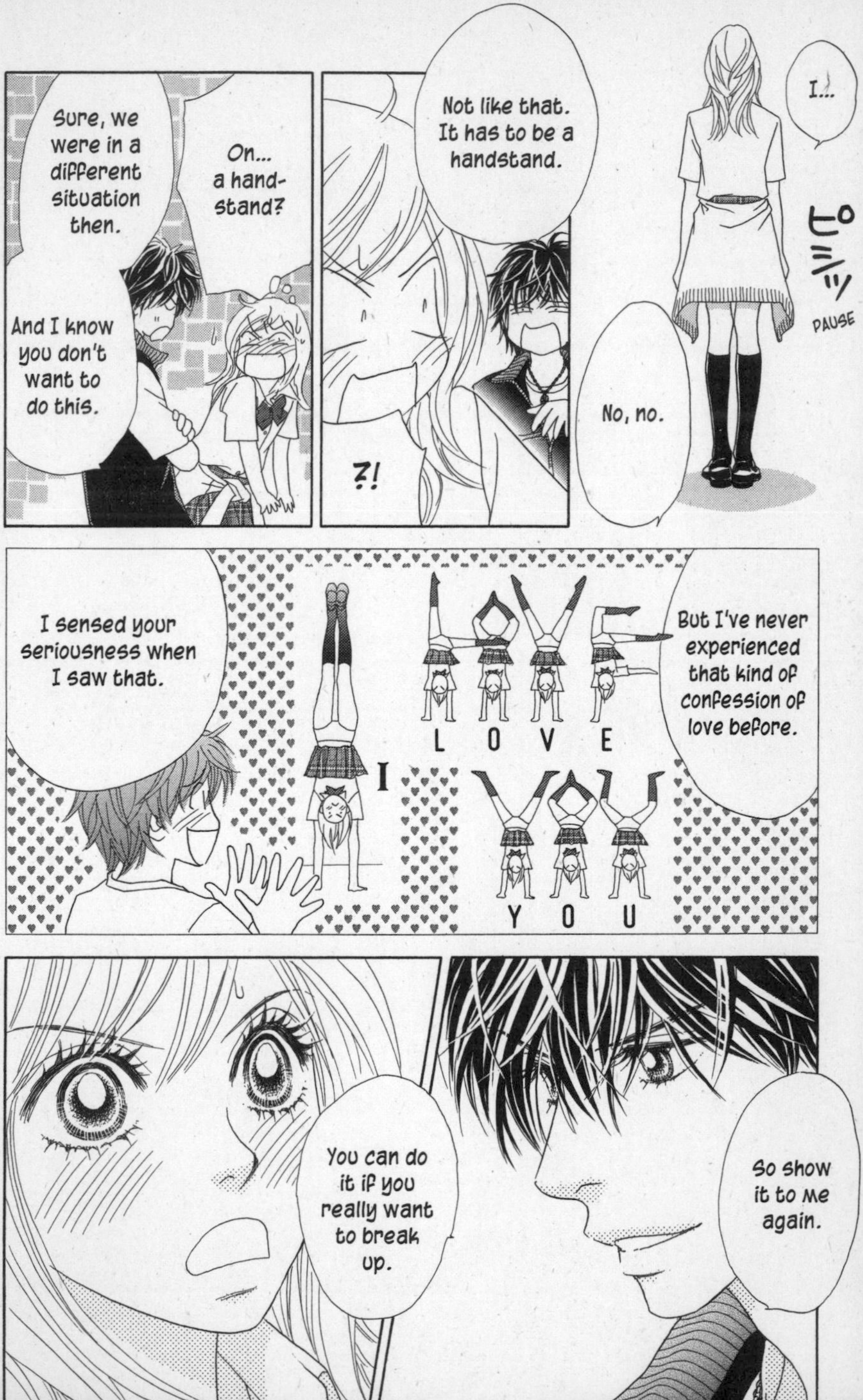
I...
ピシッ
PAUSE
No, no.
Not like that. It has to be a handstand.
?!
On... a hand-stand?
Sure, we were in a different situation then.
And I know you don't want to do this.
But I've never experienced that kind of confession of love before.
L O V E
Y O U
I
I sensed your seriousness when I saw that.
So show it to me again.
You can do it if you really want to break up.

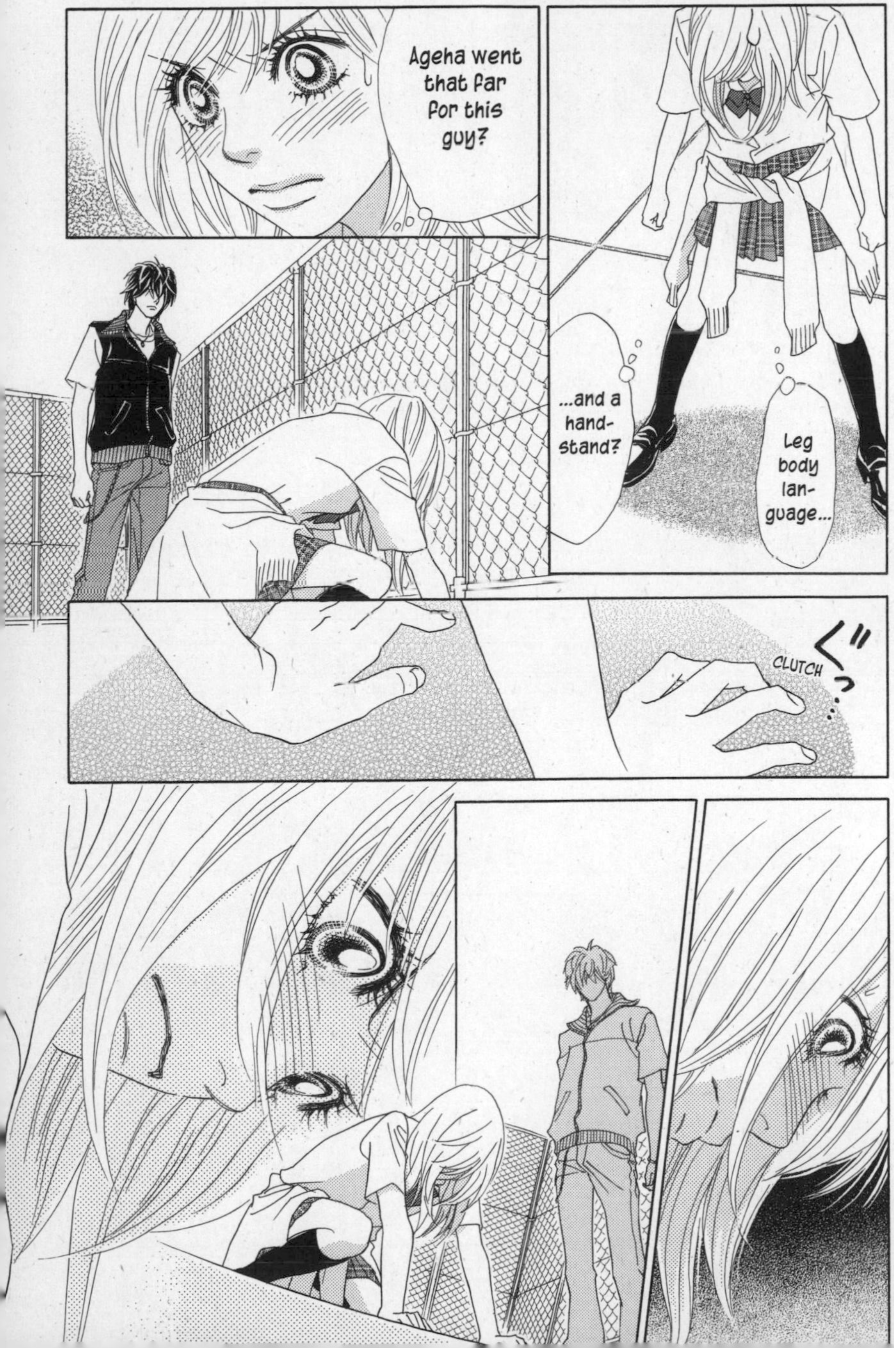
Leg body language...
...and a hand-stand?
Ageha went that far for this guy?
ぐっ
CLUTCH

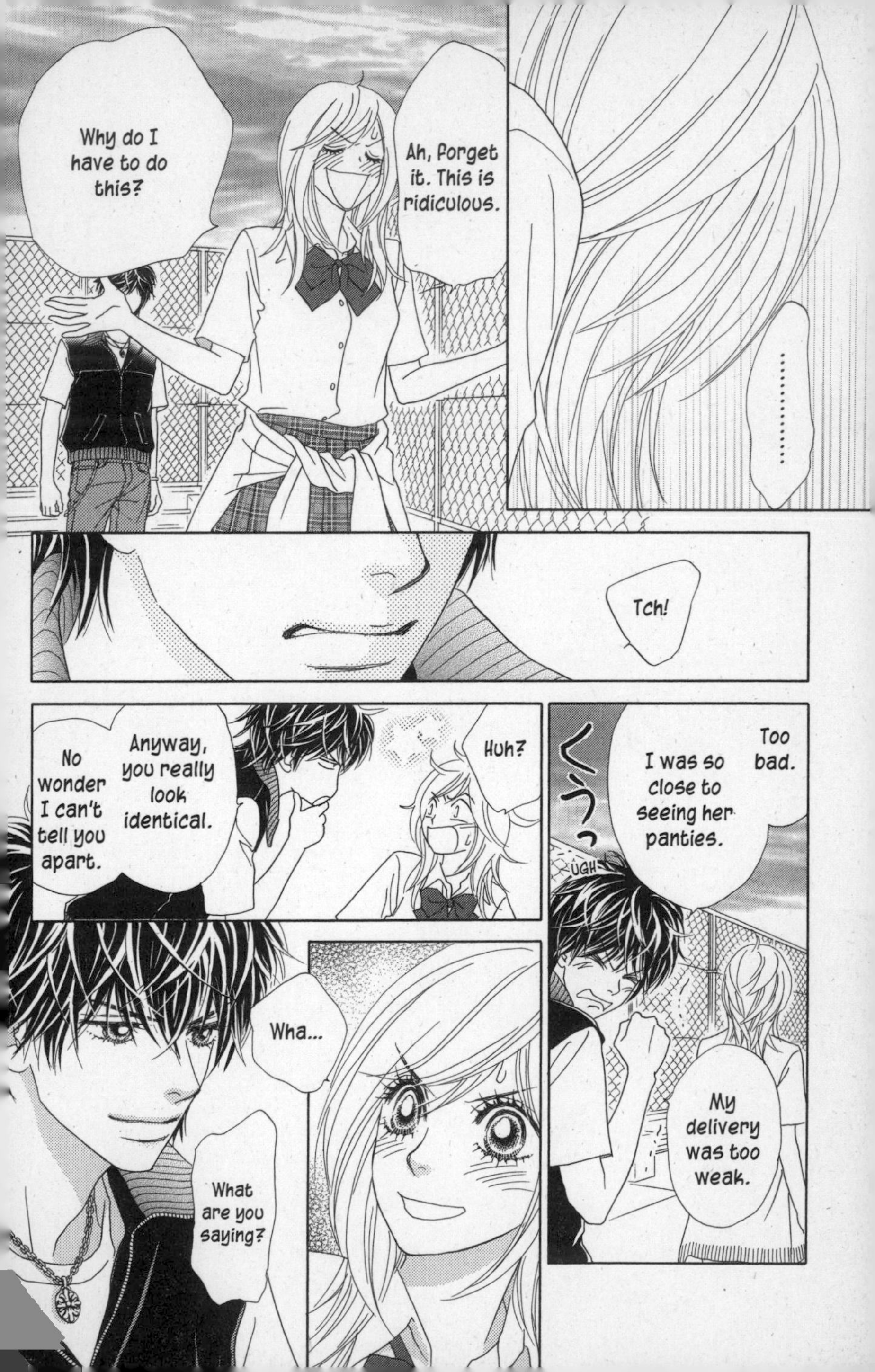
......
Ah, forget it. This is ridiculous.
Why do I have to do this?
Tch!
Too bad.
I was so close to seeing her panties.
くうっ
UGH
My delivery was too weak.
Huh?
Anyway, you really look identical.
No wonder I can't tell you apart.
Wha...
What are you saying?

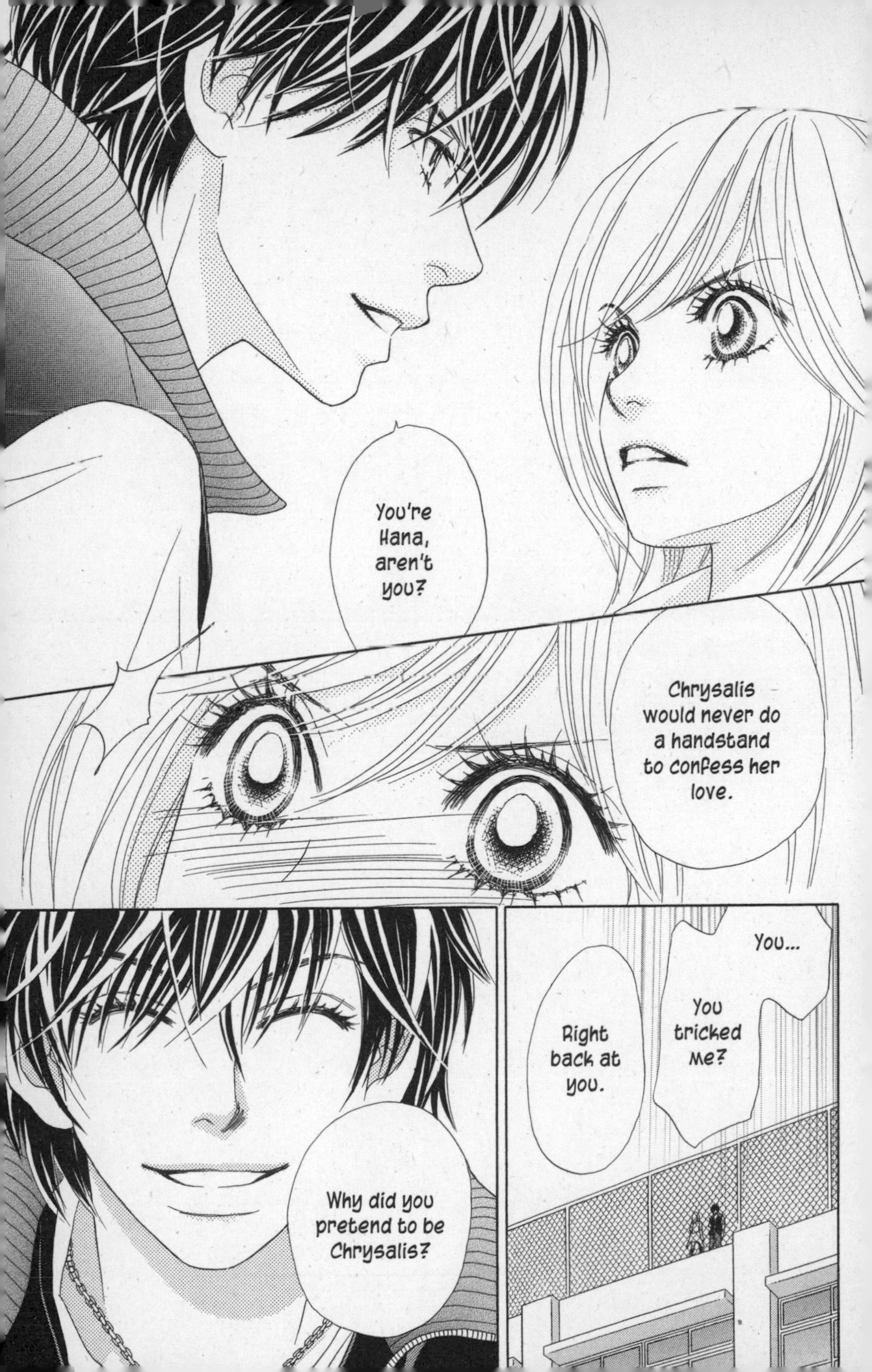
You're Hana, aren't you?
Chrysalis would never do a handstand to confess her love.
You...
You tricked me?
Right back at you.
Why did you pretend to be Chrysalis?

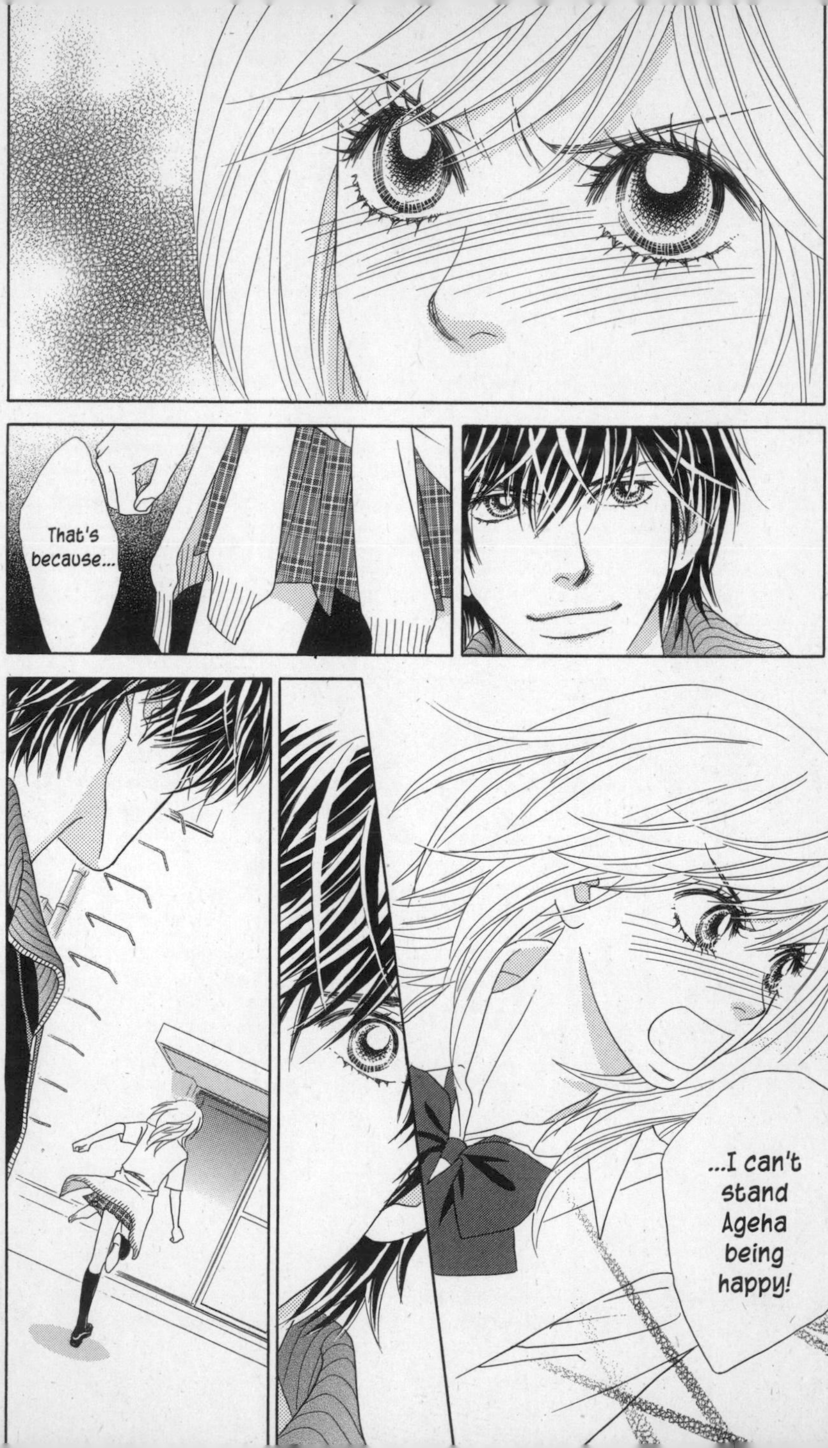
That's because...
...I can't stand Ageha being happy!

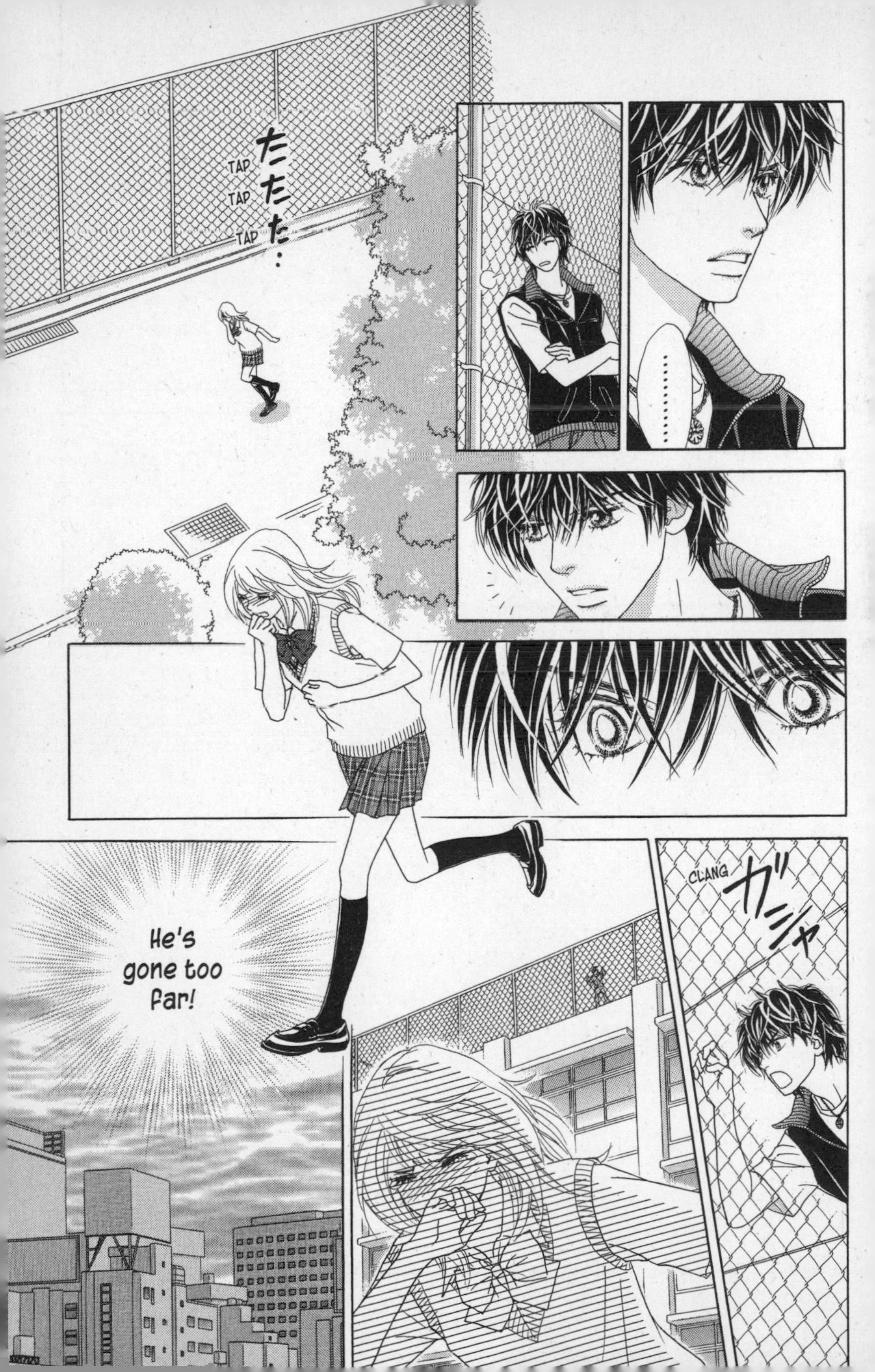

......
たたた…
TAP TAP TAP
ガシャ
CLANG
He's gone too far!

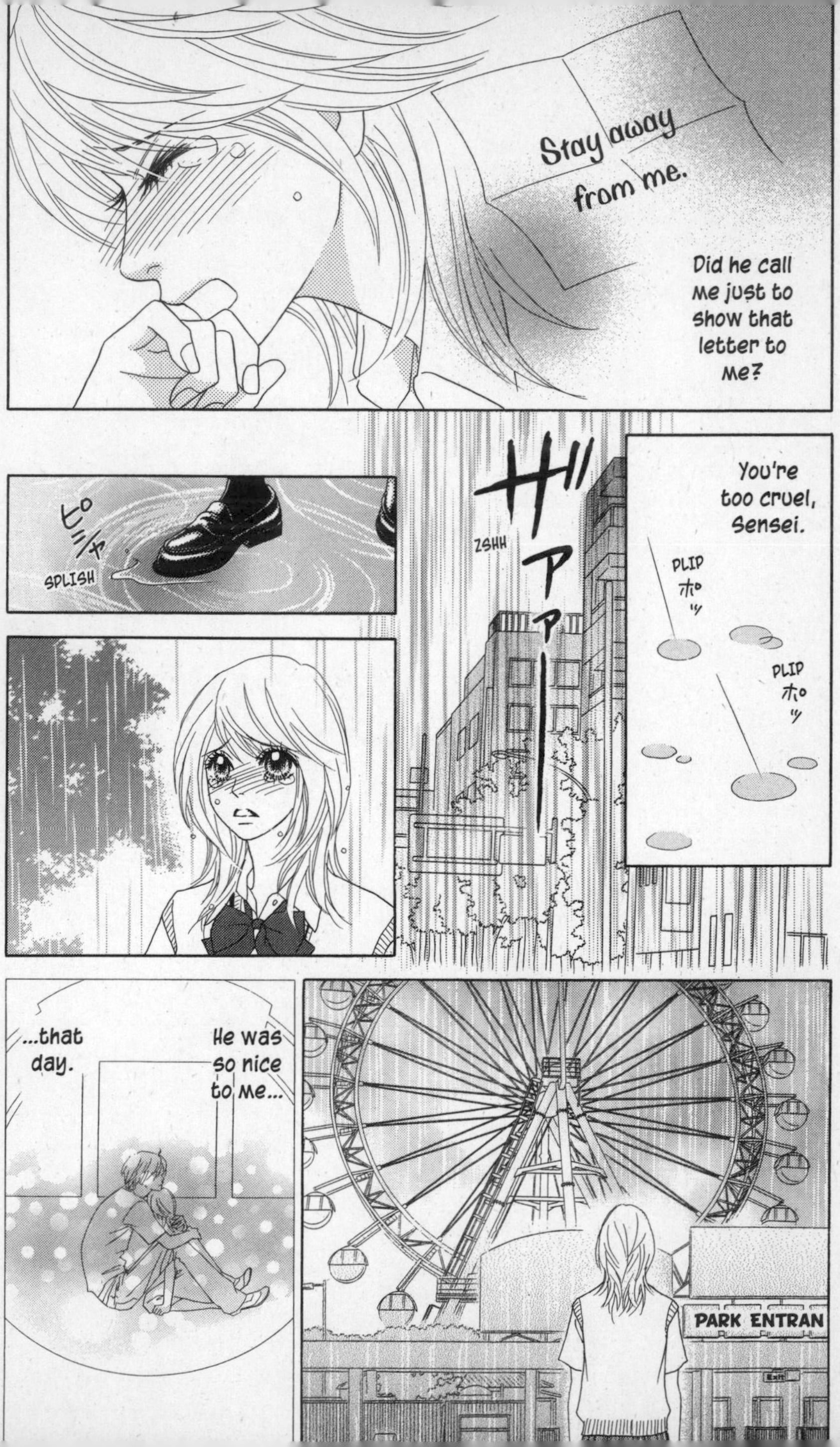
Stay away from me.
Did he call me just to show that letter to me?
You're too cruel, Sensei.
PLIP
ポッ
PLIP
ポッ
ザァー
ZSHH
ピシャ
SPLISH
PARK ENTRAN
He was so nice to me...
...that day.

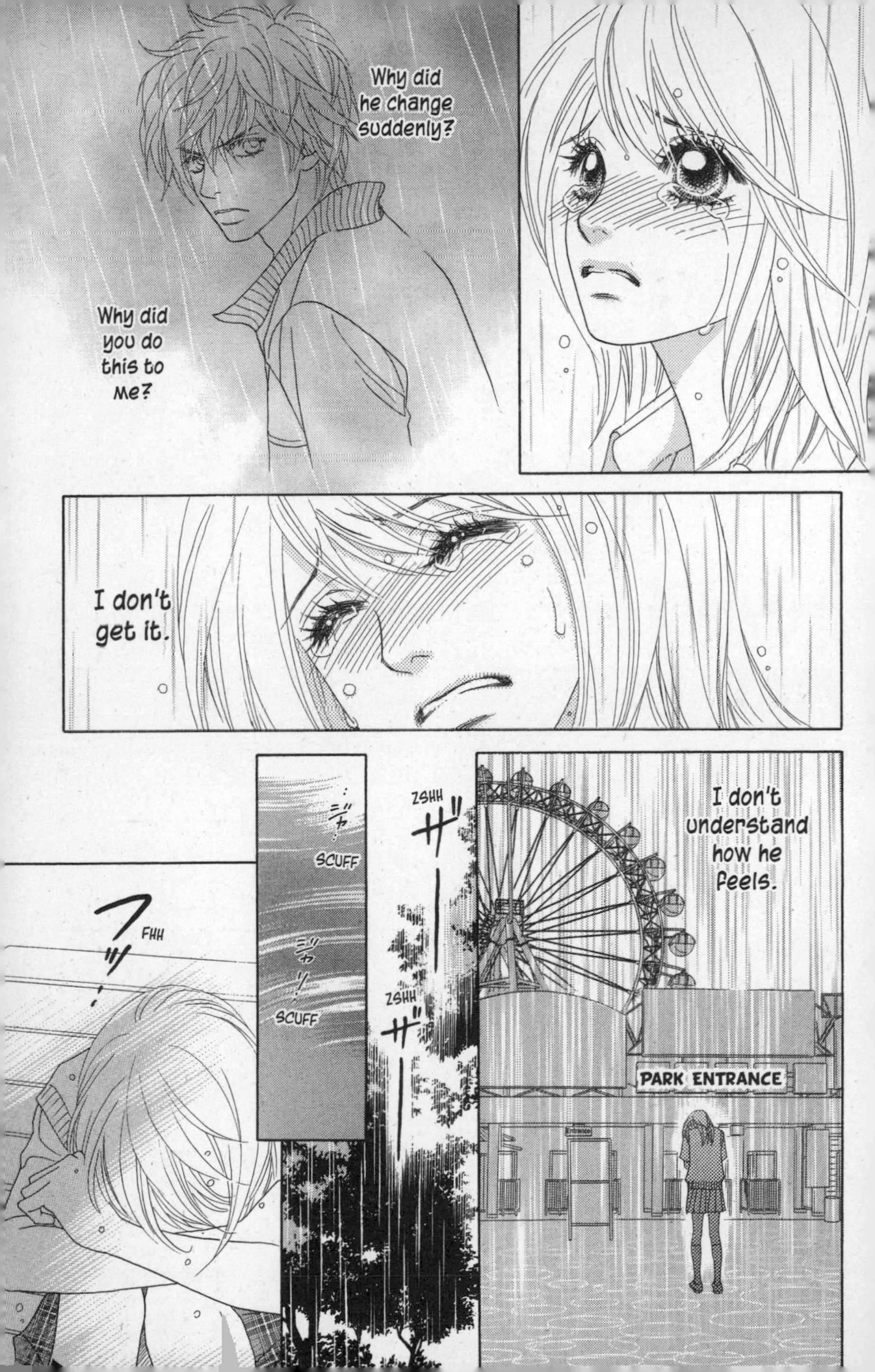
Why did he change suddenly?
Why did you do this to me?
I don't get it.
I don't understand how he feels.
ZSHH
ザー
ZSHH
ザー
PARK ENTRANCE
SCUFF
SCUFF
FHH

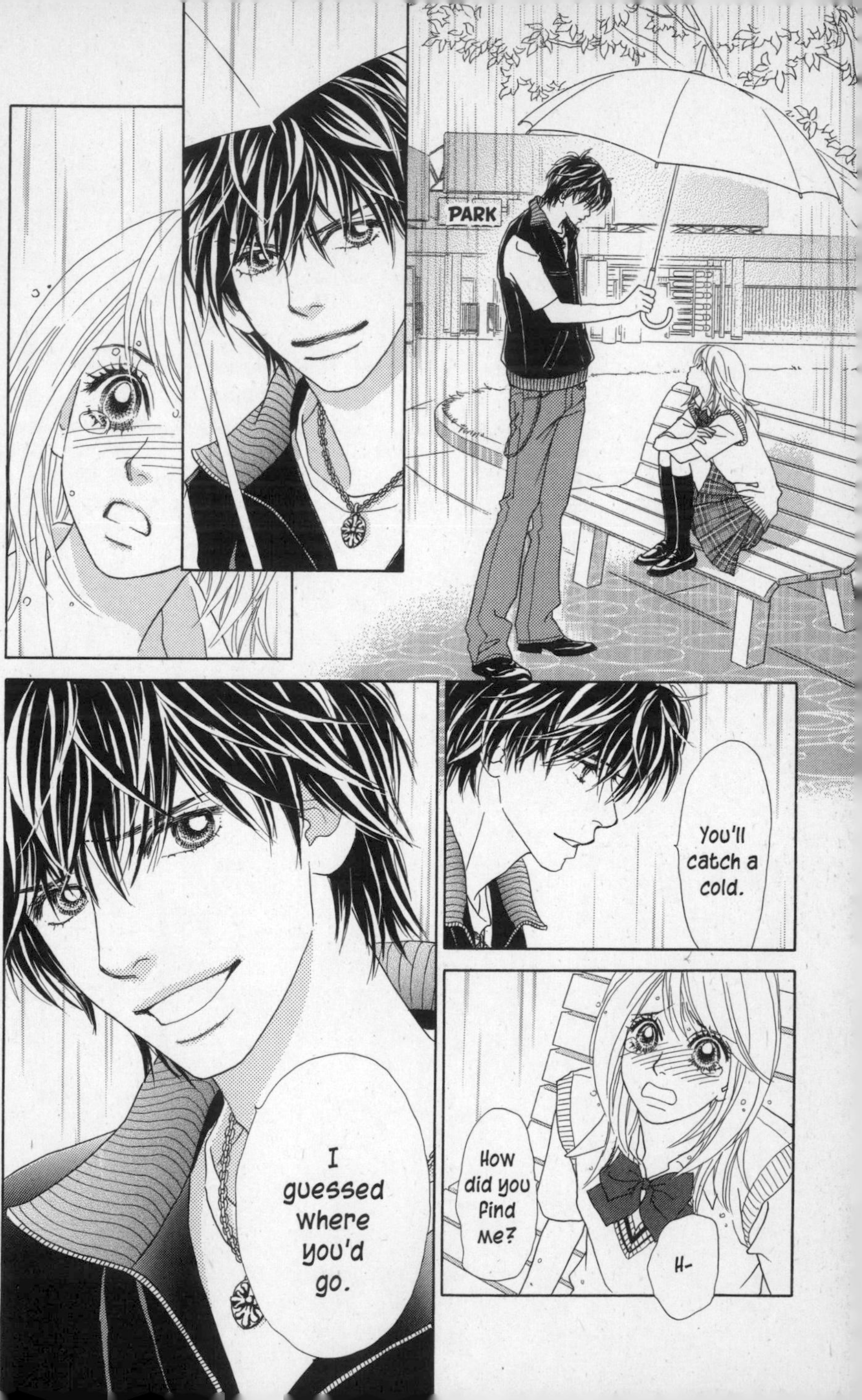
PARK
You'll catch a cold.
H-
How did you find me?
I guessed where you'd go.

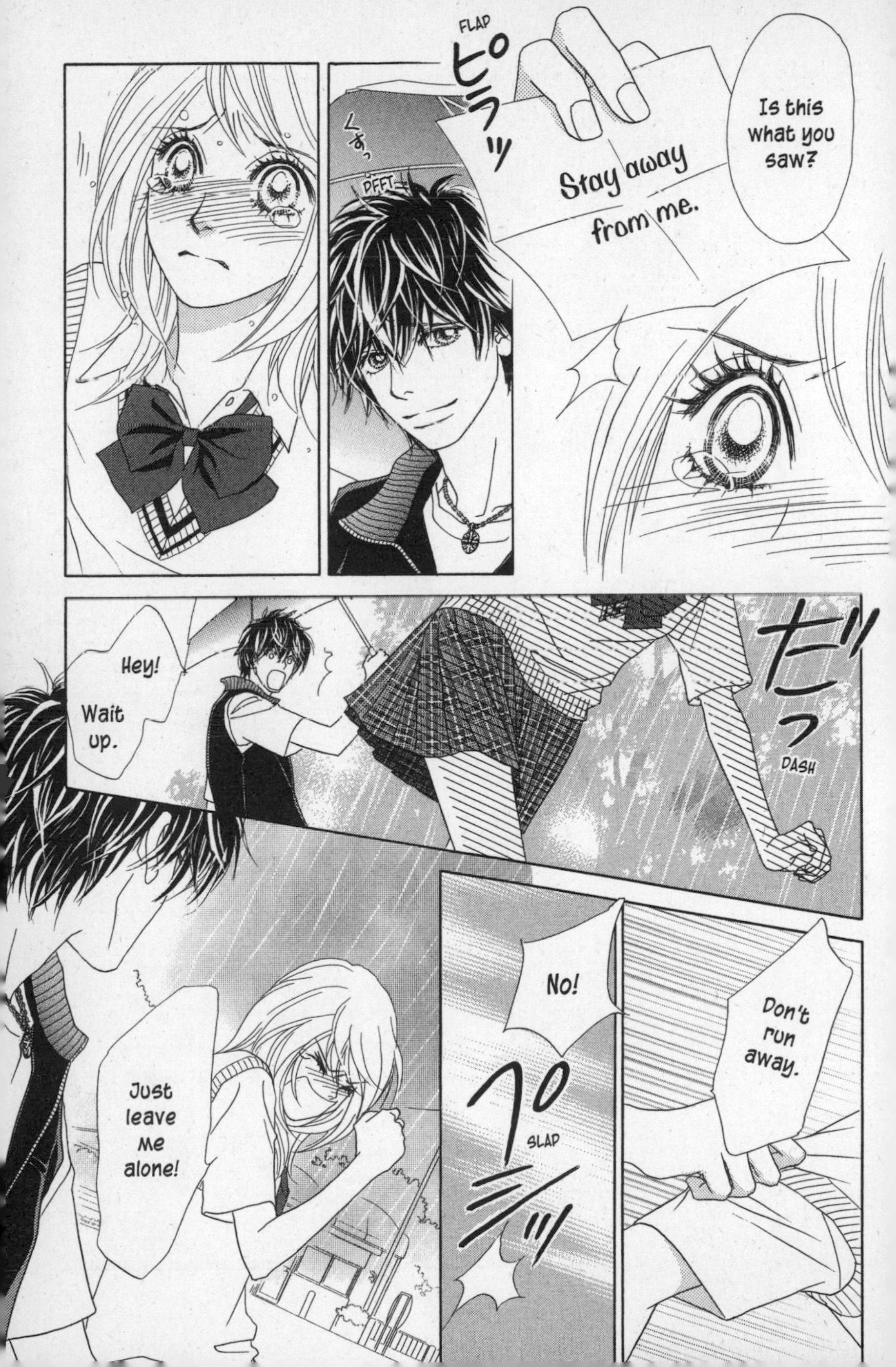
Is this what you saw?
Stay away from me.
FLAP
ピラッ
くすっ
DFFT
だっ
DASH
Hey!
Wait up.
Don't run away.
No!
パシッ
SLAP
Just leave me alone!

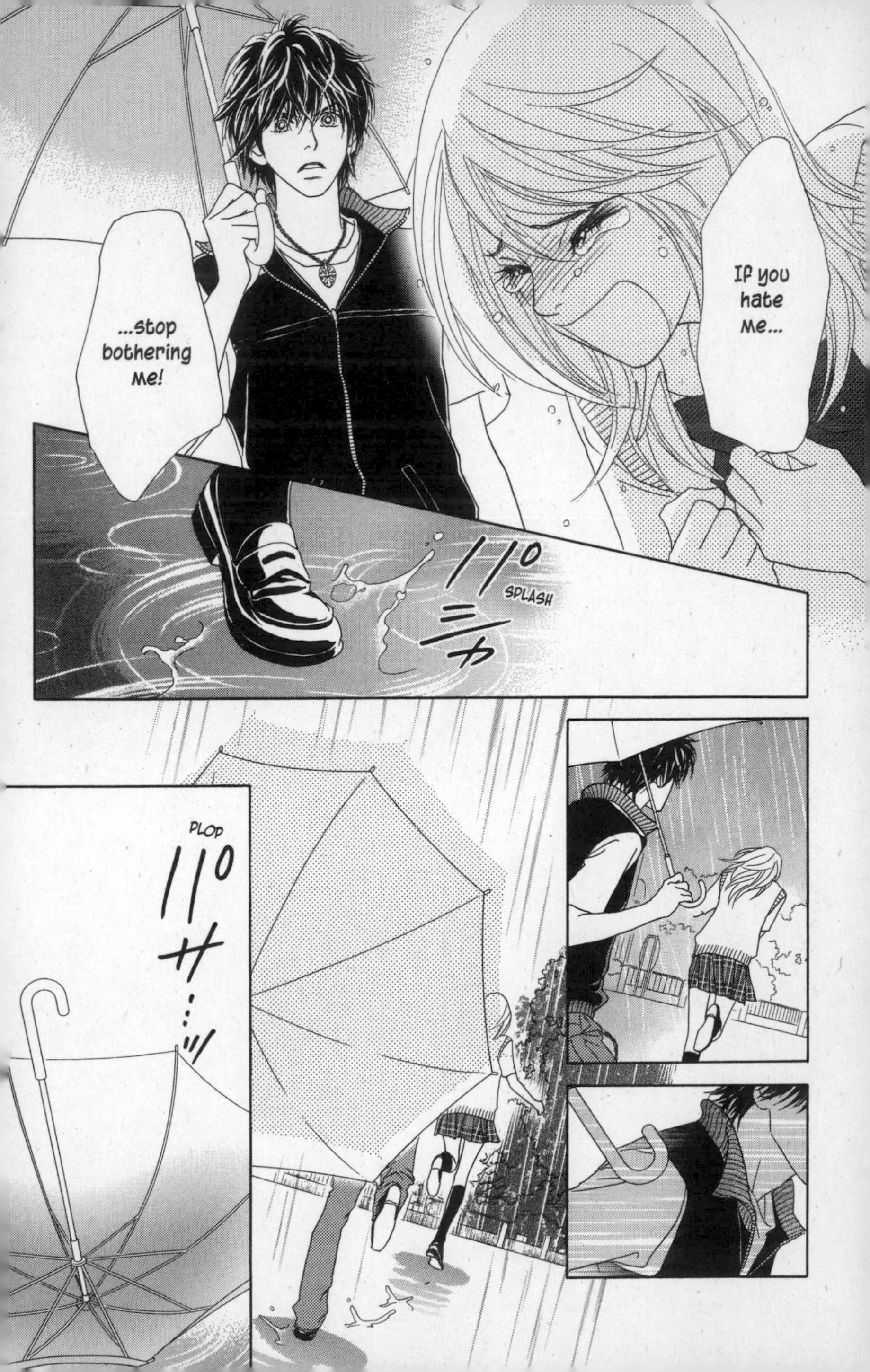
If you hate me...
...stop bothering me!
パシャ
SPLASH
PLOP
パサ…ッ

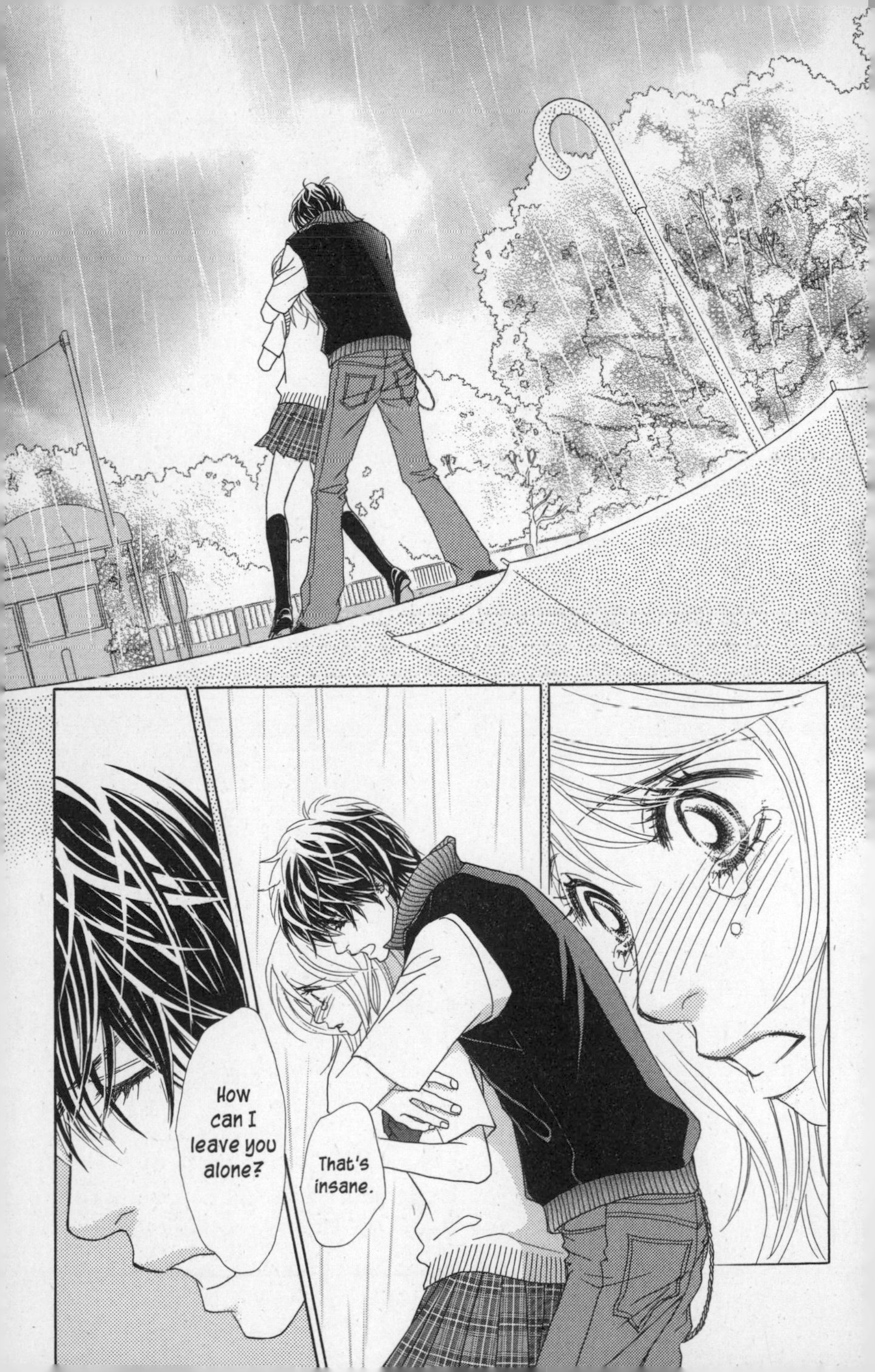
That's insane.
How can I leave you alone?

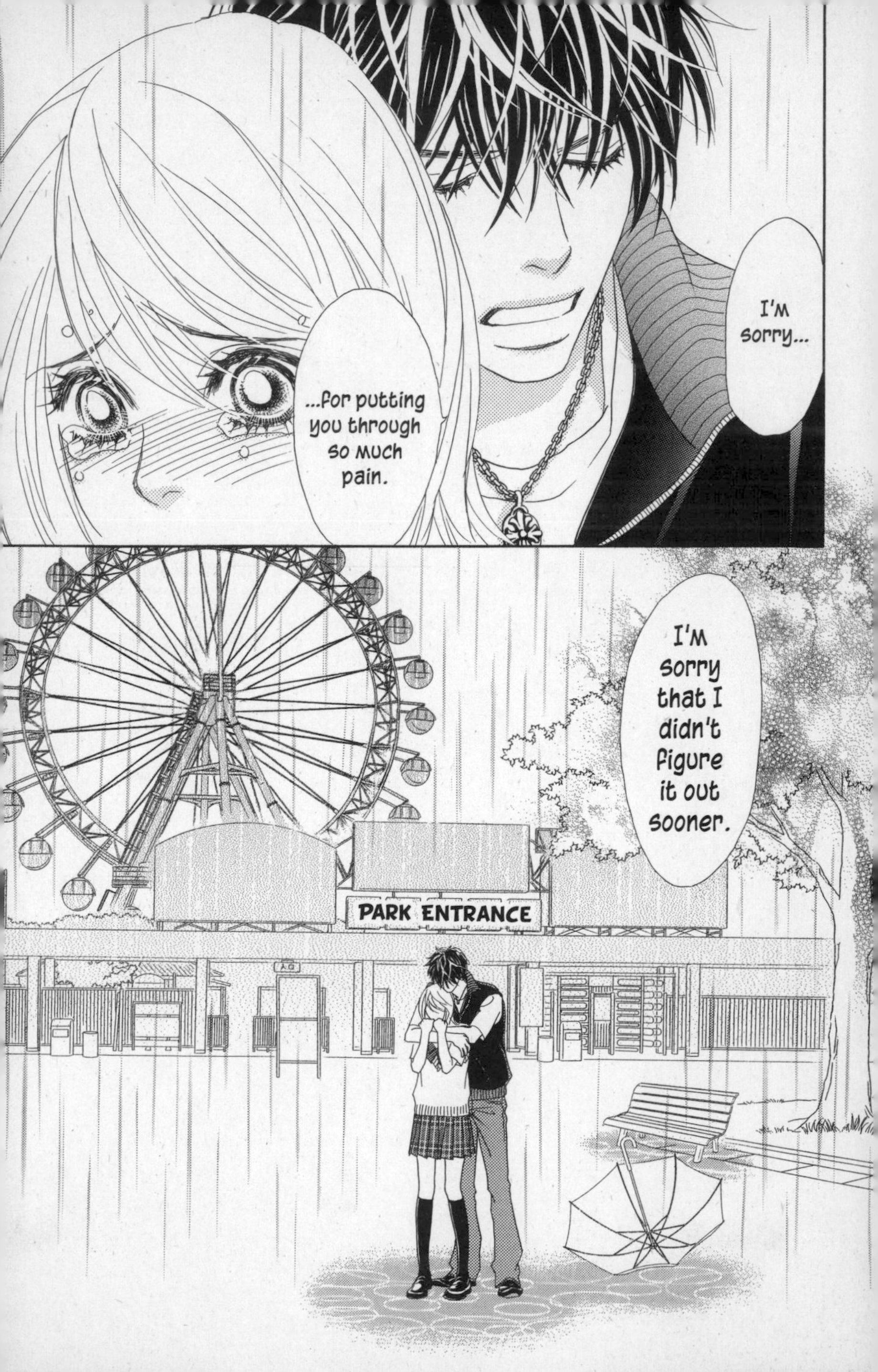
I'M sorry...
...for putting you through so much pain.
I'M sorry that I didn't figure it out sooner.
PARK ENTRANCE

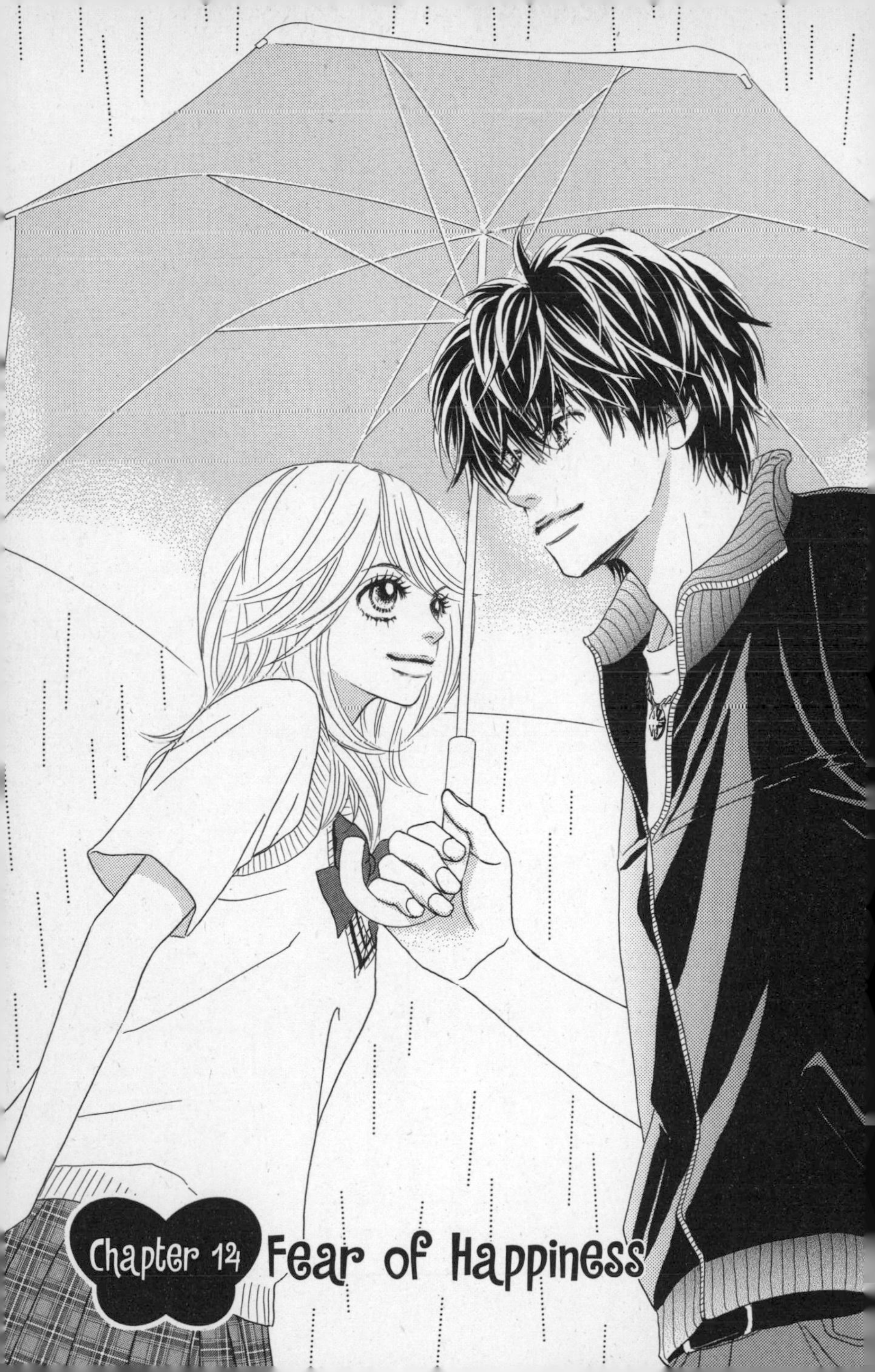
Chapter 14
Fear of Happiness

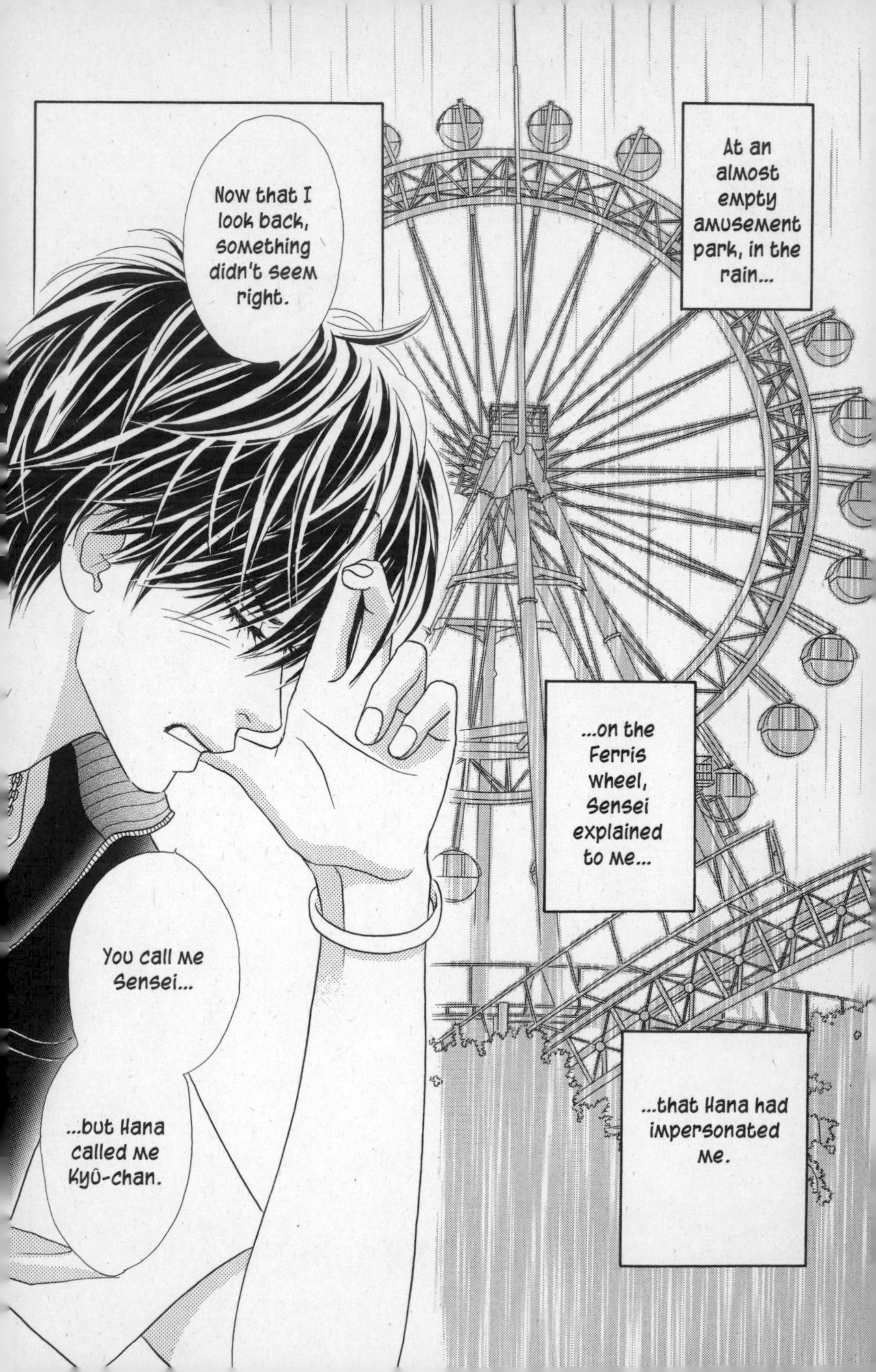
At an almost empty amusement park, in the rain...
...on the Ferris wheel, Sensei explained to me...
...that Hana had impersonated me.
Now that I look back, something didn't seem right.
You call me Sensei...
...but Hana called me Kyû-chan.

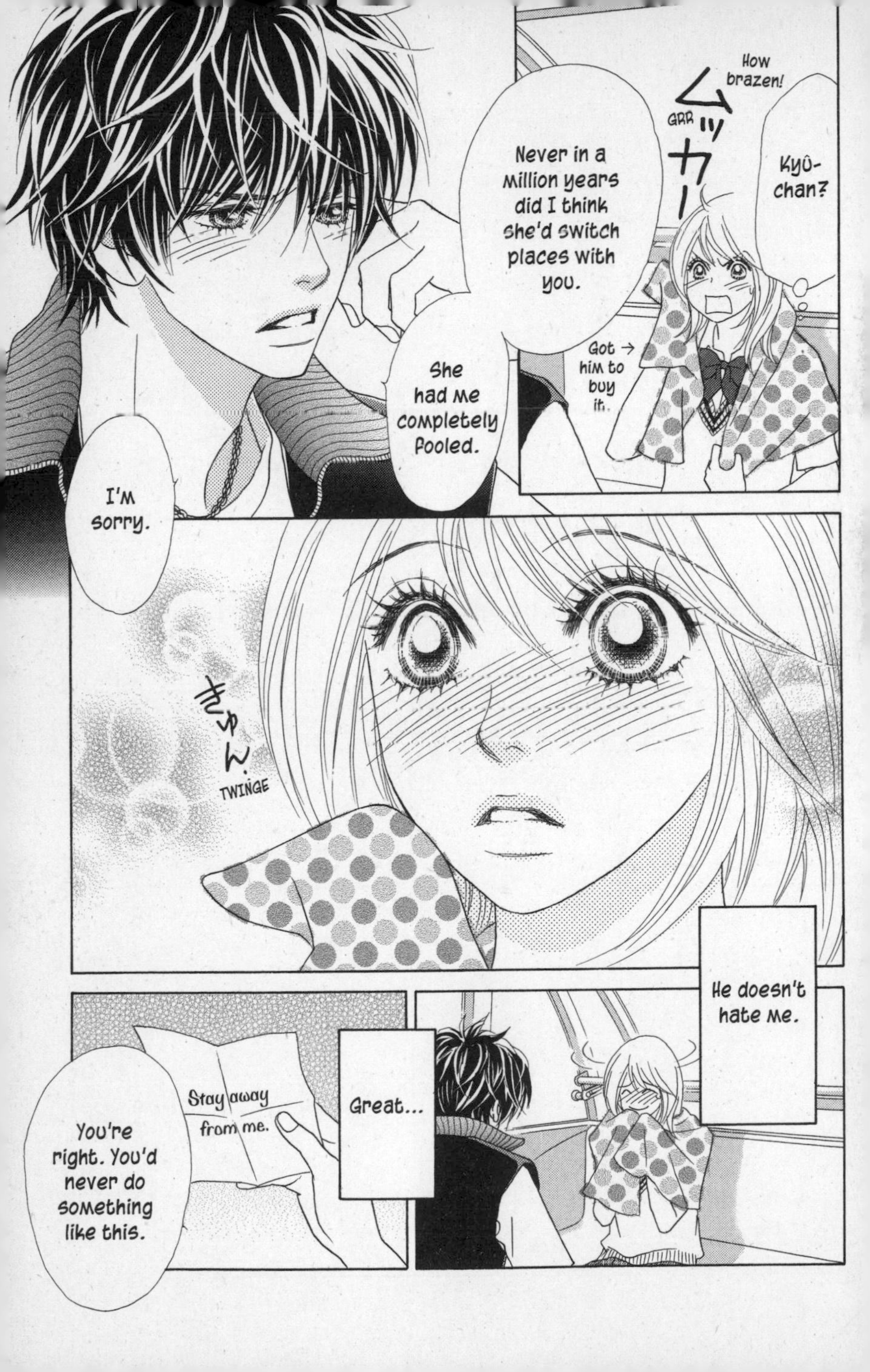
Kyû-chan?
How brazen!
ムッカー
GRR
Got → him to buy it.
Never in a million years did I think she'd switch places with you.
She had me completely fooled.
I'm sorry.
きゅん.
TWINGE
He doesn't hate me.
Great...
Stay away from me.
You're right. You'd never do something like this.

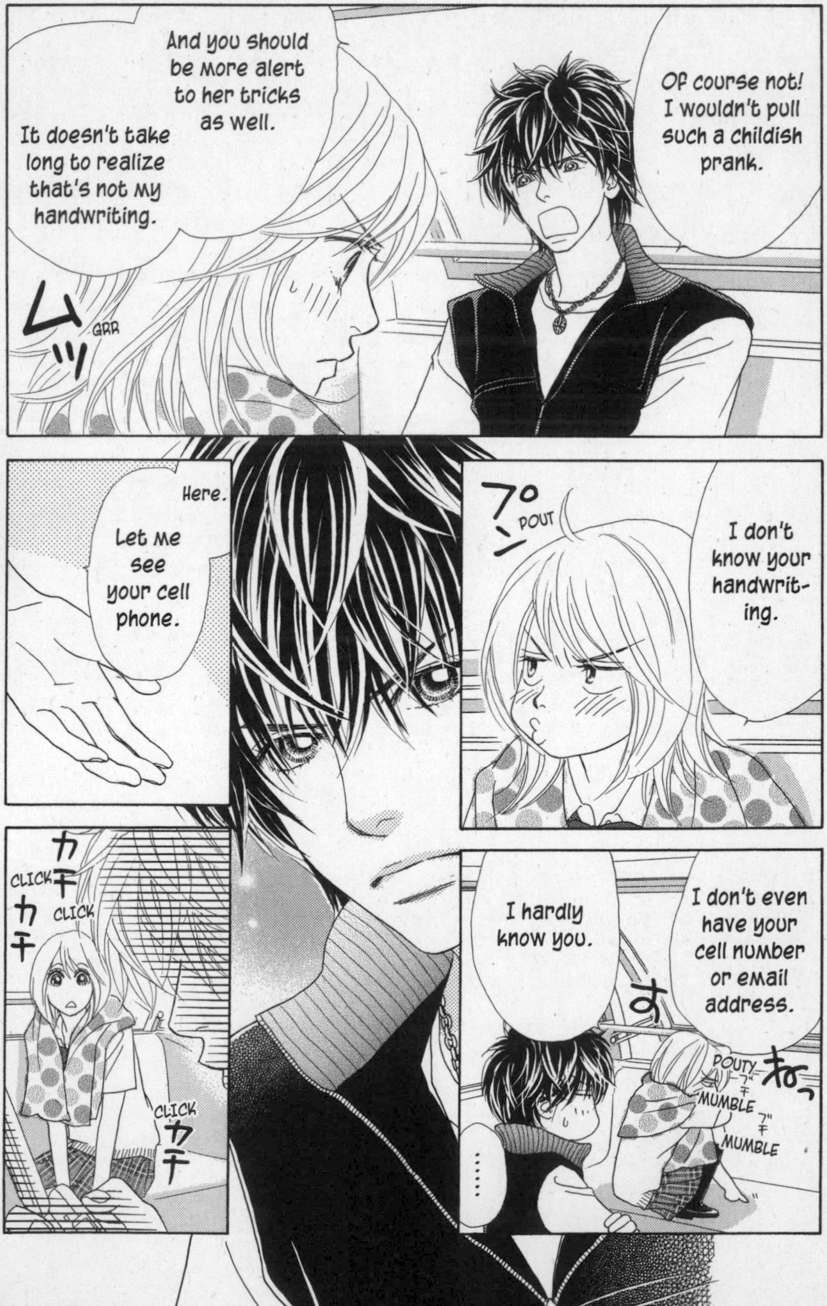
Of course not! I wouldn't pull such a childish prank.
And you should be more alert to her tricks as well.
It doesn't take long to realize that's not my handwriting.
ムッ GRR
プン POUT
I don't know your handwrit-ing.
I don't even have your cell number or email address.
ねっ
POUTY ブー MUMBLE
ブー MUMBLE
I hardly know you.
す
......
Here.
Let me see your cell phone.
カチ CLICK
カチ CLICK
カチ CLICK

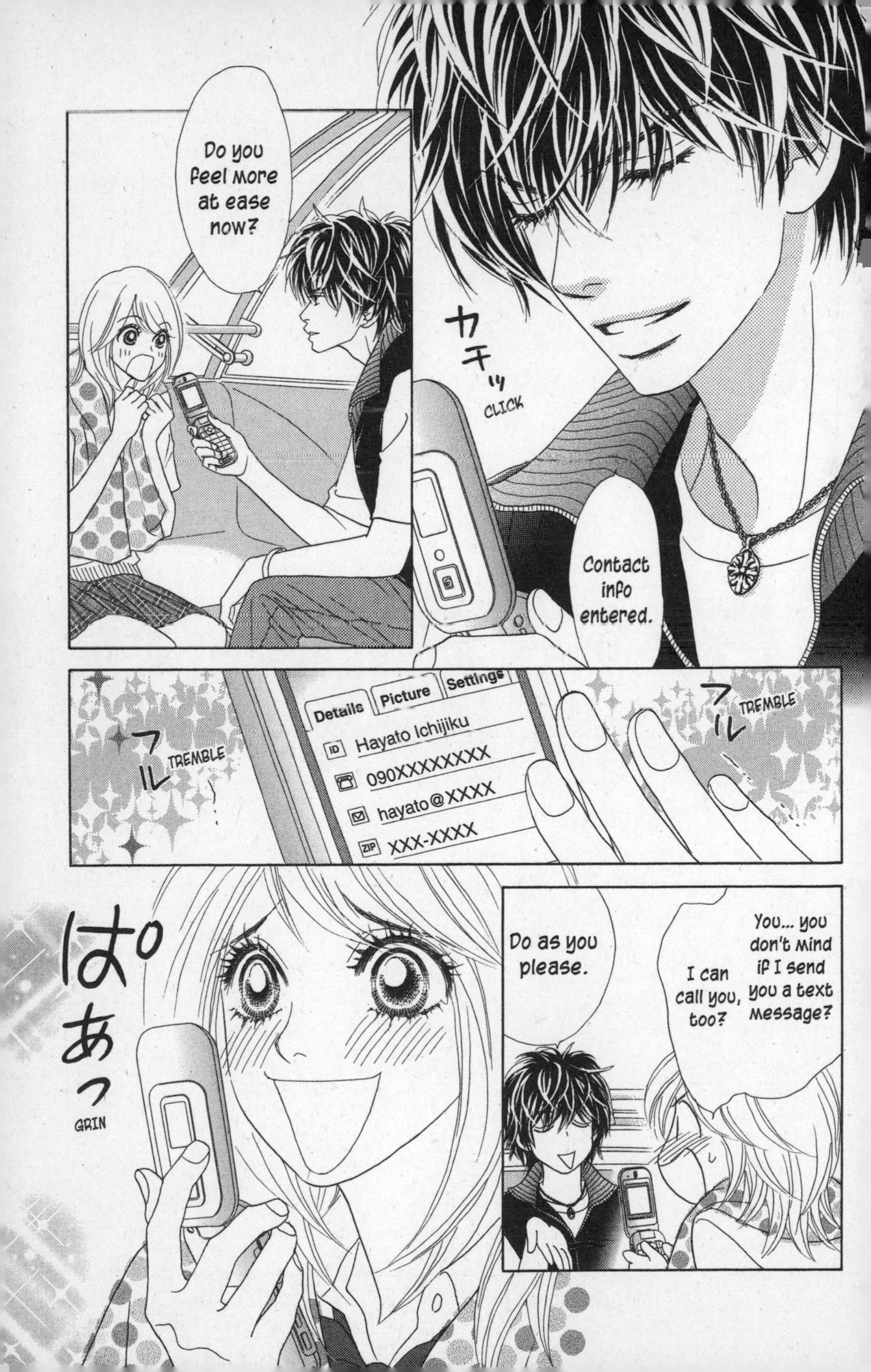
カチッ
CLICK
Contact info entered.
Do you feel more at ease now?
フル
TREMBLE
Settings
Picture
Details
Hayato Ichijiku
090XXXXXXXX
hayato@XXXX
XXX-XXXX
フル
TREMBLE
You... you don't mind if I send you a text message?
I can call you, too?
Do as you please.
ぱあっ
GRIN

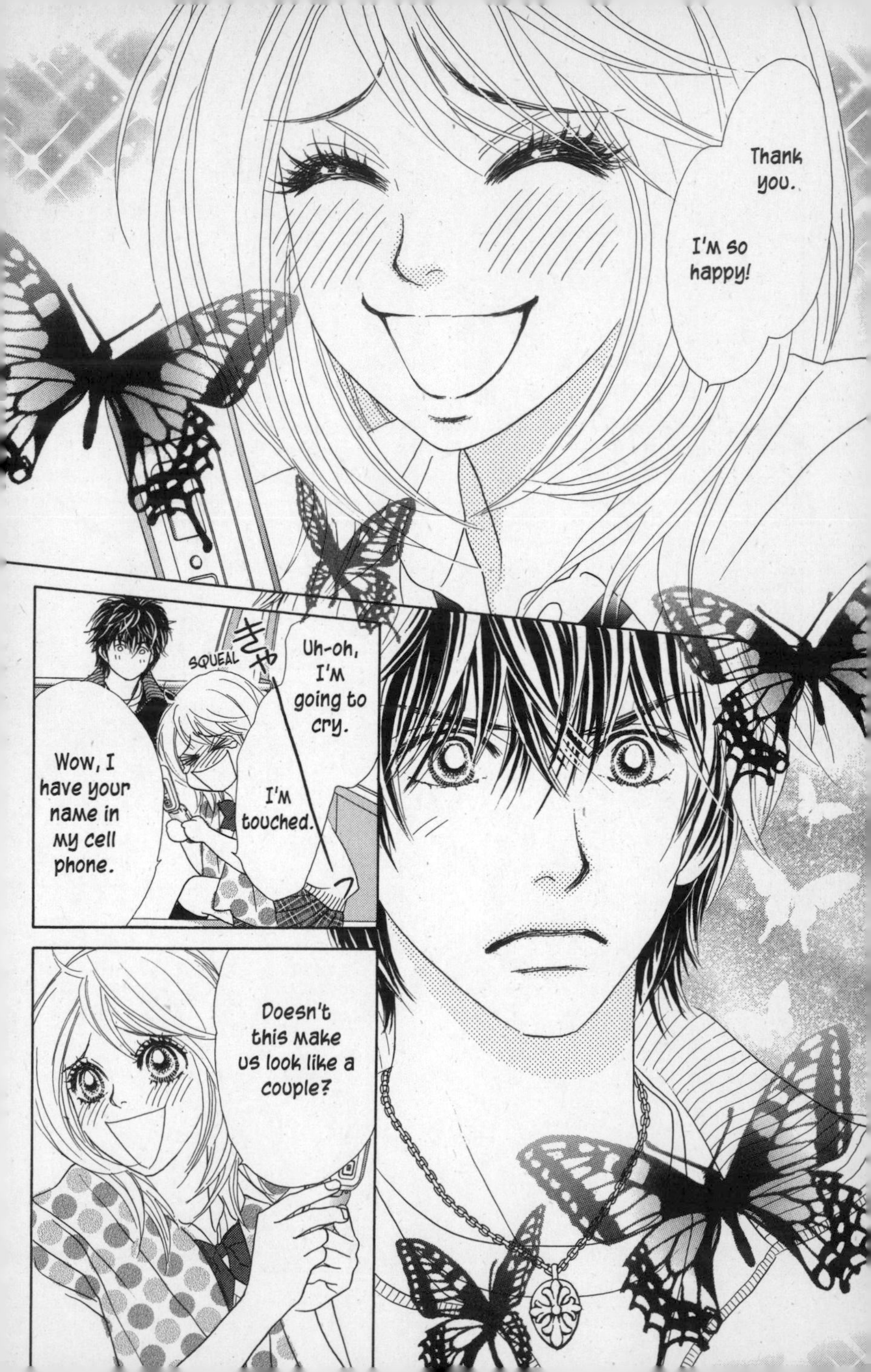
Thank you.
I'm so happy!
きゃ
SQUEAL
Uh-oh, I'm going to cry.
I'm touched.
Wow, I have your name in my cell phone.
Doesn't this make us look like a couple?

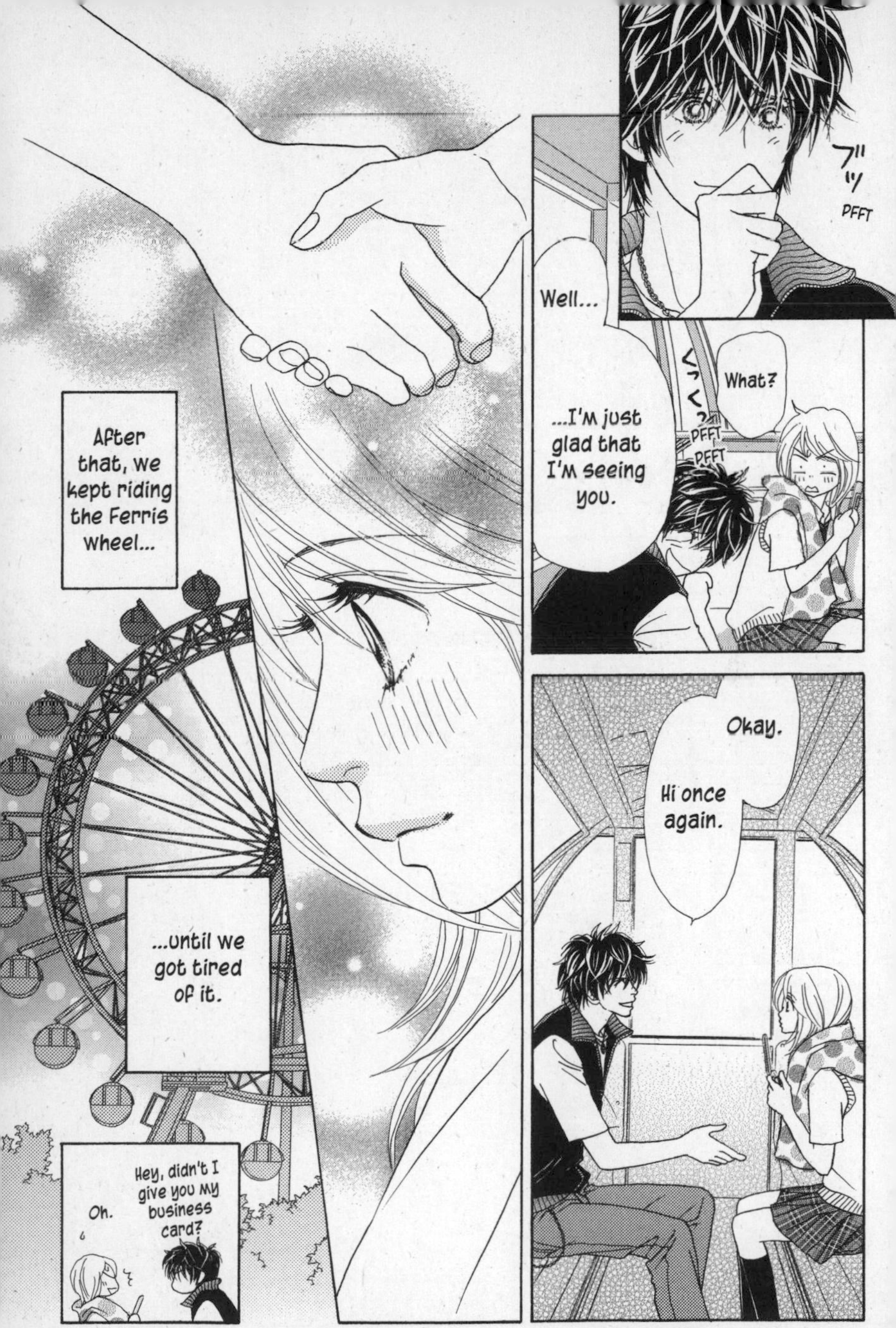
ブツ
PFFT
Well...
What?
PFFT
PFFT
...I'm just glad that I'm seeing you.
Okay.
Hi once again.
After that, we kept riding the Ferris wheel...
...until we got tired of it.
Hey, didn't I give you my business card?
Oh.

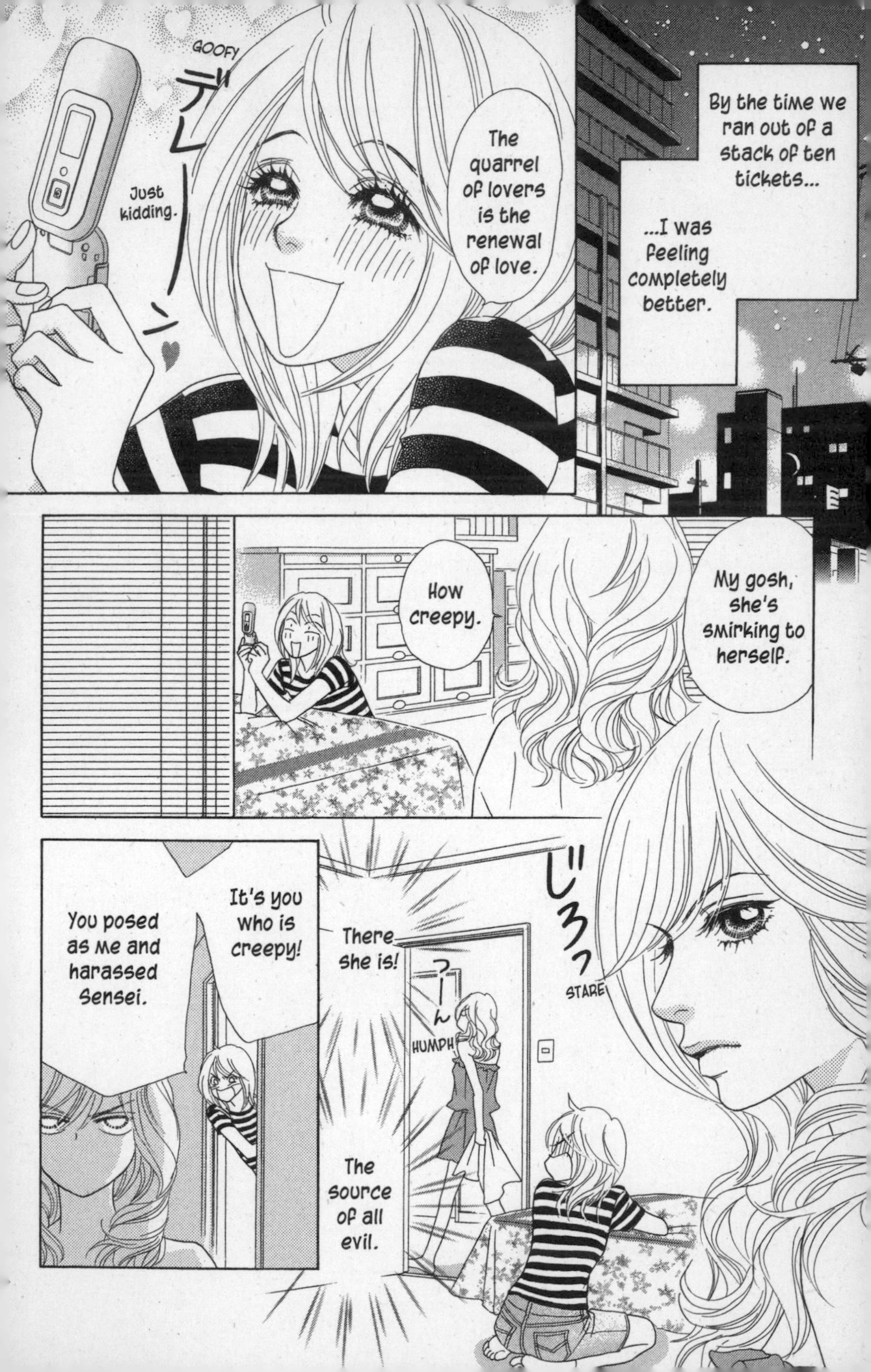
By the time we ran out of a stack of ten tickets...
...I was feeling completely better.
The quarrel of lovers is the renewal of love.
GOOFY
デレーン
Just kidding.
My gosh, she's smirking to herself.
How creepy.
じろっ
STARE
There she is!
つーん
HUMPH
The source of all evil.
It's you who is creepy!
You posed as me and harassed Sensei.

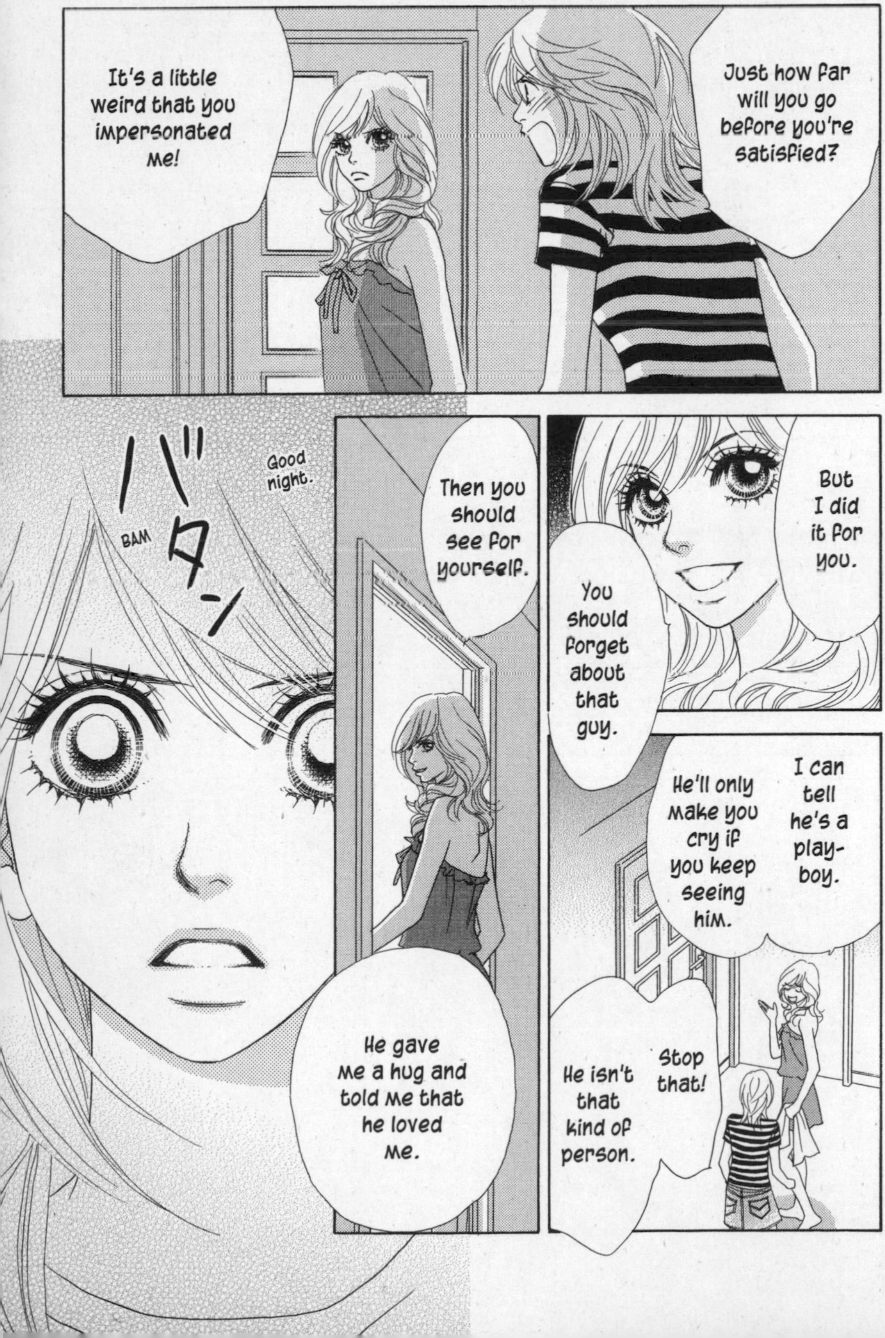
Just how far will you go before you're satisfied?
It's a little weird that you impersonated me!
But I did it for you.
You should forget about that guy.
I can tell he's a playboy.
He'll only make you cry if you keep seeing him.
Stop that!
He isn't that kind of person.
Then you should see for yourself.
He gave me a hug and told me that he loved me.
Good night.
バタン
BAM

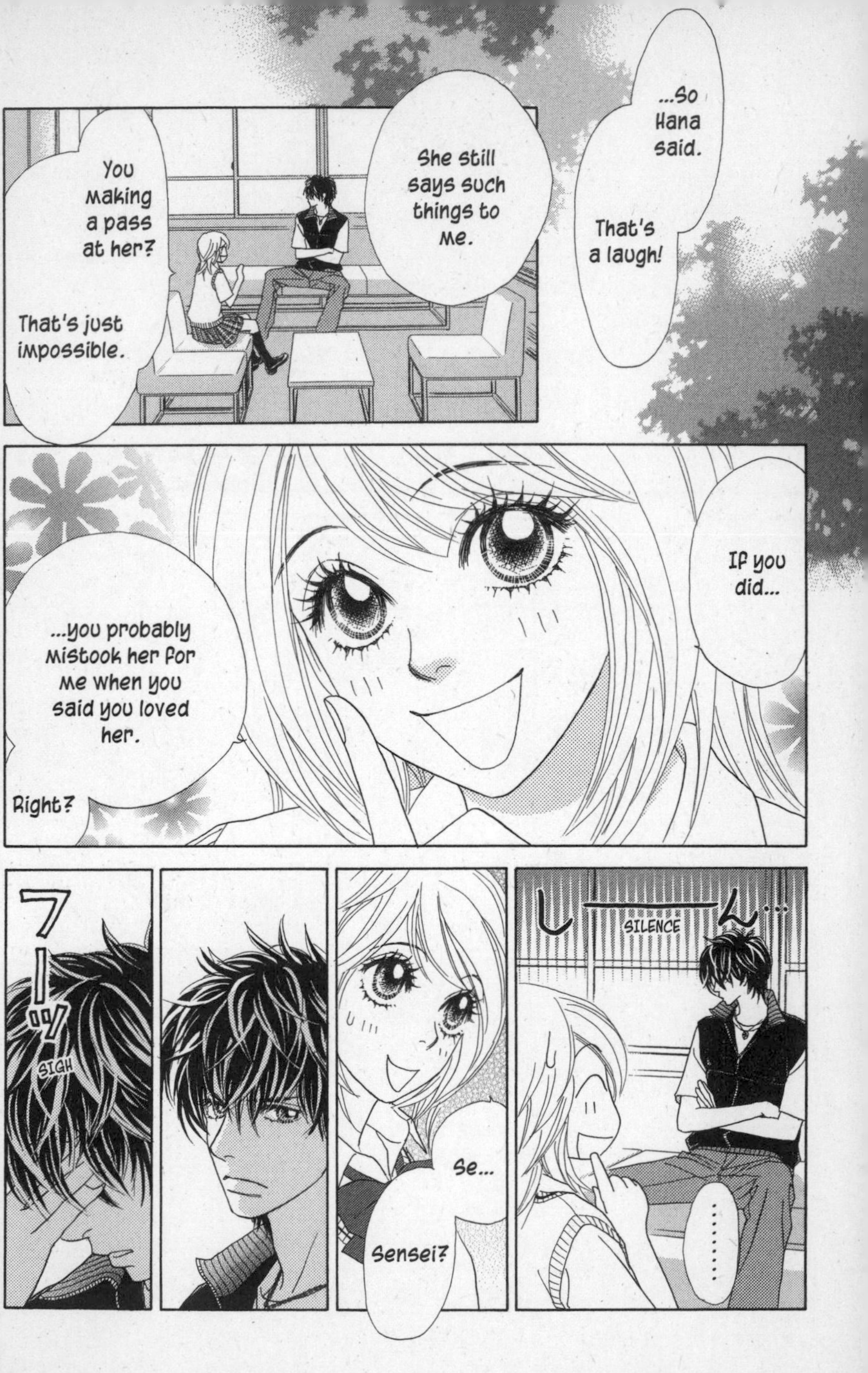
...So Hana said.
That's a laugh!
She still says such things to me.
You making a pass at her?
That's just impossible.
If you did...
...you probably mistook her for me when you said you loved her.
Right?
SILENCE
....
Se...
Sensei?
SIGH

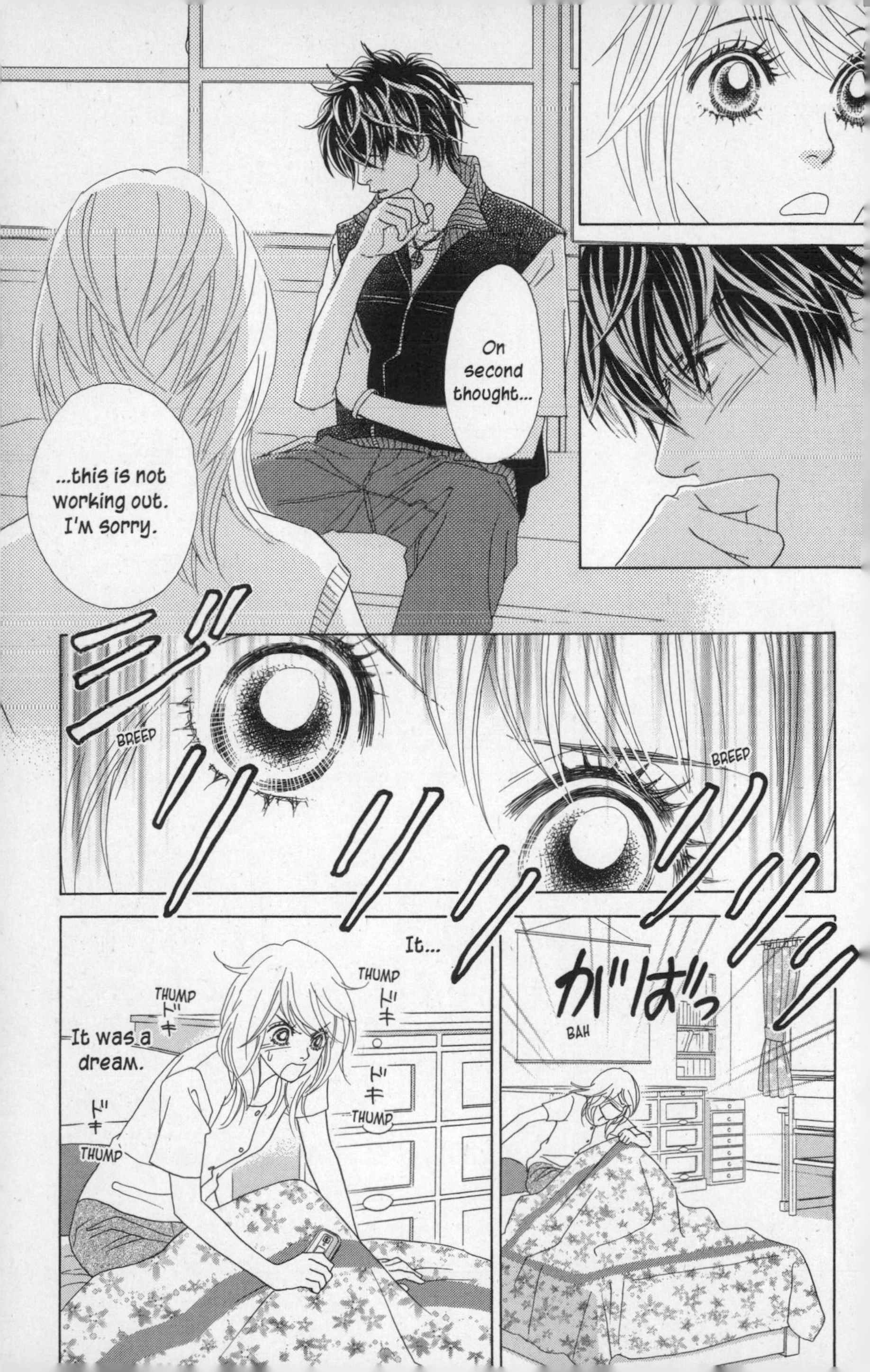
On second thought...
...this is not working out. I'm sorry.
BREEP
BREEP
がばっ
BAH
It...
ドキ
THUMP
ドキ
THUMP
It was a dream.
ドキ
THUMP
ドキ
THUMP

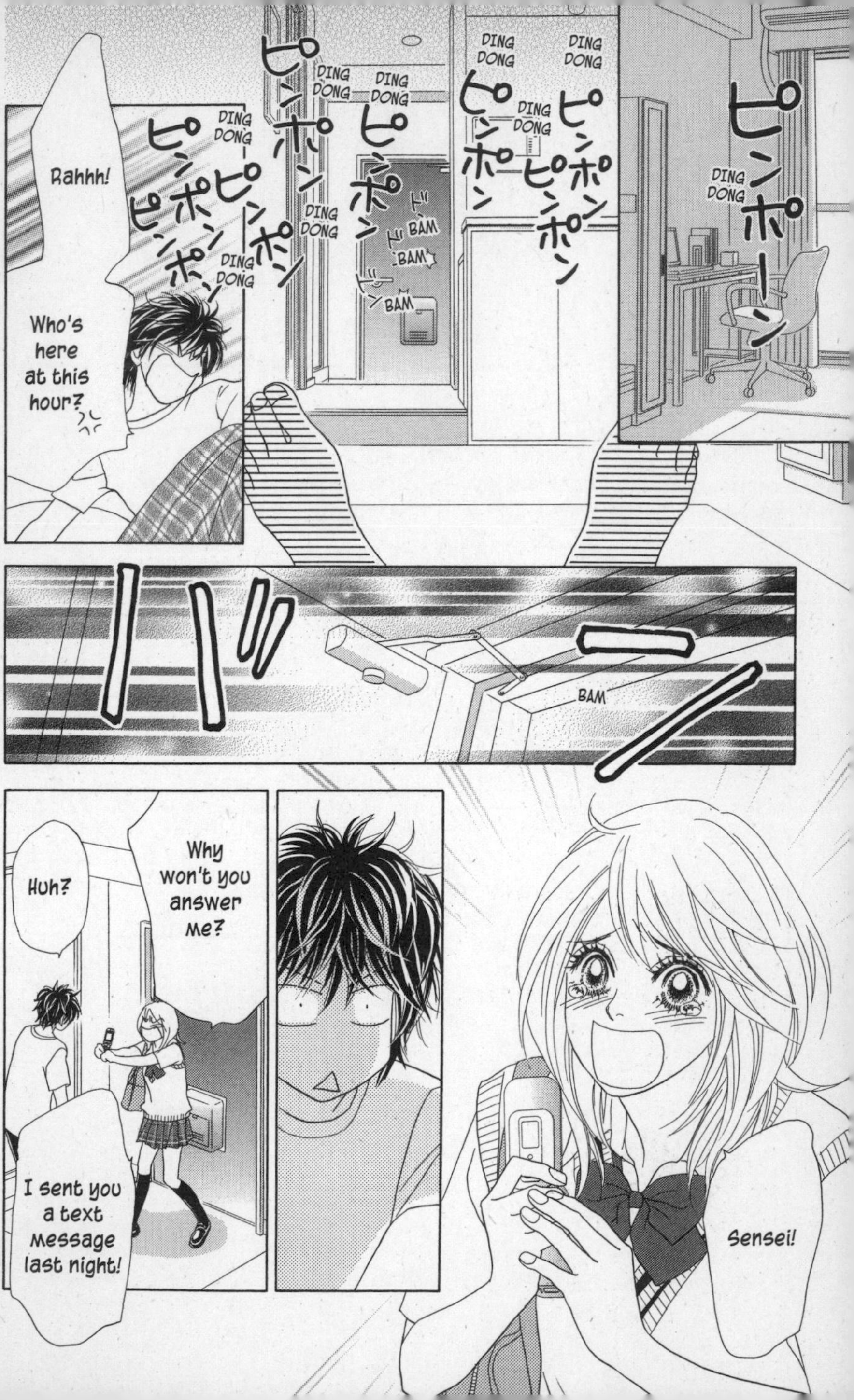

ピンポーン
DING DONG
ピンポン
DING DONG
ピンポン
DING DONG
ピンポン
DING DONG
ピンポン
DING DONG
ピンポン
DING DONG
ピンポン
DING DONG
ピンポン
DING DONG
ピポピポ
DING DONG
ド BAM
ド BAM
ド BAM
Rahhh!
Who's here at this hour?
BAM
Sensei!
Why won't you answer me?
Huh?
I sent you a text message last night!

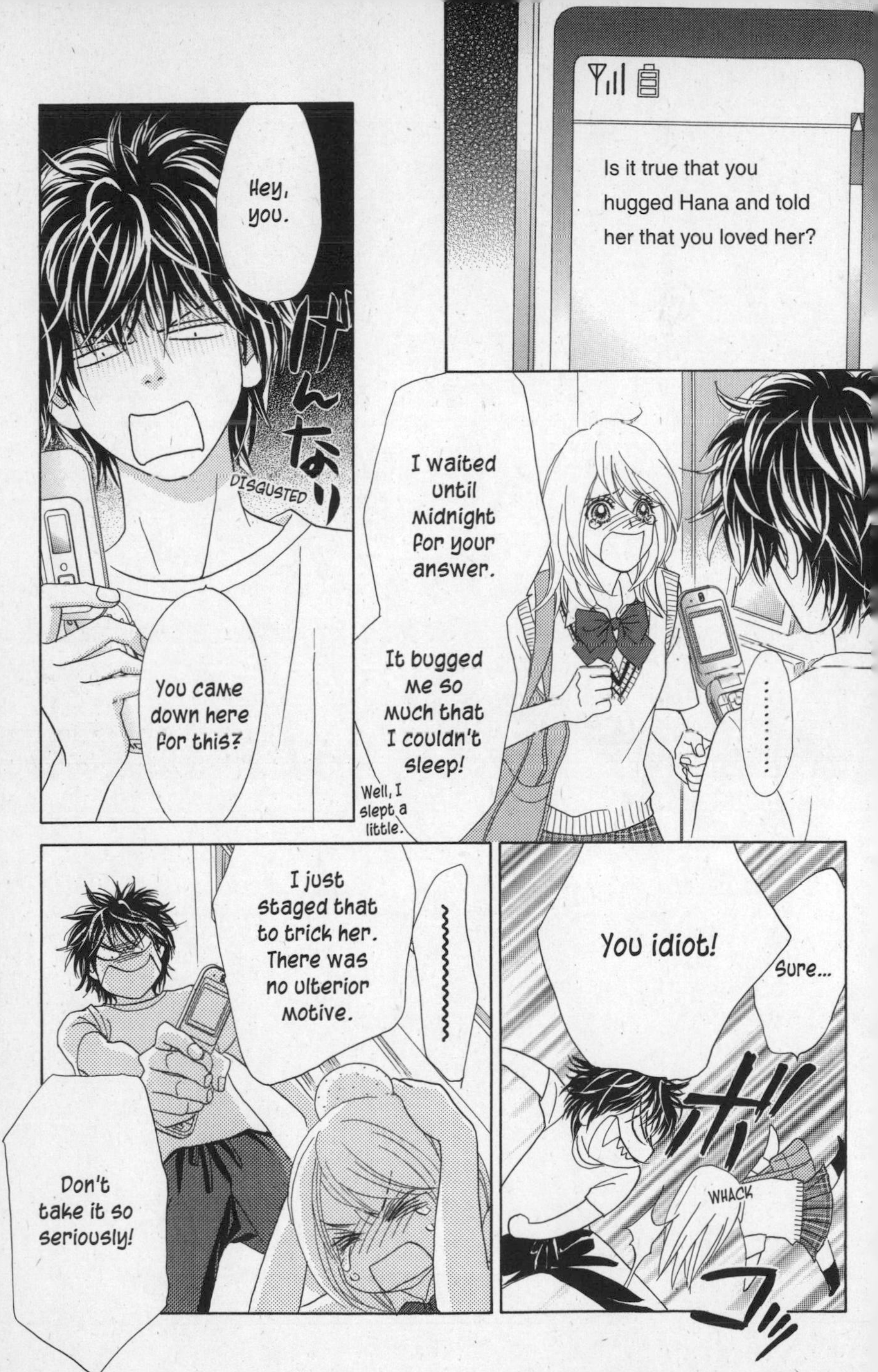

Is it true that you hugged Hana and told her that you loved her?
......
I waited until midnight for your answer.
It bugged me so much that I couldn't sleep!
Well, I slept a little.
Hey, you.
げんなり
DISGUSTED
You came down here for this?
Sure...
You idiot!
WHACK
I just staged that to trick her. There was no ulterior motive.
Don't take it so seriously!

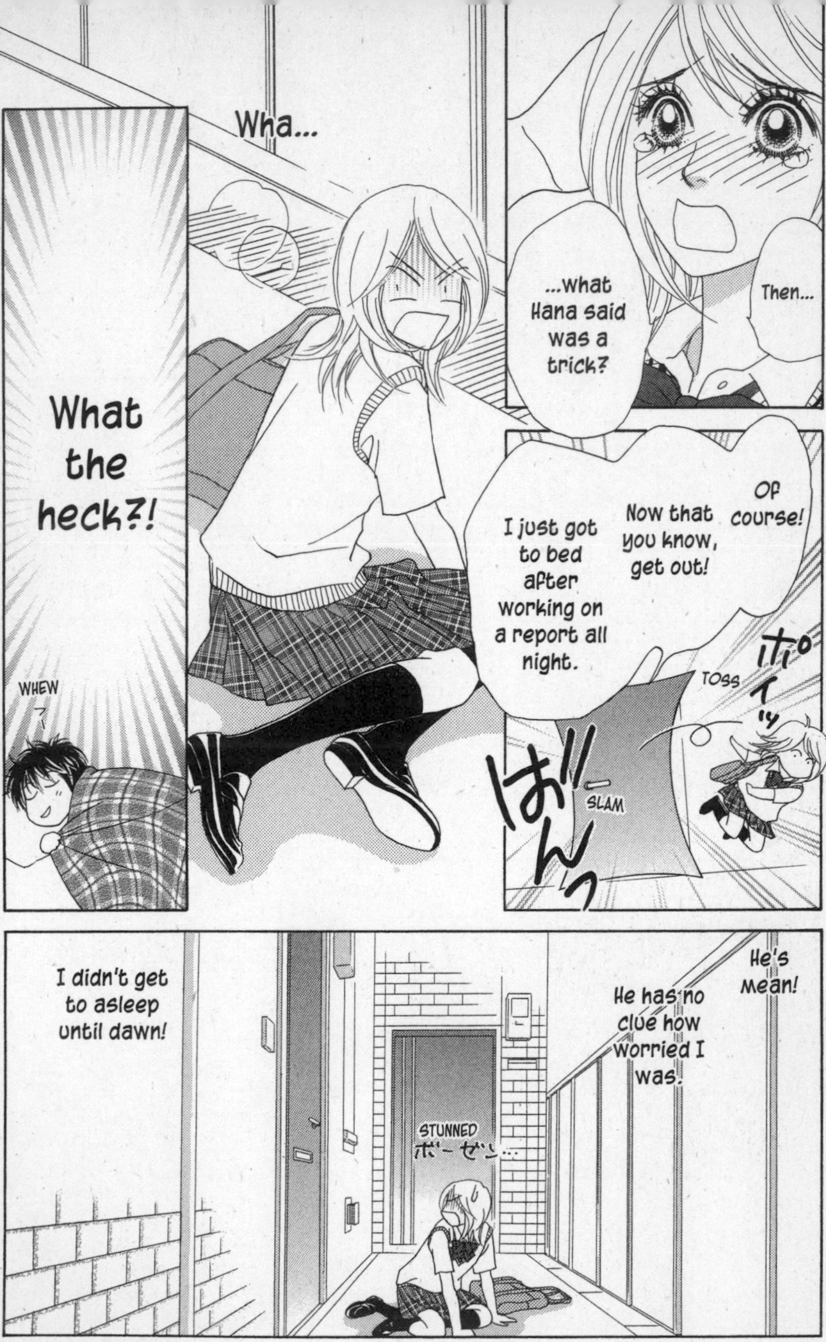
Then...
...what Hana said was a trick?
Of course!
Now that you know, get out!
I just got to bed after working on a report all night.
TOSS
ポイッ
SLAM
ばんっ
Wha...
What the heck?!
WHEW
He's Mean!
He has no clue how worried I was.
STUNNED
ボーゼン…
I didn't get to asleep until dawn!

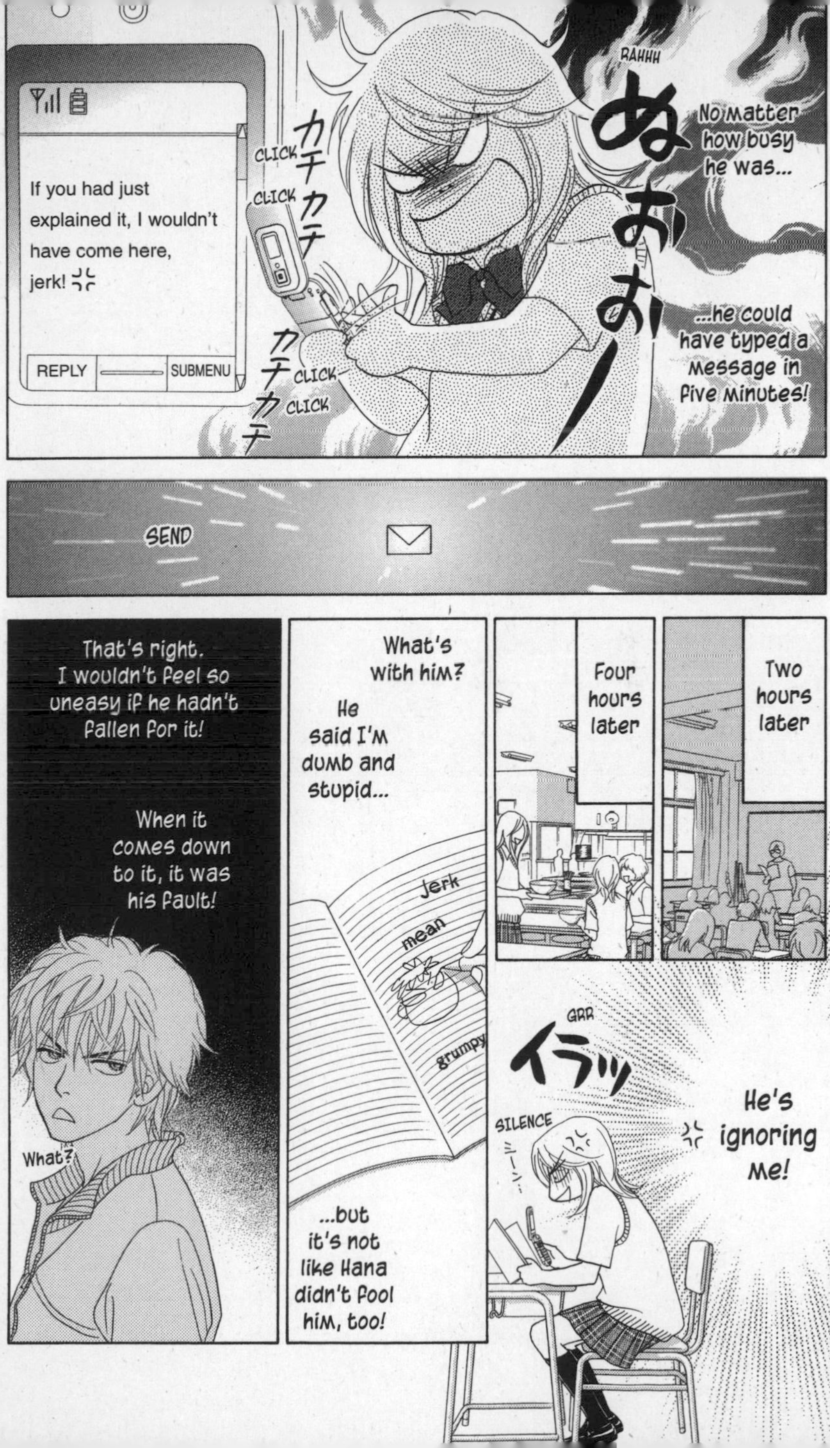
RAHHH
ぬおお!
No matter how busy he was...
...he could have typed a message in five minutes!
CLICK
カチ
CLICK
カチ
CLICK
カチ
CLICK
カチ
If you had just explained it, I wouldn't have come here, jerk!
REPLY
SUBMENU
SEND
Two hours later
Four hours later
GRR
イラッ
He's ignoring me!
SILENCE
シーン
What's with him?
He said I'm dumb and stupid...
jerk
mean
grumpy
...but it's not like Hana didn't fool him, too!
That's right. I wouldn't feel so uneasy if he hadn't fallen for it!
When it comes down to it, it was his fault!
What?

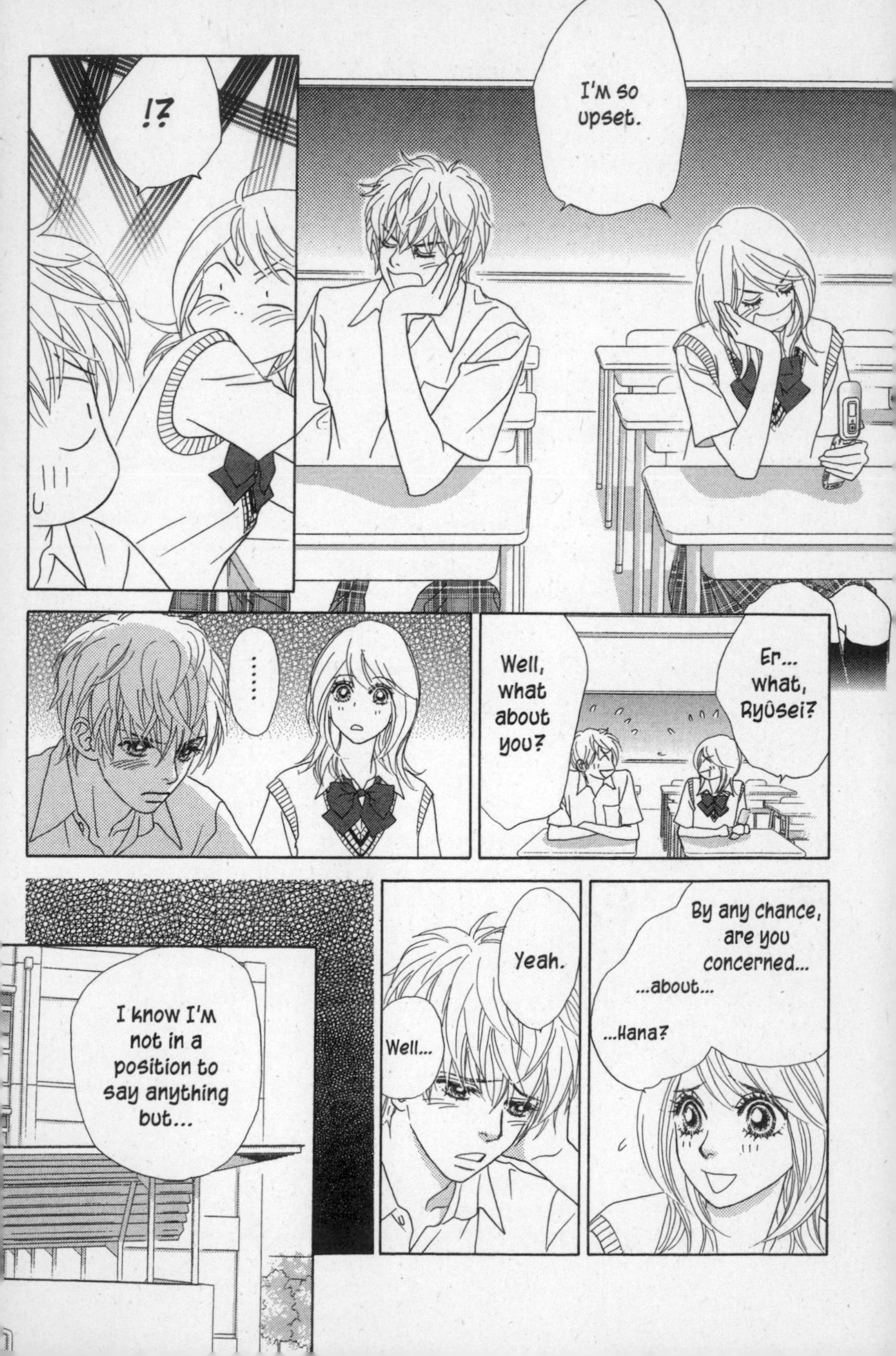
I'm so upset.
!?
Er... what, Ryûsei?
Well, what about you?
......
By any chance, are you concerned...
...about...
...Hana?
Yeah.
Well...
I know I'm not in a position to say anything but...

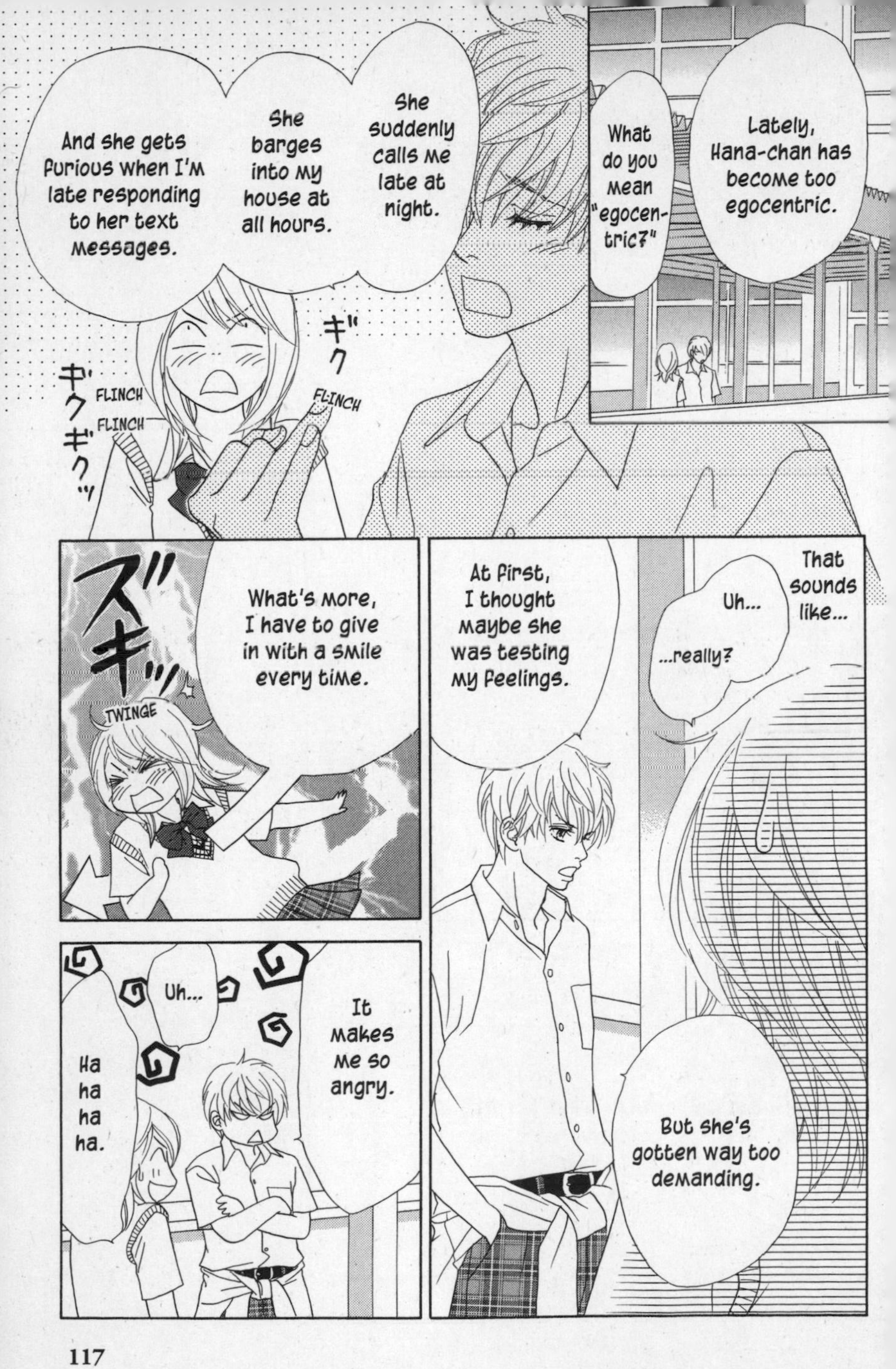
Lately, Hana-chan has become too egocentric.
What do you mean "egocentric?"
She suddenly calls me late at night.
She barges into my house at all hours.
And she gets furious when I'm late responding to her text messages.
ギク
FLINCH
ギクギクッ
FLINCH
FLINCH
That sounds like...
Uh...
...really?
At first, I thought maybe she was testing my feelings.
But she's gotten way too demanding.
What's more, I have to give in with a smile every time.
ズキッ
TWINGE
It makes me so angry.
Uh...
Ha ha ha ha.

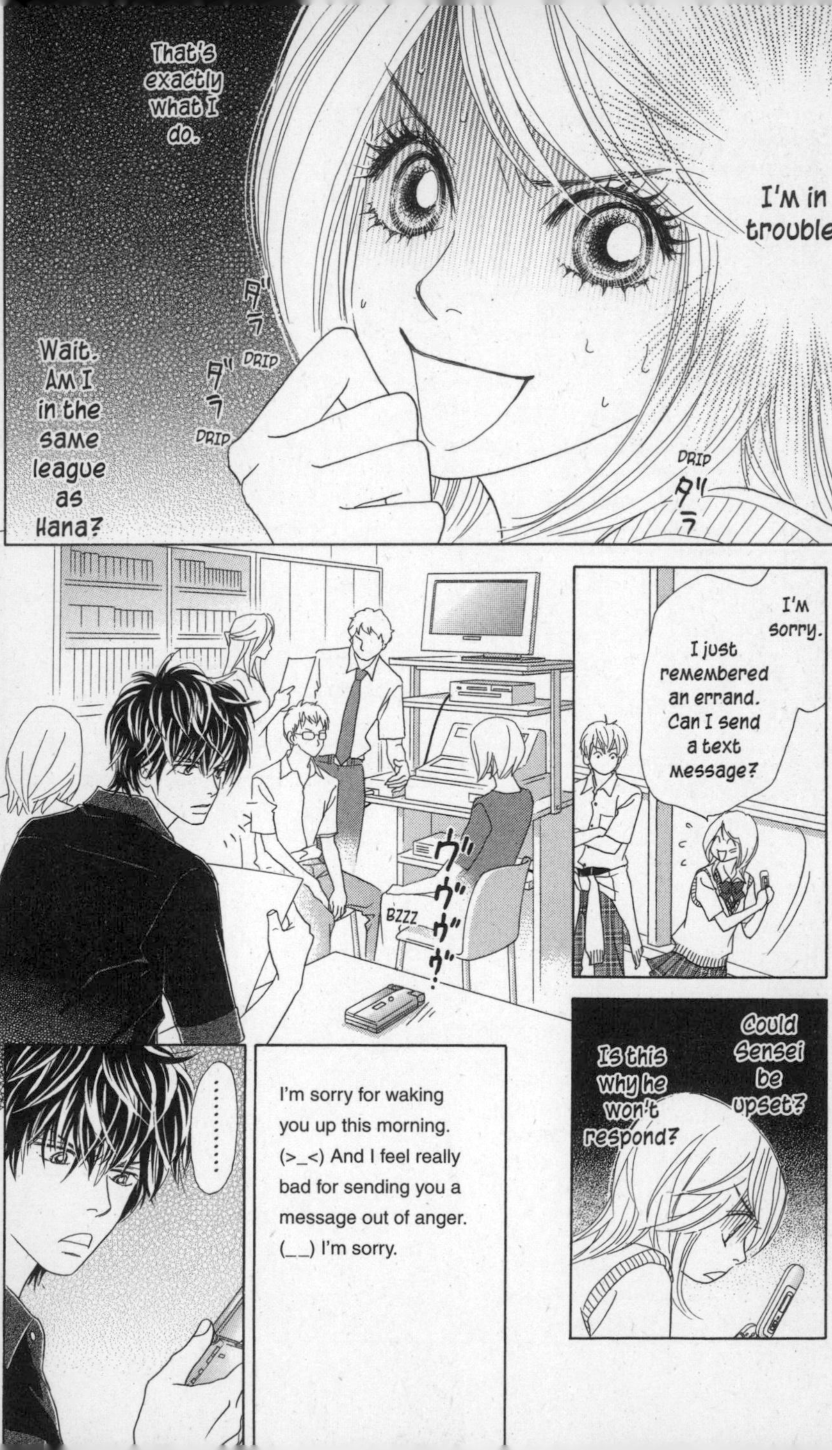
That's exactly what I do.
Wait. Am I in the same league as Hana?
ダラ
DRIP
ダラ
DRIP
I'm in trouble!
DRIP
ダラ
I'm sorry.
I just remembered an errand. Can I send a text message?
ヴヴヴヴ
BZZZ
Could Sensei be upset?
Is this why he won't respond?
I'm sorry for waking you up this morning. (>_<) And I feel really bad for sending you a message out of anger. (__) I'm sorry.
......

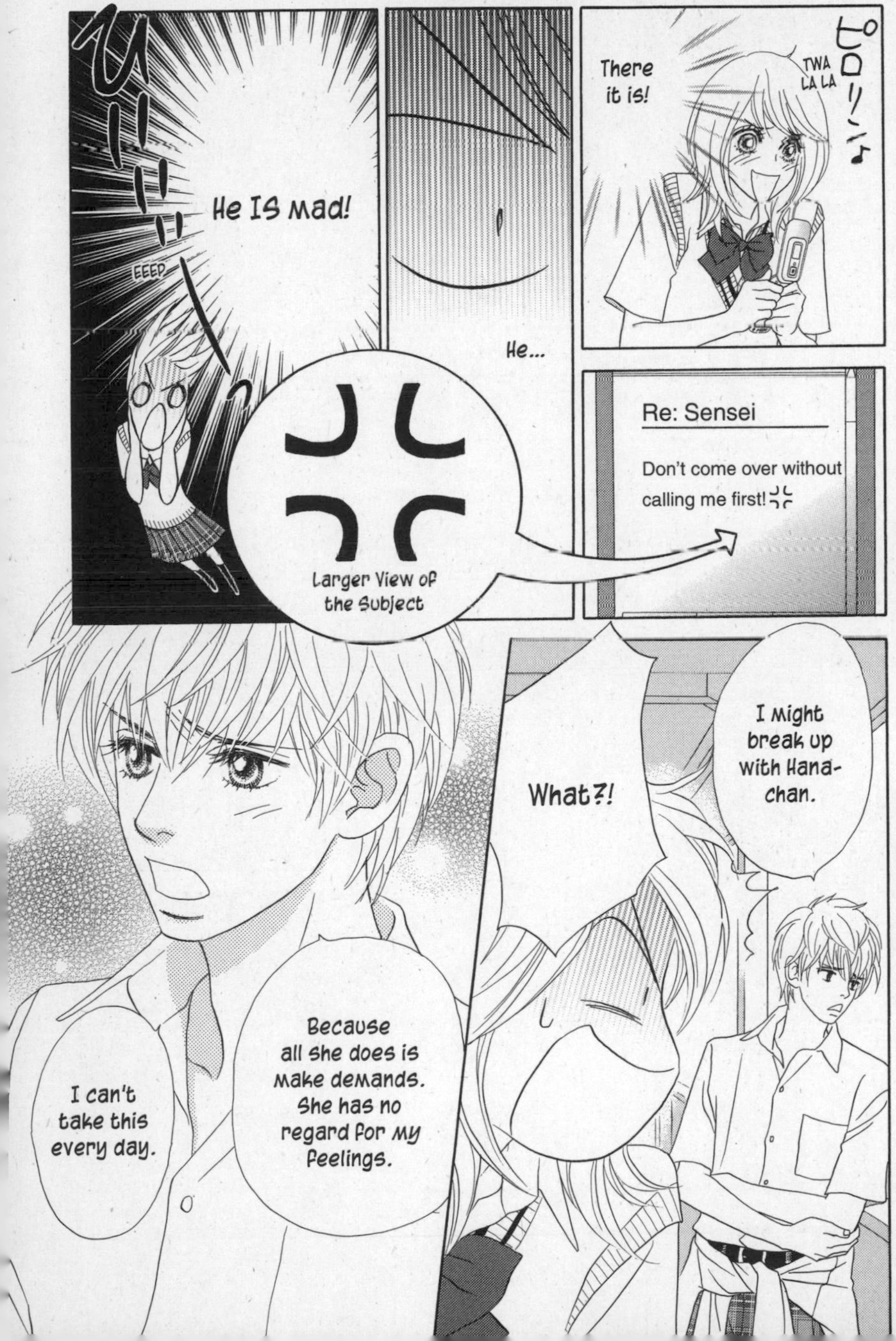
There it is!
TWA LA LA
Re: Sensei
Don't come over without calling me first!
He...
He IS mad!
EEEP
Larger View of the Subject
I might break up with Hana-chan.
What?!
Because all she does is make demands. She has no regard for my feelings.
I can't take this every day.

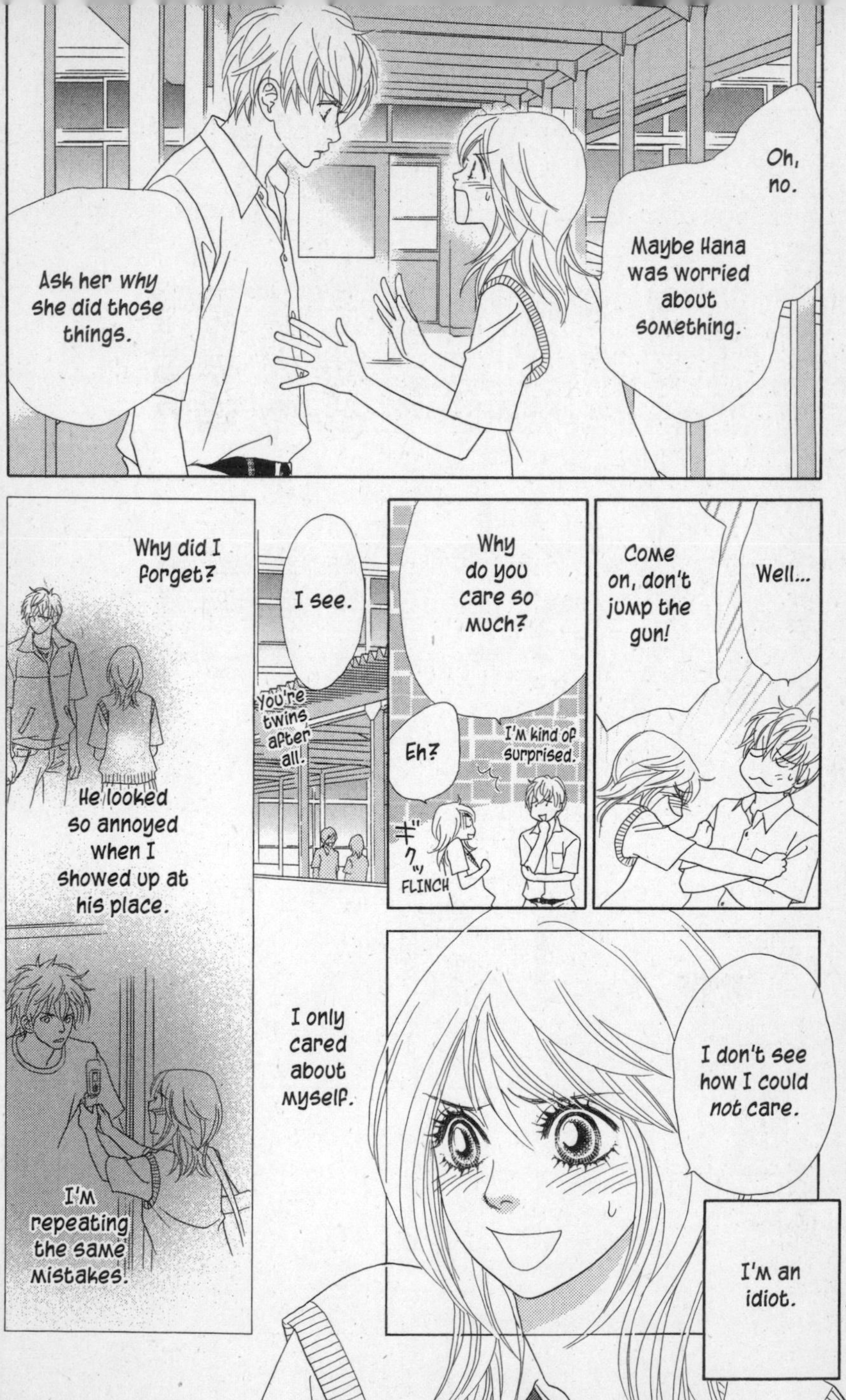
Oh, no.
Maybe Hana was worried about something.
Ask her why she did those things.
Well...
Come on, don't jump the gun!
Why do you care so much?
I'm kind of surprised.
Eh?
ギクッ FLINCH
I see.
You're twins after all.
I don't see how I could not care.
I'm an idiot.
I only cared about myself.
Why did I forget?
He looked so annoyed when I showed up at his place.
I'm repeating the same mistakes.

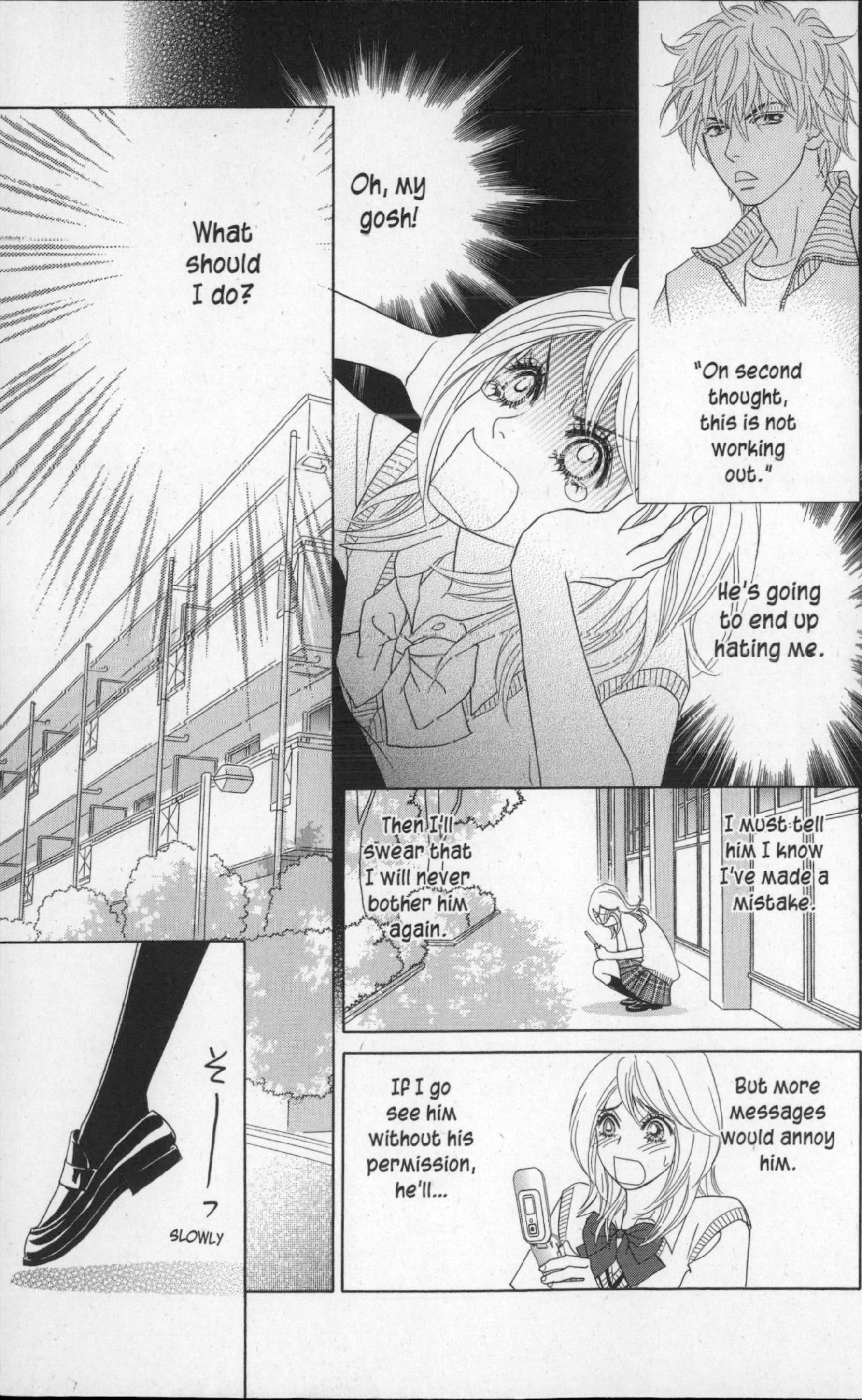

"On second thought, this is not working out."
Oh, my gosh!
He's going to end up hating me.
I must tell him I know I've made a mistake.
Then I'll swear that I will never bother him again.
But more messages would annoy him.
If I go see him without his permission, he'll...
What should I do?
SLOWLY

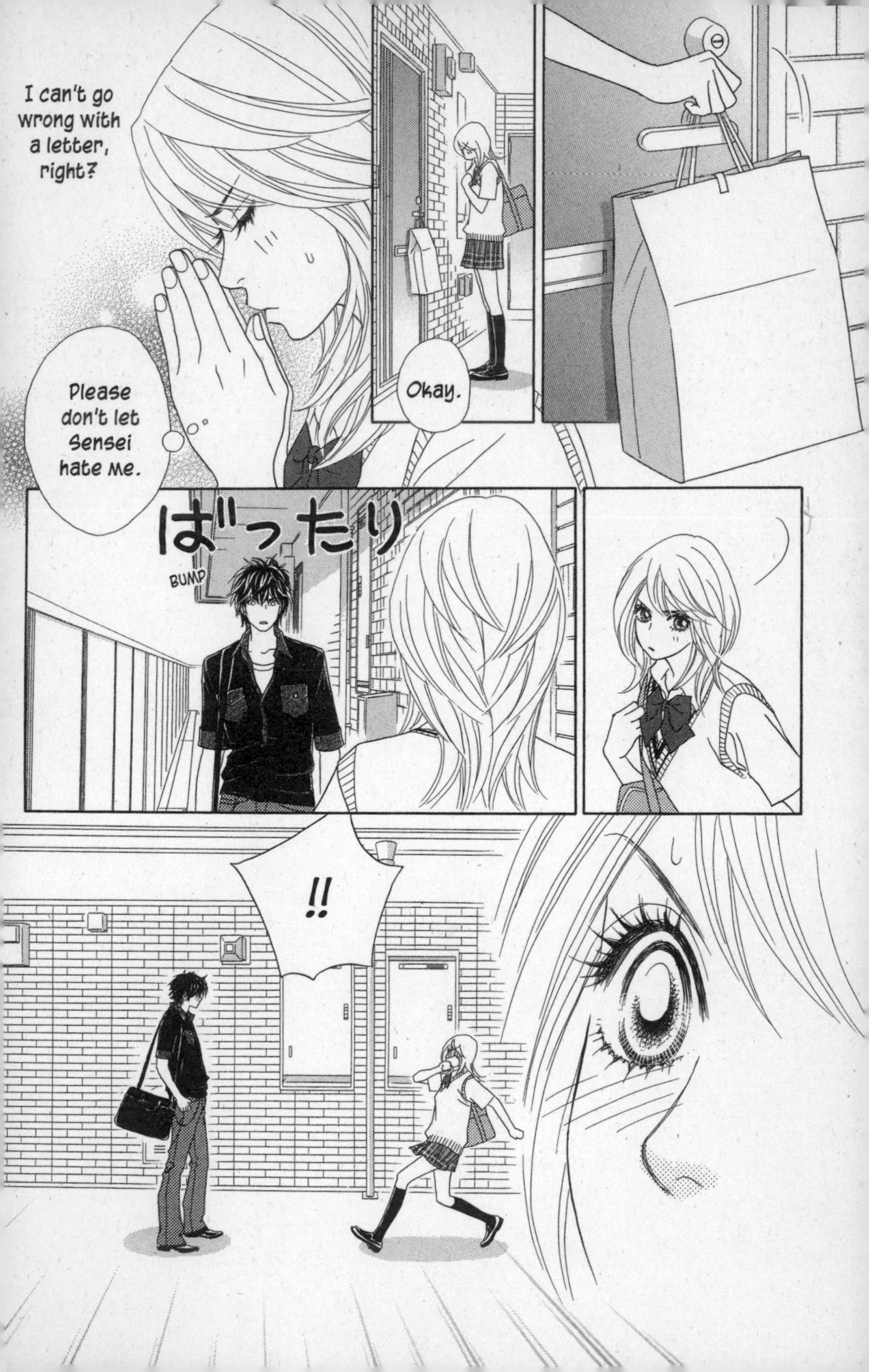
Okay.
I can't go wrong with a letter, right?
Please don't let Sensei hate me.
ばったり
BUMP
!!

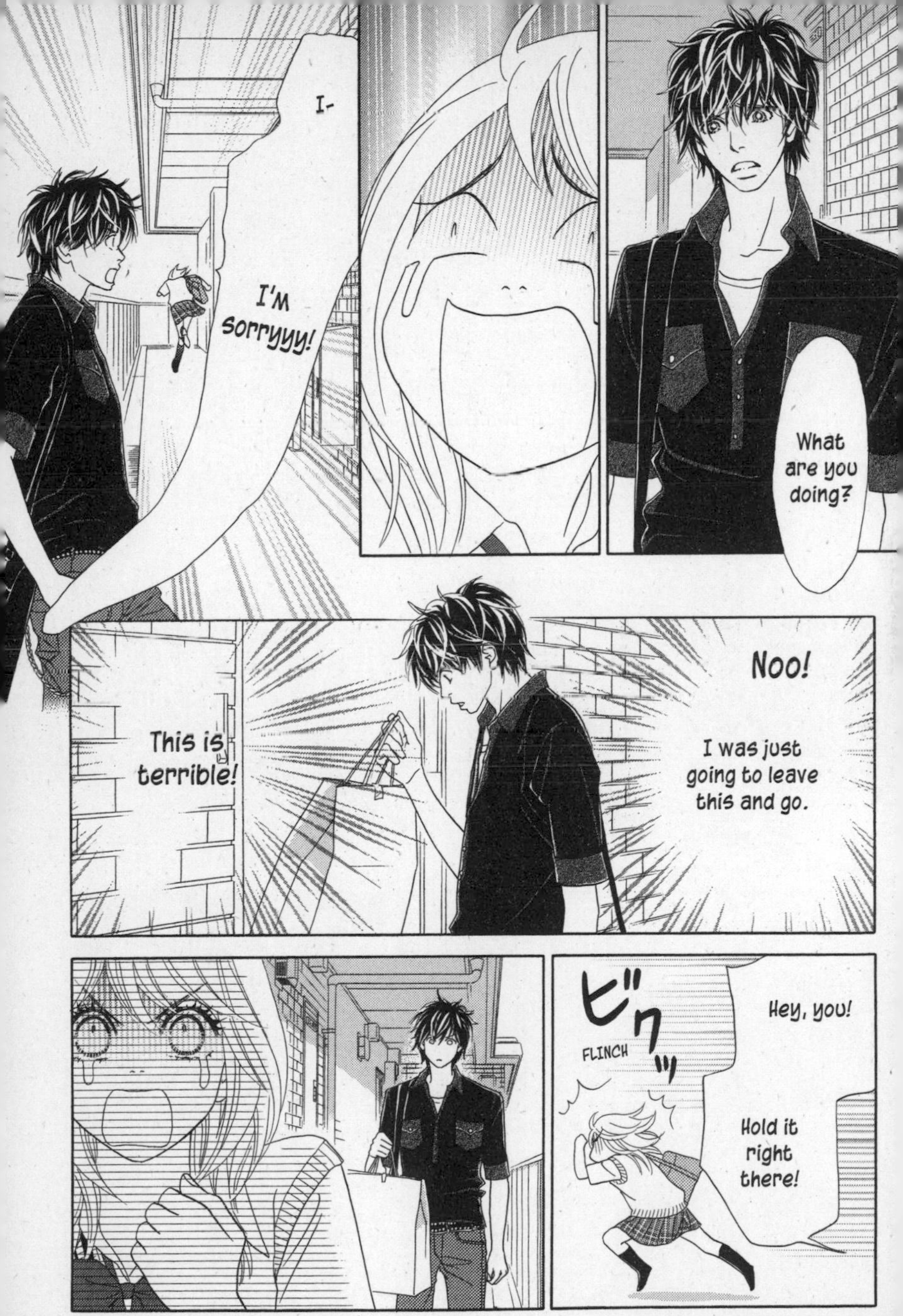
What are you doing?
I-
I'M sorryyy!
Noo!
I was just going to leave this and go.
This is terrible!
Hey, you!
Hold it right there!
ビクッ
FLINCH

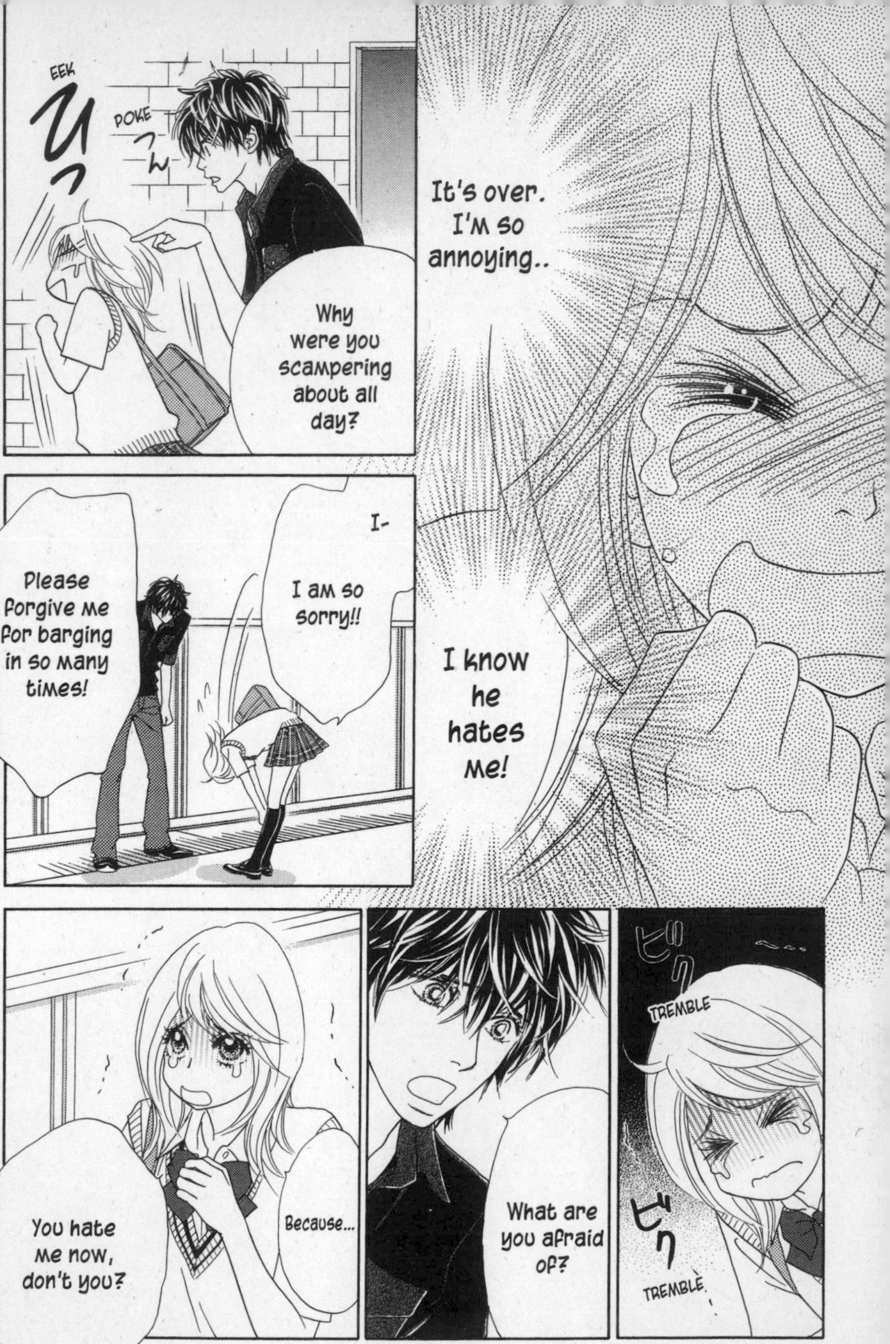
It's over. I'm so annoying..
I know he hates me!
EEK
POKE
Why were you scampering about all day?
I-
I am so sorry!!
Please forgive me for barging in so many times!
TREMBLE
TREMBLE
What are you afraid of?
Because...
You hate me now, don't you?

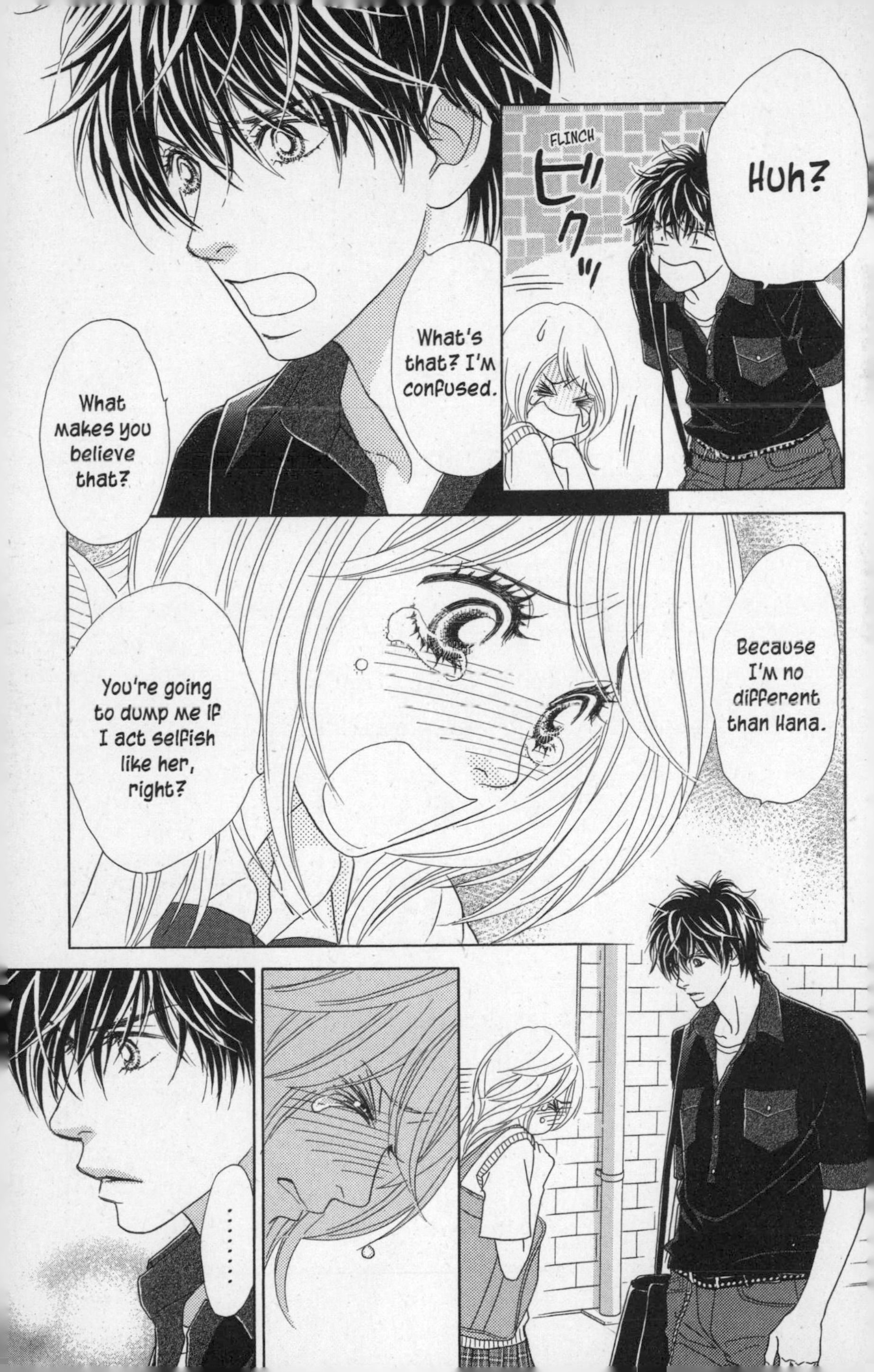
FLINCH
ビクッ
HUH?
What's that? I'm confused.
What makes you believe that?
Because I'm no different than Hana.
You're going to dump me if I act selfish like her, right?
......

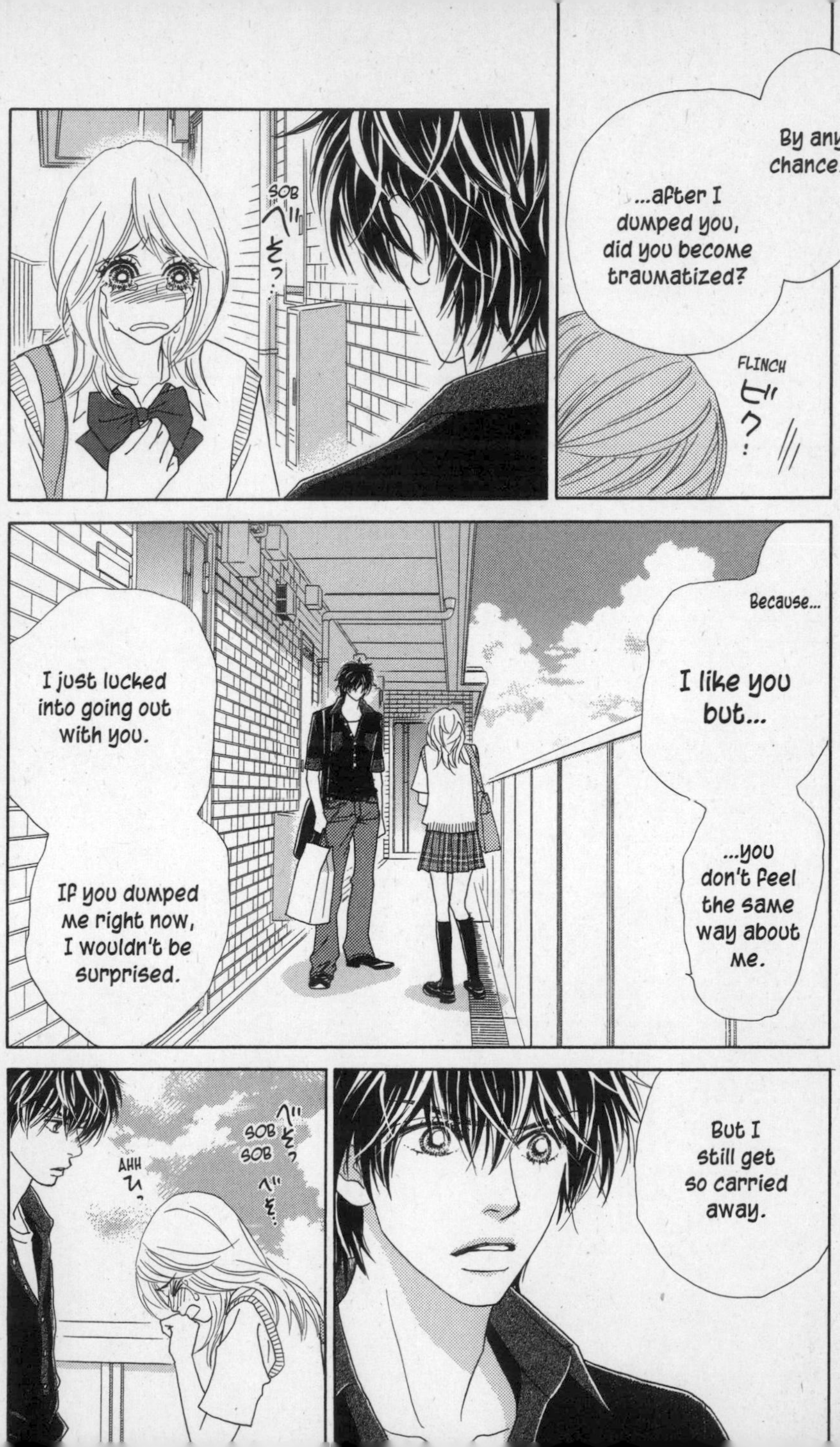
By any chance...
...after I dumped you, did you become traumatized?
FLINCH
SOB
Because...
I like you but...
...you don't feel the same way about me.
I just lucked into going out with you.
If you dumped me right now, I wouldn't be surprised.
But I still get so carried away.
SOB SOB
AHH

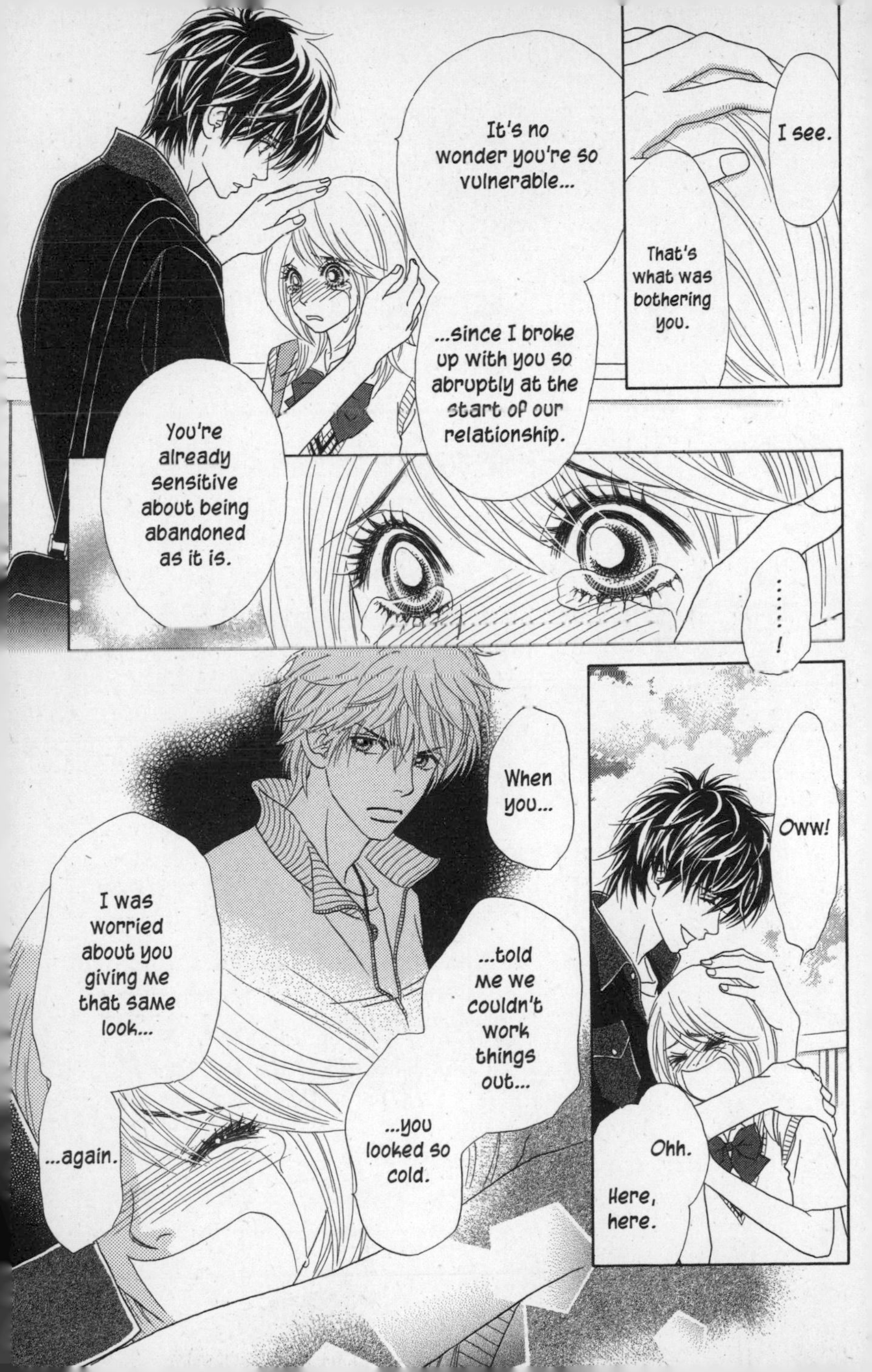
I see.
That's what was bothering you.
It's no wonder you're so vulnerable...
...since I broke up with you so abruptly at the start of our relationship.
You're already sensitive about being abandoned as it is.
......!
Oww!
Ohh.
Here, here.
When you...
...told me we couldn't work things out...
...you looked so cold.
I was worried about you giving me that same look...
...again.

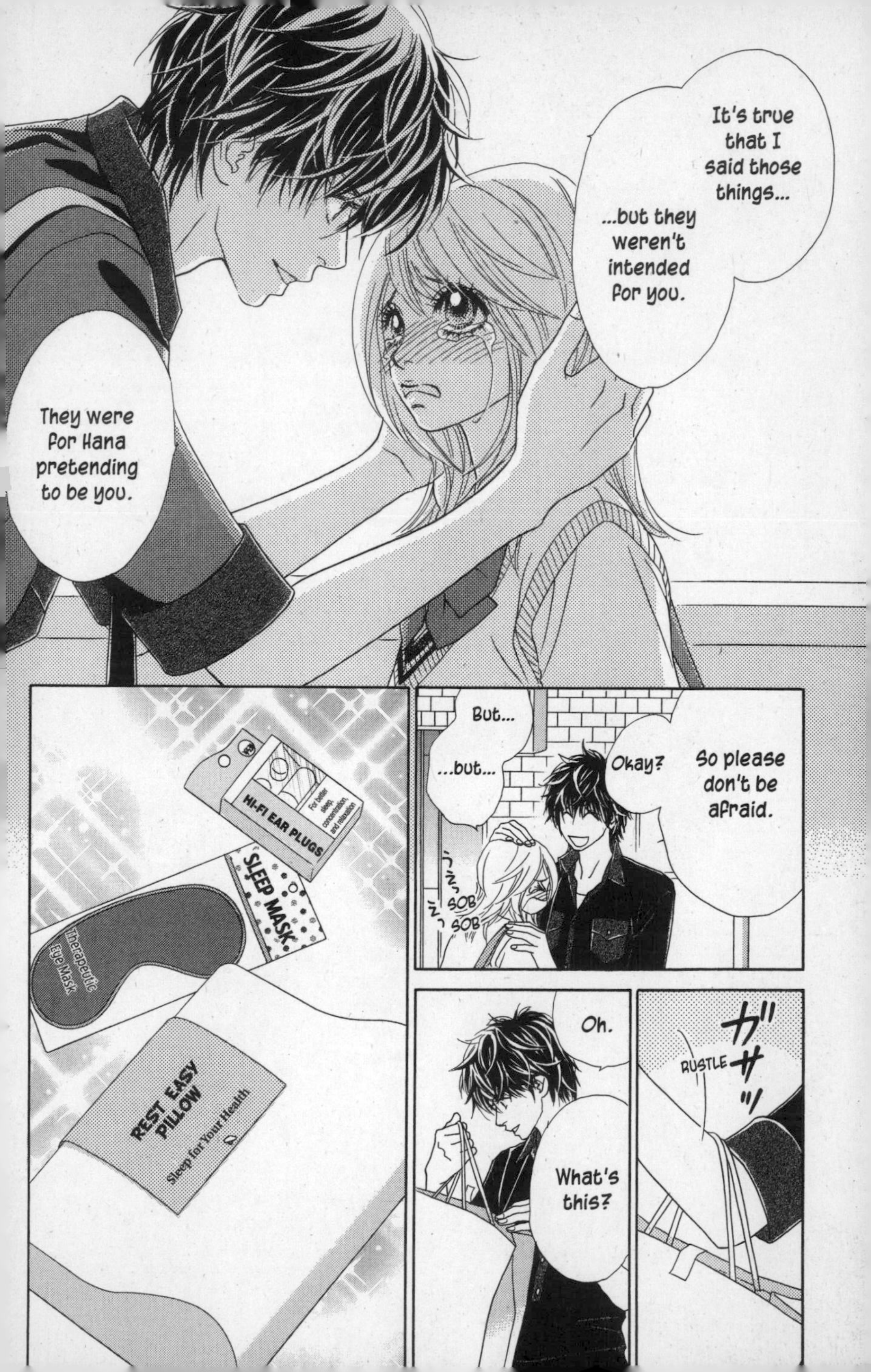
It's true that I said those things...
...but they weren't intended for you.
They were for Hana pretending to be you.
So please don't be afraid.
Okay?
But...
...but...
SOB SOB
ガサッ
RUSTLE
Oh.
What's this?
HI-FI EAR PLUGS
For better sleep, concentration, and relaxation
SLEEP MASK
Therapeutic Eye Mask
REST EASY PILLOW
Sleep for Your Health

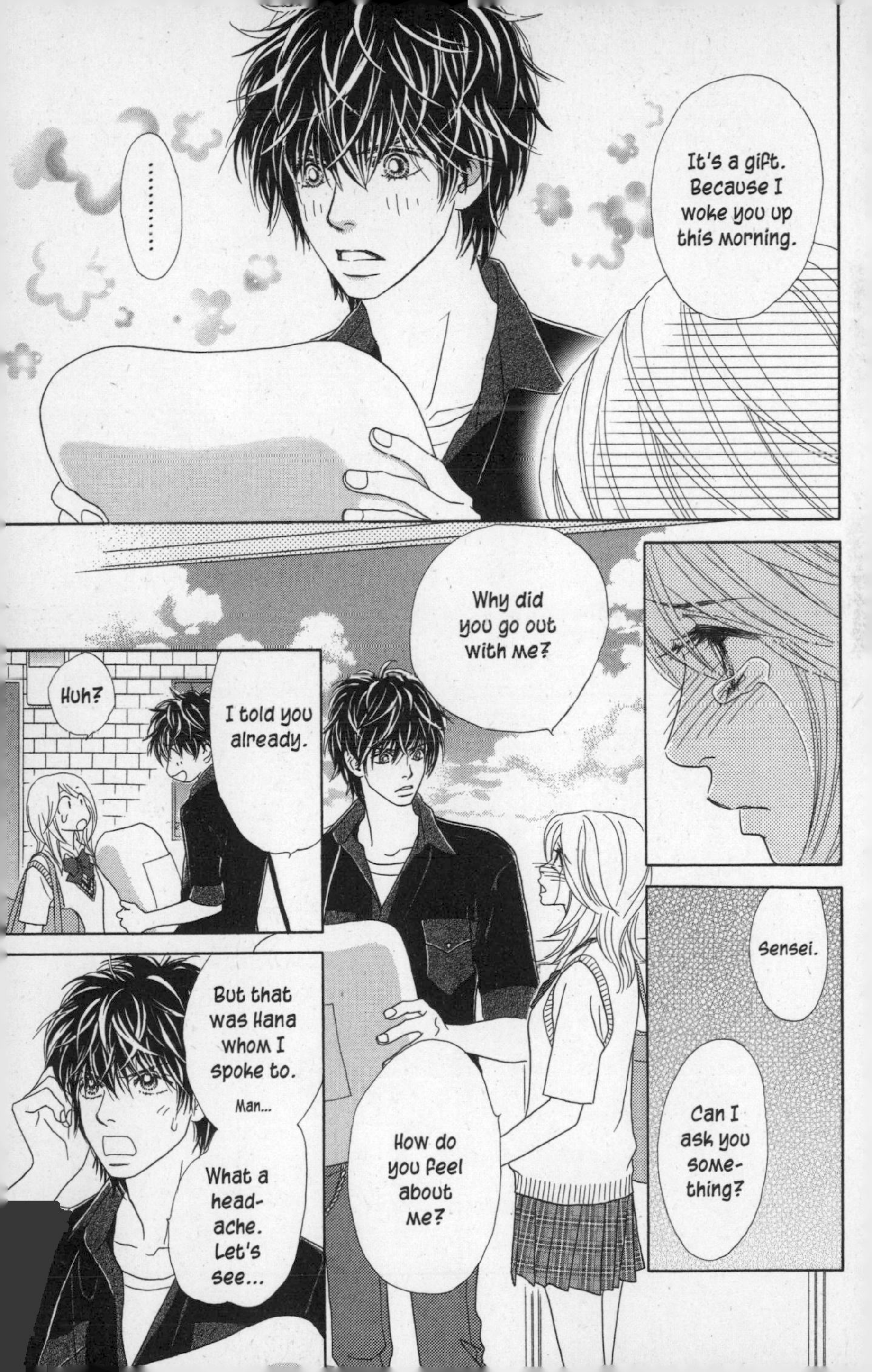
It's a gift. Because I woke you up this morning.
……
Sensei.
Can I ask you something?
Why did you go out with me?
How do you feel about me?
Huh?
I told you already.
But that was Hana whom I spoke to.
Man...
What a headache. Let's see...

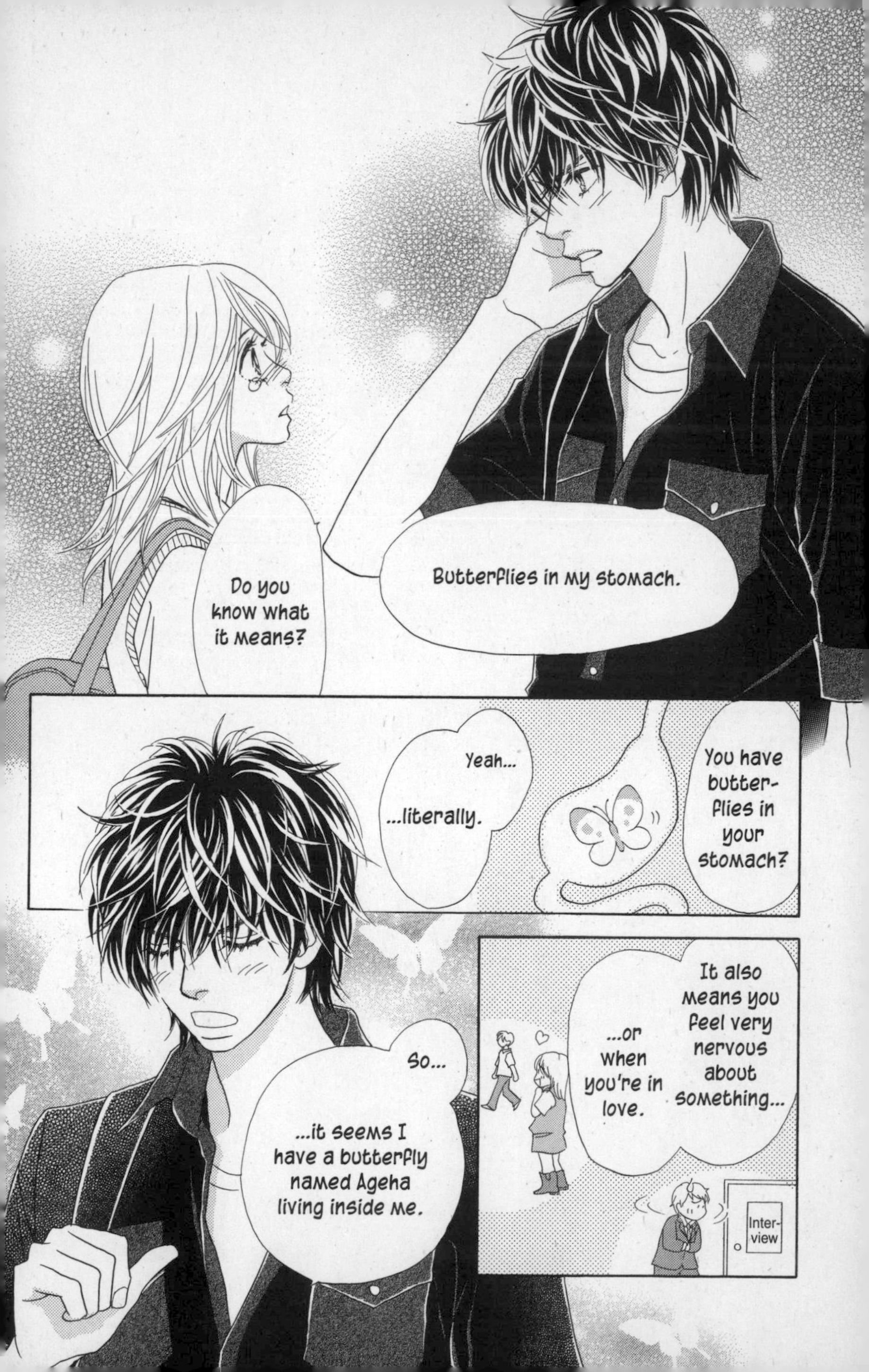
Butterflies in my stomach.
Do you know what it means?
You have butter-flies in your stomach?
Yeah...
...literally.
It also means you feel very nervous about something...
...or when you're in love.
Inter-view
So...
...it seems I have a butterfly named Ageha living inside me.

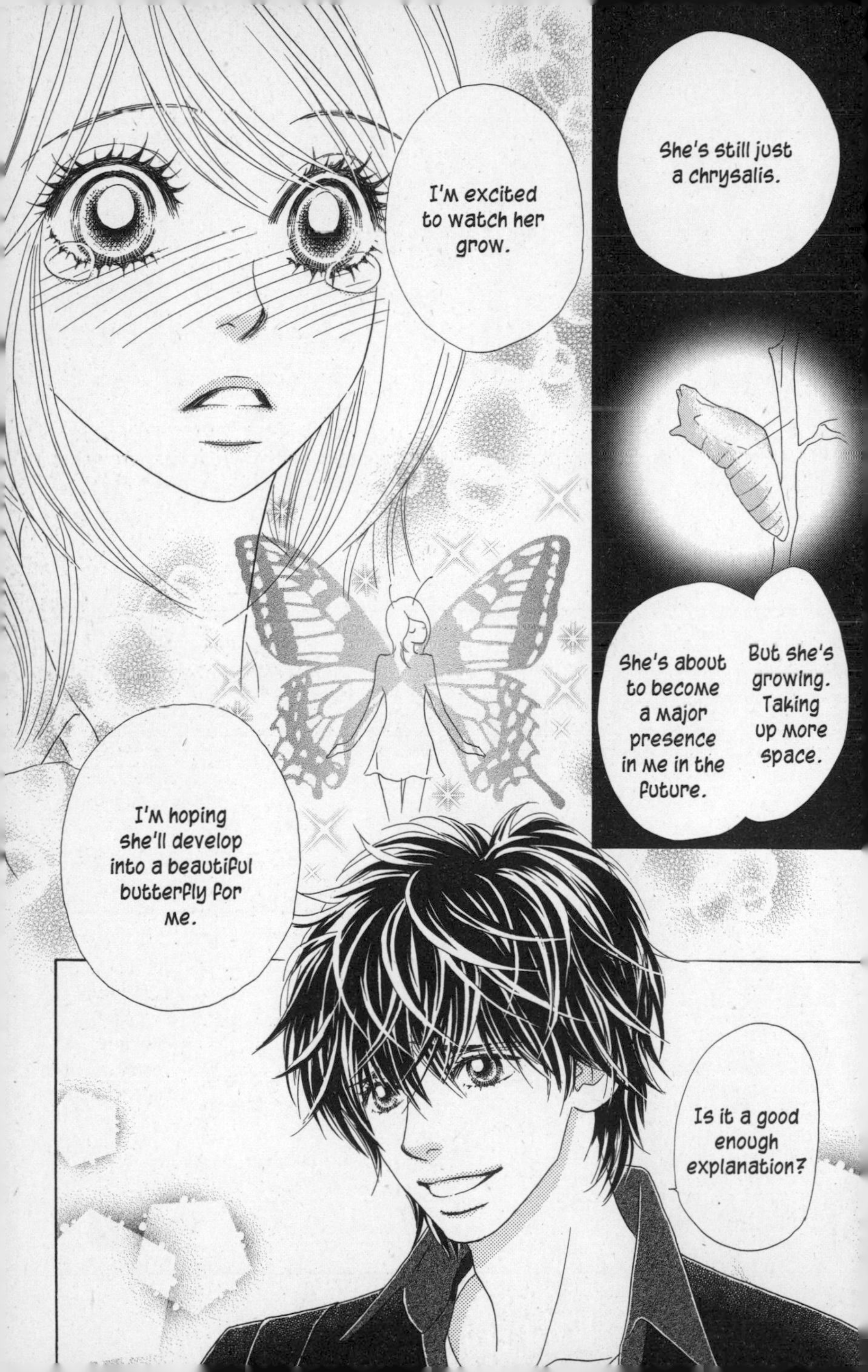
She's still just a chrysalis.
But she's growing. Taking up more space.
She's about to become a major presence in me in the future.
I'm excited to watch her grow.
I'm hoping she'll develop into a beautiful butterfly for me.
Is it a good enough explanation?

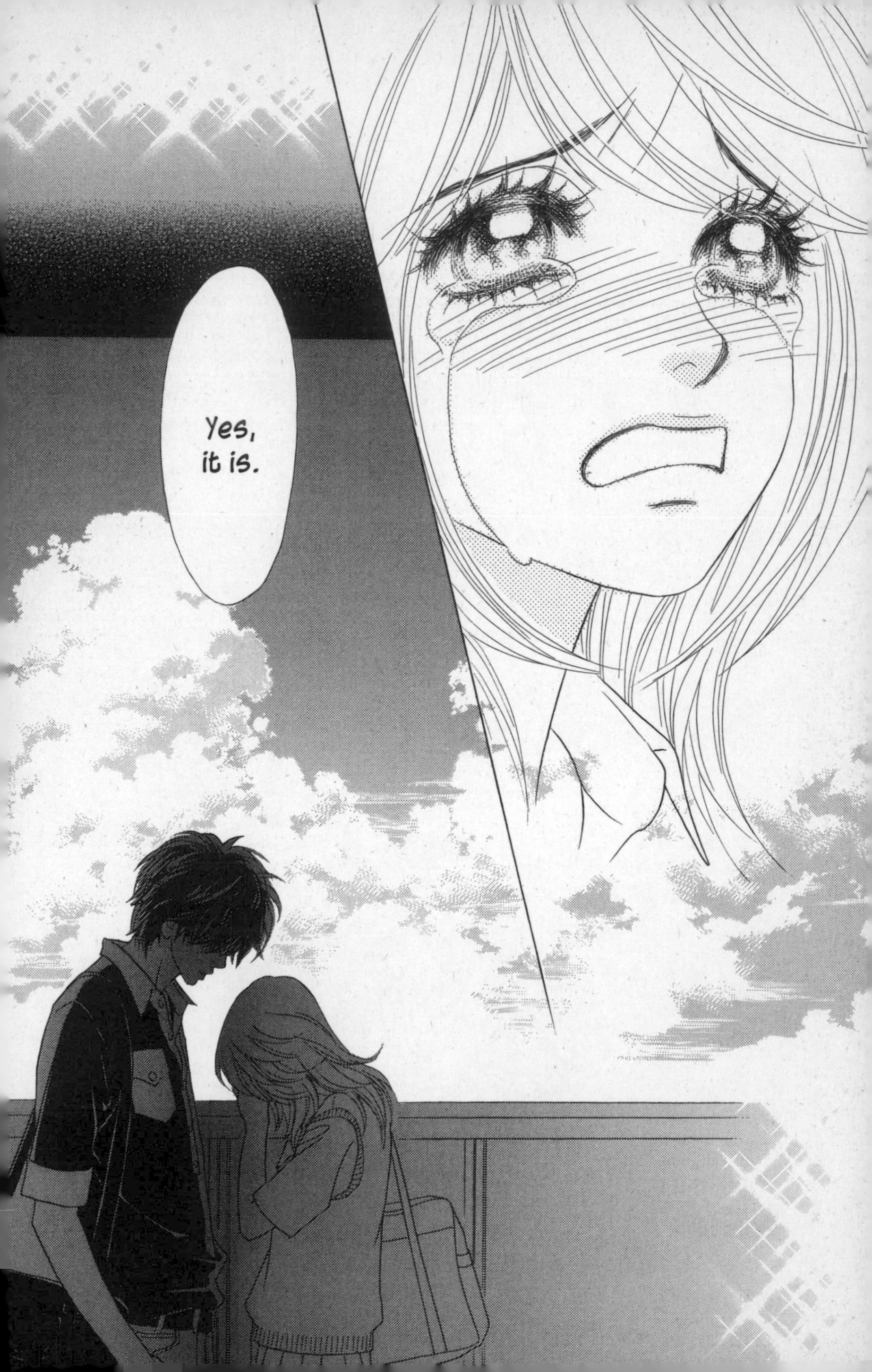
Yes, it is.

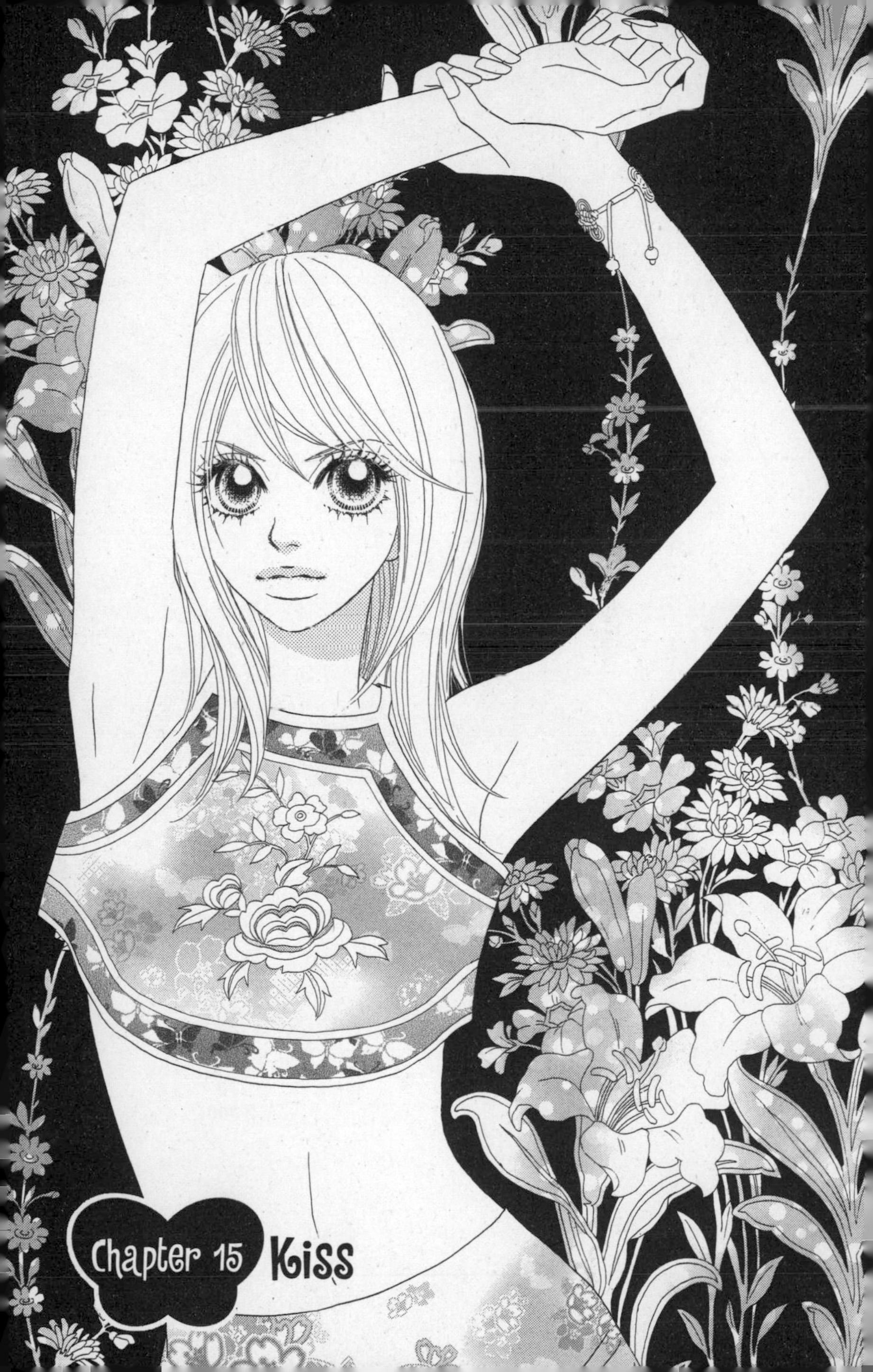
Chapter 15 Kiss

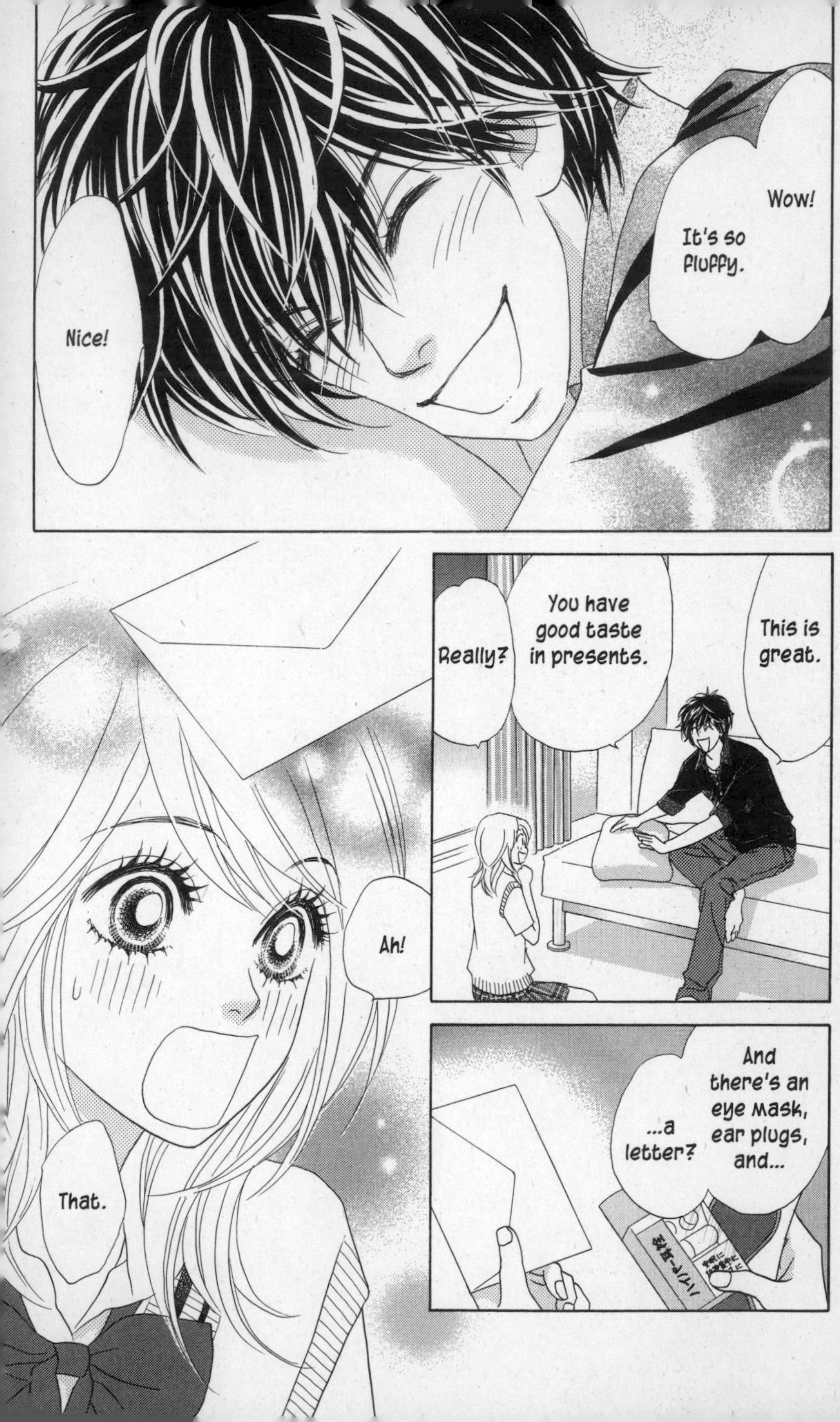

Wow!
It's so fluffy.
Nice!
This is great.
You have good taste in presents.
Really?
And there's an eye mask, ear plugs, and...
...a letter?
Ah!
That.

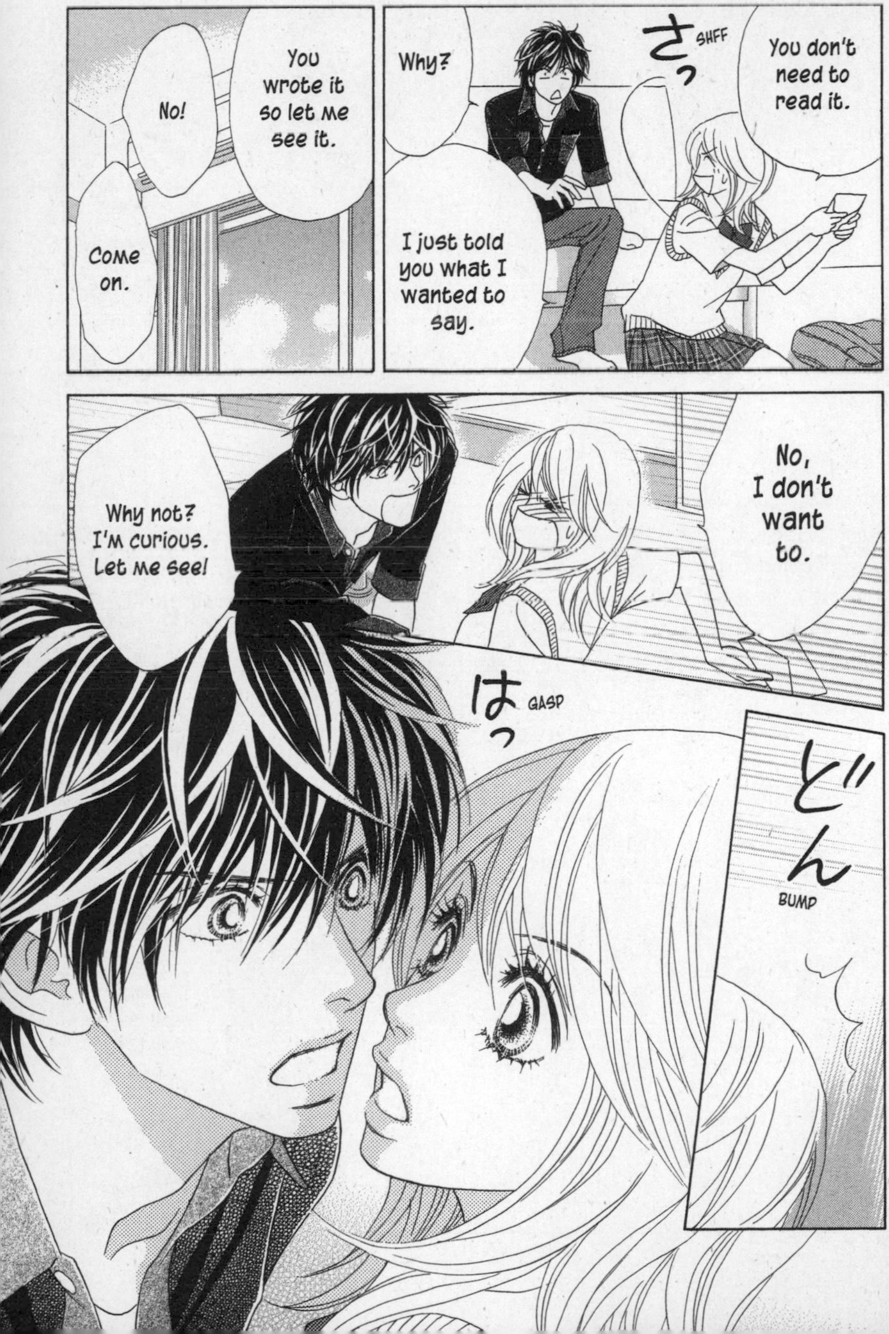
さっ
SHFF
You don't need to read it.
Why?
I just told you what I wanted to say.
You wrote it so let me see it.
No!
Come on.
No, I don't want to.
Why not? I'm curious. Let me see!
どん
BUMP
はっ
GASP

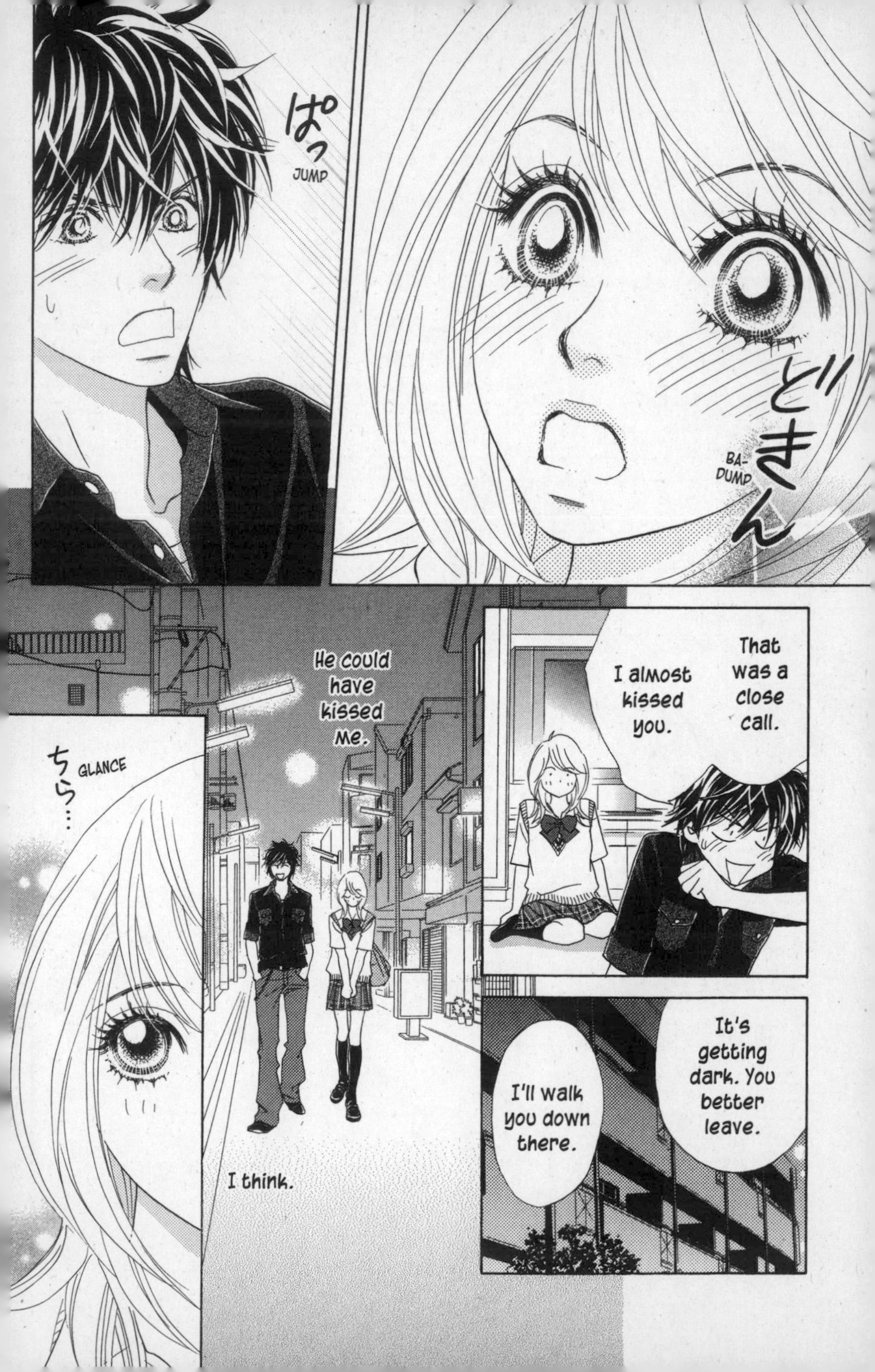
どきん
BA-DUMP
ぱっ
JUMP
That was a close call.
I almost kissed you.
It's getting dark. You better leave.
I'll walk you down there.
He could have kissed me.
I think.
ちら…
GLANCE

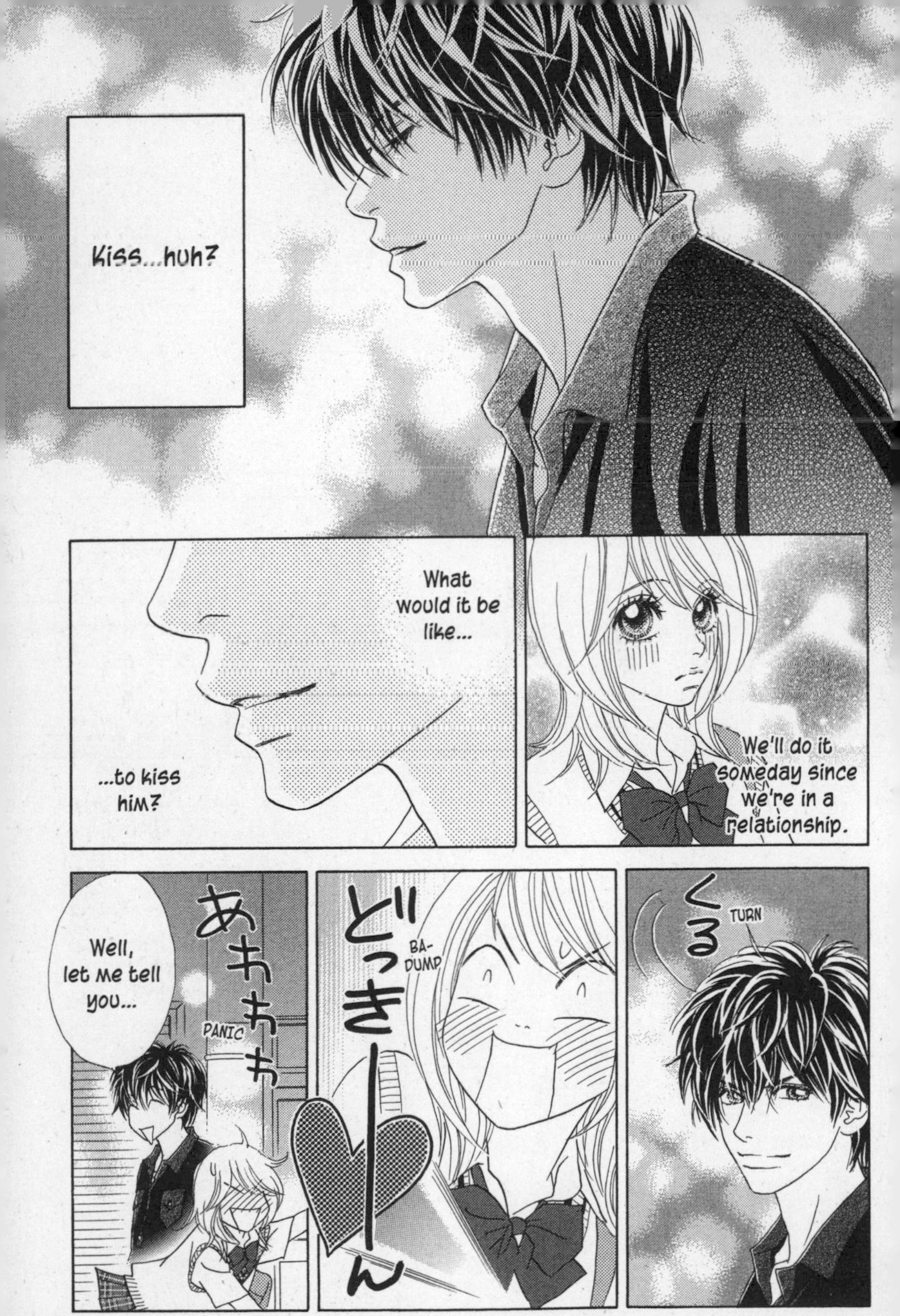
Kiss...huh?
We'll do it someday since we're in a relationship.
What would it be like...
...to kiss him?
くる
TURN
どっきーん
BA-DUMP
Well, let me tell you...
あわわわ
PANIC

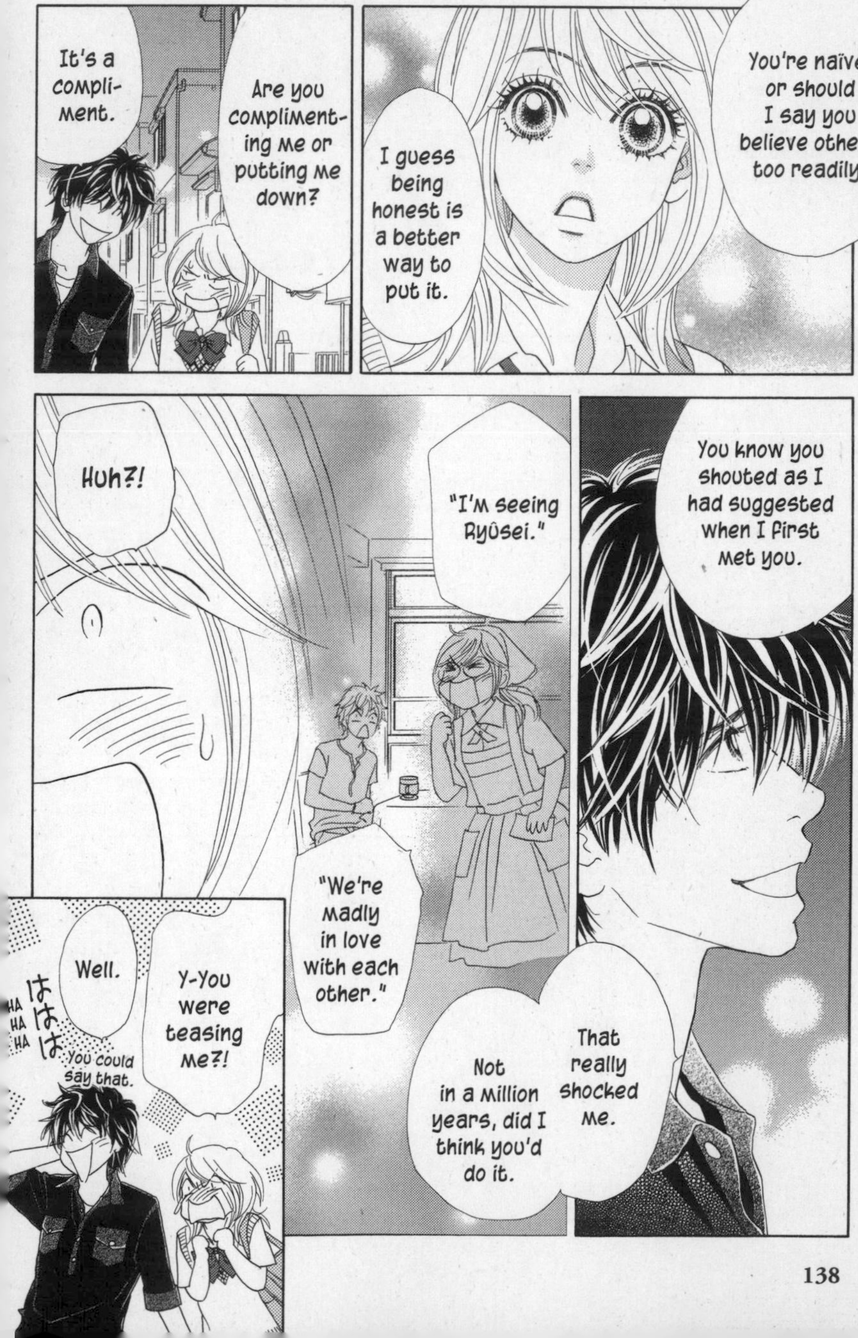
You're naïve, or should I say you believe others too readily.
I guess being honest is a better way to put it.
Are you complimenting me or putting me down?
It's a compliment.
You know you shouted as I had suggested when I first met you.
That really shocked me.
Not in a million years, did I think you'd do it.
"I'm seeing Ryûsei."
"We're madly in love with each other."
Huh?!
Y-You were teasing me?!
Well.
ははは HA HA HA
You could say that.

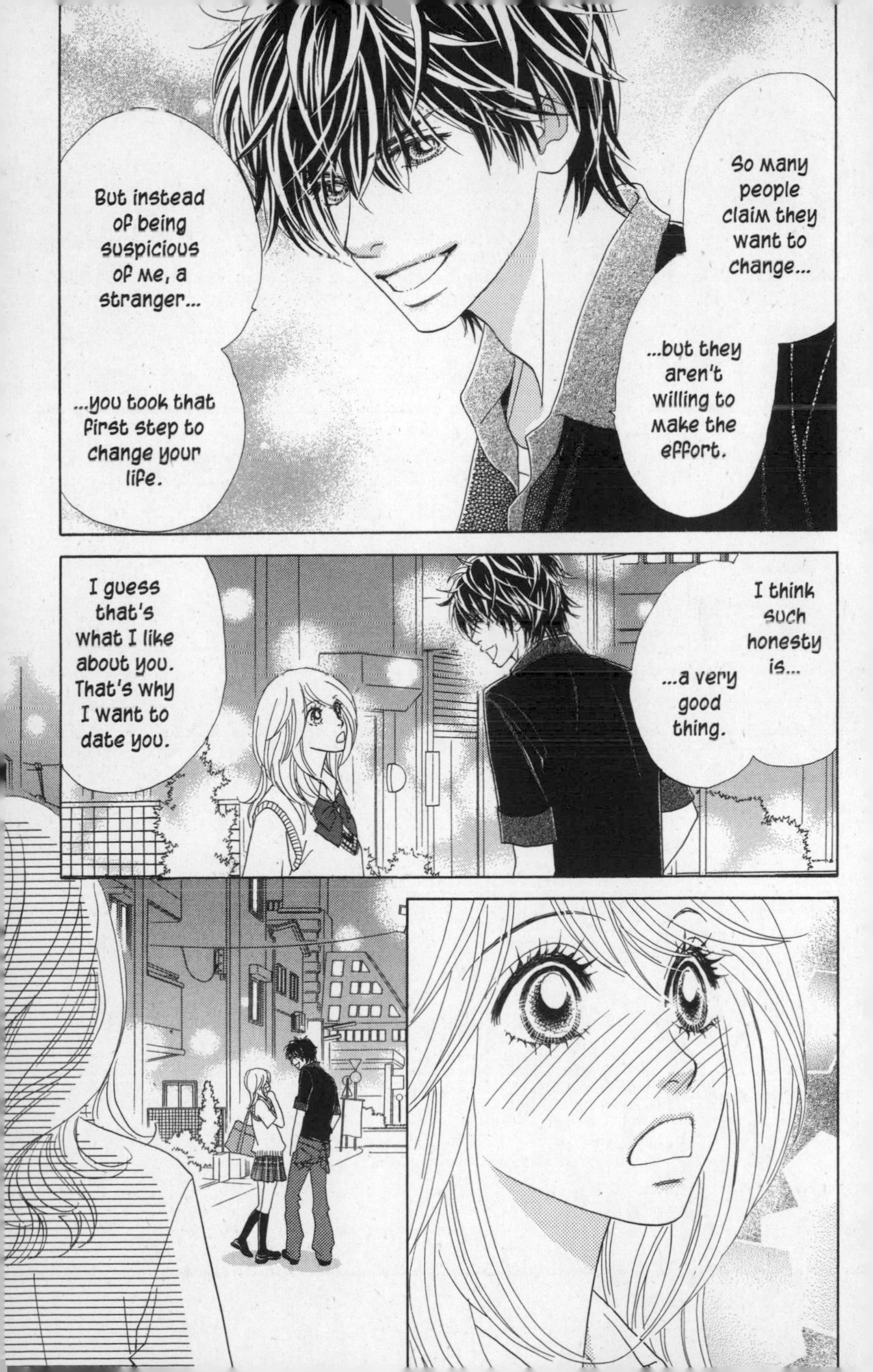
So many people claim they want to change...
...but they aren't willing to make the effort.
But instead of being suspicious of me, a stranger...
...you took that first step to change your life.
I think such honesty is...
...a very good thing.
I guess that's what I like about you. That's why I want to date you.

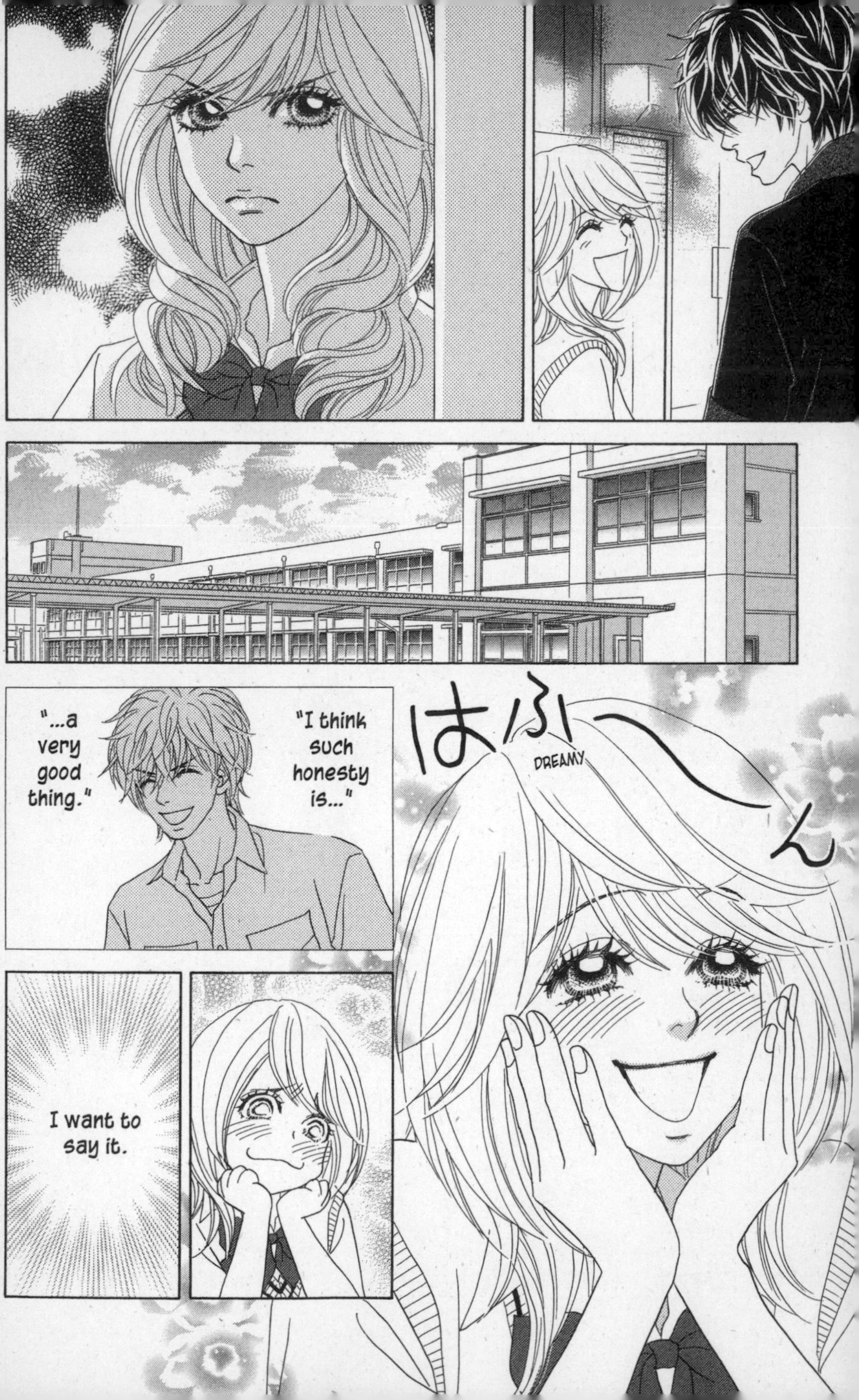
はふ～ん
DREAMY
"I think such honesty is..."
"...a very good thing."
I want to say it.

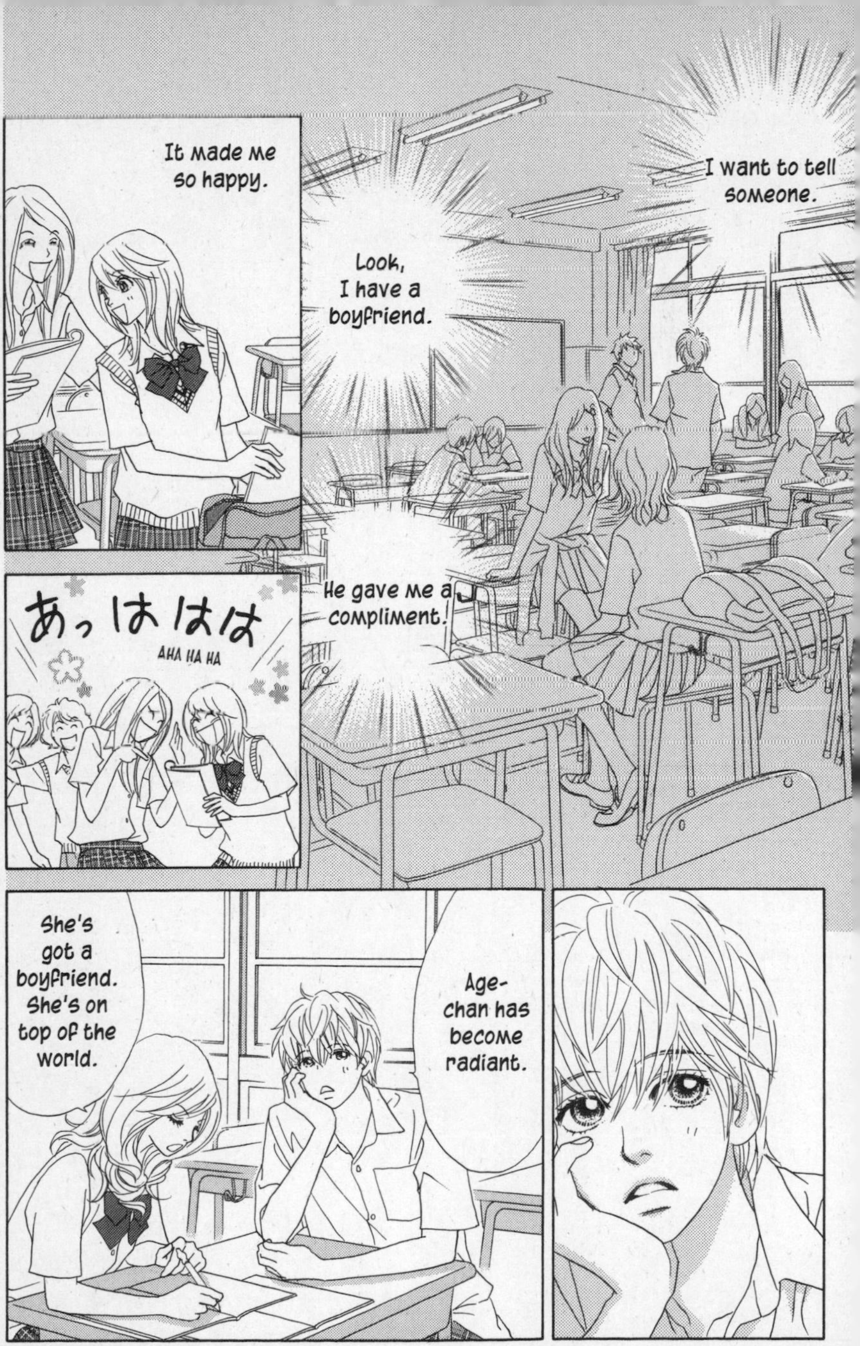
I want to tell someone.
Look, I have a boyfriend.
He gave me a compliment!
It made me so happy.
あっははは
AHA HA HA
Age-chan has become radiant.
She's got a boyfriend. She's on top of the world.

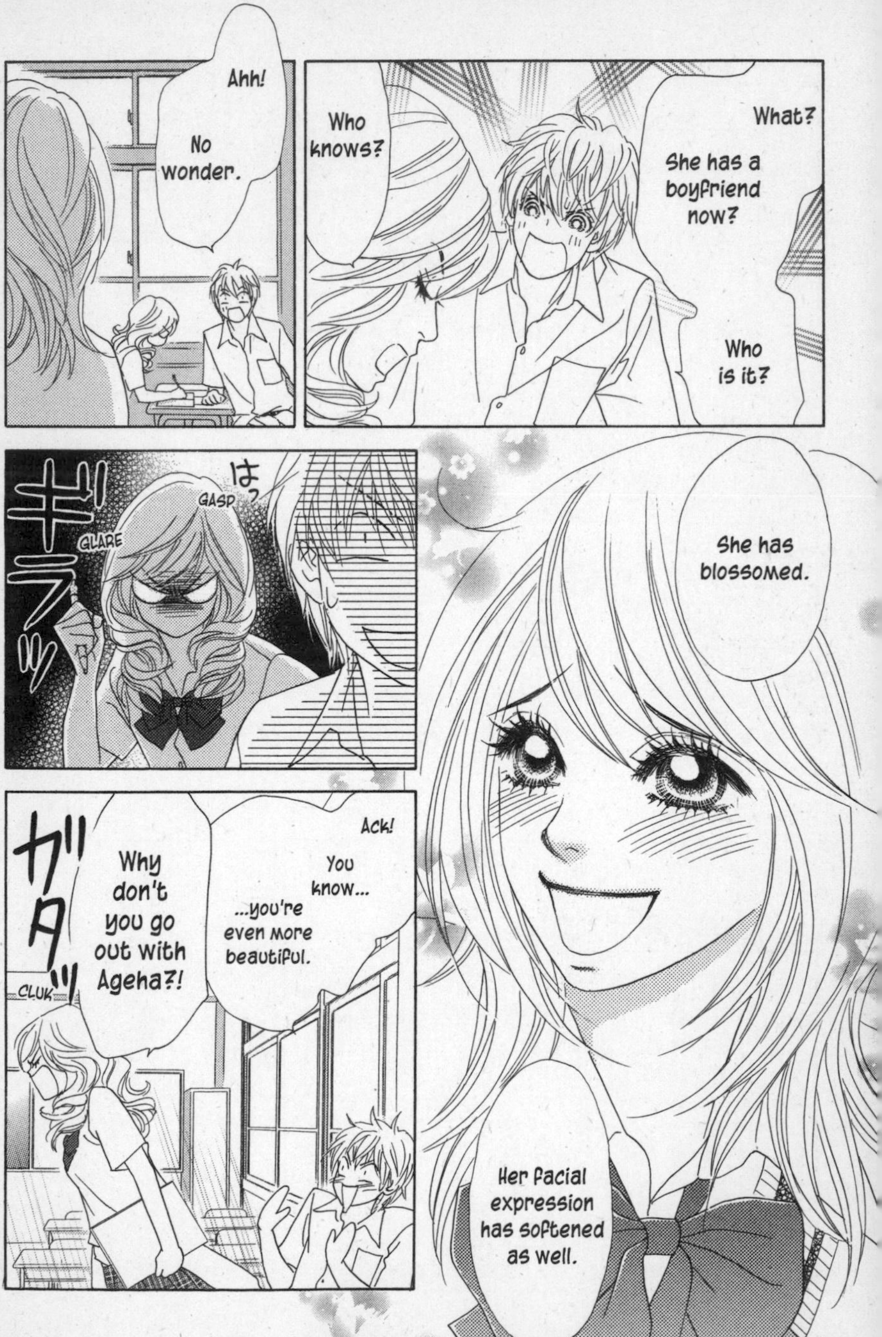
What?
She has a boyfriend now?
Who is it?
Who knows?
Ahh!
No wonder.
She has blossomed.
Her facial expression has softened as well.
はっ
GASP
ギラッ
GLARE
Ack!
You know...
...you're even more beautiful.
Why don't you go out with Ageha?!
ガタッ
CLUK

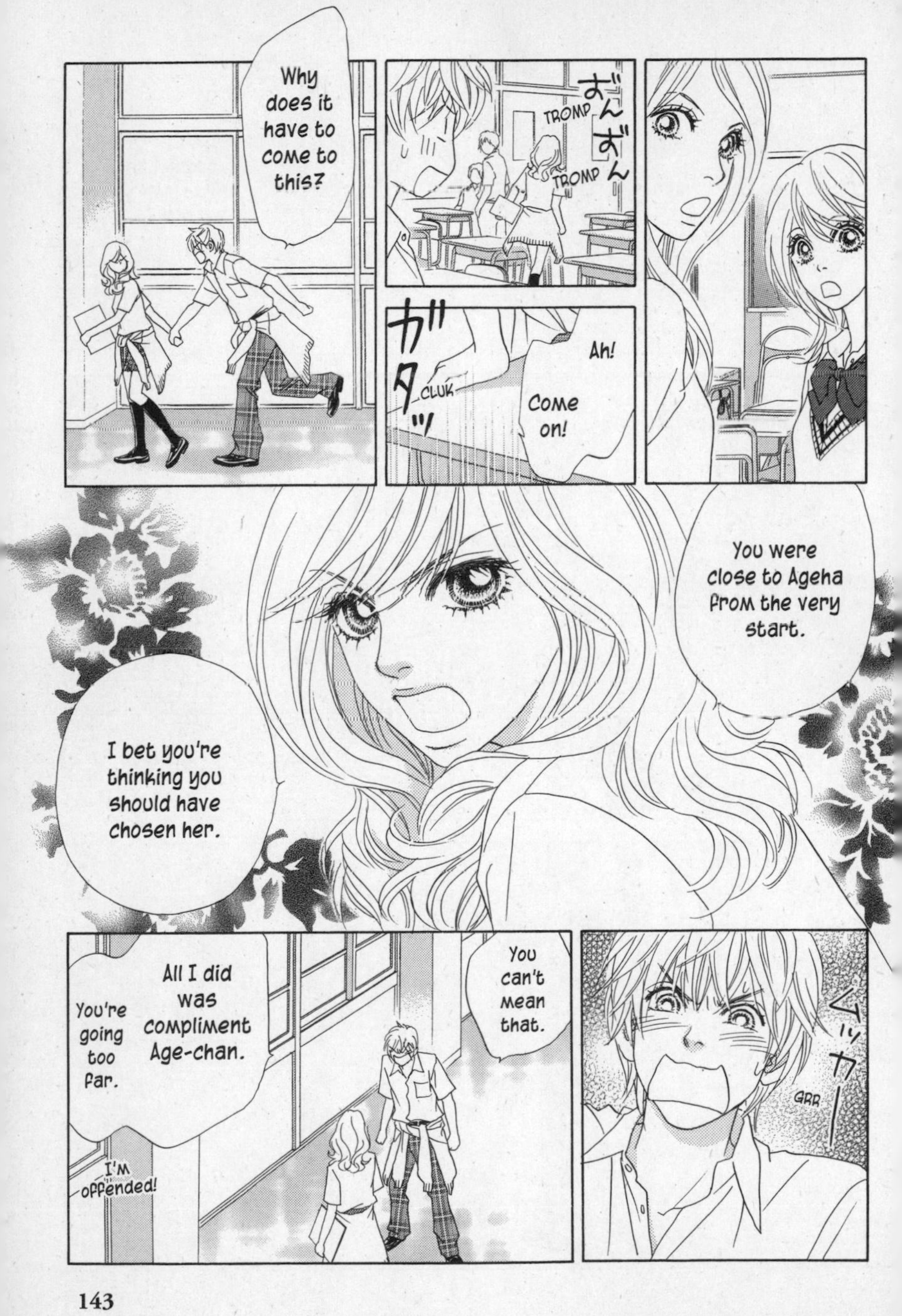
ずんずん
TROMP
TROMP
ガタッ
CLUK
Ah!
Come on!
Why does it have to come to this?
You were close to Ageha from the very start.
I bet you're thinking you should have chosen her.
ムッカー
GRR
You can't mean that.
All I did was compliment Age-chan.
You're going too far.
I'm offended!

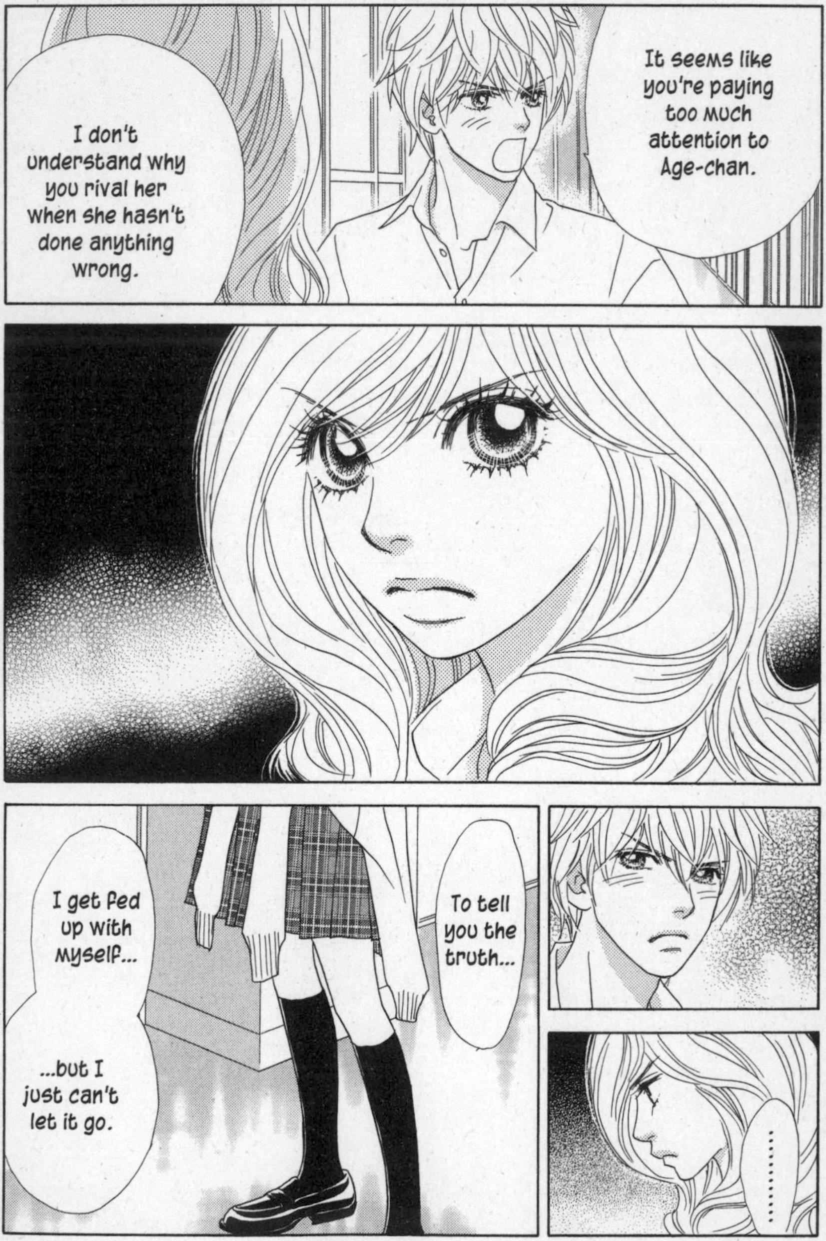
It seems like you're paying too much attention to Age-chan.
I don't understand why you rival her when she hasn't done anything wrong.
......
To tell you the truth...
I get fed up with myself...
...but I just can't let it go.

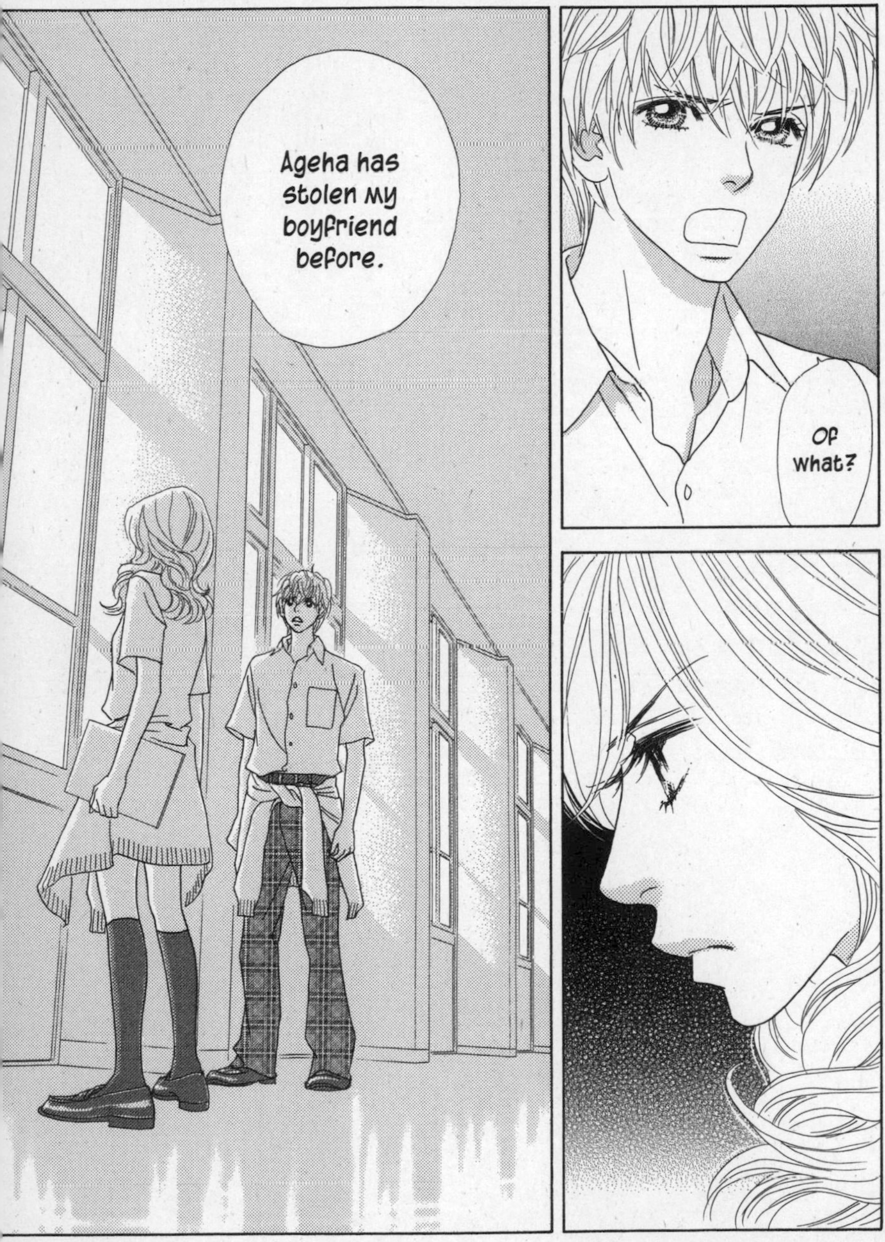
Of what?
Ageha has stolen my boyfriend before.

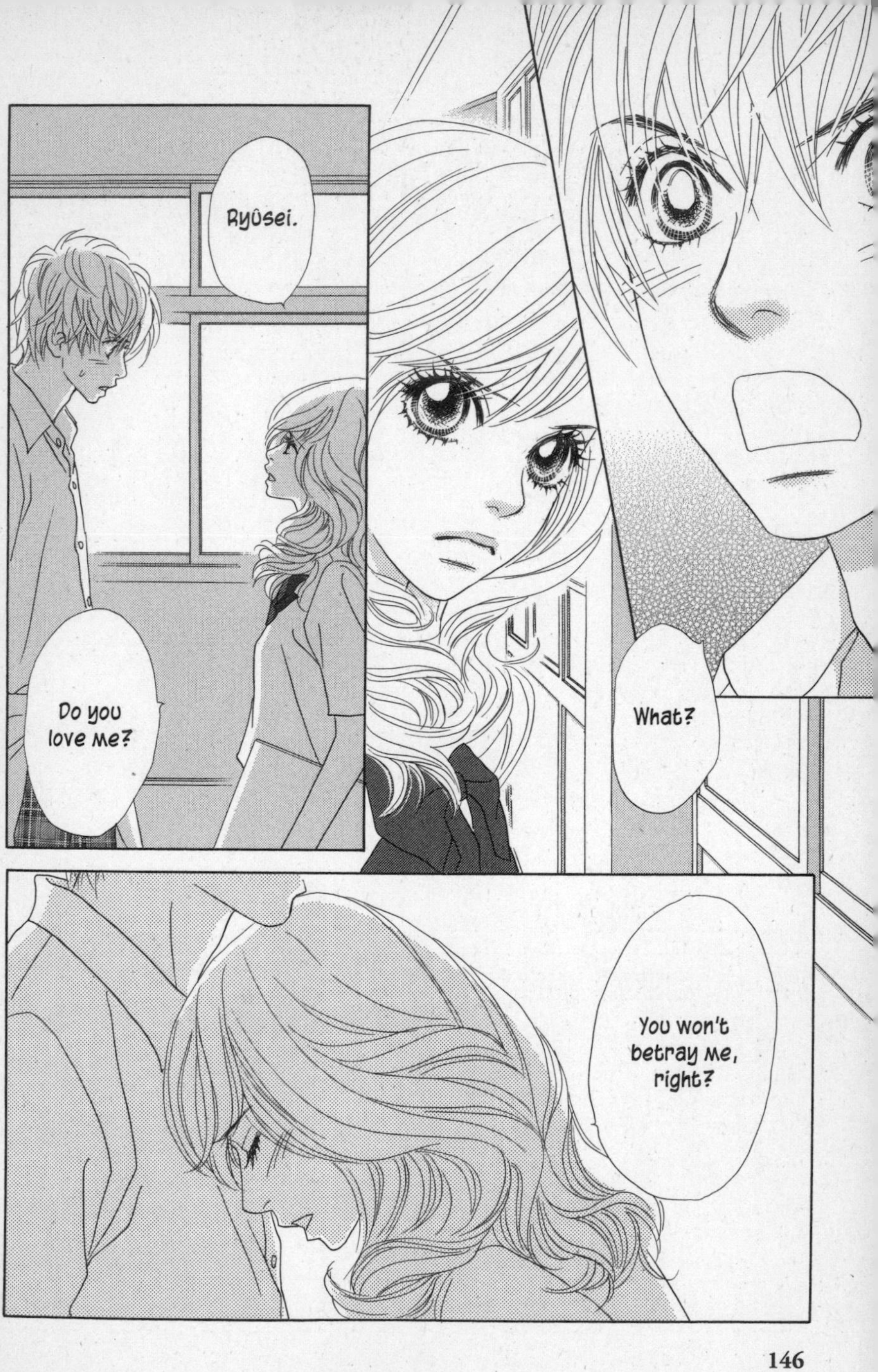
What?
Ryûsei.
Do you love me?
You won't betray me, right?

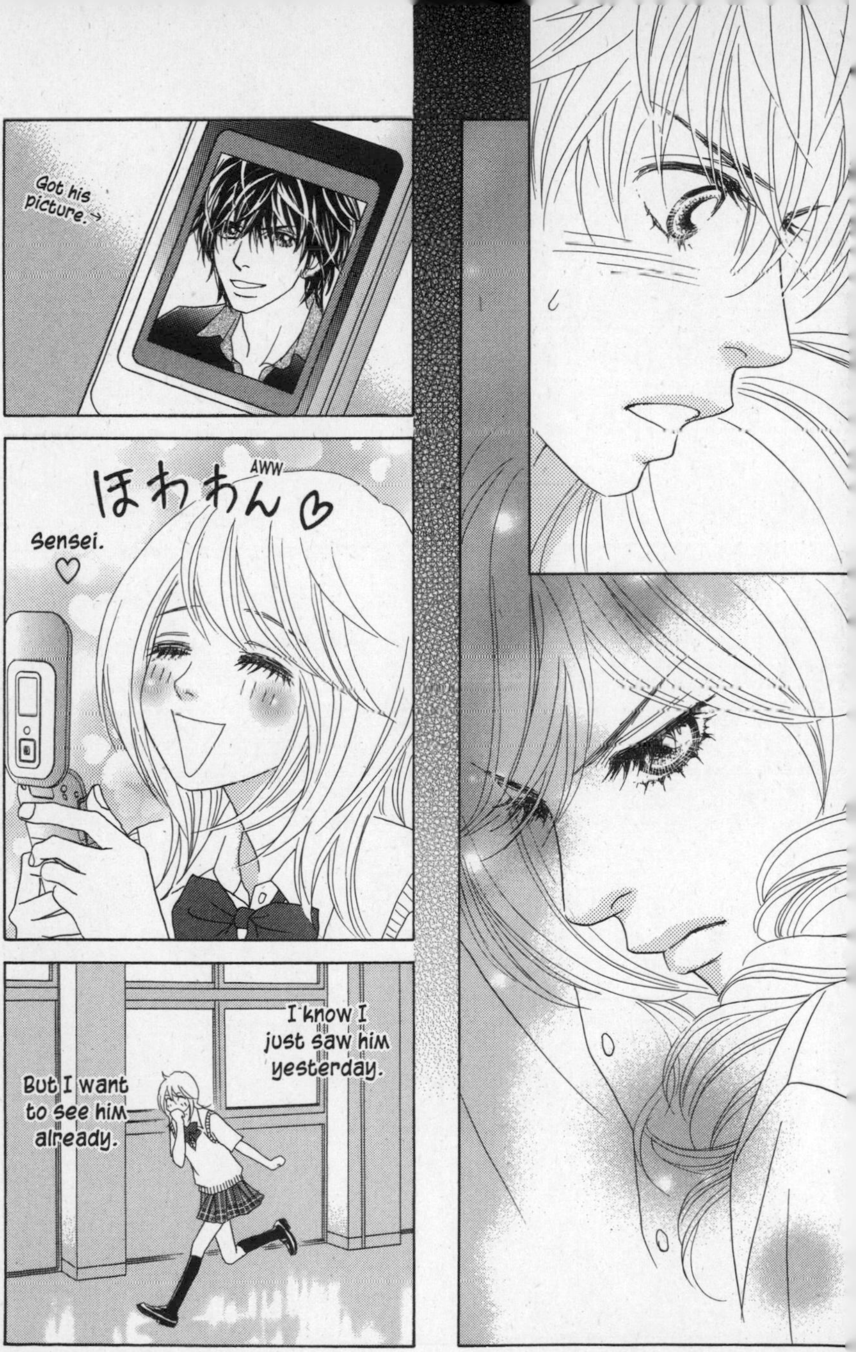
Got his picture.→
ほわわん
AWW
Sensei. ♡
I know I just saw him yesterday.
But I want to see him already.

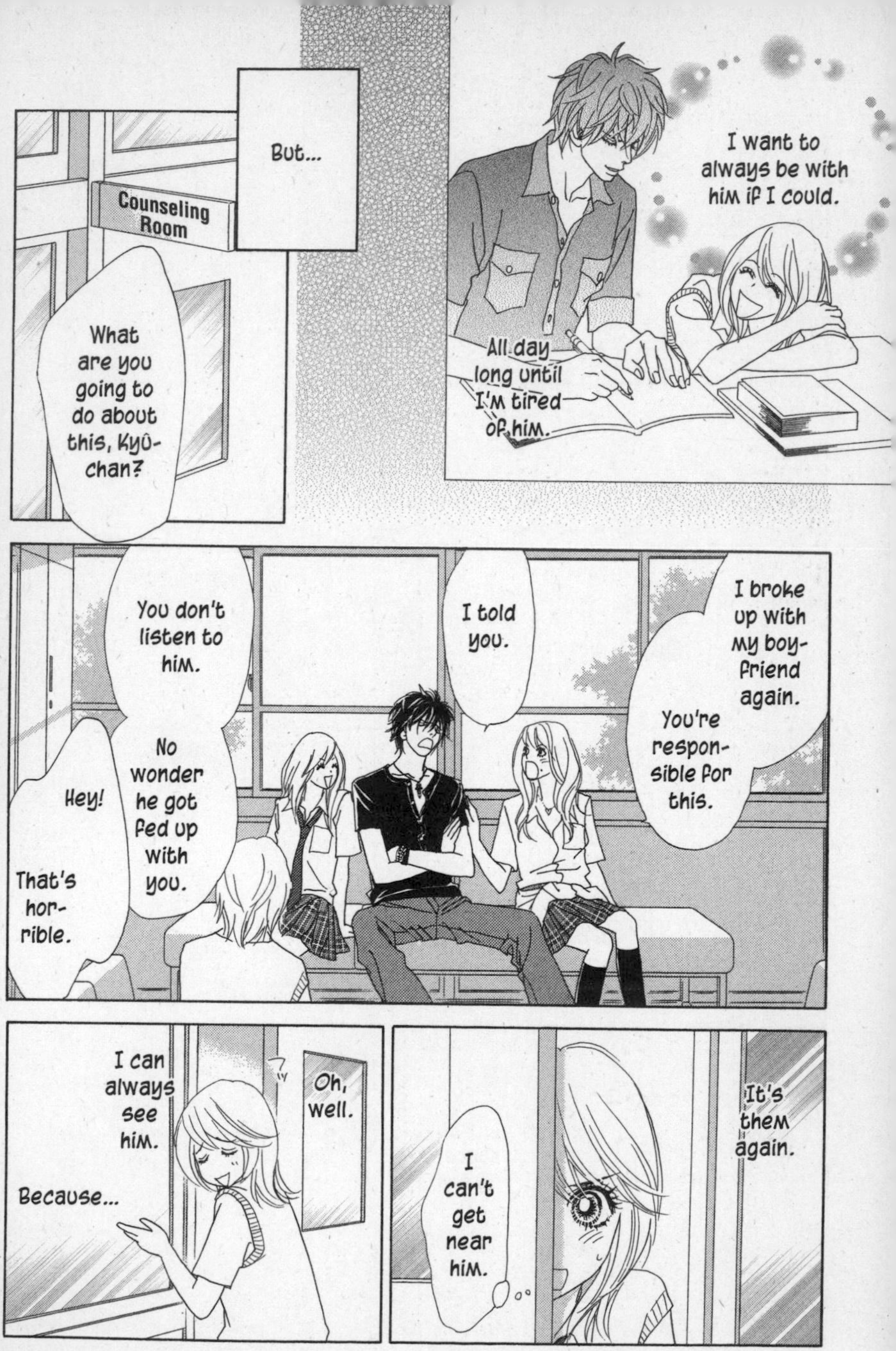
I want to always be with him if I could.
All day long until I'm tired of him.
But...
Counseling Room
What are you going to do about this, Kyû-chan?
I broke up with my boy-friend again.
You're respon-sible for this.
I told you.
You don't listen to him.
No wonder he got fed up with you.
Hey!
That's hor-rible.
It's them again.
I can't get near him.
Oh, well.
I can always see him.
Because...

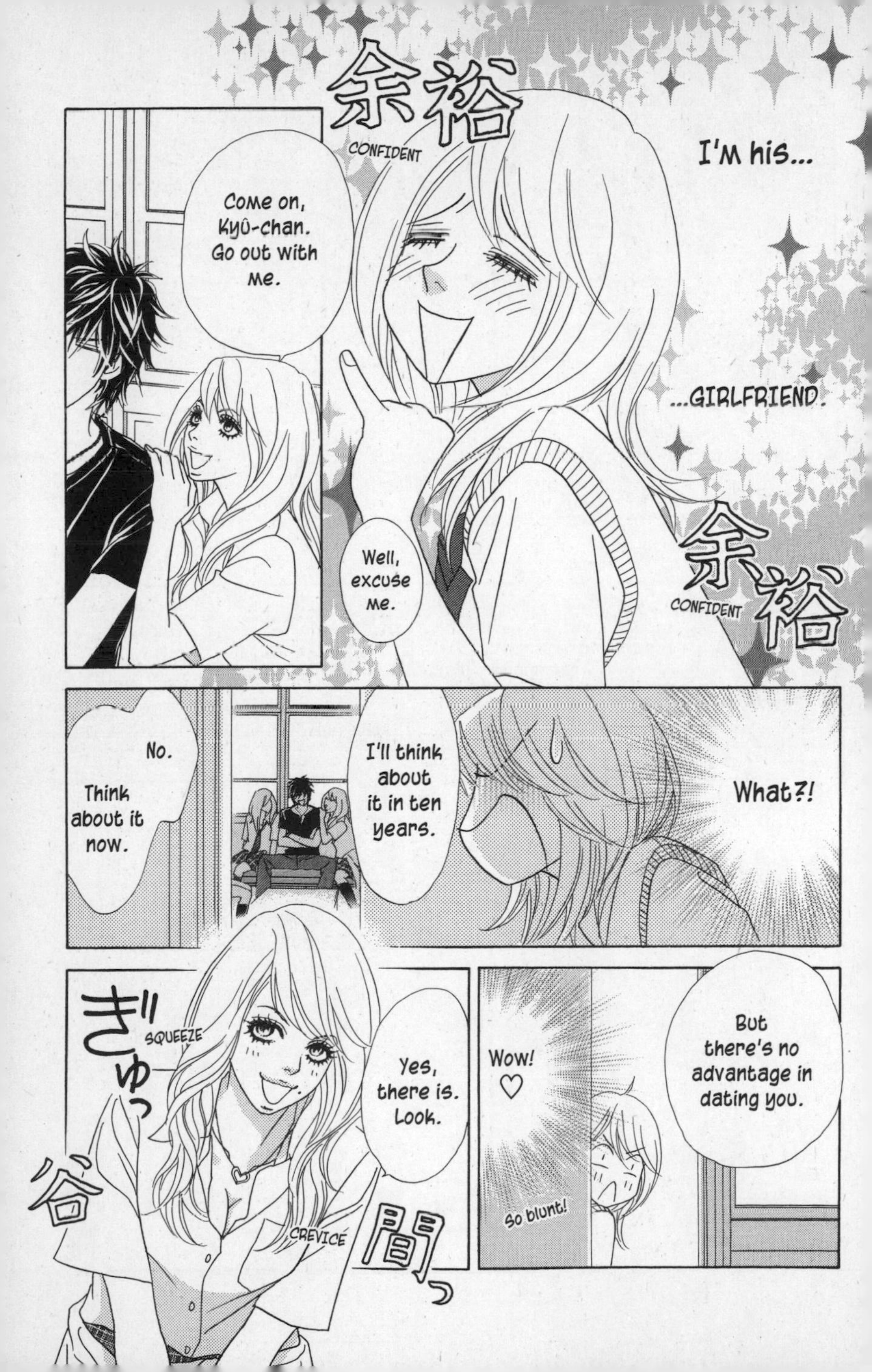
余裕
CONFIDENT
I'M his...
...GIRLFRIEND.
Well, excuse me.
余裕
CONFIDENT
Come on, Kyû-chan. Go out with me.
What?!
I'll think about it in ten years.
No.
Think about it now.
But there's no advantage in dating you.
Wow! ♡
So blunt!
Yes, there is. Look.
ぎゅっ
SQUEEZE
谷間っ
CREVICE

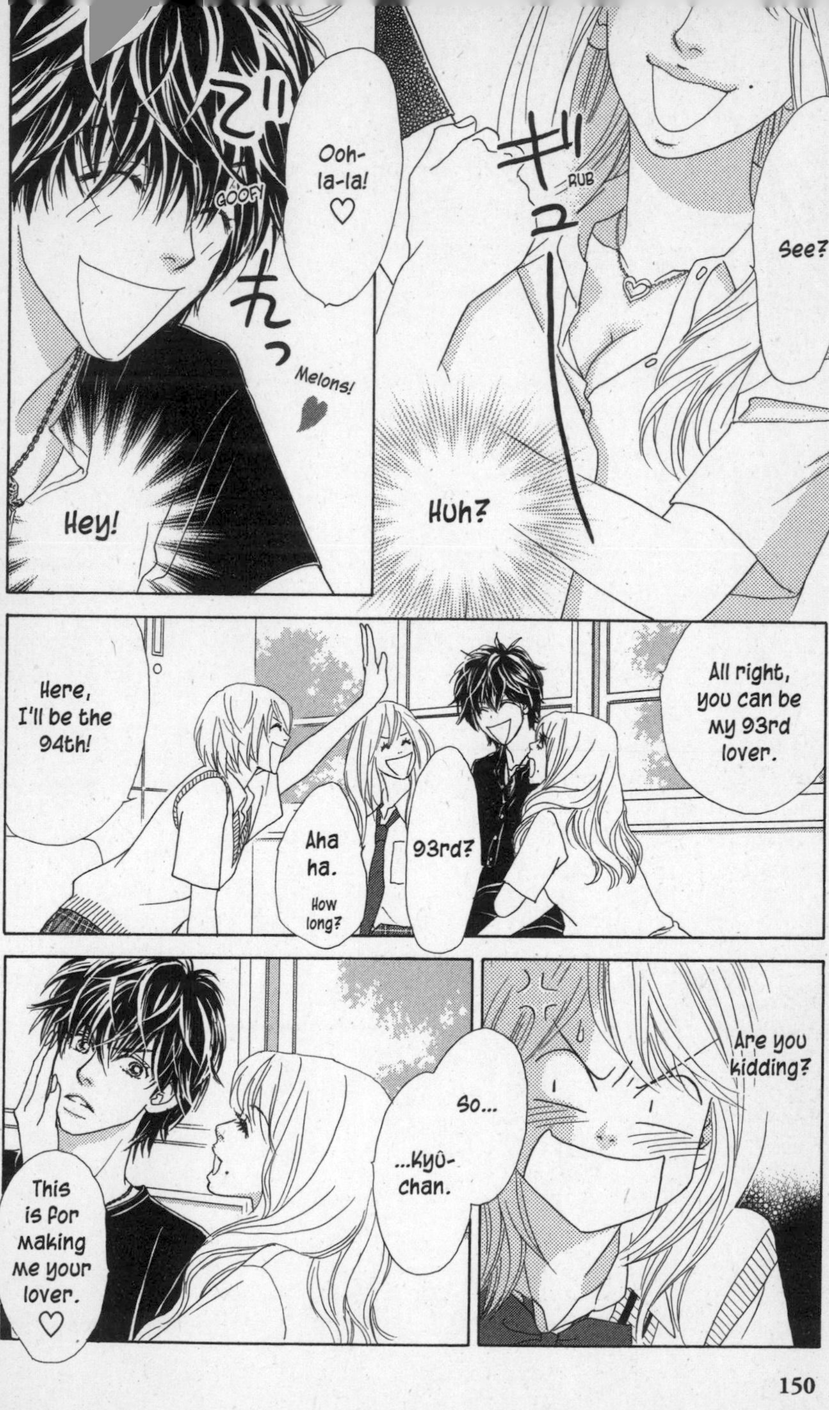
See?
RUB
Huh?
Ooh-la-la! ♡
GOOFY
Melons! ♥
Hey!
All right, you can be my 93rd lover.
93rd?
Aha ha.
How long?
Here, I'll be the 94th!
Are you kidding?
So...
...Kyû-chan.
This is for making me your lover. ♡

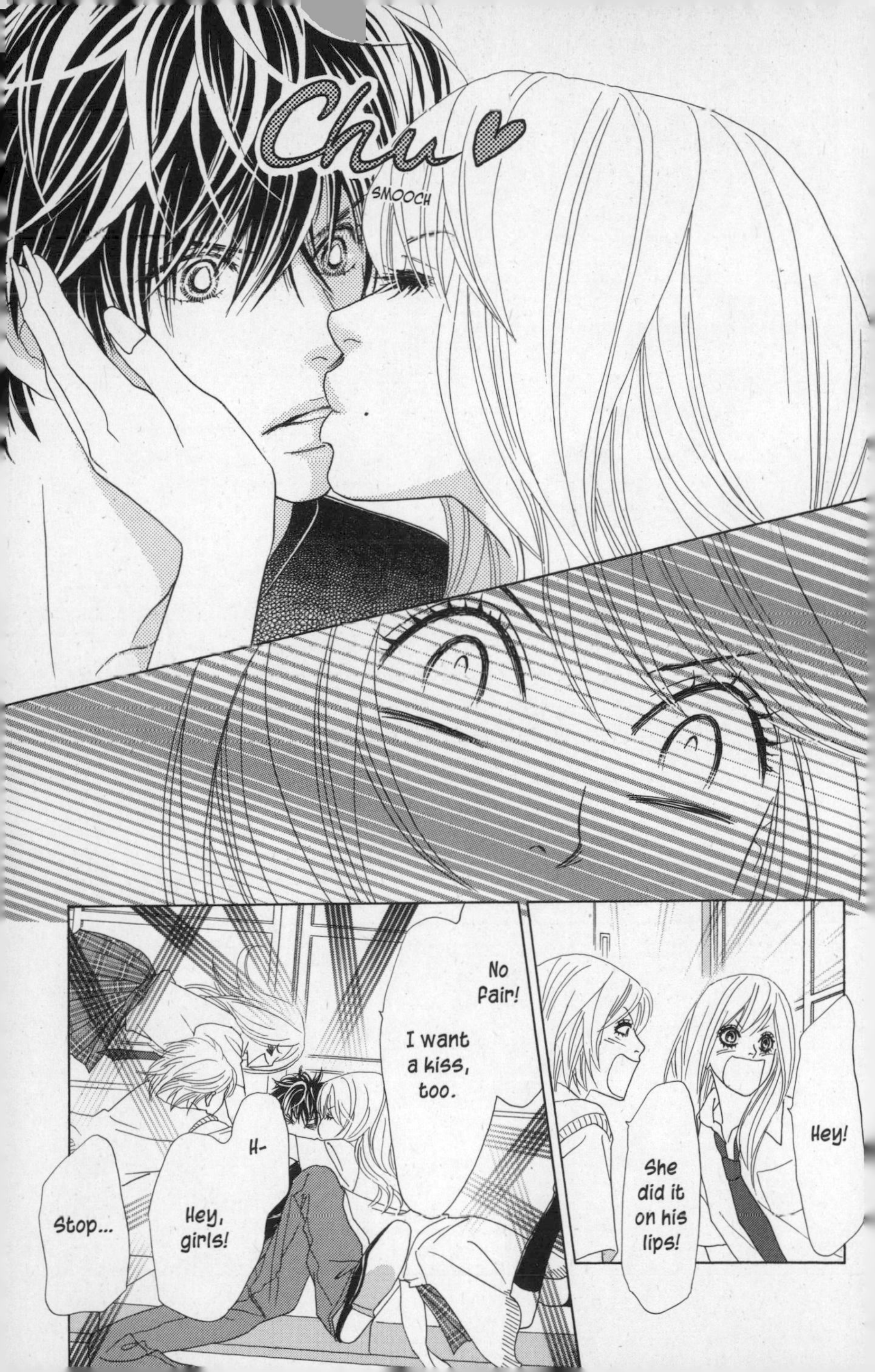
Chu♥
SMOOCH
Hey!
She did it on his lips!
No fair!
I want a kiss, too.
H-
Hey, girls!
Stop...

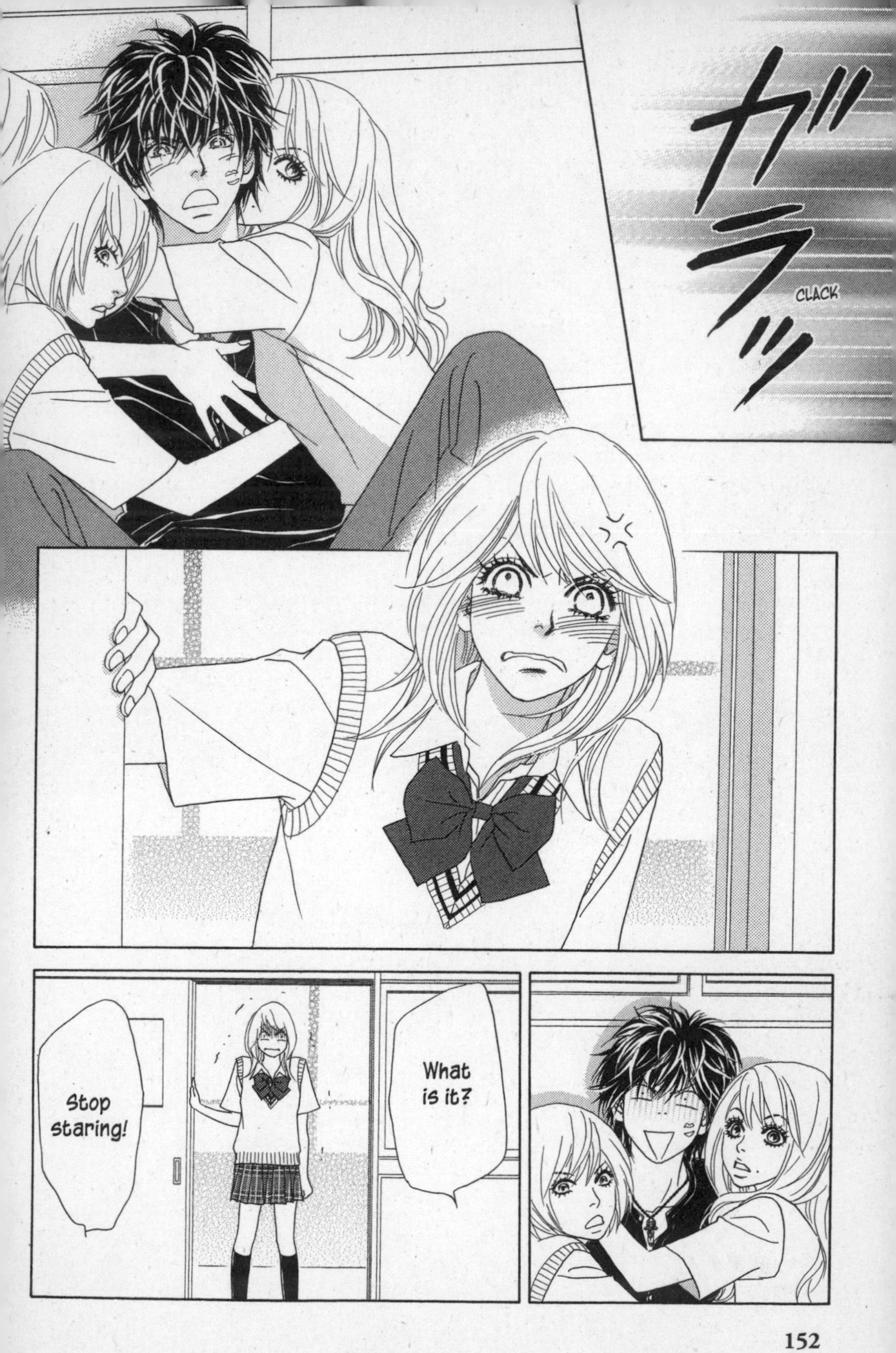
ガラッ
CLACK
What is it?
Stop staring!

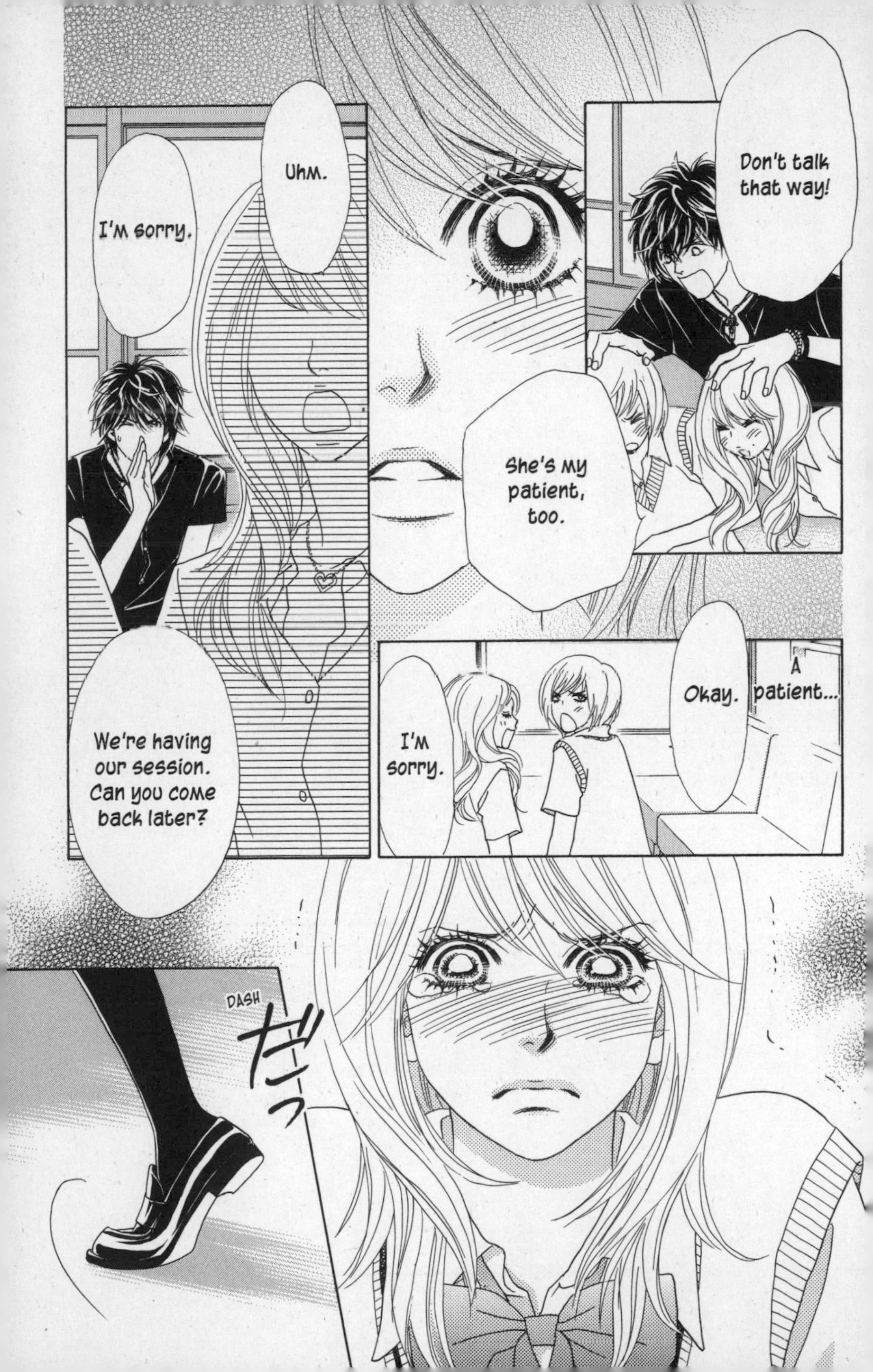
Don't talk that way!
She's my patient, too.
Uhm.
I'm sorry.
A patient...
Okay.
I'm sorry.
We're having our session. Can you come back later?
DASH
だっ

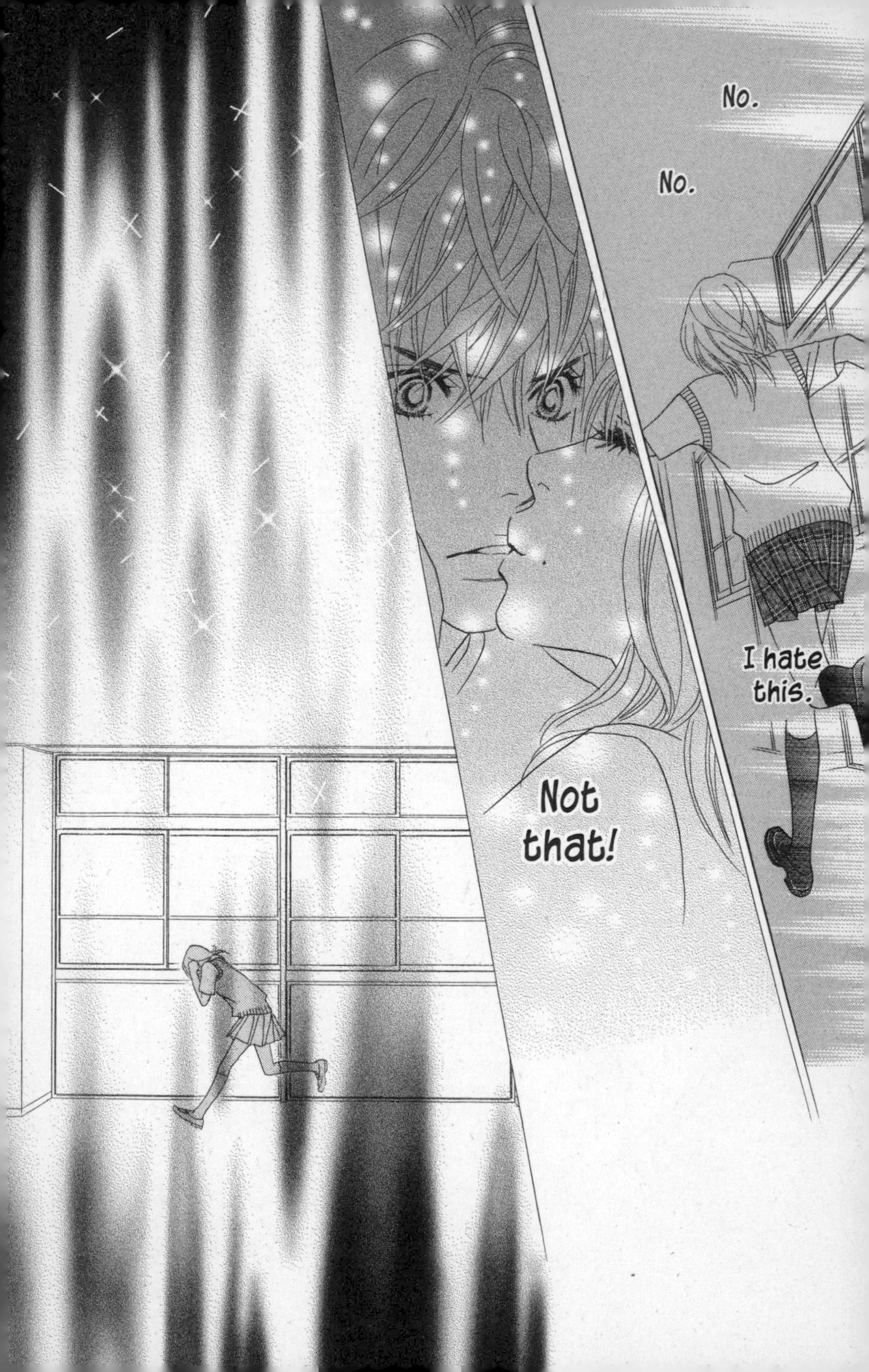
No.
No.
I hate this.
Not that!

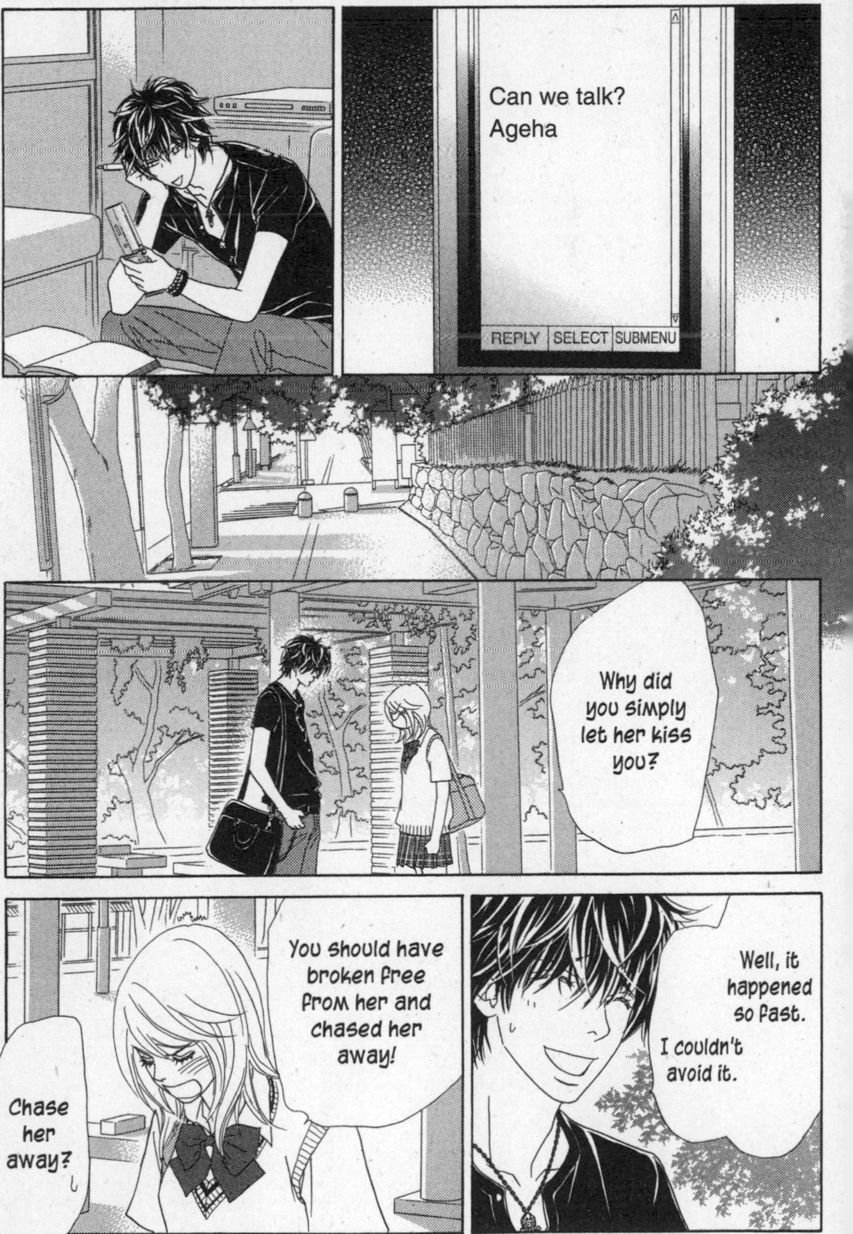
Can we talk?
Ageha
REPLY
SELECT
SUBMENU
Why did you simply let her kiss you?
Well, it happened so fast.
I couldn't avoid it.
You should have broken free from her and chased her away!
Chase her away?

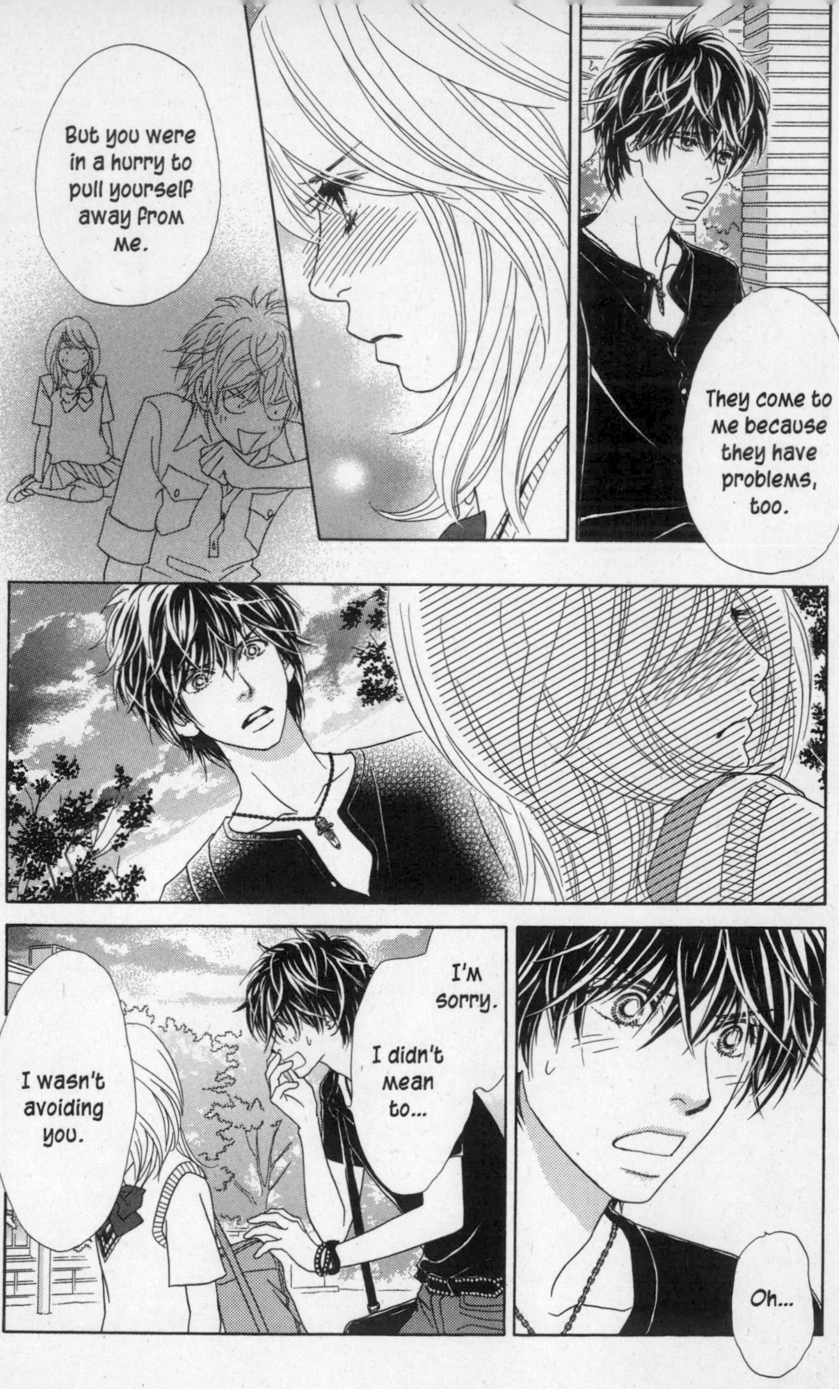
They come to me because they have problems, too.
But you were in a hurry to pull yourself away from me.
Oh...
I'm sorry.
I didn't mean to...
I wasn't avoiding you.

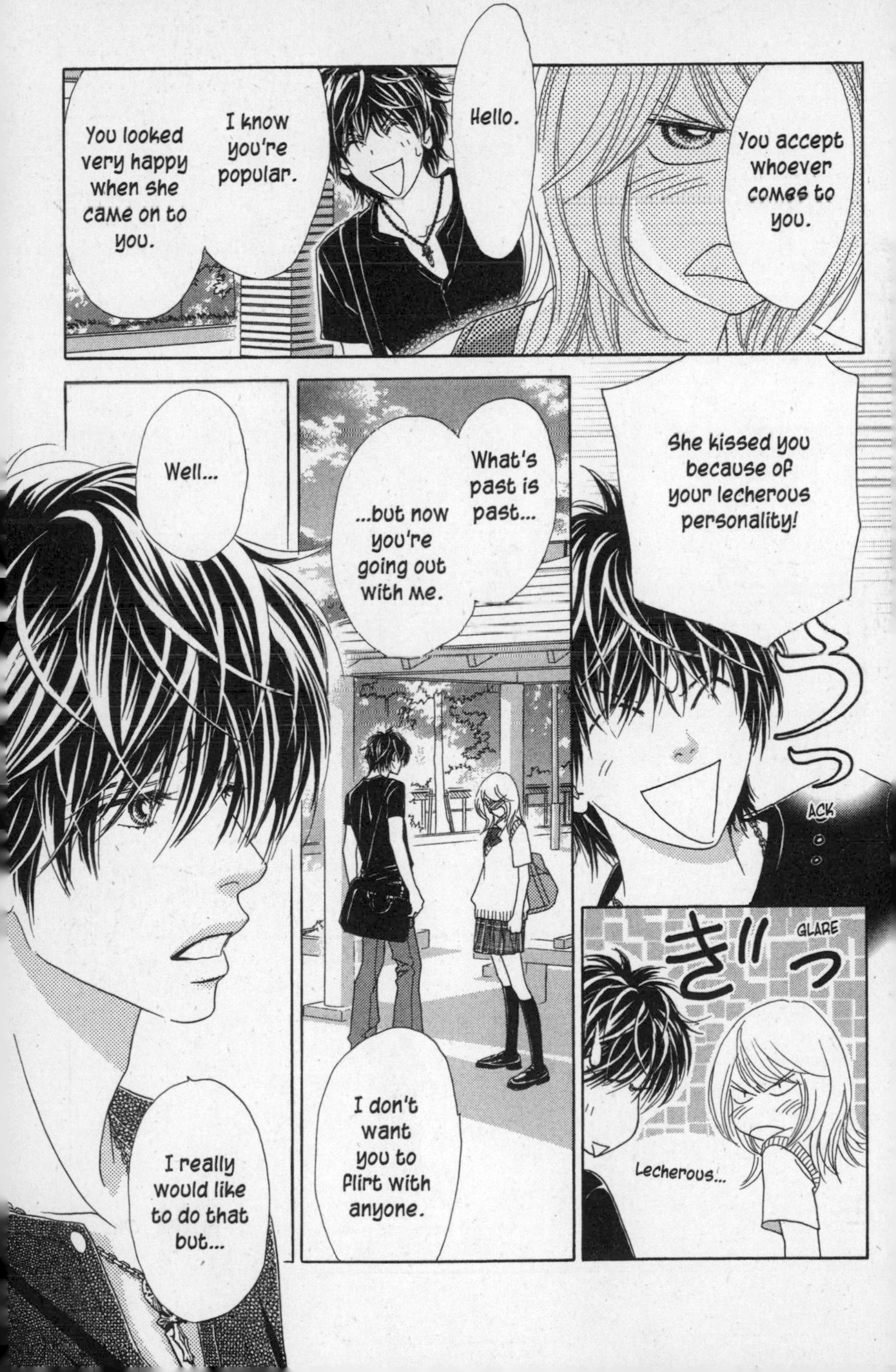
You accept whoever comes to you.
Hello.
I know you're popular.
You looked very happy when she came on to you.
She kissed you because of your lecherous personality!
うっ
ACK
きっ
GLARE
Lecherous...
What's past is past...
...but now you're going out with me.
I don't want you to flirt with anyone.
Well...
I really would like to do that but...

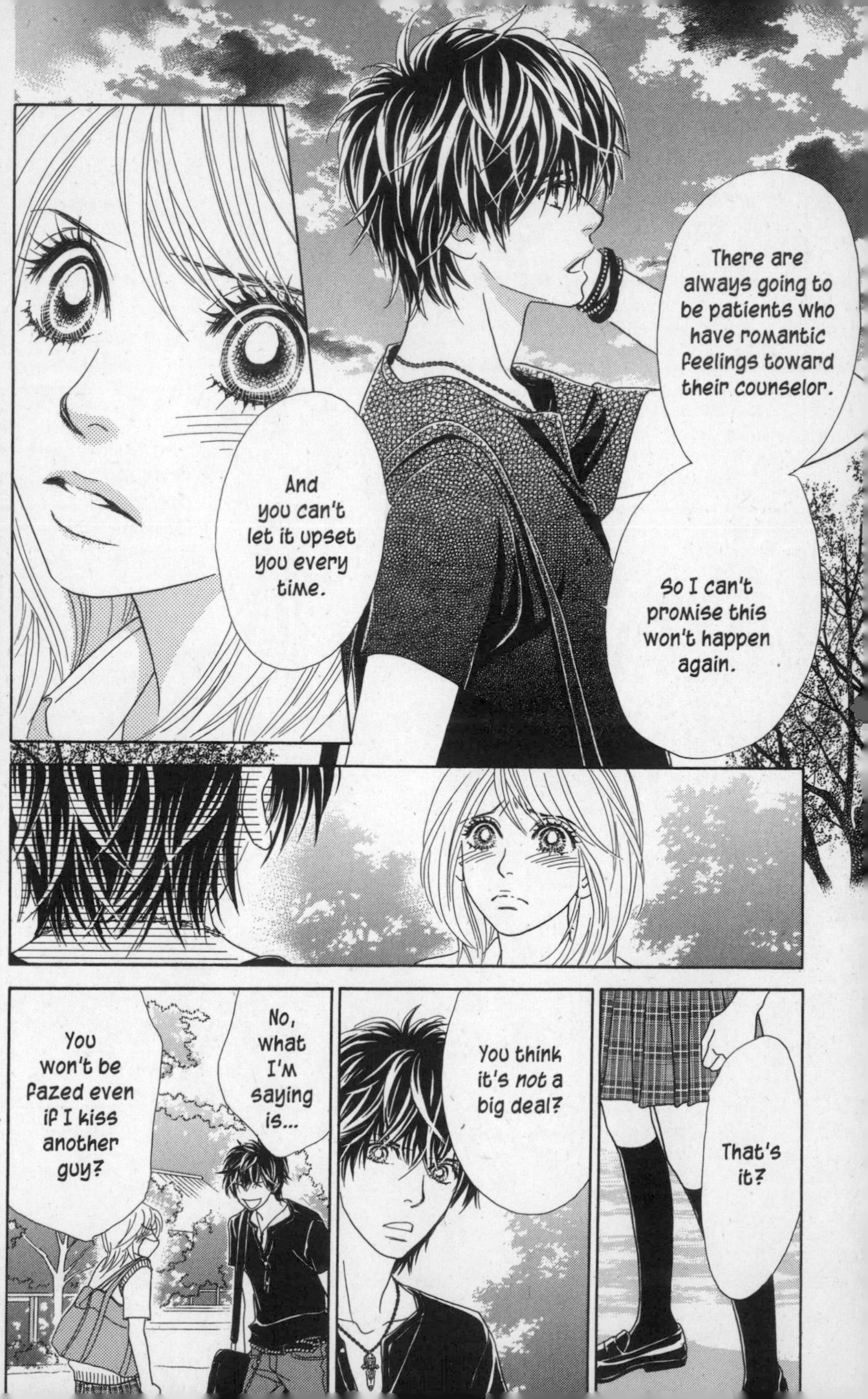
There are always going to be patients who have romantic feelings toward their counselor.
So I can't promise this won't happen again.
And you can't let it upset you every time.
That's it?
You think it's *not* a big deal?
No, what I'M saying is...
You won't be fazed even if I kiss another guy?

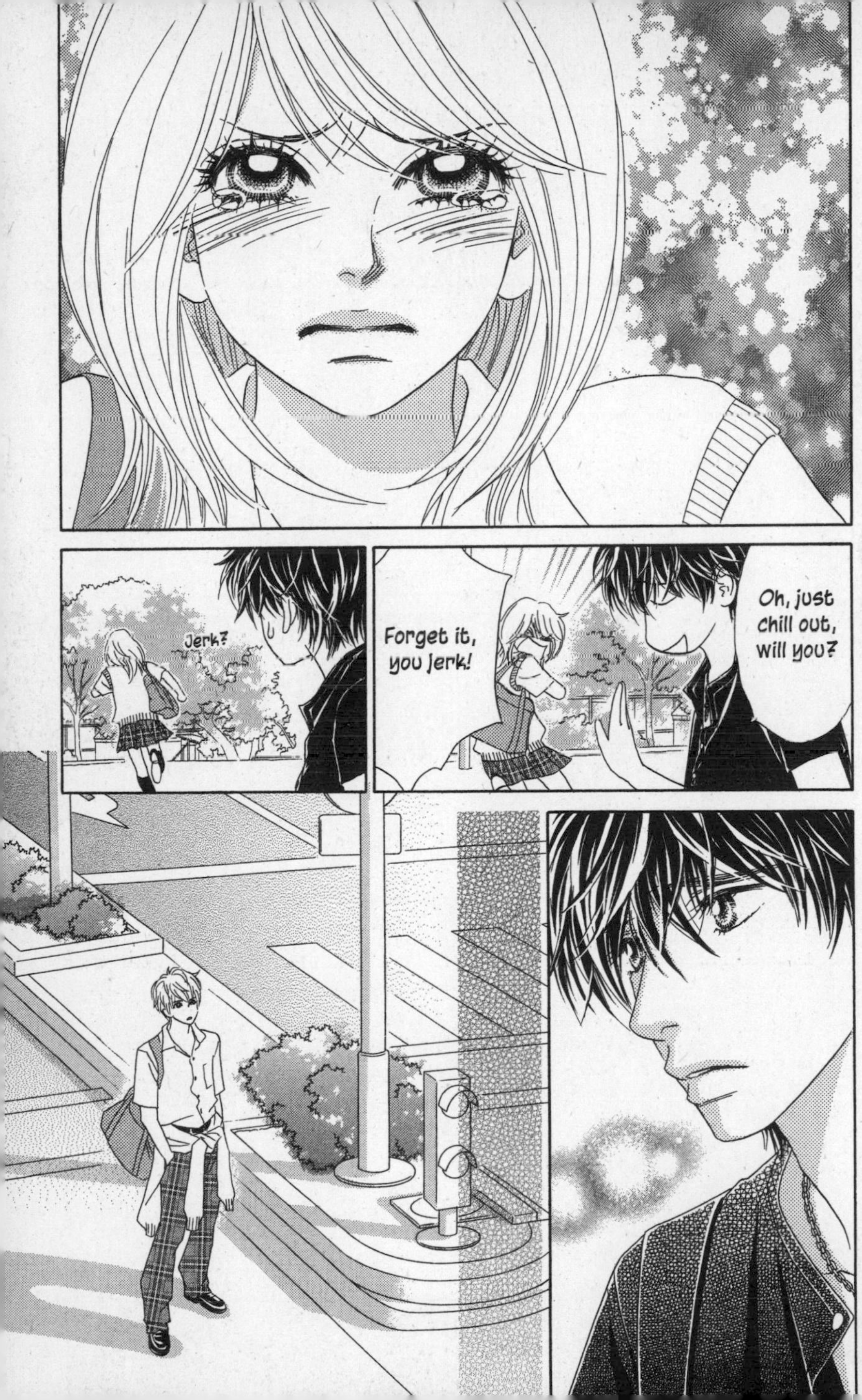
Oh, just chill out, will you?
Forget it, you jerk!
Jerk?

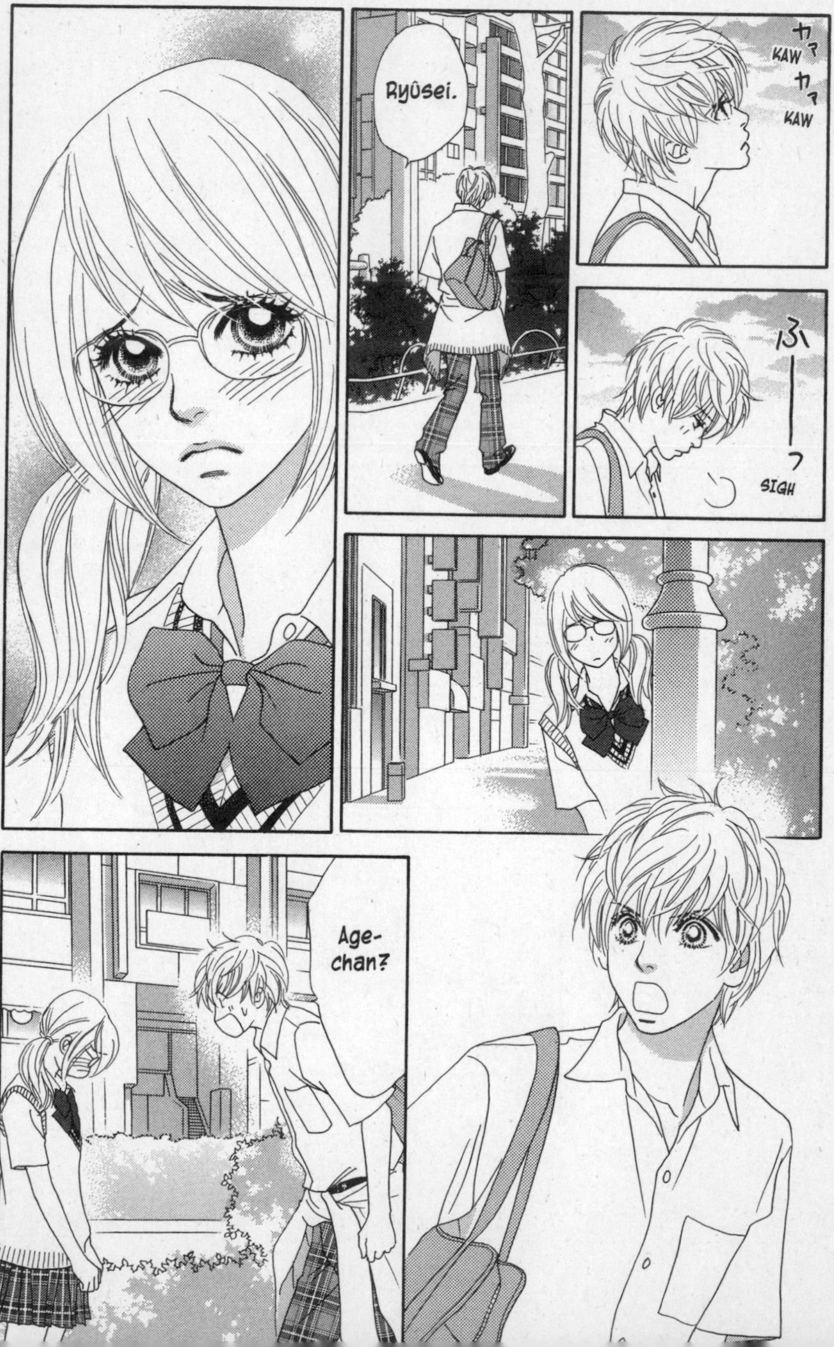
KAW
KAW
SIGH
Ryûsei.
Age-chan?

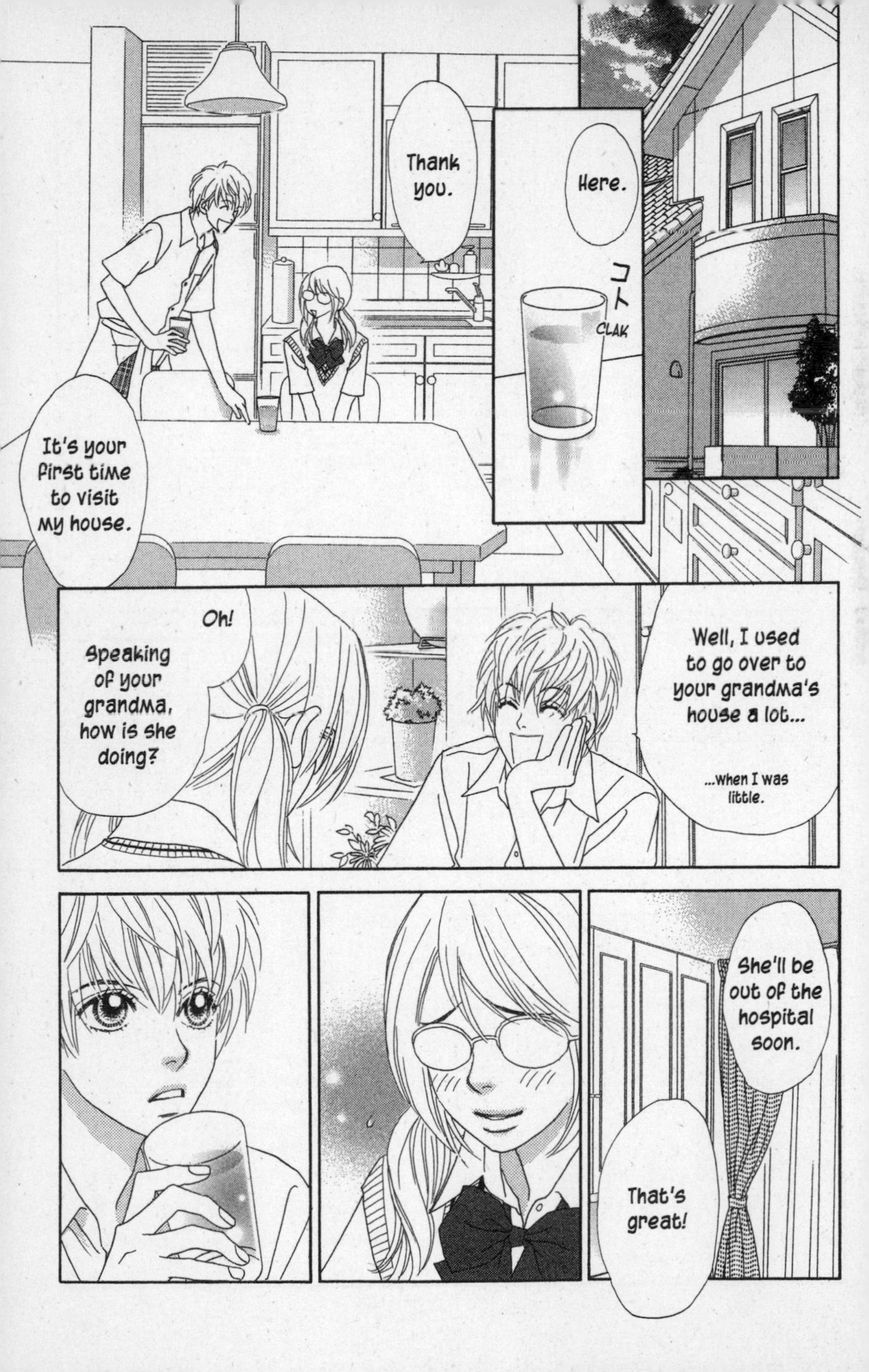
Here.
コト
CLAK
Thank you.
It's your first time to visit my house.
Well, I used to go over to your grandma's house a lot...
...when I was little.
Oh!
Speaking of your grandma, how is she doing?
She'll be out of the hospital soon.
That's great!

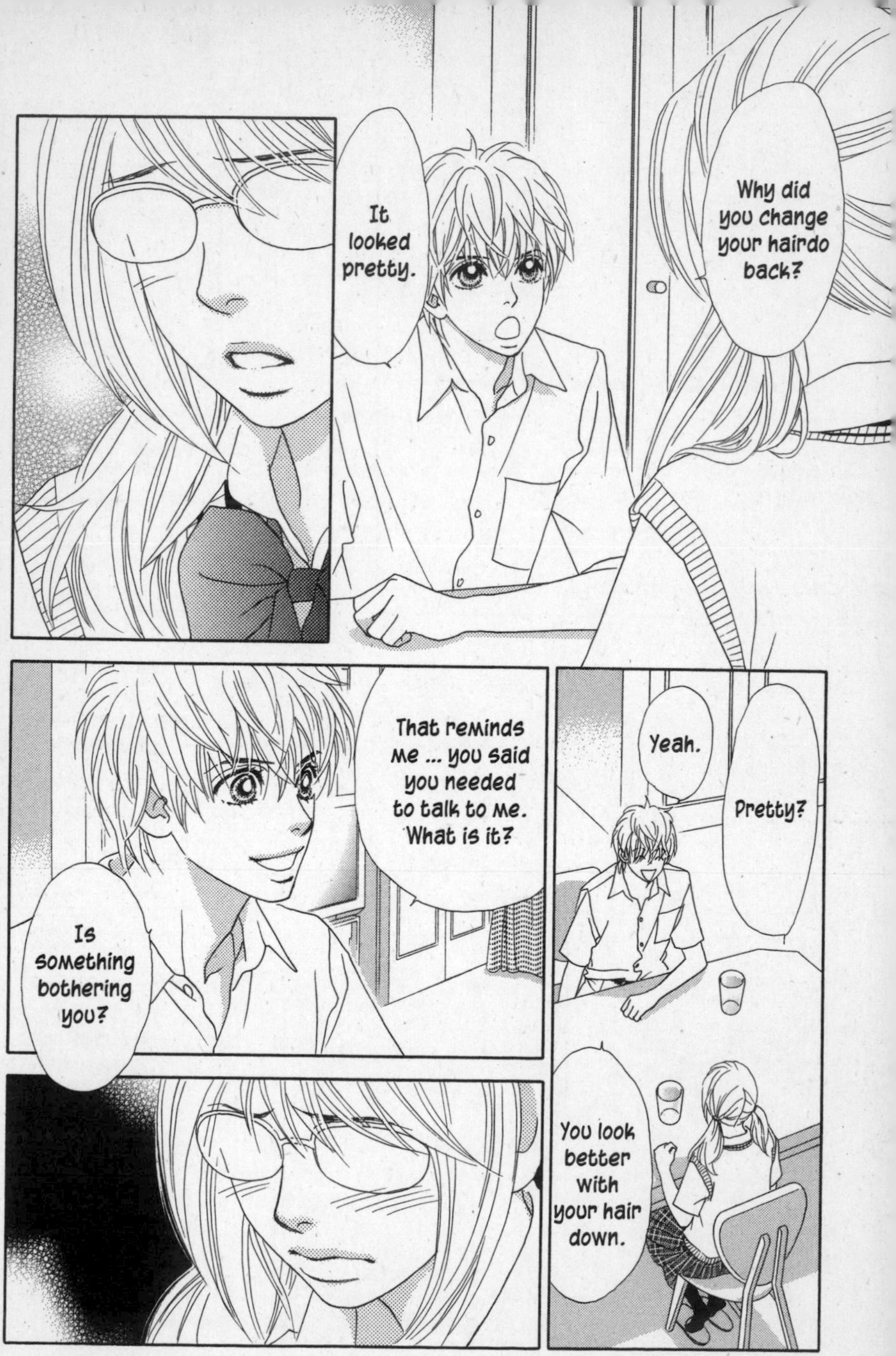
Why did you change your hairdo back?
It looked pretty.
Pretty?
Yeah.
You look better with your hair down.
That reminds me ... you said you needed to talk to me. What is it?
Is something bothering you?

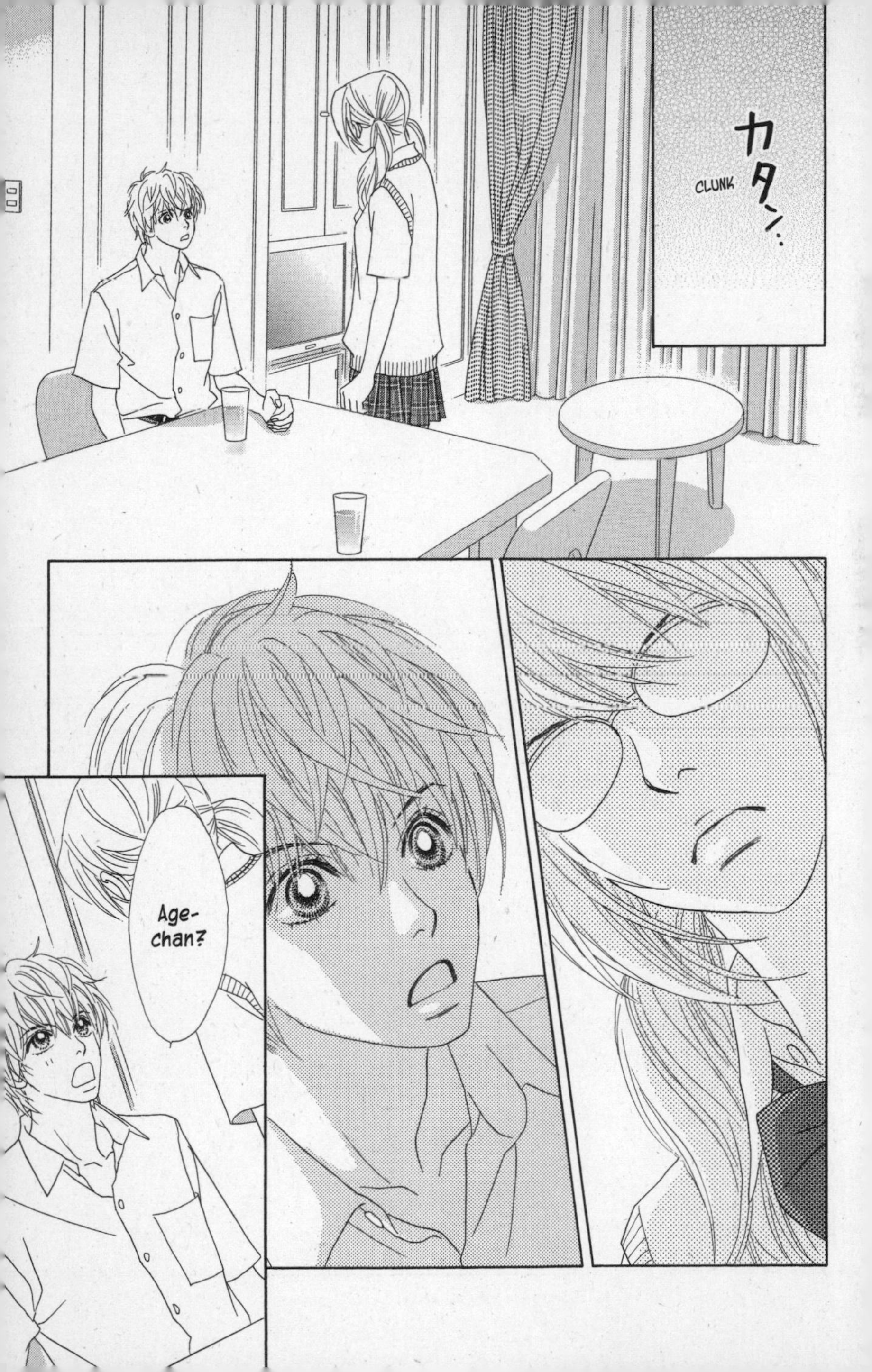
カタン…
CLUNK
Age-chan?

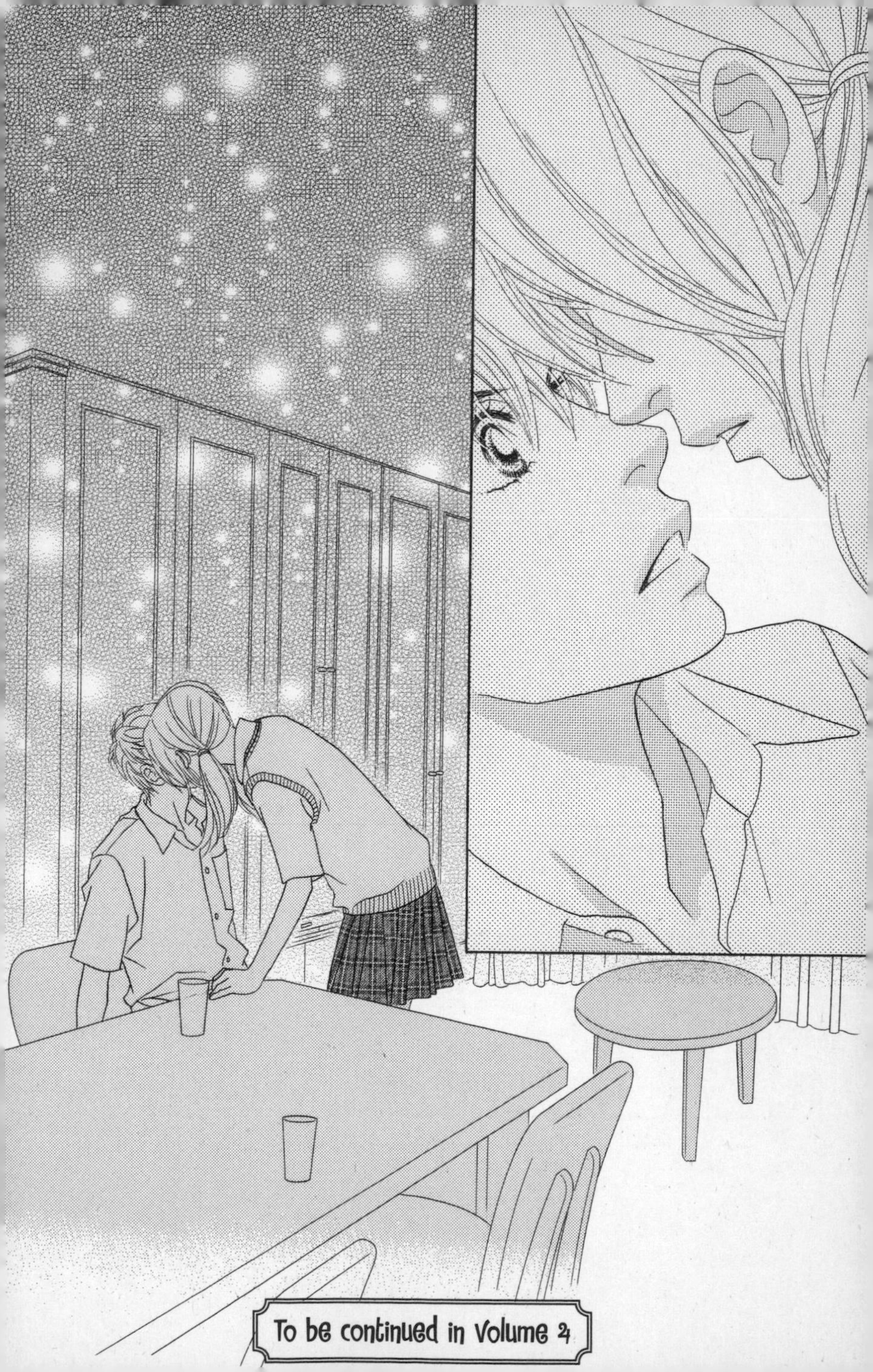
To be continued in Volume 4

Staff

Aiko   Amemori
Tomomi   Kasue
Satsuki   Furukawa
Akiko   Kawashima
Ayumi   Yoshida

Editor
Toshiyuki   Tanaka

October 26, 2007

Miwa   Ueda

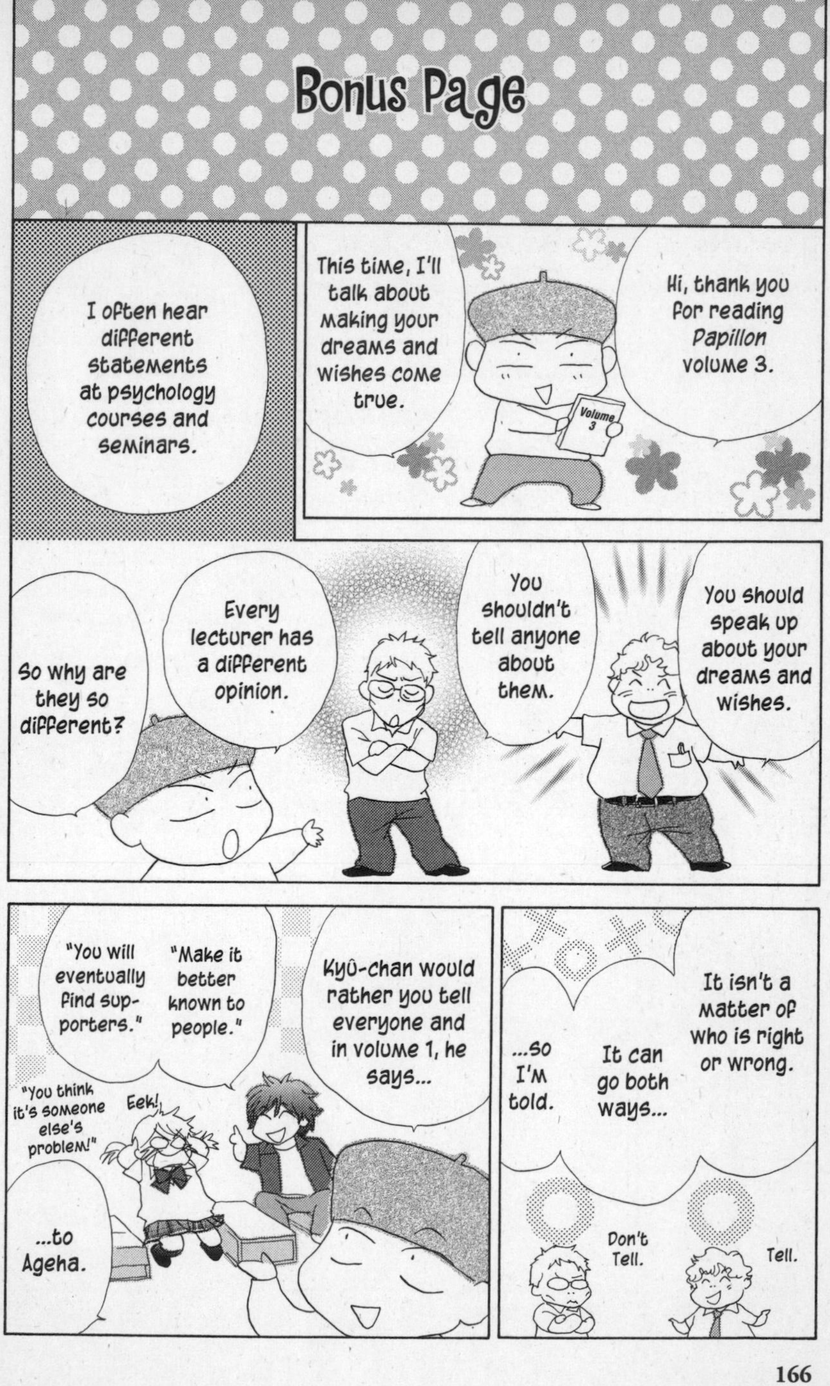
Bonus Page
Hi, thank you for reading *Papillon* volume 3.
This time, I'll talk about making your dreams and wishes come true.
Volume 3
I often hear different statements at psychology courses and seminars.
You should speak up about your dreams and wishes.
You shouldn't tell anyone about them.
Every lecturer has a different opinion.
So why are they so different?
It isn't a matter of who is right or wrong.
It can go both ways...
...so I'm told.
Tell.
Don't Tell.
Kyû-chan would rather you tell everyone and in volume 1, he says...
"Make it better known to people."
"You will eventually find supporters."
Eek!
"You think it's someone else's problem!"
...to Ageha.

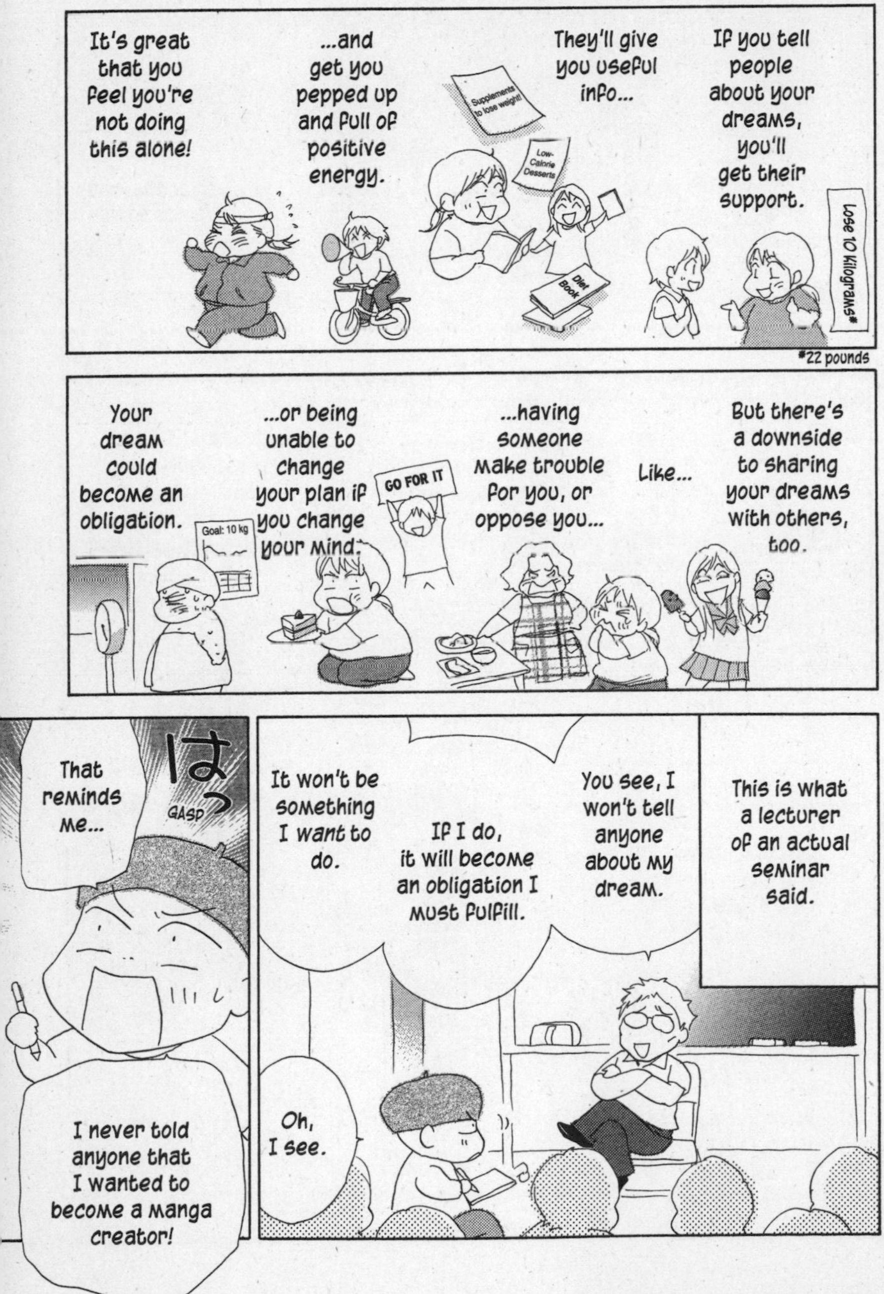

If you tell people about your dreams, you'll get their support.
Lose 10 kilograms*
They'll give you useful info...
Supplements to lose weight!
Low-Calorie Desserts
Diet Book
...and get you pepped up and full of positive energy.
It's great that you feel you're not doing this alone!
*22 pounds
But there's a downside to sharing your dreams with others, too.
Like...
...having someone make trouble for you, or oppose you...
GO FOR IT
...or being unable to change your plan if you change your mind.
Goal: 10 kg
Your dream could become an obligation.
This is what a lecturer of an actual seminar said.
You see, I won't tell anyone about my dream.
If I do, it will become an obligation I must fulfill.
It won't be something I *want* to do.
Oh, I see.
はっ
GASP
That reminds me...
I never told anyone that I wanted to become a manga creator!

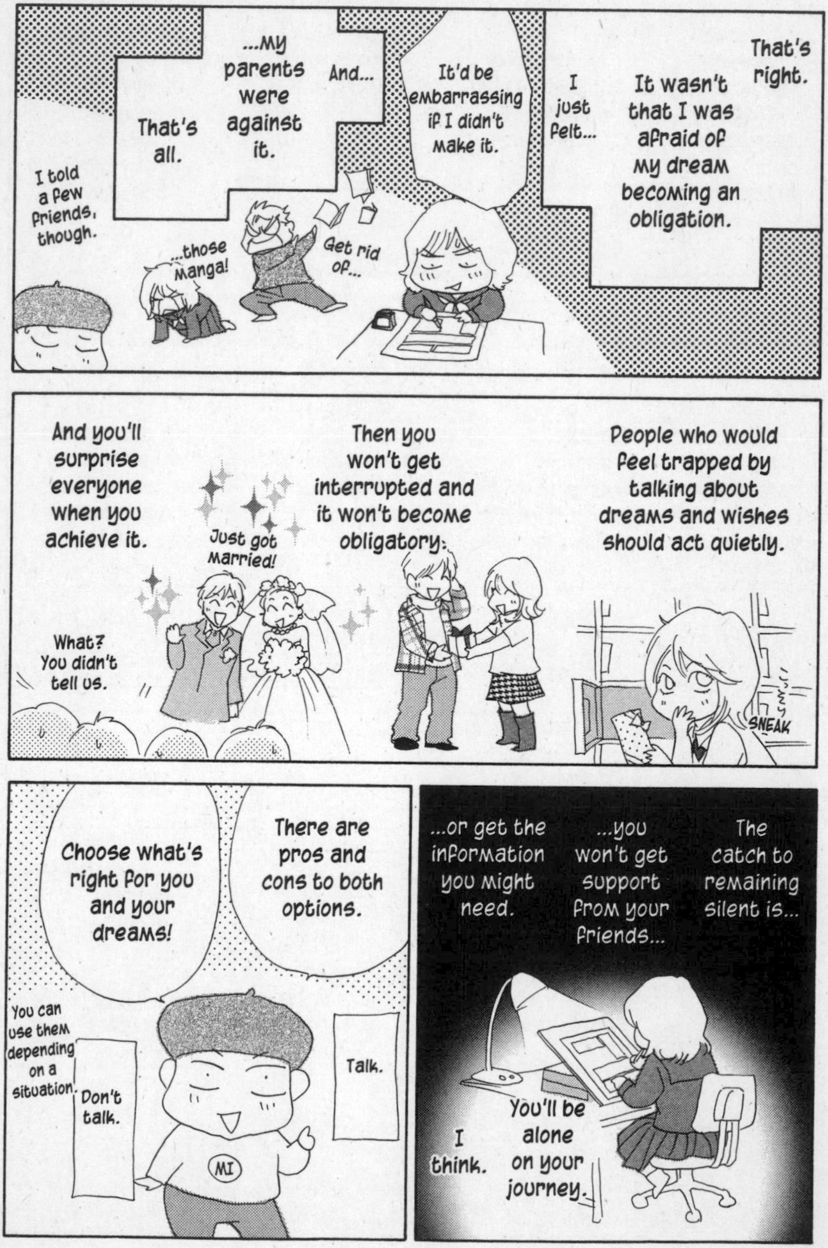
That's right.
It wasn't that I was afraid of my dream becoming an obligation.
I just felt...
It'd be embarrassing if I didn't make it.
And...
...My parents were against it.
That's all.
Get rid of...
...those Manga!
I told a few friends, though.
People who would feel trapped by talking about dreams and wishes should act quietly.
SNEAK
Then you won't get interrupted and it won't become obligatory.
And you'll surprise everyone when you achieve it.
Just got Married!
What? You didn't tell us.
The catch to remaining silent is...
...you won't get support from your friends...
...or get the information you might need.
You'll be alone on your journey.
I think.
There are pros and cons to both options.
Choose what's right for you and your dreams!
Talk.
Don't talk.
You can use them depending on a situation.
MI

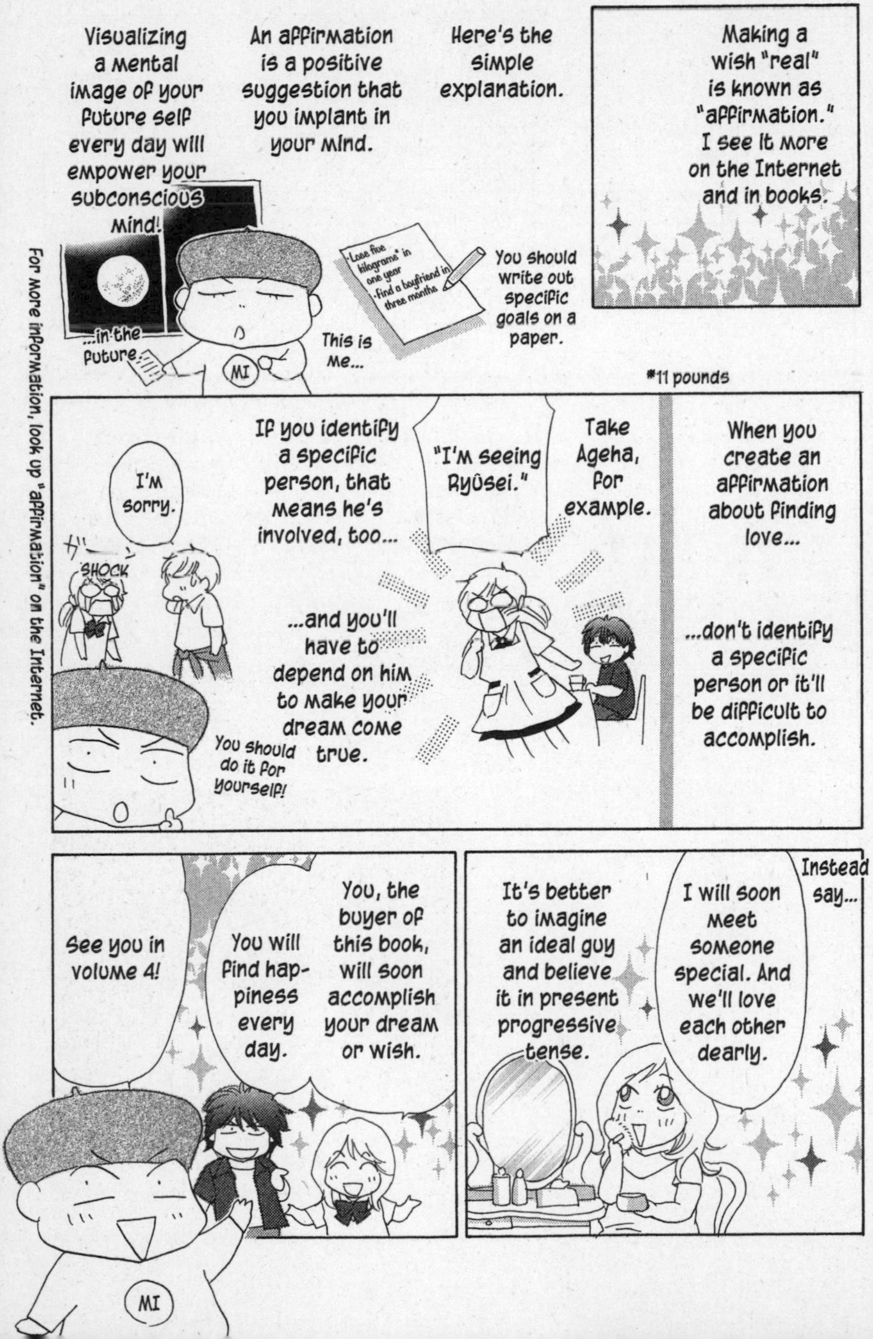
Making a wish "real" is known as "affirmation." I see it more on the Internet and in books.
Here's the simple explanation.
An affirmation is a positive suggestion that you implant in your mind.
Visualizing a mental image of your future self every day will empower your subconscious mind!
You should write out specific goals on a paper.
·Lose five kilograms* in one year
·Find a boyfriend in three months
This is me...
...in the future.
*11 pounds
When you create an affirmation about finding love...
...don't identify a specific person or it'll be difficult to accomplish.
Take Ageha, for example.
"I'm seeing Ryûsei."
If you identify a specific person, that means he's involved, too...
...and you'll have to depend on him to make your dream come true.
I'm sorry.
SHOCK
You should do it for yourself!
Instead say...
I will soon meet someone special. And we'll love each other dearly.
It's better to imagine an ideal guy and believe it in present progressive tense.
You, the buyer of this book, will soon accomplish your dream or wish.
You will find happiness every day.
See you in volume 4!
MI
For more information, look up "affirmation" on the Internet.

About the Creator

MIWA UEDA was born on September 29, in Hyogo, Japan.
Her original series, *Peach Girl*, won the Kodansha Shojo Manga
of the Year Award in 1999. *Papillon* is her latest creation.

Translation Notes

Japanese is a tricky language for most Westerners, and translation is often more art than science. For your edification and reading pleasure, here are notes on some of the places where we could have gone in a different direction with our translation of the work, or where a Japanese cultural reference is used.

Butterfly and Flower

The full Japanese title of this series is *Papillon: Chô to Hana*. Ageha and Hana's names contain the Japanese characters *chô* and *hana*, which mean "butterfly" and "flower" respectively. The title, *Papillon*, is French for "butterfly"—a good title for a story about a girl undergoing an amazing transformation, like a caterpillar becoming a butterfly.

Kyû-chan

Ichijiku's nickname comes from a Japanese character in his last name, which can also be read as *kyû*.

Hospital, page 14

People, particularly in cities, in Japan go to a clinic or a hospital for the treatment of any symptoms, including a common cold.

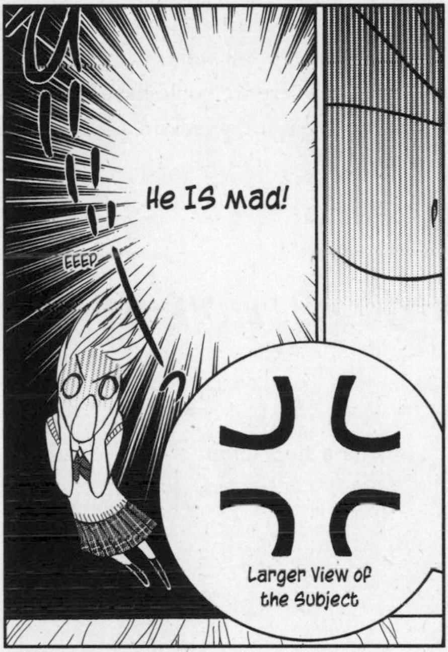
He IS mad!
EEEP
Larger View of the Subject

Angry Emoticon, page 119

The Japanese have created different variations of emoticons adapted to their culture. Here Kyû-chan is using a popping vein emoticon that shows he is enraged.

Preview of *Papillon*, Volume 4

We're pleased to present you a preview from volume 4. Please check our website (www.delreymanga.com) to see when this volume will be available in English. For now you'll have to make do with Japanese!

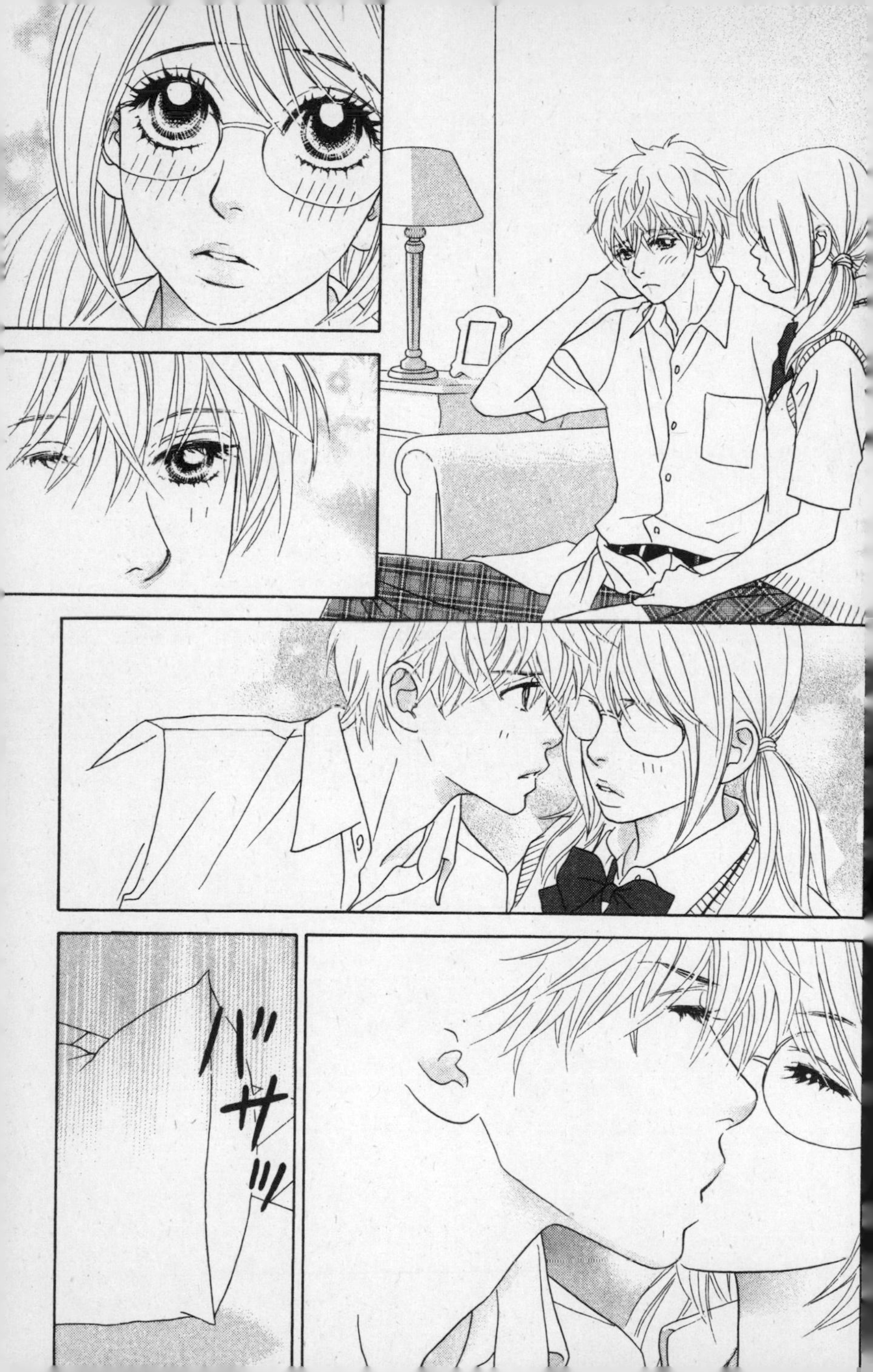
バサッ

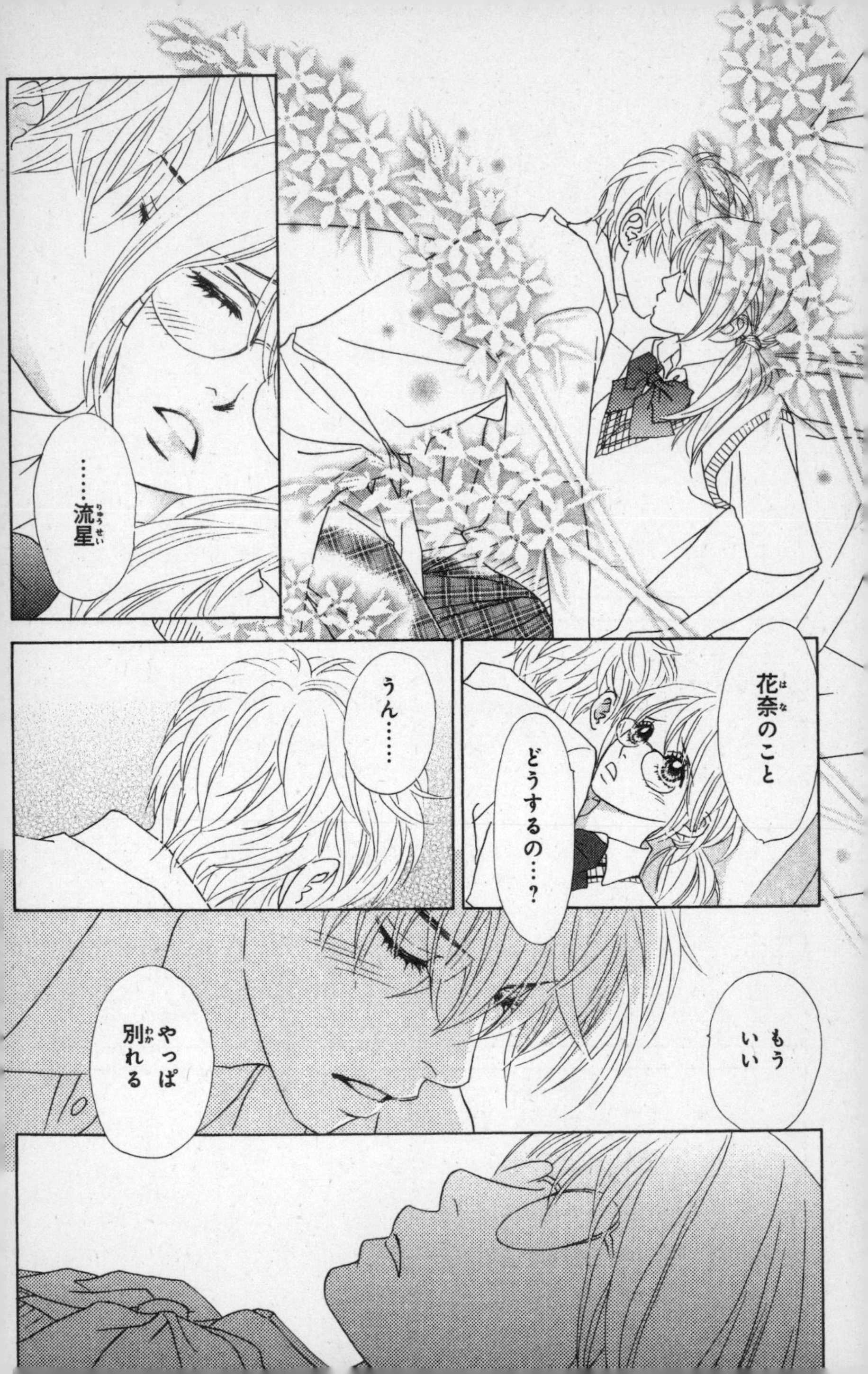
……流星
花奈のこと
どうするの…？
うん……
もう
いい
やっぱ
別れる

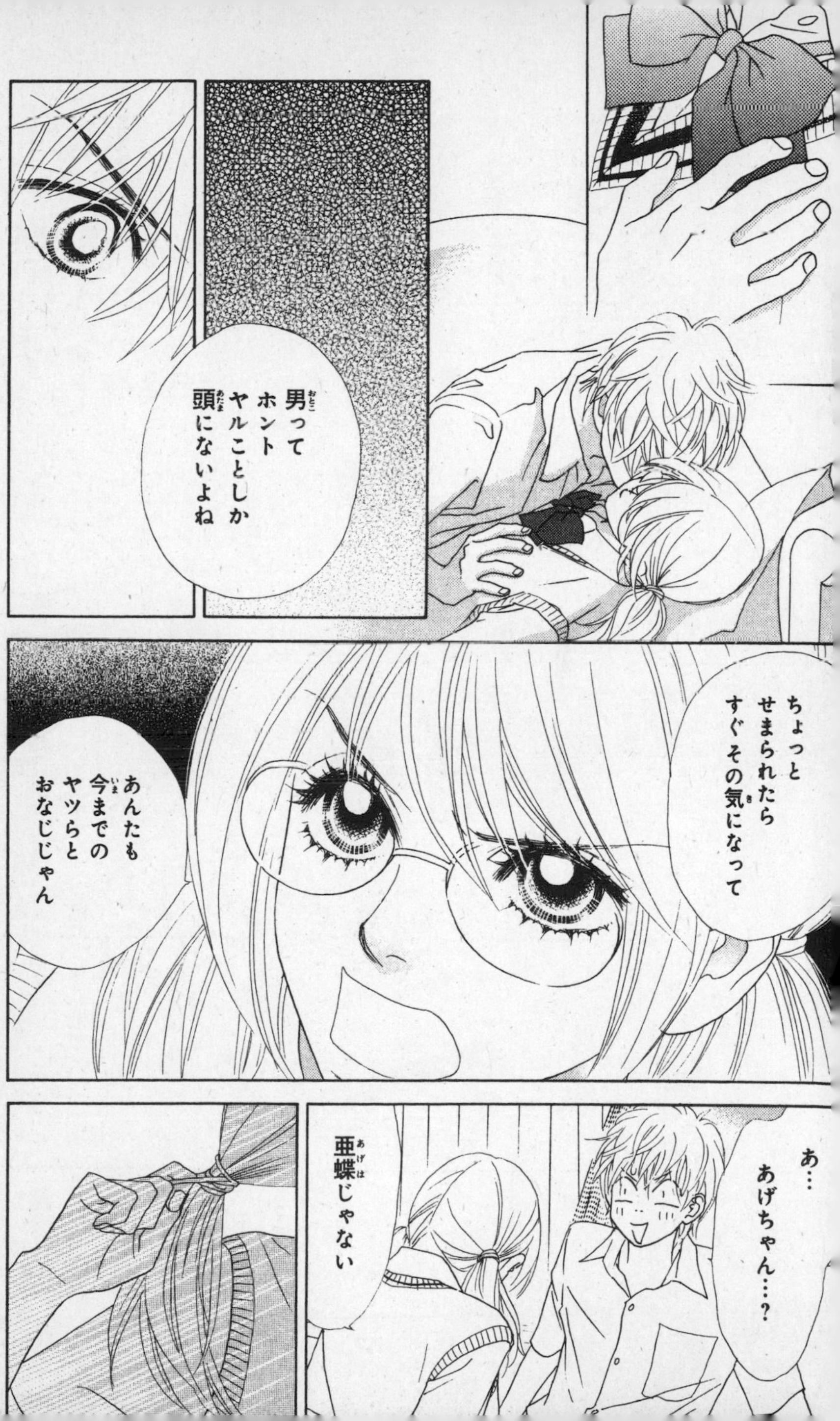
男ってホントヤルことしか頭にないよね
ちょっとせまられたらすぐその気になって
あんたも今までのヤツらとおなじじゃん
あ…あげちゃん…？
亜蝶じゃない

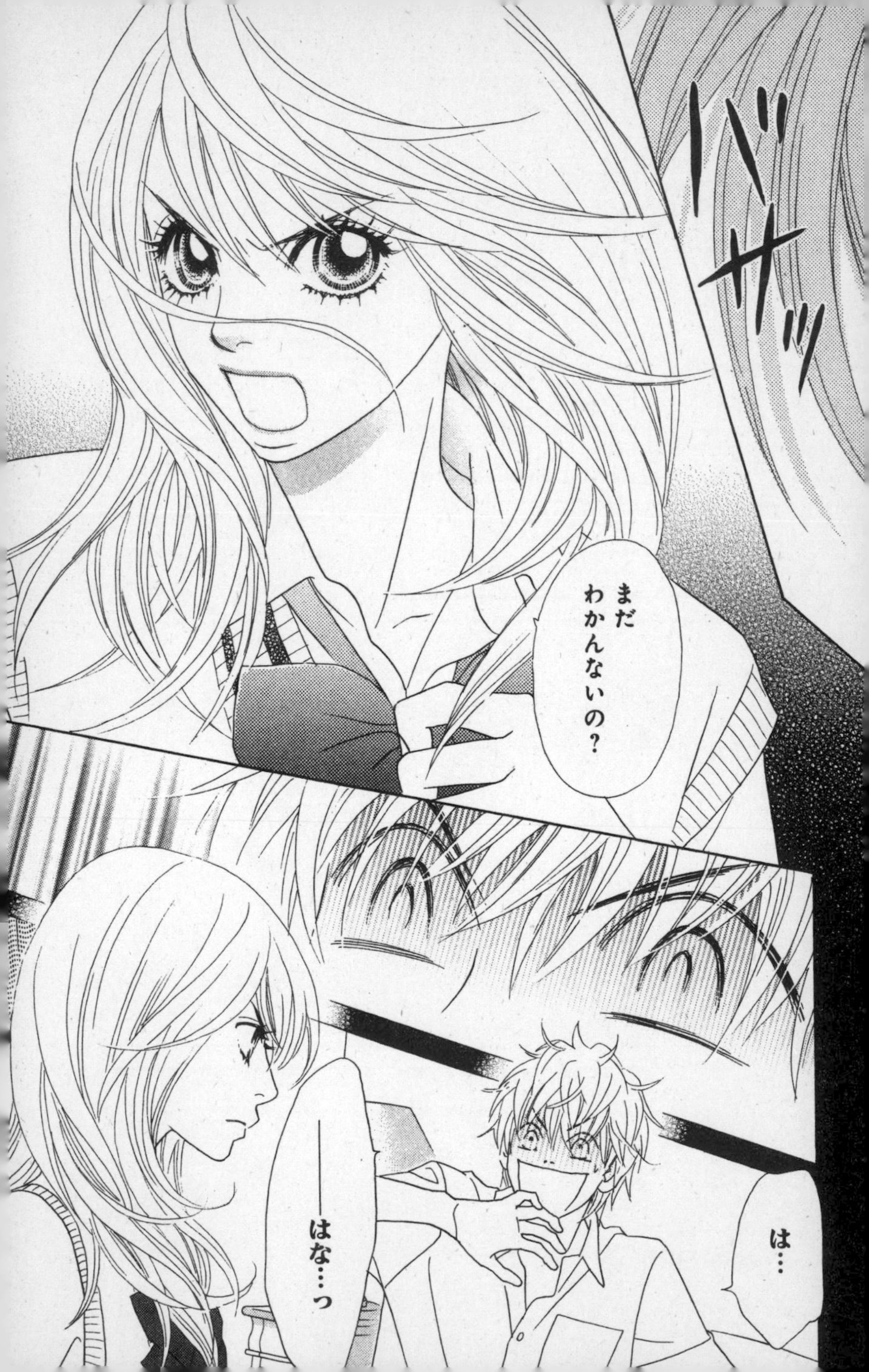
バサッ
まだわかんないの?
は…
──はな…っ

KITCHEN PRINCESS

STORY BY MIYUKI KOBAYASHI
MANGA BY NATSUMI ANDO
CREATOR OF ZODIAC P.I.

HUNGRY HEART

Najika is a great cook and likes to make meals for the people she loves. But something is missing from her life. When she was a child, she met a boy who touched her heart—and now Najika is determined to find him. The only clue she has is a silver spoon that leads her to the prestigious Seika Academy.

Attending Seika will be a challenge. Every kid at the school has a special talent, and the girls in Najika's class think she doesn't deserve to be there. But Sora and Daichi, two popular brothers who barely speak to each other, recognize Najika's cooking for what it is—magical. Could one of the boys be Najika's mysterious prince?

Special extras in each volume! Read them all!

Kamichama Karin Chu

BY KOGE-DONBO

A GODDESS IN LOVE!

Karin is your lovable girl next door—if the girl next door also happens to be a goddess! Karin has a magic ring that gives her the power to do anything she'd like. Though what she'd like most is to live happily ever after with Kazune, the boy of her dreams. Magic brought Kazune to her, but it also has a way of complicating things. It's not easy to be a goddess and a girl in love!

• Sequel series to the fan-favorite *Kamichama Karin*

Special extras in each volume! Read them all!

VISIT WWW.DELREYMANGA.COM TO:
• Read sample pages
• View release date calendars for upcoming volumes
• Sign up for Del Rey's free manga e-newsletter
• Find out the latest about new Del Rey Manga series

RATING T AGES 13+

The Otaku's Choice.™

SHUGO CHARA!

PEACH-PIT

Creators of *Dears* and *Rozen Maiden*

Everybody at Seiyo Elementary thinks that stylish and super-cool Amu has it all. But nobody knows the *real* Amu, a shy girl who wishes she had the courage to truly be herself. Changing Amu's life is going to take more than wishes and dreams—it's going to take a little magic! One morning, Amu finds a surprise in her bed: three strange little eggs. Each egg contains a Guardian Character, an angel-like being who can give her the power to be someone new. With the help of her Guardian Characters, Amu is about to discover that her true self is even more amazing than she ever dreamed.

PEACH-PIT
CREATORS OF DEARS AND ROZEN MAIDEN
SHUGO CHARA!
1

Special extras in each volume! Read them all!

VISIT WWW.DELREYMANGA.COM TO:

- Read sample pages
- View release date calendars for upcoming volumes
- Sign up for Del Rey's free manga e-newsletter
- Find out the latest about new Del Rey Manga series

RATING T AGES 13+

DEL REY MANGA デルレイ

The Otaku's Choice

BY MACHIKO SAKURAI

A LITTLE LIVING DOLL!

What would you do if your favorite toy came to life and became your best friend? Well, that's just what happens to Ame Oikawa, a shy schoolgirl. Nicori is a super-cute doll with a mind of its own—and a plan to make Ame's dreams come true!

Special extras in each volume! Read them all!

VISIT WWW.DELREYMANGA.COM TO:
- Read sample pages
- View release date calendars for upcoming volumes
- Sign up for Del Rey's free manga e-newsletter
- Find out the latest about new Del Rey Manga series

RATING T AGES 13+

DEL REY MANGA
The Otaku's Choice™